CIMA EXAMINATION TEXT

Intermediate Level

Paper 10

Systems and Project Management

ISBN 1 84390 250 8

British Library Cataloguing-in-Publication data

A catalogue record for this book is available from the British Library.

We are grateful to the Chartered Institute of Management Accountants and the Association of Chartered Certified Accountants for permission to reproduce past examination questions. The solutions have been prepared by The Financial Training Company.

Published by

The Financial Training Company
22J Wincombe Business Park
Shaftesbury
Dorset
SP7 9QJ

Contents

How to use this examination text

Objective

The aim of this Examination Text is a simple one: to give you the best possible chance of achieving the pass mark when you attempt the CIMA Paper 10 Systems and Project Management examination. To do this, we follow three main principles:

♦ The texts cover **all** areas of the syllabus with sufficient depth to ensure that you are fully prepared. However, we use our knowledge and experience to home in on the key syllabus areas and give these areas extra attention.

♦ We use our extensive experience of teaching CIMA students to assess how much the majority of students can assimilate. We do not make the mistake of overloading you with material that you will find worthless in the examination room.

♦ We believe that the best way to prepare for an examination is by practice. We intersperse explanatory text with frequent examples for you to try your hand at. Full solutions are provided in all cases.

Using the Examination Text

Each chapter begins with a section headed 'Exam Focus'. This reflects our key objective: we are interested above all in your examination success.

We set out CIMA's own Learning Outcomes and the main structural divisions into which the chapter is organised. This gives you a clear picture of what you should be aiming to achieve as you work through the text, and guidance on the steps to follow on the way.

The main body of each chapter consists of very full explanation of all syllabus areas. We concentrate on clear explanations of what really matters. We emphasise drills — standardised approaches that you can follow for typical questions. Never again need you ask: 'Where do I begin?'

Each chapter includes practice questions. These are graded: earlier questions involve material from the earlier sections of the chapter, while in later questions we progress to include more complex examples, including exam-standard questions. To get the best from the text you should make a serious attempt to tackle all the practice questions. Only then should you refer to our suggested solutions, which are contained in the final chapter of the text.

Each chapter ends by summarising the main points that you should have digested as you worked your way through.

Key features

The text is written in an interactive style:

♦ key terms and concepts are clearly defined

♦ 'pitfalls' and 'examination tips' help you avoid commonly made mistakes and help you focus on what is required to perform well in your examination

♦ frequent practice examples throughout the chapters ensure that what you have learnt is regularly reinforced

Icons

Throughout the text we use symbols to highlight the elements referred to above.

  Key facts

  Examination tips and techniques

  Pitfalls

  Practice questions

Syllabus

Syllabus overview

This syllabus introduces students to the concepts, tools and issues of the management of information technology and systems, the process and tools of project management, and the control of organisational systems. It is assumed that students will have basic knowledge and understanding of the following areas, either from their earlier studies or from their work experience, prior to commencing study for this examination.

♦ The features and functions of common IT hardware, software, peripherals and networks, and their application to management accounting and other parts of the organisation.

♦ The characteristics and components of a simple information system (data input, processing, storage, information output).

♦ The most common controls in computerised systems (security measures, verification, validation, access controls, back-up).

Although Chartered Management Accountants are finance specialists they are often given early responsibility for the design, development, implementation and control of information systems. This work normally consists of a series of projects, of which the Chartered Management Accountant may be manager.

Another major aspect of the work of the Chartered Management Accountant is control. Either through their day-to-day activities, or as part of an internal audit function, Chartered Management Accountants are tasked with ensuring that the various systems within an organisation achieve their objectives.

One of the objectives of this syllabus is to introduce and develop some of the skills required for success in the case study at the Final level.

Aims

This syllabus aims to test the student's ability to:

♦ contribute to the management of projects;

♦ evaluate an organisation's information systems and recommend appropriate solutions;

♦ recommend improvements to the control of organisational activities and resources;

♦ advise management on the audit of systems and activities;

♦ evaluate and recommend improvements in the management of quality.

Assessment

There will be a written paper of three hours, which will include a substantial scenario. The paper will consist of two sections. Section A consists of three compulsory questions and accounts for 80% of the marks. Section B consists of a choice of one question from two and accounts for 20% of the marks.

Learning outcomes and syllabus content

	Chapter where covered in this textbook

10(i)   Project management - 30%

Learning outcomes

On completion of their studies students should be able to:

♦ explain the skills required of a project manager	2
♦ evaluate the project management process	1
♦ produce a management plan for a simple project	2
♦ apply project management tools	3
♦ analyse the issues relating to the selection and management of an effective project team	2
♦ evaluate the relationships between the project manager, the project team and organisational project sponsors	2
♦ identify problems with the interpersonal relationships of project staff and recommend solutions to those problems	2
♦ explain why meetings are commonly used in organisations	4
♦ evaluate the planning and conduct of a meeting and the roles of the various participants in a typical meeting	4
♦ identify the main problems associated with meetings and recommend how these problems might be avoided or solved	4
♦ recommend changes to the management and conduct of a meeting in order to avoid or solve problems identified	4
♦ produce a presentation on a management accounting topic	4
♦ explain the process of post-completion audit and its importance in the project management process	3

Syllabus content

♦ The skills of a project manager	2
♦ The scope of project management	1
♦ Project objectives, performance measurement and control	1
♦ Building and managing a project team	2
♦ The stages of a project (eg initiation, formation, objective setting, planning, feasibility, fact finding, position analysis, options generation, options evaluation, design and development, implementation, review, completion)	1, 3
♦ The major tools and techniques used at each of the project stages (ie project initiation document, SWOT analysis, critical path analysis, Gantt chart, resource histogram, budget, progress report, completion report)	3
♦ The purpose, conduct and limitations of meetings in a business context	4

	Chapter where covered in this textbook
♦ The roles which may be adopted by participants in a business meeting (eg chair, secretary, facilitator, advisor, protagonist, antagonist) and how the chair should manage those participants to retain control of the meeting	4
♦ The stakeholders of a project (eg organisation, customers, steering committee, project manager, project team, vendors, specialists, users) and the relationships between them	2
♦ Managing project stakeholder conflict	2

10(ii) Information technology and systems - 35%

Learning outcomes

On completion of their studies students should be able to:

♦ explain the features and operation of commonly-used information technology hardware and software	5
♦ evaluate the use and relative merits of different hardware and applications architectures	5
♦ identify opportunities for the use of information technology in organisations, particularly in the implementation and running of the information system	5
♦ apply general systems theory to the design of information systems in organisations	6
♦ recommend how the value of information can be increased by careful design of an organisation's data and information architecture	7
♦ explain the importance of effective communication and the consequences of failure in the communication process	8
♦ analyse communication problems in a range of organisational situations	8
♦ recommend changes or actions to avoid or correct communication problems	8
♦ evaluate the operation of the various parts of the information system of an organisation and the relationships between them	9
♦ explain the issues involved in planning and managing an information systems project and produce a management plan for such a project	9
♦ apply the main tools and techniques used in the gathering, recording and analysis of information relating to an existing information system	10
♦ explain the processes of system design and development and analyse the issues arising at those stages	9
♦ identify and evaluate the main issues relating to the development of an information systems solution, and the risks involved in implementation	11
♦ explain the nature and purpose of systems maintenance and performance evaluation	11

	Chapter where covered in this textbook

Syllabus content

♦ The various types of information technology hardware and software in common use in organisations — 5

♦ The different hardware and applications architectures (ie centralised, distributed, client-server) available to organisations, and the information technology required to operate them (eg PCs, servers, networks, peripherals) — 5

♦ The concepts of general systems theory and their application to information systems (ie system definition, system components, system behaviour, system classification, entropy, requisite variety, coupling and decoupling) — 6

♦ The qualities of information — 7

♦ Designing data and information architectures to assist and improve planning, decision-making and control — 7

♦ The use of information for decision-making at the various levels of the organisation, and the components of the information system which can support those decisions (ie transaction processing systems, management information systems, decision support systems, executive information systems, expert systems) — 7

♦ The purpose and process of communication — 8

♦ Communication problems and solutions — 8

♦ The main communication tools (ie conversation, meeting, presentation, memorandum, letter, report, telephone, facsimile, electronic mail, video-conference), their features and limitations — 8

♦ Systems evaluation — 10

♦ The concept of the systems development life-cycle when applied to an information systems project — 9

♦ The stages in the systems development life-cycle — 9

♦ Assessing the feasibility of systems projects (ie cost-benefit analysis, technical feasibility, time feasibility) — 10

♦ Information gathering techniques (ie interviews, questionnaires, observation, simulation, document review) — 10

♦ Recording and documenting tools used during the analysis and design of systems (ie entity-relationship model, logical data structure, entity life history, dataflow diagram, and decision table) — 10

♦ Databases and database management systems (Note: Knowledge of database structures will not be required) — 9

♦ The nature and purpose of data normalisation and Structured English (Note: students will not be expected to apply these techniques) — 9

♦ Performance and technical specification (Note: Knowledge of computer programming is not required) — 9

	Chapter where covered in this textbook

10(iii)   Control of activities and resources - 10%

Learning outcomes

On completion of their studies students should be able to:

Syllabus content

	Chapter where covered in this textbook

10(iv)   Audit of activities and systems - 15%

Learning outcomes

On completion of their studies students should be able to:

◆ explain the process of internal audit	13
◆ produce a plan for the audit of various organisational activities including management, accounting and information systems	13
◆ analyse problems associated with the audit of activities and systems, and recommend action to avoid or solve those problems	13
◆ recommend action to improve the efficiency, effectiveness and control of activities	13
◆ evaluate specific problems associated with the audit of systems which use information technology	14

Syllabus content

◆ The process of review and audit of internal controls	13
◆ The major tools available to assist with such a review (eg audit planning, documenting systems, internal control questionnaires, sampling and testing)	13
◆ The identification and prevention of fraud	14
◆ The role of the internal auditor and the relationship between the internal auditor and external audit	13
◆ The techniques available to assist audit in a computerised environment	14
◆ The use of information technology to assist the audit process (ie CAATs)	14
◆ The operation of internal audit, the assessment of audit risk and the process of analytical review	13
◆ The different types of benchmarking, their use and limitations	15
◆ The analysis of business risks and approaches to risk management	13
◆ Value for money audit and management audit	13

10(v)   Management of quality - 10%

Learning outcomes

On completion of their studies students should be able to:

◆ analyse problems with the management of quality in an organisation	15
◆ evaluate the features, benefits and drawbacks of contemporary approaches to the management of quality	15
◆ produce and communicate a plan for the implementation of a quality improvement programme	15

	Chapter where covered in this textbook

Syllabus content

Meaning of CIMA's examination requirements

CIMA use precise words in the requirements of their questions. In the schedule below we reproduce the precise meanings of these words from the CIMA syllabus. You must learn these definitions and make sure that in the exam you do precisely what CIMA requires you to do.

Learning objective	Verbs used	Definition
1 Knowledge What you are expected to know	List	Make a list of
	State	Express, fully or clearly, the details of/facts of
	Define	Give the exact meaning of
2 Comprehension What you are expected to understand	Describe	Communicate the key features of
	Distinguish	Highlight the differences between
	Explain	Make clear or intelligible/state the meaning of
	Identify	Recognise, establish or select after consideration
	Illustrate	Use an example to describe or explain something
3 Application Can you apply your knowledge?	Apply	To put to practical use
	Calculate/compute	To ascertain or reckon mathematically
	Demonstrate	To prove with certainty or to exhibit by practical means
	Prepare	To make or get ready for use
	Reconcile	To make or prove consistent/compatible
	Solve	Find an answer to
	Tabulate	Arrange in a table
4 Analysis Can you analyse the detail of what you have learned?	Analyse	Examine in detail the structure of
	Categorise	Place into a defined class or division
	Compare and contrast	Show the similarities and/or differences between
	Construct	To build up or compile
	Discuss	To examine in detail by argument
	Interpret	To translate into intelligible or familiar terms
	Produce	To create or bring into existence
5 Evaluation Can you use your learning to evaluate, make decisions or recommendations?	Advise	To counsel, inform or notify
	Evaluate	To appraise or assess the value of
	Recommend	To advise on a course of action

CHAPTER 1

Project management

EXAM FOCUS

This chapter presents an overview of project management concepts, the nature of projects and their underlying attributes. Because this is a new subject, there are a few areas where you will have a knowledge gap. The examiners have outlined some syllabus topics that require specific study. The scope of project management and the stages of a project are two of these topics that we will be covering in this chapter.

LEARNING OUTCOMES

This chapter covers the following Learning Outcome of the CIMA syllabus

> Evaluate the project management process

In order to cover this learning outcome the following topics are included

> The scope of project management

> Project objectives, performance measurement and control

> The stages of a project (eg initiation, formation, objective setting, planning, feasibility, fact finding, position analysis, options generation, options evaluation, design and development, implementation, review, completion)

---

1 The scope of project management

1.1 The nature of a project

 A project can be defined simply as an activity which has a start, middle and end, and consumes resources.

Project management may be defined as 'the management and control of activities', and is concerned with the allocation of resources in the most effective manner, and ensuring the following.

- The right people at the right time
- The correct sequence of activities
- Adherence to the project timetable
- Adoption of a formal project plan

A project manager must be appointed who will be responsible for control of the overall project. This person should possess effective communication skills to enable him or her to communicate with all different levels of management - strategic, tactical, and operational. The overriding responsibility of the project manager is to ensure that effectiveness and efficiency are achieved throughout the entire project.

Consequently, we may consider a project to be a collection of temporary 'packets' of effort that in combination:

◆ have a specific objective
◆ have a defined start and end date
◆ consume resources
◆ are unique
◆ require organisation

Thus a project defines 'what' it is that is to be achieved (the objective), 'when' it is to be achieved by (timescale) and the people, equipment and finance required to achieve the what and when (resources).

Importantly, projects represent a one-time-only configuration of these elements; they are consequently unique and require organisation to enable the objective to be met. The element of organisation relates to the management aspect in our triad of terms above and is broadly concerned with the planning, monitoring and control of the project.

1.2 Sources of projects

The most common sources of projects are as follows:

◆ From a strategy process.

◆ From a customer or client who requests help, particularly if the business of the organisation is the provision of project-based services.

◆ From a 'project champion' – an individual who believes that the project is a good thing and persuades the organisation of its merits. The champion may go on to become the project sponsor or project manager.

◆ From a 'user', who recognises a problem that needs solving or a need that is unsatisfied.

1.3 Characteristics of a project

A project is a unique undertaking, ie a non-repetitive activity, to accomplish a specific goal, which requires resources and effort. According to Trevor Young (*The Handbook of Project Management: A Practical Guide To Effective Policies and Procedures*, Trevor L Young, 1999) it has the following characteristics:

◆ a specific purpose/objective which can be readily defined

◆ a focus on the customer and customer expectations

◆ not usually routine work but may contain some routine-type tasks

◆ a series of activities that are linked together because they all contribute to the desired result

◆ clearly defined time constraints, ie a date when the results are required

◆ frequently complex because the work involves people in different departments and even on different sites

◆ flexibility - enough to accommodate change as the work proceeds

◆ many unknowns within the work itself, within the skills of the people doing the work and in the external influences on the project

◆ cost constraints which must be clearly defined and understood to ensure the project remains viable

◆ a unique opportunity to learn new skills

♦ it forces you to work in a different way because the 'temporary' management role is directly associated with the life of the project

♦ it challenges traditional lines of authority with perceived threats to the *status quo*

♦ it involves risk at every step of the process which must be managed to sustain the focus on the desired results

In a real business situation it may sometimes be difficult to determine whether a job is a project or not but in the examination the examiner will tell you what the project is. The characteristics of the project, outlined above, may help you find a solution to one or more of the problems identified in the scenario.

Practice question 1 *(The answer is in the final chapter of this book)*

Project

Required

Give some examples of projects ranging from simple to complex.

1.4   The project lifecycle

Projects can be divided into several phases to provide better management control. These phases are collectively known as the project lifecycle.

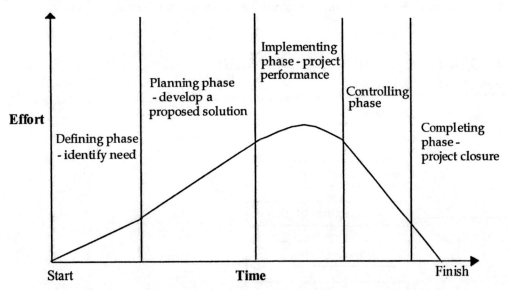

As shown in the diagram, effort such as resource use is low at the start of the project, higher towards the end and then falls away rapidly as the project comes to the end.

Risk and uncertainty are highest at the start of the project and the probability of successfully completing it are at their lowest. As the project progresses, the likelihood of successful completion increases.

The stages in the lifecycle are:

♦ The defining phase - involves identification of a need, opportunity or problem. This process will form the basis for the organisation to establish its own requirements and find out whether they are achievable.

- The planning phase - will result in the submission of proposals to the customer by the organisations that want to perform the project. The proposals will be evaluated and the most appropriate solution chosen. A feasibility study and cost benefit analysis is generally used in the option evaluation process. The customer and contractor will then sign a contract.

- The implementing phase - is the actual performance of the project, resulting in the accomplishment of the project objective.

- The controlling phase - involves monitoring and controlling the project, with vetting on progress, milestones achieved or missed, costs of equipment and labour compared to budget.

- The completing phase - involves the confirmation that all the deliverables have been provided and accepted, all payments have been made and received and performance has been evaluated and appraised.

We will look at these stages later in the chapter when we are discussing the project management stages.

Practice question 2 *(The answer is in the final chapter of this book)*

Project lifecycle

Required

Use a personal example, such as a holiday, to describe the stages of the project lifecycle.

---

2 Project objectives, performance measurement and control

2.1 Project management plan

The stages of the plan can be shown as a system, as shown below.

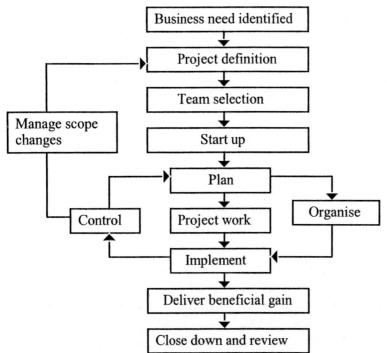

2.2 Identification of a business need

This is really the first stage in a systems project - the actual selection of the task to be performed. Projects arise from someone attempting to solve a problem or seeing an opportunity for a business venture – a new idea. Not all ideas will result in viable projects. Some organisations will apply a 'reality test' to all ideas. This is not a feasibility study but will eliminate concepts that are obviously not practical. The criteria for selecting a project include the following:

Priority - there may be a number of different projects being considered at one time. Several of these may be justified, but resources are not sufficient to carry them all out. There are both formal and informal methods of ranking which projects should be completed first.

Integration requirement - perhaps other, urgent systems cannot be installed unless a particular system is established from the beginning, even though that special system may not, in itself, be 'profitable'.

Availability of appropriate personnel - it may be that systems staff are working to a full schedule already, and/or that they do not have the relevant experience to be of use (eg perhaps an on-line real-time system is to be considered for the first time). In such cases, external consultants may be called in, although this adds to the cost.

Expected return on investment - this could only be very roughly assessed at this stage, of course, and only the full feasibility study would produce a confirmation or denial of the preliminary ideas about the expected return.

Management stimulus - management cooperation and commitment must be sought.

2.3 Project definition

Clear and accurate definition of a project is one of the most important actions you can take to ensure the project's success. The clearer the target the more likely you are to hit it. Defining a project is a process of selection and reduction of the ideas and perspectives of those involved into a set of clearly defined objectives, critical success factors and evaluated risks.

The examiner may use the term 'critical success factors' or 'key success criteria' or a combination of both.

The way to define a project is to ask a standard set of questions. They fall into the categories given below.

(a)   The **Purpose** (or mission) - is the reason for doing the project and is a statement of its overall aims, expressed in the most general of terms

♦   What is the project about in broad terms?
♦   Who wants it done and why?
♦   What is its title?

(b)   The **Goals** - these are the targets we want to meet

♦   What is it we want to achieve?
♦   When do we want to achieve it?
♦   What are our specific aims?
♦   Why are these goals essential to the project?

(c)   **Milestones** - in order to monitor and control progress in a project, a series of project milestones will be established. A milestone is a point in a project which provides an absolute measure of progress. Generally, milestones are the completion of tasks or stages of the project with clear 'deliverables' (tangible items that are given to the users or sponsor), such as a report.

Milestones allow the time spent on a project to be controlled more effectively, as it is easy to compare the actual time of milestone achievement with the planned time.

(d)   The **Beneficial Gains** or Scope - this is how the organisation will gain. Here we define the performance criteria and set our quality standards for the project.

- ♦ How will things be different if the project is successfully completed?
- ♦ Is there a clear need and can it be quantified?
- ♦ Who will benefit, how will they benefit and what will they gain?
- ♦ Do the beneficiaries agree about the need and the proposed solution?
- ♦ Is the project to identify that need and/or that solution?
- ♦ How will they react to that solution?
- ♦ What are the alternatives?
- ♦ Are those alternatives more or less acceptable (satisfactory)?

2.4   Project objectives

The project objectives are the anticipated result or final outcome and must be clearly understood at the outset. They are usually defined in terms of scope, schedule and cost and the management of them is often a delicate balancing act, as the various objectives normally conflict with one another.

These objectives will tell us if we have met our goals and to what standard. From our list of specific goals for the project we must develop a set of measurable objectives that will confirm that we have reached certain project milestones (or way points) including the final one of project completion.

The measurable objectives (when achieved) demonstrate the extent to which the beneficial gains have been achieved, the goals have been met and that the purpose of the project has been achieved.

Example

Aim: A Local Authority has a statutory duty to provide accommodation for homeless people. It needs to develop a temporary housing strategy that removes the need for expensive bed and breakfast accommodation for homeless people.

Measurable Objectives:

- ♦ Develop links with Housing Associations and Shelters to ensure that we have sufficient capacity to meet our expected (150 per annum) homeless needs.

- ♦ Reduce the number of bed and breakfast lets over 2 years from 100 to 0.

- ♦ Verify that the annual cost of accommodating homeless people has reduced by at least 10%.

2.5   Critical success factors (CSFs)

These are the objectives that, if all else fails, we must meet and/or those that we must meet for the project to be deemed successful even if other objectives are met and achieved.

From the list of objectives, it is essential that the project manager identifies and selects the CSFs of the project, as activities leading to the achievement of these will necessarily require more management time and effort. These are the items that are critical to those who will benefit from the project and those with the responsibilities for judging success criteria (Managers, Customers, Members, Shareholders, Stakeholders, etc). The purpose of this is twofold:

- ♦ to clarify in the minds of the project team and service managers what are the essential benefits that the project will deliver.

♦   if circumstances change within the life of the project then it is often extremely useful to see what were the agreed success criteria at the start of the project. The project may then be re-planned to ensure the CSFs are met or the CSFs may be formally changed (by senior managers in the light of changed circumstances) and the project redefined and re-planned to ensure they are met.

Practice question 3 *(The answer is in the final chapter of this book)*

Project objectives

Required

Define the terms 'project' and 'project objective' and give examples of each.

2.6   Deliverables

The fundamental objective of a project is to deliver something new. If the project is to create new products or modify existing ones, then the list of deliverable items may be as simple as a set of parts or product numbers.

However, the deliverable items may be less easy to distinguish in some projects. A project to deliver the implementation of a new integrated housing management computer system will deliver parameter set-up, data transfer, staff training, etc.

In the first example, a new product will have a specification (or a set of specifications), which defines its essential elements, its functions, its quality standards, its marketing requirements, etc. Thus the deliverables may be reduced to a simple set of inventory numbers.

The deliverables of the second project should concentrate on the qualitative and quantitative aspects of the project. For example, the set-up phase will deliver the responsive repairs functions of the *Repairs Module* but not the programmed works functions. The data transfer will deliver the defect description but not the itemised repair for completed and paid orders for the last 4 years. The training in July will not include the production of statistical data.

In effect, the deliverables list becomes a set of specified outputs (a quantity and quality specification) for each milestone or way-point of the project.

2.7   Project constraints

Every project has constraints. The primary ones are the trade off between Time, Resources and Performance Criteria (or time, cost and scope), often referred to as the 'project triangle', shown below. The project must be defined to manage these constraints.

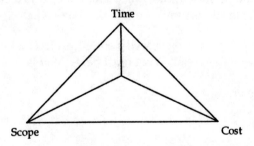

Time - there are two aspects to the time dimension of a project:

♦   an overall time constraint on a project (sometimes called a deadline) by when the project must be completed.

♦   a 'time budget' for the project. This is often expressed in terms of resource availability and measured in labour hours or worker days.

The time objective or schedule is the timetable of activities involved in achieving the project's objectives. It helps to plan for a firm delivery date, which will make the project viable and minimise disruption time, optimise cash flow and co-ordinate the availability of resources.

If the organisation chooses to reduce the resource days by increasing the resource capability, this will not necessarily reduce the total cost because the reduction in resource days may be out-weighed by the increased resource cost. However, improved resource capability will reduce the task time and there is often a delivery time cost associated with a project so that the cost to the organisation will be less or its income improved. This is the so-called 'window of opportunity' factor.

 Project scope - there are two aspects to the scope dimension of a project.

♦ a certain series of tasks or activities to be performed in reaching the project solution.

♦ an expected quality level associated with each task. It is important that the tasks are performed well, and that the sponsor's quality expectations are met.

The aim of the scope objective is to ensure that the project's purpose is achieved, specify the work that must be done and specifically exclude work that is superfluous or otherwise unnecessary. Developing the scope of the project means planning for quality. In project terms this means delivering a project which satisfies the customer and is 'fit for the purpose'.

Examples

(i)   Where the objective is to build a house, the project scope will include clearing the land, laying on all the necessary services, building the house and landscaping, all within the agreed quality standards expected by the NHBC and the customer.

(ii)   A project to connect travelling or home workers to the corporate computer network may have three possible sets of performance criteria:

♦ Every external employee must have modem access to corporate and external e-mail via the Internet

♦ Every external employee must have access to corporate e-mail and one departmental server via ISDN connections

♦ Every employee must have access to all corporate computer systems via ISDN (from home) and modem (from hotels)

The equipment costs, the number and complexity of tasks and the knowledge requirement associated with each of these performance criteria is very different. For example, it is not possible to deliver the same performance using a modem as it is using an ISDN line so further definition is required if the third performance criteria above is selected.

One of the main reasons for producing a well-defined project definition is to ensure that the performance criteria are set and agreed. What must be defined is

♦ what it will NOT deliver
♦ what it will deliver
♦ to what quality standard

 Cost - there are two aspects to cost

♦ a budget available for project completion, which the project manager should not exceed without authorisation.

♦ the need, in most projects, to prove that the benefits of the project exceed the costs.

The project cost is based on the budget, which includes an estimate of the resources that will be used in the project.

Costs and resources - include people, equipment and money. They may be internal or external and include suppliers, contractors, partners, statutory bodies, governments, banks, loans, grants, expert opinion (lawyers, accountants, consultants), etc. Generally, organisations are reasonably good at estimating or obtaining estimates for the use and costs of external resources and, if needs be, they can obtain the opinion of an expert (another cost). Where they often fail is in estimating the cost of the use of their internal resources, particularly people.

Aside from the employment costs, there are:

♦ the costs to the service provision they normally perform

♦ the cost of substitution to maintain the service

♦ the loss of opportunity for them to work on other projects (ie, the loss of the benefit those projects would deliver)

♦ the cost of training associated with the project work.

Because internal resources are so constrained it is vital that projects are selected with the utmost care to maximise the use of that resource. Defining projects helps to make this selection objective and rational.

The significant aspect of the project triangle is that it illustrates a relationship between the elements that, in the practical context of project management, often requires a trade-off. Each element is constrained at the outset but, should change occur to one aspect during the project, there is generally an impact on one or both of the remaining aspects.

For example, a change to the specification that increases its scope will logically require that either the timescale is extended or that resources are added to cater for the new parts of the specification in the same timescale. Conversely, a reduction in timescale will logically require that either the specification is reduced in scope or that resources are added to complete the same amount of work in less time. Again, this may be argued to portray a simplistic understanding; the point of importance to remember, however, is that some form of relationship does exist.

2.8   Ranking project objectives

Projects are initiated when needs or objectives are identified. Turning the needs into realisable projects can be difficult. This can be due to the different concerns of members of the organisation making it difficult to prioritise. It could be because there is more than one way to achieve the objectives or it could be that not all the objectives can be achieved within the same time because of limited resources.

As the organisation determines its objectives and the strategies to accomplish them, the priorities will be those that are critical and those considered the most effective to realise objectives.

3   Threats to a successful project

3.1   Risk analysis

All projects, regardless of size or complexity, will contain some elements of risk, eg costs exceeding budget, unachieved project objectives, missed deadlines, business disruption.

A risk is anything that will have a negative impact on any one or all of the primary project constraints - Time, Scope and Cost. Examples include:

♦ A key person with specialist skills is required for several projects. If one of those projects overruns, then that person will be required to work on several projects at the same time. If this is not practical then the other projects will be delayed.

♦ A person selected to do work on a project may not have the skills to do the work. If this risk is identified then the project plan can allow for training time and learning curve time. Alternatively, another resource may be identified.

♦ A vital machine may be scheduled for maintenance during the time it is required for the project. The maintenance schedule must be known and the effect of early or late maintenance, or even machine substitution, must be assessed and built into the project plan.

Let us take the example of a new computer system implementation and look at what is often one of the most time consuming tasks (one that is so often prone to increased duration) and see how we might reduce the associated risks. When implementing a new computer system the quantity and difficulty of data transfer (extracting data from the existing system, reformatting it and importing it into the new system) is often grossly under-estimated. The time the work will take has a great sensitivity to:

♦ the similarity of previous transfers by the supplier for other customers (even similar ones will not be exactly the same)

♦ the similarity between the data in the old and new systems

♦ the quantity of the data to be transferred

♦ the knowledge and skill of the staff who must validate the data transferred

♦ the importance of historic data to the satisfactory operation of the new system or the service level provision to customers.

All of these will almost certainly be untried to some extent. The greater the quantity and type of data transferred the greater the work in constructing the data transfer programs and in validating the take-on data. What are the risks?

♦ That the cost of data transfer will increase.
♦ That the 'live' date will be delayed.
♦ That the system may not operate correctly.
♦ That the customers will be dissatisfied.
♦ That the organisation will be publicly criticised.
♦ That, in consequence, the organisation will lose income or market share.

Risk can be reduced by analysing what is essential data, what is accurate data and what is merely nice to have. Risk is minimised by transferring only essential data that is also accurate. Re-enter essential but inaccurate data and store the rest on CD-ROM when the data transfer part of the project is complete. You may never use this data but you will have a warm and comfortable feeling for having done it. Obviously, putting only your best people on the project will also help.

3.2   Risk management

It is important to identify risks within the project plan, and to devise ways in which these risks are to be managed.

Risk management consists of the following steps.

- Identification of the risks
- Estimates of the effects of things going wrong
- Estimation of the probabilities of the events occurring
- Ranking of the important and more likely threats
- Decision as to the way in which the risks are to be handled

Risks can be handled in a number of different ways.

- Ignore the risks and do nothing – appropriate where the effect of the risk is small and the chances of it occurring remote.

- Purchase insurance against the risk.

- Transfer the risk – eg arranging for third parties to complete the riskier parts of the project.

- Protect against the risk – arrange for additional staff to be available at critical parts of the project to minimise the possibility of the project overrunning.

3.3   Threats to the project

The following is a brief list of the types of threats that can threaten the success of a project, together with some suggestions as to how they may be avoided.

Threat	Ways of minimising threat
Poor planning	Use of CPA and Gantt charts
Few control mechanisms	Implement constant progress review, together with standardised reporting mechanisms
Specification changes	User requirements should be thoroughly examined at the systems analysis stage, using walkthroughs or prototyping
Unrealistic deadlines	The network diagram should identify the critical path on which management's attentions should be concentrated
Under-resourced budgets	Management should ensure that the budget (in terms of finance and manpower) is correctly balanced to ensure that the project can be successfully completed
Poor management	Training of project managers in management skills as well as technical skills

4   Preparing the feasibility study

4.1   An overview of the process

The development of any new project requires careful consideration and planning. It will consume large volumes of resources, both financial and non-financial, and is likely to have a major effect on the way in which the organisation will operate.

In considering the development of a project, and in order to create benchmarks to evaluate its success, the following questions must be addressed.

- What is required?
- What different ways are there to satisfy these requirements?
- Is it technically feasible?
- Does it make economic sense?
- Will it result in major changes in organisational structure or operation?

The answers to these questions can be derived from the feasibility study.

Before the feasibility study can be carried out, the personnel assigned to complete the study must have a set of guidelines and objectives to know what is required of them.

4.2 Project requirements

The requirements will be clearly defined and set out in a statement, outlining what is expected of the project or product. It is a statement of the reason for what is being done or developed. It is not a specification with detailed characteristics and size or performance criteria. It gives the customer and the project team an opportunity to agree that the requirement is appropriate and meets the organisational needs and objectives.

Once the requirements have been identified, potential projects can be investigated to examine their feasibility. The primary objective of the feasibility study is to identify the key technical and performance objectives that the project must achieve and to ensure that the technology exists to achieve these targets. The study must also determine the cost of achieving these targets. This cost information is fed into the economic feasibility assessment.

Four issues are particularly important.

- Technical feasibility
- Economic/financial feasibility
- Social feasibility
- Ecological feasibility

4.3 Technical feasibility

Technical feasibility is the matching of the project requirements to the performance that can be achieved from available material, technology and processes. In terms of a computer system, technical feasibility may be evaluated by consideration of the following factors.

- Ability to support a number of users
- Response times required
- Ability to process a certain number of transactions within a time constraint
- Capacity to hold a certain number of records on line
- Networking with distant locations

For a bridge building project technical, engineering, environmental and safety issues need to be evaluated by different experts.

4.4 Social or operational feasibility

This type of feasibility is concerned with ensuring that the project fits with the business and social organisation of the company. The new project may require new skills and attitudes. The feasibility study must assess whether the current employees have such skills and, if they do not, whether they can attain these skills and the cost of attaining them (for use in economic feasibility). Redundancies may be necessary and the feasibility study should assess both the direct and indirect (for example; in terms of morale and motivation of remaining staff) costs of such a programme.

The new project may cut across established organisational boundaries and structures. This is likely to lead to resistance and reluctance as employees see well-established procedures and career paths disappear.

Some of these social/operational feasibility issues can be directly costed (such as training costs). Others have less tangible effects that must be documented in the feasibility report.

4.5 Ecological feasibility

Ecological considerations may be stimulated by health and safety legislation. Products that are ecologically sound and less harmful to the environment will lessen the chances of customers switching to alternatives. The project feasibility should consider the raw material input, the production processes and the disposal of the product at the end of its life.

4.6 Economic feasibility

The project (proposed system) must provide a benefit to the organisation. Economic feasibility will be assessed through a process of cost benefit analysis. Costs will include:

♦ Capital costs for purchasing assets, eg equipment, plus any additional costs of installation and maintenance.

♦ Revenue costs for purchases other than assets, eg consultancy, conversion and training, staff salaries, stationery and financing costs.

The benefits may be as a result of:

♦ Direct cost savings
♦ Increased capacity
♦ Improved quality of product or service
♦ Competitive edge
♦ Improved decision-making.

These benefits must be quantified so that they can be compared with the cost. A formal cost-benefit analysis will be undertaken which takes into account the **timing** of the costs and the benefits. The results of this analysis will be assessed in the context of the criteria used by the company to give the go-ahead to projects. For example, the organisation may state that all projects must pay back within three years, and failure to achieve this may lead to the project being deemed economically infeasible.

4.7 Techniques of cost benefit analysis

After compiling all of the various costs associated with the project, and having assessed the financial benefits that should result from it, it is necessary to evaluate the overall financial viability of the project.

There are a number of commonly known methods of project evaluation that fall within the framework of cost benefit analysis, and the majority of these methods will have been encountered in your past studies.

The main methods include the following.

♦ Cashflow analysis
♦ Payback period
♦ Return on investment
♦ Discounted cashflow (net present values)

One of the main problems in project evaluation is in the calculation of future cashflows. As the future cashflows are likely to be received over a number of years, there is a high level of inherent inaccuracy in their calculation, and hence a risk of incorrect assessment. Further, a new system may bring intangible benefits such as improved staff morale and better customer satisfaction, and these benefits cannot be measured in strict financial terms.

Practice question 4 *(The answer is in the final chapter of this book)*

Project feasibility

Required

(a)   Explain the term 'feasibility'.

(b)   Discuss the aspects of feasibility you would consider in project selection.

4.8   Terms of reference for feasibility report

The terms of reference for a feasibility study might contain:

♦   **Objectives** - what is expected at the end of the feasibility study, eg to produce a feasibility report, which recommends whether the project should proceed or not and, if progression is recommended, to produce a detailed timetable for the next phase.

♦   **Scope of the study.** The terms of reference should specify what is within the scope of the feasibility study, eg the feasibility study is concerned with investigating the procedures for dealing with customer complaints made directly to head office.

♦   **Constraints** that apply to the study - the feasibility study may have to conform to company standards and its conduct and presentation has to take place in a prescribed way (perhaps to a certain quality standard). Other constraints may include time, eg the feasibility study must be concluded by 8 October.

♦   **Client of the study** - the feasibility study, and its eventual report, must be **owned** by someone within the organisation. The client or authority will agree the other aspects of the terms of reference as well as monitoring progress and signing-off the final product.

♦   **Resources** available to undertake the feasibility study - this defines the people, equipment and budget available for the study costs.

4.9   Project contract

Not all projects are internal and before some external projects can be undertaken it is necessary to draw up a project contract. This sets out the requirements and specifications for the project, both from the viewpoint of the purchaser and the vendor.

The contract will include such things as

♦   Description of service bought/supplied
♦   Timescale for project
♦   Budget for project
♦   Acceptance criteria of system
♦   List of deliverables
♦   Constraints or penalties imposed on either party
♦   Change control and the responsibility for it
♦   Payment terms.

It is likely, however, that a 'Risks Limited/Commitment Limited' contract will be signed. This means that the project will be managed in stages and either party can withdraw at the end of each stage and that payments will be in instalments.

Once the project has been agreed and the contract signed, a project plan will be drawn up, probably using a structured diagram to identify the main areas. The function of the project plan is to allow the overall project structure to be clearly defined.

Practice question 5 *(The answer is in the final chapter of this book)*

Feasibility report

Required

(a)   Outline the main sections of a feasibility report and briefly explain the purpose of the typical contents of each section.

(b)   An important part of any feasibility report is a section giving a financial justification for the proposed system. Describe in detail the costs dealt with in this section.

5   The stages of project management

5.1   Terms of reference

Before planning procedures can even commence it is important to ascertain terms of reference. The points to be covered include the following.

♦   Details of the work to be performed.
♦   The cost of the work and a mechanism for costing changes in specification.
♦   Deadlines for various stages of the project.
♦   Experience of staff available.
♦   Quality control issues, testing and acceptance.

The work to be performed will include the following.

♦   Define what is required of the system.

♦   Investigate the existing system, estimating its cost and any problems or shortcomings.

♦   Explore alternative ways of satisfying the system requirements.

♦   Select the most suitable way of satisfying those requirements.

♦   Prepare a detailed estimate of the cost of developing and operating the system.

♦   Assess and assign a value to the savings and benefits of developing the system.

♦   Recommend whether or not the project should be carried out.

♦   Specify the performance criteria for the system.

♦   Prepare a detailed time schedule for implementing the system.

♦   Recommend suitable candidates for a user group assigned to help in the development of the system.

In summary, the terms of reference will lay down the following points in advance.

♦   The reasons for undertaking the project
♦   The resources available
♦   Any financial constraints
♦   Any resultant major organisational change

Once the terms of reference have been established the project planning can begin in earnest.

Any questions in the examination on either change or project management are likely to be practical, asking you to give advice on how particular problems can be overcome.

5.2 Project management process

 The elements of the project triangle provide the complex assembly of parts and the purpose; management provides the organised means of achieving the purpose.

The general model of project management perceives that a project has certain phases of development, which are generally embodied in a process model.

 In the syllabus for this paper, CIMA identify thirteen project stages and five managerial stages. These are shown below:

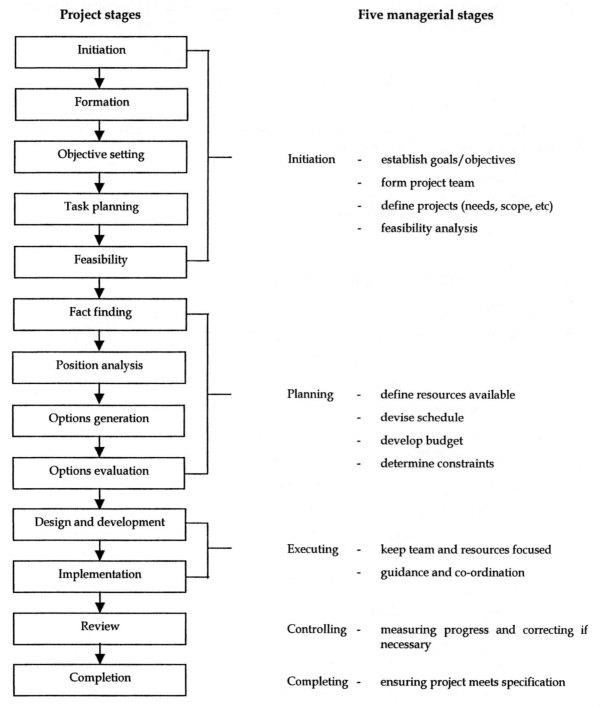

| Project stages | Five managerial stages |

Project stages

- Initiation
- Formation
- Objective setting
- Task planning
- Feasibility
- Fact finding
- Position analysis
- Options generation
- Options evaluation
- Design and development
- Implementation
- Review
- Completion

Five managerial stages

Initiation
- establish goals/objectives
- form project team
- define projects (needs, scope, etc)
- feasibility analysis

Planning
- define resources available
- devise schedule
- develop budget
- determine constraints

Executing
- keep team and resources focused
- guidance and co-ordination

Controlling - measuring progress and correcting if necessary

Completing - ensuring project meets specification

5.3   *Managerial stages*

Initiation - developing the idea, determining the needs, establishing the scope, goals, objectives and customer expectations of the project. At this stage the feasibility study will be undertaken and the project team will be brought together.

Planning - involves defining the resources to complete the project, devising a schedule and budget and negotiating with the project team the time and performance specifications required to achieve the objectives.

Executing - according to Tom Peters it means we must involve all personnel at all levels in all functions in virtually everything and be guided by the axiom 'there are no limits to the ability to contribute on the part of a properly selected, well trained, appropriately supported, and above all, committed person'. This stage requires managerial guidance and co-ordination to keep team members focused on the project tasks.

Controlling - measures the progress of the project and takes corrective action if it differs from the plan.

Completing - ensures the project is finished and conforms to the objectives.

Yeates and Cadle (Yeates, D and Cadle, J (1996), *Project Management for Information Systems*, 2nd edn, Financial Times Pitman Publishing) describe these phases in the information systems context, as follows:

♦   Initiation - What needs to be done? Why is it being done? Who is going to do it? How is it to be carried out? When is it to be carried out?

♦   Development - Requirements definition, design and implementation

♦   Completion - Delivery to the customer, end user training, acceptance testing and acceptance by the customer

♦   Operation

5.4   *Learning outcome*

You have now covered the learning outcome for this chapter.

Evaluate the project management process.

6   *Summary*

A way of describing a project is to assess the project lifecycle. This is a series of stages the project will pass through from conception to completion. Although projects can vary widely in terms of size, complexity, scope, timescales and cost, most of them will have a number of key features. These include an objective, quality criteria, customer requirements, resource constraints, a schedule and a budget. As well as resource constraints, the project may have financial limits and quality, time, legal and logical constraints.

CHAPTER 2

People and projects

EXAM FOCUS

In this chapter we will be covering several areas that the examiner has highlighted as requiring specific study. These include the skills of a project manager, building and managing a project team and the stakeholders of a project. You may be able to draw on your own experiences of team-working to help you with any questions on this topic. Even if you have not worked on specific projects, team-working skills gained in non-project environments will provide you with valuable experience that can add value to an examination answer.

LEARNING OUTCOMES

This chapter covers the following Learning Outcomes of the CIMA syllabus

> Produce a management plan for a simple project
>
> Evaluate the relationships between the project manager, the project team and organisational project sponsors
>
> Explain the skills required of a project manager
>
> Analyse the issues relating to the selection and management of an effective project team
>
> Identify problems with the interpersonal relationships of project staff and recommend solutions to those problems

In order to cover these learning outcomes, the following topics are included

> The stakeholders of a project (eg organisation, customers, steering committee, project manager, project team, vendors, specialists, users) and the relationships between them
>
> The skills of a project manager
>
> Building and managing a project team
>
> Managing project stakeholder conflict

---

1   Management plan

1.1   Introduction

Once the project need is identified and the project definition stage is complete, the next stage of the project management plan is to select the people that will be involved in the project and start up the project.

The stages of the plan were shown in a diagram in Chapter 1 and you should turn back to it occasionally to remind yourself what you have covered and what further stages you have to study.

1.2 A plan for developing an information system

The management plan for the activities involved in design, development and installation of an information system could cover the following areas:

- Detailed design work, including systems specifications, flowcharts and a list of equipment and hardware required.

- Design reviews, including modifications and design changes, may result in a change in project scope, price or schedule. It may even involve re-planning the original schedule.

- Systems testing, involving the customers who might want to participate in the testing or at least review the test procedures.

- Write and construct the software.

- Test the software.

- Purchase, assemble and test the hardware, including detailed testing of sub-assemblies of hardware, and then final test the entire hardware system interface.

- Integrate hardware and software and test the whole system.

- Plan installation - select the optimum changeover method and time.

- Prepare training materials to help users to understand, operate and maintain the system.

- Install and changeover.

- Training.

- Final acceptance testing.

1.3 Learning outcome

You have now covered the first learning outcome for this Chapter.

> Produce a management plan for a simple project.

2 Project stakeholders

2.1 Stakeholder hierarchy

There are various interested parties who are involved in or may be affected by the project activities. They are known as its 'stakeholders', as they have a 'stake' or interest in the effective completion of the project. Obviously, the number of people involved will depend on the size of the project.

 A project is much like an organisation in that it has a hierarchical set of relationships. This hierarchy is put in place for two main reasons:

- to create a structure of authority so everyone knows who can make decisions, and

- to create a series of superior-subordinate relationships so each individual or group has only one 'boss'.

Project stakeholders should all be committed to achieving a common goal - the successful completion of the project.

 The hierarchy shown below is adapted from the one shown in *Successful Project Management*, Gido J and Clements J, International Thompson Publishing, 1999.

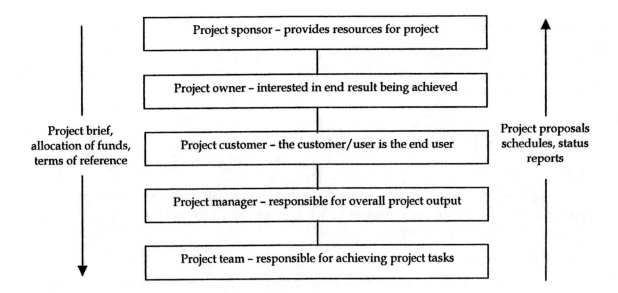

 However, in your syllabus for this paper the CIMA examiners have specified more stakeholders. Their list includes the organisation, customers, steering committee, project manager, project team, vendors, specialists and users and also the relationships between them.

 It is common for an organisation to put in place a formal organisation structure for a project. The following diagram can illustrate the relationship for this:

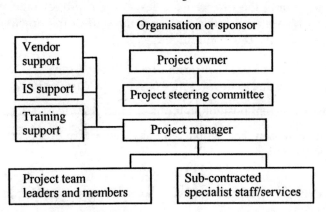

2.2   Project sponsor or organisation

The organisation is responsible for project selection and the approval of the project budget. The term 'project sponsor' is a generic term given to the source of the project manager's authority. He or she may be the owner, financier, client or their delegate. The sponsor acts as agent of the organisation to ensure that the project achieves the objectives set by the organisation (such as cost, quality and time). The sponsor is also responsible for reporting progress to the organisation and supporting the project manager. It is the sponsor's responsibility to control the project budget and ensure that the organisation's needs are met. This entails being responsible for the control of the project within the organisation, and providing a channel of communication between the project manager and senior management to report on progress and future developments.

Often a project involves change - a state that invariably meets with resistance; it is for this reason that the support of senior management is required. Ideally the project sponsor needs to be someone with sufficient authority to be able to progress the project in the face of difficulties and who has sufficient personal interest in the project to see it through.

The project sponsor:

♦ Agrees project outcomes
♦ Authorises definition of project
♦ Controls provision of resources
♦ Ensures delivery of project
♦ Promotes project at high level
♦ Owns project risks and resolves major problems

2.3 Project owner

The project owner is responsible for financing the project. He or she is the person for whom the project is being carried out and consequently will be interested in the end result being achieved and the needs/requirements met.

2.4 Project customer/user

These are the individuals or groups that will use the end product, process or service produced by the project. The user group should, ideally, consist of at least one user from each of the departments affected by the proposals, as well as the project manager and team leader(s). This group is an ideal forum for users to express their concerns; to highlight problems affecting users as the solution develops; for solutions to be explored; for obtaining user feedback.

2.5 The project steering committee

 This committee would typically consist of representatives from the user departments who are members of the user group; the project team leaders; the project manager and members of senior management who are responsible for either the staff or the functional areas affected by the project. The role of the steering committee is to:

♦ facilitate the discussion of user concerns in a discussion where recommended courses of action can be provided due to the presence of senior level staff

♦ review the project's current position in terms of time, resources, costs and scope

♦ analyse the likely reason and impact of any departure from the plan, and evaluate alternative remedial action

♦ recommend modifications to the project, with a view to remedying current or anticipated departures, or to take into account adjustments in the users' requirements from the system

♦ provide advice with regard to the formulation of policy relating to the operation of the information system within the organisation at all levels.

 Practice question 1 *(The answer is in the final chapter of this book)*

Steering committee

A steering committee is formed to monitor and control the feasibility study for the introduction of a management information system in a medium sized company.

Required

(a) Who might be a member of this committee?

(b) What might be the committee's terms of reference?

2.6   Vendors

In any project, many of the components of the solution may be bought in from suppliers or vendors. These individuals and organisations will have an interest in the project as they see it as a source of profit, and they will therefore want to ensure that they supply the right product or service and are paid on time.

2.7   Specialists

Most complex projects enlist the help and support of specialists from within the organisation. These individuals and groups will each have their own objectives, and may not see the project as their first priority. Typically, specialists come from the following departments:

◆ Human resources (personnel)
◆ Purchasing
◆ Production
◆ IT
◆ Quality
◆ Engineering

2.8   Project manager and project team

The project manager is the person who takes ultimate responsibility for ensuring the desired result is achieved on time and within budget. He or she will co-ordinate a project from initiation to completion, using project management and general management techniques.

The project team consists of individuals brought together purely for the purpose of undertaking a specific project. The size of the team and the period of their existence will be determined by the nature of the project.

With large development projects, there may be several leaders, each responsible for a part of the project team and reporting to the project manager. The team leader will typically be responsible for:

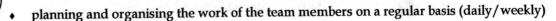

◆ planning and organising the work of the team members on a regular basis (daily/weekly)

◆ constantly supervising the activities of each individual team member

◆ providing advice or taking appropriate decisions in the case of technical difficulties

◆ co-ordinating and overseeing intercommunication between user departments and other project teams

◆ reporting to the project manager and/or user group and, where problems have been encountered, providing advice on feasible solutions

◆ reporting back to the team members any modifications to the project resulting from decisions made at a more senior level

◆ supervising the implementation of any changes to the planned activities or schedules resulting from control activities.

The project manager and the project team are considered in more detail in the next two sections of this chapter.

2.9   Learning outcome

You have now covered the following learning outcome for this chapter.

> Evaluate the relationships between the project manager, the project team and organisational project sponsors.

3 The project manager

3.1 Role and responsibilities

In the last chapter we proposed that projects were temporary packets of effort that have specific objectives, a defined start and end date, consume resources, are unique and require organisation. They also result in some form of facility or product that is operational in nature.

Given that management in the operational or 'traditional' sense revolves around control, co-ordination and communication, this implies that there are differences between project management and operational management. The first of these differences is found in the time-limited nature of project management. This difference mandates that the continuous supervision-based and appraisal-led approach of traditional management is inappropriate because the repetitive nature of work that allows performance to be noted, measured and compared with standards does not exist to the same degree.

A second difference is found in the aspect of uniqueness inherent to a project. This difference generates a higher level of risk and means that the project manager is less able to predict the outcomes of work and also has the burden of knowing that mistakes will have a higher degree of impact. A third difference is found in the purposeful change that is endemic to a project. This difference is highlighted in the fact that project management is generally designed to break the status quo, whereas operational management is designed to perpetuate it.

These differences mandate that a unique blend of skills and competencies are required in good project managers. These are discussed in detail in Yeates and Cadle (*Project Management for Information Systems*, 2nd edn, 1996, Chapter 22) who provide the following summary of the role and responsibilities of a project manager:

♦   To achieve the project's objectives within the time, cost and quality/performance constraints imposed by the sponsor.

♦   Make or force timely decisions to assure the project's success.

♦   Plan, monitor and control the project through to completion.

♦   Select, build and motivate the project team.

♦   Keep the sponsor and senior management informed of progress and alert them to problems - especially if these could have an impact on the project achieving its business objectives.

♦   Recommend termination of the project to the sponsor if necessary.

♦   Serve as the principal point of contact between the sponsor, management and contributors.

♦   Select and manage subcontractors.

The project manager has primary responsibility for organising, planning and controlling the work effort to complete the project objective. He or she is responsible for reaching and agreeing on a project objective, securing appropriate resources to achieve the project activities, tracking and monitoring project progress and implementing corrective action when necessary.

The ultimate responsibility of the project manager is to ensure the completion of the project objective to the satisfaction of the customer. He or she will take responsibility for providing leadership to the project team who will carry out the tasks to achieve the project objective. It is generally accepted that the project manager is the one person responsible for the project team's guidance, motivation, output and control. This statement implies that the project manager is all of the following:

- ♦ Leader - helps new team members to integrate into the team
- ♦ Project's technical director
- ♦ System integrator
- ♦ Project planner - takes action to keep the project on target for successful completion
- ♦ Project administrator - ensures the team has the resources to perform the tasks assigned
- ♦ Team's main communicator
- ♦ Mender of fractured relationships - provides support when members leave the team

On top of all of these responsibilities is added the task of team building. The effective project manager makes team building a part of each of the above aspects of his or her job.

 The project manager also has responsibilities to management. He or she will:

- ♦ maintain a customer (internal or external) orientation to ensure the success of the project
- ♦ ensure resources are used efficiently by striking a balance between cost, time and scope
- ♦ keep management informed with timely and accurate information
- ♦ promote the organisation's culture and policies

3.2   What does a project manager do?

Managing a project effectively can make the difference between success and failure of that project. Planning and managing a project particularly in an area which is innovative is challenging, but invaluable as a means of keeping an overview and control over the process of development.

 The project manager co-ordinates resources, controls the progress of the project, sets clear priorities and provides the formal process used to measure progress.

Typically a project manager will be nominated to lead a project and will be expected to be fully accountable for meeting its objectives. He or she will be the leader of the project team and will be responsible for ensuring the following are completed in a timely way:

- ♦ Gaining approval for the project aim and terms of reference
- ♦ Selecting and leading the team and setting individual objectives
- ♦ Ensuring a feasibility study is complete
- ♦ Ensuring that the project is planned in appropriate detail
- ♦ Allocating and monitoring the work and cost
- ♦ Motivating the team
- ♦ Reporting progress back to the organisation
- ♦ Helping the team to solve project problems
- ♦ Achieve, through the team, the goals
- ♦ Reviewing and closing down

 Practice question 2 *(The answer is in the final chapter of this book)*

Project manager

A project manager has been nominated to head a team set up to recommend the future direction and development of a sales order processing system. The individual nominated has asked for a brief description of the responsibilities of the project manager so that he understands his role before he takes on the job.

Required

In a briefing report to the project manager describe what will be his five main responsibilities.

3.3 The skills of the project manager

(a) **Core skills**

Very broad skills and a deal of experience are needed to manage a large project successfully. They include business knowledge, technical skills and individual and team leadership skills.

♦ The personal or individual skills are likely to include good presentation and persuasive skills, good written skills but allied to goal orientation, high energy and credibility. Good project managers know their own strengths and weaknesses and will compensate for these in selecting the team.

♦ Having team skills means that they will appreciate the differing needs of both individuals and the project team at different stages of the project. They will be aware of different team types.

♦ They will have technical skills in setting objectives, planning complex tasks, negotiating resources, financial planning, contract management, monitoring skills, managing creative thinking and problem solving, as well as their own specialist topic.

According to Yeates and Cadle, a project manager requires the following core skills in order to be effective.

♦ Leadership - to be able to stimulate action, progress and change.

♦ Technological understanding - to have an accurate perception of the technical requirements of the project so that business needs are addressed and satisfied.

♦ Evaluation and decision-making - the ability to evaluate alternatives and to make informed decisions.

♦ People management - to be able to motivate and enthuse their teams and have a constant personal drive towards achieving the project's goals.

♦ Systems design and maintenance - to be able to demonstrate their individual competence and have a complete working knowledge of the internal administration of their project.

♦ Planning and control - for constantly monitoring progress against the plan and taking any necessary corrective action using modern planning and monitoring methods.

♦ Financial awareness - proficient in risk management and have a broad financial knowledge.

♦ Procurement - understand the basics of procurement and be able to develop the procurement strategy for their project.

♦ Communication - able to express themselves clearly and unambiguously in speaking and writing and be able to do this in a wide range of situations and with a wide range of people.

♦ Negotiation - skilful in managing their clients and able to plan and carry out a negotiation strategy.

♦ Contractual skills - able to understand the contract that defines their project and able to manage subcontractors to ensure that the contractual terms are met.

♦ Legal awareness - an awareness of any legal issues that could affect their project.

(b)   Leadership skills

Leadership has been described as influence, or the art, skill or process of influencing people to work towards the achievement of group or larger organisational goals. There can be no leaders without followers, and such followers need to be influenced, persuaded or inspired to follow the leader. The project manager cannot achieve the project objectives without the whole project team. He or she must have the ability to motivate the project team to create a team objective that they want to be part of.

(c)   Communication skills

The progression of the project is dependent on the communication skills of the project manager. As well as the team members, he or she will communicate regularly with the customer, sub-contractors, suppliers and senior management. It means being involved in:

♦   identifying potential problems
♦   generating solutions
♦   keeping up to date with customer requirements
♦   discussions with the team on project issues
♦   giving timely feedback to both the team and the customer.

(d)   Delegation skills

The project manager will have neither the time nor the skills to carry out all of the tasks and must therefore delegate responsibility to those who do. Delegating is about empowering the project team and each team member to accomplish the expected tasks for his or her area of responsibility. The skill involved is in clarifying the overall objective to the team members and then further clarifying the individual team member's role in achieving the objectives by a process of delegation.

Delegation ensures effective performance by the project team and fosters conditions necessary for teamwork and co-ordination. It allows team members to learn from their mistakes and, if they are able, to correct them by themselves without fear of blame.

(e)   Problem-solving skills

There will be many problems during the life of a project. It is vital that the project manager gathers information about the problem so that he or she can understand the issues as clearly as possible. It is important for team members to be encouraged to identify problems within their own tasks and to try to solve them on their own initially. Where the tasks are large or critical to the overall achievement of the project, it is important the team members and the project manager get together so that they can initiate the problem-solving process.

(f)   Change management skills

The nature of a project suggests change. It may come about because it is requested by the customer or by the team. It can be caused by unexpected events during the project performance or required by the users of the final project outcome. There must be a leader of the change process who accepts the responsibility. Such a leader must have certain skills and attributes, such as:

♦   inspiration;
♦   interpersonal skills;
♦   ability to resolve a multitude of interdependent problems;
♦   ability to plan;
♦   opportunist;
♦   gift of good timing.

To maximise the advantages and minimise the disadvantages of the change process, the skills of the leader are further called into play. He or she will need to:

♦ communicate - explain as far as possible the reasons for change as the provision of both adequate and accurate information scotches rumours before they can be circulated; keep lines of communication going, monitor progress, giving regular feedback and communicate results; ensure the workforce are aware of the benefits to them of the change, eg increased responsibility, job enrichment.

♦ allow participation - give all staff concerned the maximum possible warning of impending change to give them time to get accustomed to the idea; involve individuals and/or work groups in the planning and implementing of change as much as possible. Employees will be more likely to become committed to change if they feel they can have some influence on the change and its outcome and it is also a way of gaining valuable suggestions.

♦ educate - try to introduce changes gradually; phased change stands a better chance of success; offer and provide appropriate training.

♦ counsel - where necessary, after considering the effects of change on individuals; follow up regularly and be supportive.

(g) **Negotiating skills**

Negotiating is an activity that seeks to reach agreement between two or more starting positions. Project managers will have to negotiate on a variety of project issues, eg level and availability of resources, schedules, priorities, standards, procedures, costs, and quality and people issues.

Field and Keller discuss the negotiation points that a project manager will be involved with. The table below shows the issues and negotiation points associated with specific groups:

Group to negotiate with	*Issues for project manager to negotiate*
Senior management	Resource funding and timescale Priorities over other projects/work Procedures - reporting
Line managers	Staff and equipment resources Schedules - duration and timing of activities Deadlines People - getting required skills, work allocations and effort needed
Accountants	Cost estimates and expenditure
Customers	Timescales Schedules - order, timing and duration of activities Priorities - between cost, quality and time Procedures - roles and responsibilities and reporting Quality assurance checks, performance measures and fitness for purpose Deadlines Costs - budgets and expenditure
Team and team members	Procedures - methods, role and responsibilities and relationships Priorities - between cost, quality and time Priorities - of team members' activities Schedules - order of activities Quality assurance checks, performance measures and fitness for purpose Cost estimates People - getting team to work together, getting required skills, work allocations and effort needed.

The skills of a negotiator can be summarised under three main headings:

♦ Interpersonal skills – the use of good communicating techniques, the use of power and influence, and the ability to impress a personal style on the tactics of negotiation.

♦ Analytical skills – the ability to analyse information, diagnose problems, to plan and set objectives, and the exercise of good judgement in interpreting results.

♦ Technical skills – attention to detail and thorough case preparation.

3.4 Developing the skills needed to be a project manager

The project manager may feel that he or she is lacking some of the skills required, eg the ability to develop people or to handle stress or time management skills. However, there are a number of techniques available to help the project manager develop the skill required, eg:

♦ gain experience
♦ seek out feedback from others
♦ conduct a self evaluation and learn from mistakes
♦ interview others who have the skills
♦ participate in training programmes
♦ join organisations
♦ read
♦ volunteer

You should be prepared for questions on the skills and competencies of a project manager. Part of a question might ask 'what personal skills and competencies might a project manager require and in what ways may these differ from an operational manager?'

Practice question 3 *(The answer is in the final chapter of this book)*

Project management

Developing and implementing large-scale administrative computer systems requires a formalised and disciplined approach to project management and control.

Required

Outline an approach to project management suitable for controlling the development of such a system.

3.5 Learning outcome

You have now covered the following learning outcome for this chapter.

Explain the skills required of a project manager.

4 Building and managing the project team

4.1 Project team

Two aspects that are important in this area are an understanding of both the lifecycle of teams and the characteristics of individuals that can be combined to create effective teams. The group lifecycle is encompassed in Tuckman's model of 'forming, storming, norming and performing', which is explained below. Group effectiveness is embodied in Belbin's work on team roles.

The project team is likely to be made up of a range of staff with different skills and experience. Effective team working is essential for the success of a project and it is important to foster this through regular meetings to establish team cohesion, helping to develop a team which is integrated, has common objectives and positive group dynamics.

The ideal project team will achieve project completion on time, within budget and to the required specifications. They will do all this with the minimum amount of direct supervision from the project manager.

4.2 Who is on the project team?

The basic project team consists of the project manager (and possible team leaders), and a group of specialists assigned or recruited for the project.

 The project team should include everyone who will significantly contribute to the project, both managerial and non-managerial people, whether they are full-time or part-time. The project team will obviously include all of the technical people responsible for the project's efforts toward research, design, development, procurement, production and testing. It is less obvious which of the many supporting and service functions involved with the project should be represented on the project team. This problem has no direct, easy answer, and often depends on whether there are available representatives from the support organisations who have both the time and inclination to become significantly involved with the project. However, representatives from other supporting groups such as quality control, finance and logistics should be sought when their function is vital to the project or is desired by the customer. Team members are expected to attend all project meetings, and to participate in project decision-making. Therefore, care should be taken in making sure that the team does not have any non-performing members.

4.3 Managing project teams

 In the management of project teams we must pay attention to two particular characteristics of each team:

♦ Each project is a complete entity, and unique in terms of experiences, problems, constraints and objectives.

♦ The members of the team concerned may well have not worked together as a group on any previous occasion.

The style of management for the team must be the relevant approach aimed at the creation of the appropriate internal team environment or, in other words, team climate. Some large organisations provide the team with initial status by providing it with all the necessary support and resources, such as office accommodation, a budget, support secretarial staff, and so on. Other organisations simply appoint a leader, authorised by the board to appoint team members and acquire resources at his or her own discretion.

 The planning and controlling of the team activities are vital aspects of management in that a major project cost lies in the fact that team members are not undertaking their own tasks but have been taken from these temporarily. It is essential that there should be an unambiguous statement of:

♦ the project objective(s) - what is to be achieved?
♦ the project approach, methods - how is it to be achieved?
♦ the location of activities - where is it to be achieved?
♦ the allocation of responsibilities - what is to be done by whom?
♦ the project budget - at what cost?

4.4   *Project team development*

The project team comprises people who report directly to the project manager. The success of the project depends to a large extent on the team members selected.

 B W Tuckman has formulated four stages of team development:

Forming - at this initial stage, the team members are no more than a collection of individuals who are unsure of their roles and responsibilities until the project manager clearly defines the initial processes and procedures for team activities, including documentation, communication channels and the general project procedures. The project manager must then provide clear direction and structure to the team by communicating the project objectives, constraints, scope, schedules and budget.

Storming - most teams go through this conflict stage. As tasks get underway, team members may try to test the project manager's authority, preconceptions are challenged, and conflict and tension may become evident. The conflict resolution skills and the leadership skills of the project manager are vital at this stage and he or she needs to be more flexible to allow team members to question and test their roles and responsibilities and to get involved in decision-making.

Norming - this stage establishes the norms under which the team will operate and team relationships become settled. Project procedures are refined and the project manager will begin to pass control and decision-making authority to the team members. They will be operating as a cohesive team, with each person recognising and appreciating the roles of the other team members.

Performing - once this final stage has been reached the team is capable of operating to full potential. Progress is made towards the project objectives and the team feels confident and empowered. The project manager will concentrate on the performance of the project, in particular the scope, timescales and budget, and will implement corrective action where necessary.

All teams do not automatically follow these four stages in this sequence. For example, a team where a large number of the members have worked together previously or have a much greater knowledge of the technical aspects of the problem will tend to arrive at the performing stage quickly. Of course, not all teams pass through all the stages - some get stuck in the middle and remain inefficient and ineffective.

4.5   *What is a team?*

 Teams have been described as collections of people who must rely on group collaboration if each member is to experience optimum success. Teams are groups of people who show the following characteristics:

♦   they share a common goal, and are striving to get a common job done;

♦   they enjoy working together, and enjoy helping one another;

♦   they have made a commitment to achieve the goals and objectives of the project by accomplishing their particular portion of the project;

♦   they are very diverse individuals having all kinds of different disciplinary and experiential backgrounds who must now concentrate on a common effort;

♦   they have great loyalty to the project as well as loyalty and respect for the project manager, and have a firm belief in what the project is trying to accomplish;

♦   they have attained a team spirit and a very high team morale.

To ensure that the group is truly an effective team working toward the same goals and objectives, the team members must have an overpowering reason for working together. They must need each other's skills, talent, and experience in order to achieve their mutual goals. Helping team members to achieve this goal is a key responsibility of the project manager.

4.6 Difficulties or blockages to team effectiveness

There are many aspects of the team process which might be impeding its effectiveness. Blocks to effectiveness include:

♦ objectives that are unclear or not accepted by the team members;

♦ a lack of trust or support;

♦ unsound working procedures;

♦ inadequate review of performance;

♦ problems with performance - it is slipping but no one knows why;

♦ decisions once made remain unimplemented;

♦ team members are unresponsive or apathetic to the needs of the team or of the project;

♦ team meetings are unproductive, full of conflict, and demoralising;

♦ team members withdraw into their own areas of responsibility and avoid co-operation;

♦ problem-solving activity like 'constructive conflict' is avoided;

♦ poor motivation and apathy;

♦ schedule slippages, quality problems and consequent cost escalations develop.

Practice question 4 *(The answer is in the final chapter of this book)*

Project processes

If a project is badly run then it is unlikely to gain the commitment of the people it needs for success. Poorly run projects fail to identify those whose commitment is needed to build the new system and as such individuals do not want to associate themselves with a project which is bound for failure.

Required

Describe the conditions that are necessary to manage a successful information system project.

4.7 Team building

When a new project is started, there is a great need to get everyone on the project team going in the same direction and aimed at accomplishing the same project goals. Basically the problem is that everyone on the project team sees the project in terms of their own particular discipline and background, and they will tend to go in different directions, often sub-optimising in their solution of project problems. The project manager must get the individual team members to view the project from the 'big-picture' perspective, and to concentrate on overall project goals.

Woodcock suggests that to achieve a successful team, the following nine aspects of its functioning and performance must have taken place.

♦ Clear objectives and agreed goals.

♦ Openness and confrontation.

♦ Support and trust.

♦ Co-operation and conflict.

♦ Sound procedures.

♦ Appropriate leadership.

♦ Regular reviews.

♦ Individual development.

♦ Sound intergroup relations.

If any one, or more, of these key aspects of team performance is not developed, the team may fail to achieve its full potential. The responsibility for team building falls squarely on the shoulders of the project manager, for he or she is the only person in the position of being able to ensure that team building occurs and that it is effective.

The role of the project manager in team building is to satisfy task, group and individual needs.

4.8 Action-centred leadership

Professor Adair's action-centred leadership model proposes that the effectiveness of a leader is dependent on three areas of need within a workgroup being met. These three areas are defined as

♦ the need to achieve the common task - the manager ensures that the purpose (completion of the task) is fulfilled. This entails defining the objectives, aims and goals, etc. The main tasks could include setting standards, allocating jobs and controlling the work. Other leadership skills required include problem solving and decision-making, promoting involvement and commitment, evaluating ideas and performance, negotiating and resolving conflicts.

♦ the need for team maintenance - until the task is completed the group has to be held together; the manager must maintain team spirit and build morale, concentrating on team building, developing interdependence and keeping the members of the group well informed.

♦ the individual needs of group members - the manager should consider individual needs and motivate, develop and support individuals.

Adair's action-centred leadership model

Task needs

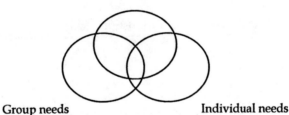

Group needs   Individual needs

 The interaction between the areas of need is commonly symbolised by three overlapping circles (see Yeates and Cadle, *Project Management for Information Systems*, 1996, p254) and the table below shows what each area involves.

Task, Team and Individual Functions

Task Functions	Team Functions	Individual Functions
- Achieving the objectives of the work group	- Maintaining morale and building team spirit	- Meeting the needs of the individual members of the group
- Defining group tasks	- Developing work methods so that the team functions cohesively	- Attending to personal problems
- Planning the work	- Setting standards and maintaining discipline	- Giving praise and status
- Allocation of resources	- Setting up and maintaining systems of communication within the group	- Reconciling conflicts between group needs and individual needs
- Organisation of duties and responsibilities	- Training the team	- Developing the individual
- Controlling quality and checking performance	- Appointing subordinate leaders	
- Reviewing progress		

Essentially, the model proposes that the three areas of need are interlinked and that an effective leader integrates them and sees that all needs are met.

A good leader does not necessarily have to be in a formal position of power to exert influence, though this is clearly a factor that can add weight. This brings into question different styles of leadership, which can be broadly classified as authoritarian (or autocratic), democratic and laissez-faire.

♦ Authoritarian places the locus of power with the manager and group interaction gravitates around them. The focus here is generally oriented toward high productivity.

♦ Democratic management devolves power and responsibility in a managed fashion and there is greater interaction within the group. The focus here is generally oriented toward high morale and productivity.

♦ Laissez-faire devolves power and responsibility to the degree where individuals have freedom of action and the manager is able to concentrate on co-ordination and support. The focus here is generally oriented toward high morale.

Effective project managers display the ability to:

♦ select the right people for the right cause
♦ evaluate progress towards objectives
♦ solve problems as they arise
♦ negotiate resolutions to conflicts
♦ heal wounds inflicted by change

Practice question 5 *(The answer is in the final chapter of this book)*

Effective teamwork

Effective teamwork is a key success factor for most projects.

Required

(a) Briefly describe some of the characteristics of effective project teams.

(b) Explain some of the barriers to effective project teams.

4.9 Learning outcome

You have now covered the following learning outcome for this chapter.

Analyse the issues relating to the selection and management of an effective project team.

5 Managing stakeholder relationships

5.1 Relationships

All of the stakeholders that we have discussed above are related to one another by their (temporary) contact with the project. They will each have different personal objectives, many of which will conflict with each other and with the objectives of the project. The authority/responsibility relationship between the various stakeholders was illustrated in the diagram earlier in this chapter (paragraph 2.1); the responsibilities include the following.

♦   The organisation is responsible for project selection and the approval of the project budget.

♦   The sponsor acts as agent of the organisation to ensure that the project achieves the objectives set by the organisation (such as cost, quality and time). The sponsor is also responsible for reporting progress to the organisation and supporting the project manager.

♦   The project manager is responsible for the delivery of an optimum project solution. The project manager is also responsible for reporting progress to the steering committee or sponsor, and communicating their views and requests to the project team and its sub-contractors.

♦   The project team and sub-contractors are responsible for delivery of the project components entrusted to them, and for the communication of issues and problems to the project manager.

At the beginning of a project potential stakeholders need to be identified and their interests in the project assessed. This is a vital project management activity to enable the relationships within the groups to be managed. A plan can be drawn up to secure and maintain their support and to foresee and react to any problems. The project manager can concentrate on the critical stakeholder relationships, assess the risks associated with certain groups, indicate where attention needs to be focused and thus reduce the vulnerability of the project.

5.2   *Stakeholder analysis*

The project manager has to balance a number of values, beliefs and assumptions in attempting to navigate a project to a successful conclusion. These values, beliefs and assumptions relate to the stakeholders in the project, who may be defined as any party with a vested interest. The ability to be able to discern stakeholder values, beliefs, assumptions and expectations is a positive tool in the project manager's 'competence toolbox', not least because they often conflict and may not always be benevolent to the project. Stakeholder analysis provides a means to discern expectation and its drivers and comprises the following stages:

♦   Stakeholder identification
♦   Stakeholder mapping

Stakeholders exist at the level of the individual, groups and organisations and can be internal or external to the project. Within a project, for example, stakeholders might exist in the form of the project sponsor, banks providing capital, suppliers and contract organisations, the client organisation, analysis and design groups and the individuals involved. All are embedded in some form of organisational culture that will fuel and/or influence the individual. Once stakeholders are identified they can be mapped in relation to:

♦   The likelihood of each stakeholder group attempting to impress their expectations on others

♦   The power and means available for them to do so

♦   The impact of stakeholder expectations on the project

Two matrices can be developed from this analysis that aid the project manager in understanding the threat and management approach to key stakeholders (following Mendelow, 1991). These are shown below. The first one maps stakeholder power against predictability and shows where political efforts are best channelled during the project. The latter maps stakeholder power against interest in the project to understand the best strategy for managing expectation.

	Predictability				Level of interest	
	High	Low			*how* High	Low *high*
Low	Few problems	Unpredictable but manageable		**Low**	Minimal effort	Keep informed
Power				**Power**		
High	Powerful but predictable	Greatest danger or opportunity		**High**	Keep satisfied	Key players

      (a) Power/Dynamism   (b) Power/Interest

5.3 Stakeholder conflict

Among the most common reasons for conflict are the following:

♦ Unclear objectives for the project.
♦ Role ambiguity within the project team.
♦ Unclear schedules and performance targets.
♦ A low level of authority given to the project manager.
♦ Remote functional groups within the project, working almost independently.
♦ Interference from local or functional management.
♦ Personality clashes, or differing styles of working.

Most conflict arises from the interaction of individuals, and a good project manager must have the interpersonal skills to be able to manage conflict.

5.4 Managing stakeholder disputes

Many of the major issues in project management arise because of the conflicting objectives of the various project stakeholders. The project manager should establish a framework to predict the potential for disputes. This involves:

♦ risk management - since an unforeseen event (a risk) has the potential to create conflict; and

♦ dispute management - matching dispute procedures with minimum impact on costs, progress and goodwill.

Risk management comprises risk assessment (identifying and analysing risk) and risk control (taking steps to reduce risk, provide contingency and monitor improvements). Risk management can be seen as a series of steps:

♦ Risk identification - producing lists of risk items

♦ Risk analysis - assessing the loss probability and magnitude for each item

♦ Risk prioritisation - producing a ranked ordering of risk items

♦ Risk-management planning – deciding how to address each risk item, perhaps by avoiding, transferring, absorbing or reducing the risk (see below)

♦ Risk resolution - producing a situation in which risk items are eliminated or resolved

♦ Risk monitoring - tracking progress toward resolving risk items and taking corrective action

Examples of risk management planning approaches would include the following:

♦ **Avoidance -** the factors that give rise to the risk are removed

- Abort the plan
- Escape the specific clause in the contract
- Leave the risk with the customer or supplier

- **Transference** - subcontract the risk to those more able to handle it, such as a specialist supplier

- **Absorption** - the potential risk is accepted in the expectation of the incidence and consequences being coped with by the organisation

- **Reduction** - analysis means that ways of reducing the incidence and/or the consequences can be identified, eg take out insurance to pay in the event of the occurrence arising or invest in additional capital equipment or security

Dispute management - whenever there is a potential for conflict, a process to resolve it should be established before it occurs. This means getting all the participants of the project together to discuss their concerns and understand the viewpoints of others. It is an opportunity to identify potential areas of conflict with a view to avoiding them. An agreed strategy for avoiding disputes can be drawn up, as well as a mechanism for avoiding them before they escalate.

Techniques for resolving conflicts include:

- Negotiation - involving the parties discussing the problem. This may or may not resolve the problem.

- Mediation or 'assisted negotiation' - involves a neutral third party (the mediator) intervening to reach a mutually agreeable solution. In practice, disputes are often resolved by accepting the view of the stakeholder that has financial responsibility for the project. In such a situation, mediation and negotiation may only deliver an outcome that is a reflection of the original power imbalance.

- Partnering - focuses on creating communication links between project participants with the intention of directing them towards a common goal - ahead of their own self-interest.

- Compromise - is the most obvious approach to conflict management, although it does imply that both parties in the conflict must sacrifice something.

5.5   Learning outcome

You have now covered the final learning outcome for this chapter.

> Identify problems with the inter-personal relationships of project staff and recommend solutions to their problems.

6   Summary

The stakeholders within a project include the owner, customer, external suppliers, the managers of the project and the project team. The project manager has primary responsibility for the organisation, planning and controlling of the work effort to complete the project objective. He or she is responsible for reaching and agreeing on a project objective, securing appropriate resources, tracking and monitoring project progress and implementing corrective action when necessary. The project team is a group of individuals working together to achieve a common objective. The team moves through a number of stages as they learn, develop and grow. Effective teams have a clear understanding of the project objective and their roles and responsibilities and have a high degree of team spirit and co-operation.

CHAPTER 3

Project management tools and techniques

EXAM FOCUS

Any project for an organisation, whether it is the reorganisation of the factory or the relocation to another area, must be planned, implemented and controlled effectively. This chapter explains the tools and techniques used by project managers in planning and controlling the activities to achieve the project objectives.

The examiner has noted that the tools and techniques mentioned in the syllabus have been introduced elsewhere in your studies, but you may not realise that they can be used at the various stages of a project as well.

LEARNING OUTCOMES

This chapter covers the following Learning Outcomes of the CIMA syllabus

> Apply project management tools

> Explain the process of post-completion audit and its importance in the project management process

In order to cover these learning outcomes, the following topics are included

> The stages of a project (eg initiation, formation, objective setting, planning, feasibility, fact finding, position analysis, options generation, options evaluation, design and development, implementation, review, completion)

> The major tools and techniques used at each of the project stages (ie project initiation document, SWOT analysis, critical path analysis, Gantt chart, resource histogram, budget, progress report, completion report)

---

1 Project stages, tools and techniques

In the first chapter of this text, we outlined the thirteen project stages and five managerial stages associated with project management. These are shown again below, identifying the tools and techniques that are used by project managers during each stage.

Project stages　　　　　　　　**Managerial stages and tools and techniques**

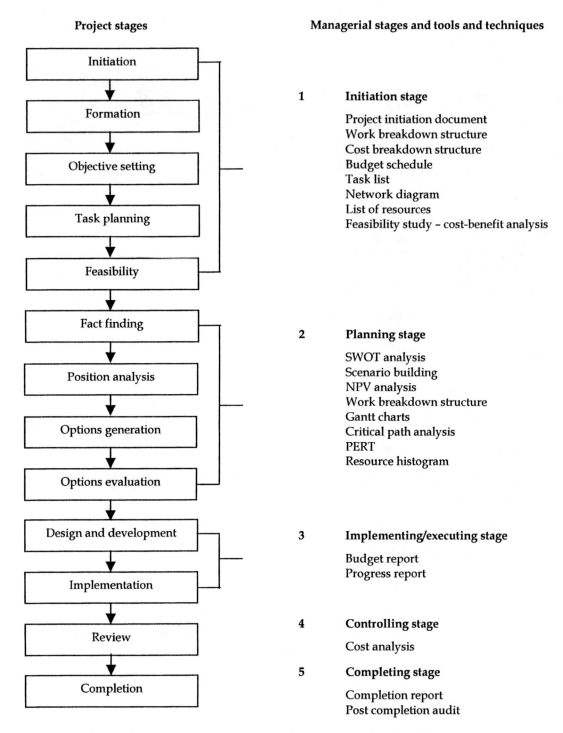

1　　**Initiation stage**

Project initiation document
Work breakdown structure
Cost breakdown structure
Budget schedule
Task list
Network diagram
List of resources
Feasibility study – cost-benefit analysis

2　　**Planning stage**

SWOT analysis
Scenario building
NPV analysis
Work breakdown structure
Gantt charts
Critical path analysis
PERT
Resource histogram

3　　**Implementing/executing stage**

Budget report
Progress report

4　　**Controlling stage**

Cost analysis

5　　**Completing stage**

Completion report
Post completion audit

 As discussed in Chapter 1 earlier, the objective of project management is to:

♦　define the project
♦　reduce it to a set of manageable tasks
♦　obtain appropriate and necessary resources
♦　build a team or teams to perform the project work
♦　plan the work and allocate the resources to the tasks
♦　monitor and control the work
♦　report progress to senior management and/or the project sponsor
♦　close down the project when completed
♦　review it to ensure the lessons are learnt and widely understood.

The project management tools available at each stage of the process are explained below.

2   Initiation stage

2.1   Introduction

This stage involves the following tasks.

♦   Establishing objectives and targets for the system.

♦   Setting a target timetable for completion of individual phases.

♦   Estimating the costs for each phase and constructing a project budget.

♦   Dividing the project into identifiable activities and using this as a basis to prepare an outline plan of the major development stages.

♦   Identifying the resources required (people, time, money). This, along with the previous task, will form the basis for any network analysis.

The following sections discuss the tools and techniques available.

2.2   Project initiation document

The first project management stage involves identification of a need, opportunity or problem. This process will form the basis for the organisation to establish its own requirements and find out whether they are achievable.

The project initiation document is sometimes called a 'statement of work' or 'project charter'. It is a formal document listing the goals, constraints and success criteria for the project. When it is written, it is subject to negotiation and modification by the various stakeholders of the project and once they formally agree its content it becomes the document that is referred to in the event of any disagreement later.

According to Eric Verzuh (*The fast forward MBA in project management*, Eric Verzuh, J Wiley, New York, 1999) a project initiation document will have the following sections:

♦   Purpose statement - explaining why the project is being undertaken.

♦   Scope statement - putting boundaries to the project by outlining the major activities of the project.

♦   Deliverables - the main outcomes expected from the project. They tend to be tangible elements of the project, such as reports, assets and other outputs and make the success of the project easier to measure.

♦   Cost and time estimates - which will be modified later in the project, but are necessary to give a starting point for planning.

♦   Objectives - clear statement of the mission, critical success factors and milestones of the project.

♦   Stakeholders - in the project.

♦   Chain of command - the project organisation structure.

2.3   Work breakdown structure (WBS)

This is a technique that analyses the content of work and cost by breaking it down into its component parts. It is produced by:

♦   Identifying the key elements

♦   Breaking each element down into component parts

♦   Continuing to breakdown until manageable work packages have been identified. These can then be allocated to the appropriate person.

The WBS needs to include all aspects of the project from planning through development to delivery. Identifying the minute stages of a project begins with the whole project, followed by breaking up into smaller parts and then continually breaking down the work until the smallest unit can be identified. This exercise is the best way of discovering the work that must be done, as well as determining the resources required. The sequencing of tasks and the priorities and pitfalls also become more apparent as the project is broken down.

Below is a work breakdown structure for the recruitment of a new person to fill a vacant post.

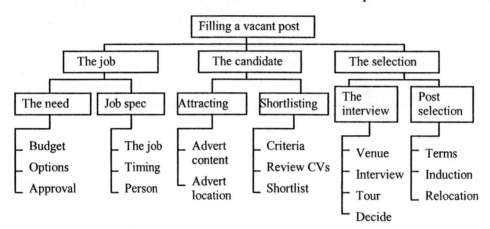

The activities in a WBS need to:

♦ be measurable in terms of cost, resources and time
♦ be the responsibility of a single individual
♦ provide an identifiable end product

The set of plans or forms produced from the work breakdown structure can then be used for estimating. A list of all the tasks, broken down into their constituent parts can be completed and analysed into direct and indirect costs, with columns for all the identifiable expenditure, including labour, materials and the project overhead costs.

2.4 Estimating resource requirements

There are different classifications to denote the accuracy of project cost estimates:

♦ **Definitive estimates** aim to be accurate to within 5% and are produced after the design stage of the project lifecycle.

♦ **Feasibility estimates** are accurate to within 10%. These are made in the early design stage.

♦ **Comparative estimates** are made when the project under review is similar to a previous one. The accuracy of this estimate depends on the similarity and the prevailing economic conditions.

♦ **Ball-park estimates** are a rough guide to the project costs and are often made before a project starts. They may be accurate to within 25%.

Cost estimation invariably involves some guesswork where the project manager is beginning a new, uncertain project. For projects where there is no margin of safety, it is crucial that the estimates are definitive. The project manager can improve the accuracy by:

♦ learning from previous mistakes;
♦ having sufficient design information;
♦ obtaining a detailed specification; and
♦ breaking the project down into smaller jobs and detailing each constituent part.

2.5   Cost breakdown structure

The normal approach to project costing is to use the work breakdown structure in order to produce the cost breakdown structure (CBS) at an increasing level of detail. This CBS will be a complete list of every item that can be classed as expenditure.

Project costs can be analysed into direct costs, including labour and materials, and indirect costs, including rent, light, heating and other overheads.

The various costs identified with each part of the work breakdown structure will be collected to provide a useful cost analysis for the various business functions and also to be a mechanism for controlling costs.

A useful means of estimating costs is to design estimation forms, based on the work breakdown structure so that by each work unit number there is a separate column for each of the costs, eg labour and materials.

Another methodology for cost planning, called the C/SPEC, combines the work breakdown structure, the organisation breakdown structure (labour, sub-contractors, materials, overheads, etc) and the cost breakdown structure. This would have to be done using a computer, because of the three dimensions.

3   Planning stage

3.1   Detailed planning

The planning phase will result in the submission of proposals to the customer by the organisations that want to perform the project. The proposals will be evaluated and the most appropriate solution chosen. The SWOT analysis and scenario building will be part of the fact-finding phase and a feasibility study with a cost benefit analysis is generally used in the option evaluation process. The customer and contractor will then sign a contract.

The initial plan is developed into a feasible action plan. The main activities during this stage are as follows.

♦   Preparing a detailed schedule of activities to be undertaken, including the logical sequence of the activities (their 'dependency'). It is important to identify those activities that are critical to meeting the overall project timetable (the activities on the critical path, as we will see when we discuss network analysis).

♦   Assessing the resources available and allocating specific resources to activities identified in the schedule. This may involve staff recruitment and training.

♦   Preparing a procurement schedule with regard to equipment, software and services required for the system.

♦   Preparing detailed budgets for both internal and external expenditure.

♦   Developing a system for monitoring and controlling the progress of the activities in terms of their time, cost, resource allocation and quality.

Practice question 1 *(The answer is in the final chapter of this book)*

Project planning

Project planning is the key activity for a project manager.

Required

What is meant by project planning, and who should be involved in the process?

3.2 SWOT analysis

This analysis consists of the internal appraisal of the organisation's **strengths and weaknesses**, sometimes called a position audit, and an external appraisal of the **opportunities and threats** open to organisations in competition within the industry. Therefore, strengths and weaknesses are peculiar to an individual organisation but opportunities and threats are open to all organisations within the market place. The purpose of SWOT analysis is to provide a summarised analysis of the company's present position in the market place.

The internal appraisal (strengths and weaknesses) should identify:

◆ the organisation's strengths that the project may be able to exploit

◆ organisational weaknesses that may impact on the project.

The main areas considered would include:

◆ products, eg age, life span, lifecycle stage, quality comparisons

◆ marketing, eg market share, presence in target segments, identifiable and non-identifiable benefits, success of promotions, advertising

◆ distribution, eg delivery promise performance, depot location

◆ production, eg age/obsolescence, valuation, capacity

◆ research and development, eg number of commercially viable products, costs/benefits, relevance of projects

◆ human resources, eg manpower plan, management in depth, training levels, morale

◆ finance, eg cash availability, risk exposure, short and long-term funding, contribution levels.

The external appraisal should identify opportunities that can be exploited by the organisation (such as growth in market demand, or new technological possibilities) and should help managers anticipate environmental threats, eg competitors' actions, declining economy, legislation, etc.

Opportunities and threats could be expected to arise in five main areas and will be available to all companies in a particular industry. These areas are:

◆ economic, eg changes expected in tax, currency rates, trade controls

◆ government, eg environmental legislation, development grants, level of government spending

◆ social, eg attitudes towards such aspects as marriage, working mothers, youth unemployment, early retirement, leisure pursuits, willingness to incur debt

◆ competitors, eg cheap imports, closure of export markets, potential entrants, sources of raw material

◆ technology, eg new products/production techniques, improved communications, transport.

Unfortunately, managers have little or no influence on external environmental factors. However, the impact and effects of external forces must be taken into account when evaluating the relevance of particular projects.

3.3   *Network analysis*

Network analysis is a general term, referring to various techniques adopted to plan and control projects. It is used to analyse the inter-relationships between the tasks identified by the work breakdown structure and to define the dependencies of each task. Whilst laying out a network it is often possible to see that assumptions for the order of work are not logical or could be achieved more cost effectively by re-ordering them. This is particularly true whilst allocating resources; it may become self evident that two tasks cannot be completed at the same time by the same person due to lack of working hours or, conversely, that by adding an extra person to the project team several tasks can be done in parallel thus shortening the length of the project.

Below is the WBS shown for the recruitment of a new person to fill a vacant post after network analysis as been applied.

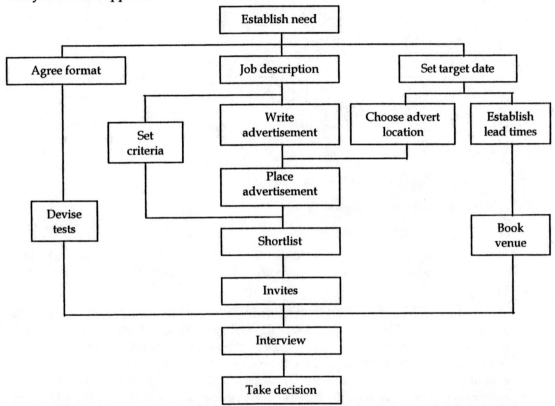

One of the component parts of network analysis is critical path analysis or CPA. This means breaking down a project into its constituent activities, presenting the activities in diagrammatic form, and identifying the critical path.

The following steps are used in CPA.

◆   Analyse the project. The project is broken down into its constituent tasks or activities. The way in which these activities relate to each other is examined: which activities cannot be undertaken until some previous activity or activities are complete?

◆   Draw the network. The sequence of activities is shown in a diagrammatic form called the 'network diagram'.

◆   Estimate the time and costs of each activity. The amount of time that each activity will take is estimated, and where appropriate the associated costs are estimated.

◆   Locate the critical path. This is the chain of events that determines how long the overall project will take. Any delay to an activity on the critical path will delay the project as a whole; delays to other activities may not affect the overall timetable for completion. That is the distinction between critical and non-critical activities.

◆ Schedule the project. Determine the chain of events that leads to the most efficient and cost effective schedule.

◆ Monitor and control the progress of the project. This implies careful attention to the schedule and any other progress charts that have been drawn up, to monitor actual progress in the light of planned achievement.

◆ Revise the plan. The plan may need to be modified to take account of problems that occur during the progress of the project.

3.4 Drawing the network diagram

The key to drawing these diagrams is to follow a number of simple rules. A network diagram looks like this:

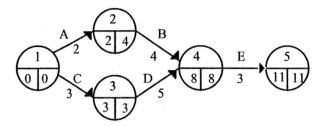

The rules referred to above are as follows.

1   The network diagram is written and read from left to right.

2   A network should have a beginning and an end.

3   Networks are not drawn to scale.

4   The event symbol (a circle) shows the beginning or end of an activity, and each event symbol is numbered for reference purposes. The event symbol represents a point in time.

5   The left hand side of the event symbol details the earliest start time (EST), which is the earliest time at which an activity can begin. ESTs are entered during a 'forward pass' through the network; in other words, once all the event symbols have been plotted we work from left to right through the network, entering ESTs as we go. The right hand side of the event symbol details the latest start time (LST), which is the latest time an activity can commence without the project exceeding its estimated duration. LSTs are entered during a 'backward pass' through the network; in other words, once we have entered ESTs we work back through the diagram from right to left entering LSTs as we go.

6   The 'activity' line connecting the event symbols shows the time taken to complete an activity. Each activity line is referenced.

7   All activity lines should have an arrowhead at one end indicating the sequence of activities.

8   Lines that cross should be avoided.

9   Every activity must have a preceding event (the tail), and a following event (the head).

10   Several activities may use the same tail event, and several the same head, but no two activities can share the same head and tail events. For example, the following connection would not be allowed.

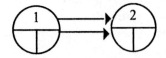

It would be redrawn as follows using a *dummy activity*.

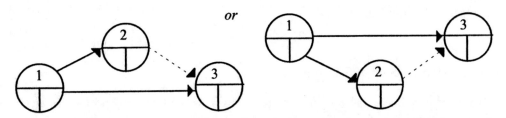

or

Dummy activities do not consume any time or resources and are drawn in the diagram to make the diagram clearer. They ensure that the rules for drawing network diagrams are not breached.

11   Loops are not allowed: you cannot have a series of activities leading from one event and back to the same event. For example, the diagrams below are not allowed.

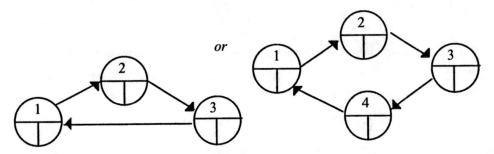

or

12   'Danglers' are not allowed: all of the activities must be connected. For example, the diagram below is not allowed.

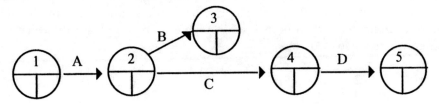

3.5   The critical path

The critical path through the network is the chain of activities whose times determine the overall minimum duration of the project. Activities on the critical path are known as critical activities; any increase in the duration of a critical activity will result in an increase in the planned minimum duration of the whole project.

The following example illustrates the principles explained above.

Example

Activity	Preceding activity	Duration (weeks)
A	–	8
B	A	10
C	–	6
D	C	4
E	B, D	8

You are required to draw the network chart and identify the critical path.

Solution

We will tackle the problem in stages.

Stage 1

Identify the starting point of the diagram.

This is where activities have no preceding activities, ie activities A and C start from time 0. Draw activity times A and C at 45° to the first event symbol.

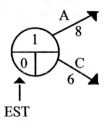

- Label the left hand side of the first event symbol with a 0 representing the commencement of the project.

- Label the event symbol '1' being the first event.

- Label the activity lines together with their estimated duration.

Stage 2

From the question identify the next activities that follow on in sequence from activities A and C. These will be activities B and D but before updating the diagram consider whether the next activity can only proceed when all other activities have been completed. In this question activity E can only commence when both B and D have been completed in which case the network diagram will now look like this.

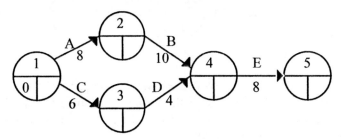

- Label each event with a reference number
- Label all activity lines together with their estimated duration

Stage 3

Now carry out the forward pass through the network by starting at the left hand side of the diagram and filling in the left hand side of the event symbols with the 'earliest start time' - this being the earliest time at which the following activity can commence. The network diagram now looks like this.

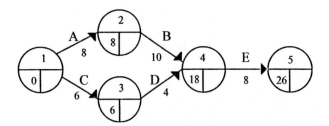

Stage 4

Then carry out the 'backward pass', by starting at the right hand side of the diagram and filling in the right hand side of the event symbol with the latest start time (LST), the latest time at which an activity can commence without the project exceeding the overall estimated project duration of 26 weeks.

Note that the first event symbol should always have a zero value for both the EST and the LST.

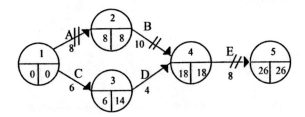

Stage 5

The critical path is the path through the network such that if any of the activities exceed their estimated duration then the overall estimated project duration of 26 weeks would be exceeded.

In this example the critical path is A, B, E. This path can also be identified from the diagram as the activities at the beginning or end of which the event symbols show the same EST and LST. The critical path can be marked by double lines on each activity line that lies on the critical path.

Stage 6

The 'float' or spare time on activities is found by identifying those event symbols that have different values for EST and LST. In our example event symbol 3 has a float of 8 weeks (ie 14 - 6). This can be interpreted to mean that the time taken to complete activity C or D can take up to 8 weeks longer in total than budgeted and the estimated project duration of 26 weeks would not be exceeded.

Practice question 2 (The answer is in the final chapter of this book)

Feasibility

During the feasibility study the major activities involved in a project have been identified and listed with their estimated durations and the order of tasks. The information is shown in the table below.

Activity	Description	Duration (days)	Preceded by
A	Draw up detailed specification	15	Start of project
B	Modify software	10	A
C	Wiring and cabling offices	4	A
D	Install new office furniture	3	C
E	Install and test hardware	5	D
F	Install and test software	4	B, E
G	Training	5	F
H	Data conversion	3	F
I	Changeover using parallel running	20	G, H
J	Acceptance testing	2	I

The computer systems manager was not able to start his employment as soon as the company would have liked. He is naturally very keen to make a good impression by getting the project completed smoothly and quickly. However, he is particularly concerned that activity B (modify software) is not directly under his control since it will be carried out by the system's suppliers. He is also concerned that there may not be sufficient slack time to cope with any problems that may arise.

Required

Draw a network chart of the project's activities as listed in the feasibility study report and identify the critical path. Comment on the computer system manager's concerns about completing the project smoothly and on time.

3.6 Disadvantages of critical path analysis

Critical path analysis has the following disadvantages.

♦ Activities do not always start and end cleanly.
♦ The critical path is necessarily based on estimates, which may not be accurate.
♦ The chart can be difficult to follow.
♦ The chart purely relates to 'time' and does not reflect the amount of work undertaken.

3.7 Network analysis - PERT

Programme evaluation and review technique is very similar to CPA. The difference lies in timings. In the PERT network, there are three times developed for each activity:

(a)   an optimistic time (assuming all goes well);
(b)   a realistic estimate (updating occurring as progress is made); and
(c)   a pessimistic time (assuming all possible problems arise).

PERT is generally used for R & D planning, major construction work, etc. For small projects PERT is rarely used.

All network planning, irrespective of the technique used, requires a review of the critical path, including comparison with the actual progress made. This is so that any necessary action can be taken to correct a deviation. Where there is a critical path delay, then the float on the other activities is increased. If the critical path is improved upon, another line could be critical as the float reduces. The review must be undertaken or network analysis cannot be regarded as a successful management technique.

Properly used network analysis provides these advantages to management:

♦ identification of both the duration and critical path;

♦ provision of an analytical device for any project which has an introduction (start) time and a finishing point;

♦ progress control is emphasised;

♦ an early indication is given of crises in the project; and

♦ the technique stresses and encourages careful appraisal of activities and stages of projects on the part of managers.

3.8 Gantt charts

Gantt charts (named after the inventor), sometimes called bar charts, are used to display and communicate the results of PERT and Critical Path Analysis in a simple bar chart format that can be readily understood by those not involved in the detail of the project. The example we considered above on recruitment and selection is now displayed as a Gantt chart below:

ID	Task name	Duration in days	w/e 28th July					w/e 4th August					w/e 11th August				
			M	T	W	T	F	M	T	W	T	F	M	T	W	T	F
1	Establish the need	2	■	■													
2	Set target date	1			■												
3	Establish lead times	1				■											
4	Book venue	1					■										
5	Choose advert location	1				■											
6	Agree format	2				■	■										
7	Devise tests	5						■	■	■	■	■					
8	Job description	2			■	■											
9	Set criteria	1						■									
10	Write advert	2						■	■								
11	Place advert	1								■							
12	Shortlist	3									■	■	■				
13	Invite candidates	1												■			
14	Conduct interviews	3													■	■	■
15	Take decision	1															■

3.9   Gantt charts and resource histogram

 The following example can be used to illustrate the use of Gantt charts and resource histograms in project management.

Example

Furnite plc are to initiate a project to study the feasibility of a new product. The end result of the feasibility project will be a report recommending the action to be taken for the new product. The activities to be carried out to complete the feasibility project are given below.

Activity	Description	Immediate predecessors	Expected time (wks)	Number of staff required
A	Preliminary design	-	5	3
B	Market research	-	3	2
C	Obtain engineering quotes	A	2	2
D	Construct prototype	A	5	5
E	Prepare marketing material	A	3	3
F	Costing	C	2	2
G	Product testing	D	4	5
H	Pilot survey	B, E	6	4
I	Pricing estimates	H	2	1
J	Final report	F, G, I	6	2

The first step is to draw the network and identify its critical path thus:

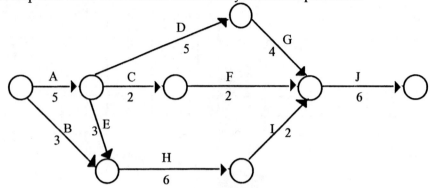

The numbers are the expected durations in weeks.

The critical path (by inspection) is A, E, H, I, J.

Total expected duration = 5 + 3 + 6 + 2 + 6 = 22 weeks

 The Gantt chart is constructed with reference to the earliest start times for each activity, the duration of each activity and the number of staff required for each activity thus:

Time wks / Activity	1	2	3	4	5	6	7	8	9	10	11	12	13	14	15	16	17	18	19	20	21	22
A			3																			
B		2																				
C						2																
D							5															
E							3															
F								2														
G											5											
H									4													
I															1							
J																			2			
No. staff	5	5	5	3	3	10	10	10	11	9	9	9	9	9	1	1	2	2	2	2	2	2

Note that activity C cannot commence until activity A is complete and is therefore drawn as starting at the end of week 5 on the chart. You will also see that the number of staff required each week is simply obtained by adding the staff requirements per activity for the relevant week number.

From the network chart, particularly in the Gantt chart form, the total resources in use at any one time can be added up from the tasks that are in progress at that time (assuming that the task's use of resources is more or less constant). If this is done for the whole project, the result is a Resource Histogram for the project. The cost of the project is likely to be less if peaks and troughs in resource use can be evened out, and, of course, the estimated use of resources at any one time must never exceed what is in fact available. The number of staff required at Furnite plc is shown in the resource histogram below:

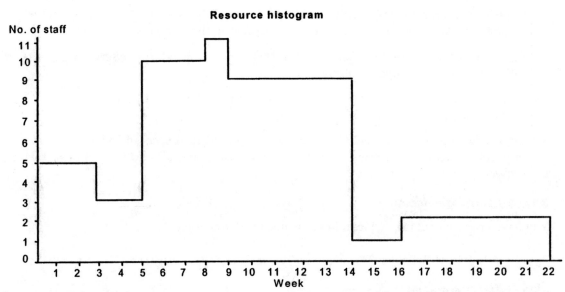

The Gantt chart and histogram will indicate the resource requirements needed to successfully complete the project.

Practice question 3 *(The answer is in the final chapter of this book)*

Order entry system

A new on-line order entry system is currently being developed in your organisation. As part of the implementation procedures, users of the new system will require a number of training activities. The following table lists the activities, their duration, and the most appropriate sequence.

Activity	Preceding activity	Duration (weeks)
A	–	4
B	–	3
C	A	6
D	B	8
E	C, D	3

Required

(a)   Produce a network chart from this information, identifying the critical path through the network.

(b)   Explain how a Gantt chart might also be of use in this context, and identify any extra information which would then be required.

3.10   Advantages of project management tools

Project management tools such as critical path analysis and Gantt charts have the following advantages.

♦   Easier visualisation of relationships. Network diagrams show how the different tasks and activities relate together and make it easier to communicate to interested parties.

♦   More effective planning. CPA forces management to think a project through thoroughly, which requires careful and detailed planning.

♦   Better focus on problem areas. This allows management to pinpoint likely bottlenecks and problem areas before they occur.

♦ Improved resource allocation. Resources are allocated to those parts of the project which will have most effect in reducing cost and speeding up the completion.

♦ Studying alternative options. Management can simulate the effect of alternative courses of action and make contingency plans.

♦ Management by exception. Management attention can be focused on important (critical) areas of the project.

♦ Improved project monitoring. Comparison of actual against schedule enables recognition of problem areas as they occur, which enables the early identification of problems that are important to the project.

3.11   Learning outcome

You have now covered the first learning outcome for this chapter.

Apply project management tools.

4   Implementing stage

4.1   Introduction

 The implementing phase is the actual performance of the project, resulting in the accomplishment of the project objective. It is the project team that delivers the implementation, not the project manager. However, it is the responsibility of the project manager to ensure that the team's output meets the performance requirements stated in the project definition and delivers the goals of the project. How the implementation is managed has a direct relationship to the quality, time scale and cost of the project.

Regular reviews of task outcomes from the work being done, training methods and their effectiveness (where applicable), and the comparison between the work completed to date with the project definition and plan are the important items to monitor. Ratios are very useful for monitoring. For example, if your team estimates that half the work has been done (on any stage or task) and you know that 60% of the budget has been spent, then you have a problem that must be addressed immediately and action taken. The project sponsor (or budget owner) should always be kept informed because surprises are more detrimental than budget over-runs. If this pattern is being repeated elsewhere then the cost over-runs could spiral out of control.

The same goes for time scales. Maybe you are ahead on time but over budget. Cutting back on labour may balance this out. If the extra expenditure has reduced the project risks then maybe no action is necessary. If you are over time and over budget you have a serious problem that must be addressed, probably at a very senior level.

The monitoring process is the feedback element of the control cycle. Various types of reporting are used at this stage.

4.2   Types of reporting

 (a)   Exception reporting - assumes that everything is in accordance with plan. Only exceptions are reported.

(b)   Effort reporting is often handled on a 'completed/to go' basis. This has the effect of re-estimating the work content of an activity.

(c)   Progress reporting – reporting everything that has occurred to those that need to know.

The periodic progress report is sent from the project manager to the project sponsor or steering committee, often on a monthly basis. A typical progress report will contain the following sections:

♦ A report identifier – the project name, report sequence number and date.

♦ A short review of progress since the last report.

♦ Problems encountered and actions taken or planned.

♦ Revised plans for cost and time, together with details of any agreed variations to scope.

♦ A SWOT analysis.

The progress report will often be used as the basis of discussion at a meeting between the project manager and the project sponsor or steering committee.

5 Controlling stage

 The controlling phase involves monitoring and controlling the project, with vetting on progress, milestones achieved or missed, costs of equipment and manpower compared to budget. This takes place on a continuous basis throughout the system development and implementation phases. The controlling activities within this stage will include the following.

♦ Prevention of deviations from the planned activities.

♦ Correction of deviations from the plan.

♦ Prevention of any future deviations by revising future plans, targets, performance standards and monitoring systems.

♦ Implementation of conclusions from monitoring, reviewing or evaluating the project.

 The evaluation and review process measures actual performance against planned performance, with particular emphasis on time, resources, costs and quality. It involves the following tasks.

♦ Measuring progress to meet targets of time, cost, resources and quality, both in the current period and cumulatively to date.

♦ Assessing the implications of carrying forward work scheduled for the current period to the next period.

♦ Devising a range of actions to be taken to overcome current or potential future problems or delays.

Control procedures for the control of projects and their development are established in very many organisations to varying degrees and under various titles (eg, DP Standards or Project Control). All projects tend to be expected to create a return on investment and this requires accurate estimates of various costs (development, running) and savings arising from operating the system. There may have been, and might be, a number of failures to meet set targets of cost/time, but there is no set 'formula' to avoid these.

6 Completing stage

6.1 Completion report

 This is undertaken once the project has been completed, with the objective of adding to the organisation's knowledge and experience. The assessment will include consideration of the following points.

- The project objectives and the outcomes achieved.

- The extent to which the required quality has been achieved.

- System efficiency during live operation compared with the agreed levels of performance.

- The cost of the system in comparison with budgeted cost, and explanations for variances.

- Comparison of actual time taken to complete the project with the budgeted time anticipated.

- The effectiveness of the management process.

- The significance of the problems encountered, and the effectiveness of the solutions generated to overcome them.

6.2 Post-completion audit

A post-completion audit is important because a project cannot be said to be successful until management is assured that all the benefits promised at the evaluation stage can be shown to have been subsequently realised.

The audit should be conducted by staff experienced in appreciating the financial and/or production implications of the project and who are independent of the original commissioning team. Two purposes will be served by this audit.

- It checks whether benefits have been achieved and draws management's attention to unsuccessful projects.

- It reduces the tendency in many organisations to be over-optimistic with the data when presenting projects for evaluation.

The information will be presented in a report, which should contain the following:

- A summary that emphasises any areas where the structure and the tools used by management have been found to be unsatisfactory.

- A review of the end results of the project compared with the results expected. Reasons for any discrepancies between the two will be identified, preferably with suggestions as to how future projects could prevent these problems occurring again.

- A cost-benefit review comparing the forecast costs and benefits identified at the time of the feasibility study with the actual costs and benefits.

- Recommendations as to any steps that should be taken to improve the project management procedures used.

6.3 Project closure meeting

The completing phase involves the confirmation that all the deliverables have been provided and accepted, all payments have been made and received, and performance has been evaluated and appraised.

It is important to ensure that a project is properly closed for two reasons. Firstly, there is a tendency for projects to drift on and become, or develop into, other projects. Secondly, it is important to ensure that the work of the project team is acknowledged and that the lessons to be learned from the project are formally investigated and recorded for use on the next project.

Most texts recommend that a project closure meeting should be held at the end of the project. The objectives of the meeting are as follows:

- To bring the project to an orderly close.
- To confirm that all the planned work has been carried out.
- To check that all technical and quality issues have been resolved.
- To agree that all documentation required is available.
- To confirm that the project has been signed off.
- To review any lessons learned from the project for future reference.

A report is completed at the meeting, summarising the matters considered. This report is distributed to the steering committee and any other organisational stakeholders such as the director responsible for the project.

Practice question 4 *(The answer is in the final chapter of this book)*

Network

The following details relate to a computer systems installation.

Activity	Description	Duration (days)	Preceded by
A	Install hardware	4	–
B	Train staff	4	–
C	Load all software	3	A
D	Transfer data from old system to new	9	B, C
E	Run test data	21	D
F	Identify and correct errors	12	E

Required

(a) Prepare the network diagram.

(b) Identify the critical path and the estimated project duration.

6.4 Learning outcome

You have now covered the final learning outcome for this chapter.

> Explain the process of post-completion audit and its importance in the project management process.

7 Project management software

7.1 Software packages

Because project management techniques can be complicated and involve large amounts of data that is constantly changing, a number of software packages have been developed to cope with the work. Project management software packages can be bought for the PC for a few hundred pounds. The features they offer include:

- access to graphical user interface
- planning activities
- work scheduling facilities
- ability to view relationships amongst tasks and other projects
- resource management
- project progress monitoring and control

7.2 Examples of project management tools

 Project management software recognises that there is a sequence in which activities need to be performed. The software package will require four items of information.

- The duration of each activity
- Dependencies of activities
- The resources available
- At what stage the resources will become available

The type of output produced by the package will vary depending upon the package being used.

 Examples of available packages include the following.

- AMIS Schedule Publisher
- Texim Project
- WinProject
- Milestone
- Project for Windows
- Masterplan
- Ultra Planner
- Auto Plan
- Open Plan
- X Plan
- RAD Path

 When choosing project management software (or indeed any software package) there are a number of important points to address.

- Determine the requirements of the organisation, including its current and future needs.

- Document the requirements, distinguishing functions that are essential, those that are important, and those that are merely desirable.

- Review the available packages to identify three or four products which meet the essential functions and fall within budget.

- Attend a demonstration of the packages or use on a trial basis if possible.

- Select the package and develop a 'roll out' strategy (including installation, training, etc).

Practice question 5 *(The answer is in the final chapter of this book)*

Project software

The development of computer systems is a project-based activity. The development project has a start and, once it has met its objectives, an end.

Required

Explain how computer software can be used to help in the planning, estimating, monitoring and reporting of project progress.

---

8   Summary

In this chapter we looked at the steps in the project lifecycle. Part of project management is the estimating of resources and the time needed to complete parts of the project. We outlined some of the techniques used for estimating, eg Gantt charts, network analysis and critical path analysis.

It must be possible to measure progress made in acceptable terms, determine and report any deviations, undertake corrective action as necessary and issue specific reports.

The evaluation of a project takes into account the total costs and total resource usage and assesses problems encountered. Eventually there will be a general appraisal of the whole project results undertaken formally, followed by regular project reviews.

CHAPTER 4

Project communication

EXAM FOCUS

Communication is an integral theme that runs through the entire syllabus. You must be able to recognise the key methods of communication and be able to recommend the most effective communication tool within the given scenario in the exam.

LEARNING OUTCOMES

This chapter covers the following Learning Outcomes of the CIMA syllabus

Explain why meetings are commonly used in organisations

Evaluate the planning and conduct of a meeting and the roles of the various participants in a typical meeting

Identify the main problems associated with meetings and recommend how those problems might be avoided or solved

Recommend changes to the management and conduct of a meeting in order to avoid or solve problems identified

Produce a presentation on a management accounting topic

In order to cover these learning outcomes, the following topics are included

The purpose, conduct and limitations of meetings in a business context

The roles, which may be adopted by participants in a business meeting (eg chair, secretary, facilitator, advisor, protagonists, antagonists) and how the chair should manage those participants to retain control of the meeting

---

1 Communication

1.1 Definition

 Communication in business can be defined as the transmission of information so that it is received, understood and leads to action.

This definition enables us to understand some of the key aspects of business communication:

♦ Information, and not data, should be communicated. Information is active, relevant and prompts action; data, on the other hand, is passive, may be historical or irrelevant and does not lead to action.

♦ Clearly, if information has not been received or is not understandable by the receiver, then communication has not taken place.

♦ The communication should lead to action; this action may take the form of a positive decision or a change in attitude. If the communication does not lead to any action then, probably, it ought not to have taken place.

So communication means transmitting messages to people in a manner that stimulates response. In some cases, the response will be direct to the sender, as when two people are engaged in debating the merits and demerits of some proposition. In other cases the response will be indirect as when transfer of the information gives rise to some independent action on the part of the recipient or when he merely stores it for future reference.

 Communication methods are often determined by the information sources and information requirements of the organisation. You need to analyse the scenario in the exam to ascertain the information problems and requirements and make appropriate comments and recommendations.

1.2 Verbal, written and visual methods

Communication within the organisation can take place through different media and methods, each of which has its advantages and disadvantages.

 Written communication - should be used when the situation is formal, official, or long term; or when the situation affects several people in related ways. Inter office memos are used for recording informal inquiries or replies. Letters are formal in tone and addressed to an individual. They are used for official notices, formally recorded statements, and lengthy communications. Reports are more impersonal and more formal than a letter. They are used to convey information, analyses, and recommendations. Written communications to groups include bulletin-board notices, posters, exhibits, displays, and audio and visual aids.

Communication and the need to exchange information are no longer constrained by place and time. E-mail, voice mail, and facsimile have facilitated communications and the sharing of knowledge. E-mail is the computer transmission and storage of written messages. Voice mail is the transmission and storage of digitised spoken messages. Facsimile (fax) is the transmission of documents.

 Verbal or spoken communication - includes informal staff meetings, planned conferences, and mass meetings. Voice and delivery are important. Informal talks are suitable for day-to-day liaison, directions, exchange of information, progress reviews, and the maintenance of effective interpersonal relations. Planned appointments are appropriate for regular appraisal review and recurring joint work sessions. Planning for an appointment includes preparing, bringing adequate information, and limiting interruptions. Telephone calls are used for quick check-ups and for imparting or receiving information.

Teams using information technology have access to information, share knowledge, and construct documents. Meetings take place electronically from multiple locations, saving the organisation's resources in both the expenses of physically bringing people from different locations together, and the time lost by employees travelling. Teleconferencing is simultaneous group verbal exchanges. Videoconferencing is group verbal and visual exchanges.

 Visual communication - examples include posters, charts, graphs, video, TV, slide projection and product demonstrations. The main advantages are:

♦ Impact - you will notice and remember the picture long after you have forgotten the words and figures.

♦ Visual has the highest retention rate (ie. recall after the event).

♦ The availability of colour and moving images enables the communicator to add drama and grab attention.

♦ They facilitate the understanding of complex material and are comprehensible by those of poor linguistic ability - they can be international in their meaning.

Practice question 1 *(The answer is in the final chapter of this book)*

Communication

Required

Why is communication necessary in a business organisation? Is it possible to formulate rules to provide better communication? If so, how?

2 Project meetings

2.1 Purpose of meetings

Meetings can be held for a wide range of purposes, but it is important that the purpose of the meeting is made clear to the participants in advance. If this is done, the meeting is more likely to be a success. The most common reasons for holding a meeting are the following:

♦ To give or obtain information.
♦ To address a problem, grievance or complaint for resolution.
♦ To make a series of specific decisions about an issue.
♦ To generate creative ideas, for development outside the meeting.
♦ To present a proposal for discussion and approval.
♦ To secure certain attitudes.

2.2 Types of formal project meeting

Regular team meetings are an important way to improve team relationships and to communicate the objectives of the project to the whole team. There are many types of project team meeting - the project design review, the project status, the project problem solving and the post project evaluation meetings are the main ones.

Project design review meetings - will be called frequently where a project involves a design element. The meeting might be a forum to present new technical specifications for the client's approval or to present problems for solving.

Project problem solving meetings - are called whenever a problem occurs within a project. The team members who are affected by the problem will attend the meeting to resolve the issue. It is important that there is a quick response to the identification of the problem and that the appropriate team members participate in the search for a solution. The project manager should provide clear guidelines on the problem solving programme and make decisions on who should take responsibility for the implementation of the solution.

Project status review meetings - are called regularly to inform others about the project status to date. Many project stakeholders will be present, especially the project leader, the team members and the customer. These meetings will identify any issues or problems associated with the scope, time or cost of the project and will reach a decision on the subsequent action plans for the rest of the project.

Post project evaluation meetings - all the team members will attend this meeting at the end of a project. Its purpose is to assess the team's overall contribution and make recommendations for the future. All parties involved in the project will evaluate their own performance and the team will learn valuable lessons for future projects.

The agenda for the meeting will cover the following topics:

♦ Project performance - scope, cost and schedule
♦ Project planning
♦ Customer relationships
♦ Team relationships
♦ Problem identification.

The questions and issues raised at the meeting might include:

♦ Whether the objective of the project was achieved.

♦ Whether the original plans were drawn up in sufficient detail and whether performance was monitored against the plan.

♦ Whether the customer was happy with the performance and felt fully informed and sufficiently involved.

♦ Whether the communications were effective and if the team worked well together.

♦ Whether there were sufficient mechanisms in place to allow team members to identify problems early and whether they were solved effectively.

The outcome of this meeting will be a report sent to senior management by the project manager. It will summarise the project performance and advise on improvements for future reference.

2.3   Informal project meetings

A major need of any formal meeting is to arrive at a decision: if it fails in this, then the time spent in the meeting has been largely wasted. Most meetings tend to be informal and are held to co-ordinate activities, exchange information and develop a team approach. Informal meetings can also be held in a participative fashion to solve problems, agree action or formulate decisions.

Such meetings can have important benefits, namely:

♦ stimulate new ideas
♦ provide information and explain reasons for policies
♦ test ideas
♦ ensure co-operation and agreement in sensitive matters
♦ provide a forum for exchange of views and feedback.

2.4   Learning outcome

You have now covered the first learning outcome for this chapter.

Explain why meetings are commonly used in organisations.

3   The conduct of meetings

3.1   Procedure

As we have already noted, there are different types of meeting and each has a different procedure.

Formal meetings generally conform to a system where there is usually a chairperson who guides the proceedings and aims to maintain order. They generate formal documentation for the announcement, planning, conduct and recording of the proceedings. These include the following:

♦ Notice - the invitation or announcement of the meeting, which is prepared and circulated in advance. The communication can be by e-mail, a personal letter, a memo, a notice on the internal notice board or an official card like an invitation.

♦ Agenda - the items of business to be discussed at the meeting. This is often attached to the notice to give participants a guide to the business that will be discussed and the preparations they will need to make. The minutes of the previous meeting might also be included so that any queries or objections relating to them may also be prepared.

The agenda of a meeting is essentially a list of points to be covered. It should be short, professional and clear. Often the previous agenda and minutes are used in its preparation. Many organisations have standard pro-formas for use in all meetings. Any agenda should show the details of the venue and time of the meeting, and should also give some indication of the expected duration of the meeting. Points for discussion should be placed in a logical order, with related points near each other to recognise that decisions may depend on previous items.

♦ Minutes - the written record of the proceedings at the meeting, approved by those present. They provide a source of reference, particularly with regard to decisions and action points agreed by participants.

 Convening a meeting means making arrangements for people to attend. This can be by issuing a notice of each meeting or, if the meeting is one of a series of similar gatherings (eg a regular Monday morning project status review meeting), it can be convened automatically.

A meeting may only proceed if it has been properly constituted, ie meets criteria laid down regarding attendance and conduct. Regarding attendance, the organisation may specify the minimum number of people that must be present for certain types of meeting. This is called a quorum. If there is no quorum, the meeting must be suspended or adjourned.

Procedures may also be defined regarding the conduct of the meeting. Each item of business may be required to be put before the meeting as a proposal or motion. This usually requires a proposer and a seconder. If it is carried (or approved), the motion becomes a resolution (or decision). The participants will vote for or against a motion. This can be by a show of hands, a poll, a ballot, a division or a voice vote.

A point of order is an objection about a perceived irregularity in the convening, constitution or conduct of the meeting. It is made to the chairperson, who makes an immediate ruling.

 Practice question 2 *(The answer is in the final chapter of this book)*

Project meeting agenda

Required

Draw up an agenda for a project status review meeting.

3.2   *Arrangements for meetings*

Meetings are an effective communication method for all of the project stakeholders. Arrangements for meetings can be split into three stages and the following points are common to all meetings whatever their purpose or form and will help ensure that the meeting is effective and useful.

 (i)   *Preparation*

♦ Establish valid purpose of meeting and consider whether this could not be achieved by other means.

- Consider the day on which the meeting should be held. The date of the meeting must not be after the date the decision has to be taken. There should be time to give appropriate notice. Remember Fridays are popular for day conferences etc.

- Determine who should attend - ensure quorum for decisions.

- Book room with due regard for ventilation, noise, refreshment, seating and security.

- Prepare agenda - even if informal for own purposes itemise with most controversial matters neither at beginning nor end.

- Publicise. Inform participants well in advance (if possible), giving details of the time, venue and purpose of the meeting.

(ii) *Conducting meeting (as chairperson)*

- Start on time.
- Put members at their ease and focus minds on purpose of meeting – informal call to order.
- Outline procedure to be followed (if irregular) and define technical terms.
- Direct a general or specific question to get meeting started.
- Ensure fair play - link speakers and deter verbosity.
- Summarise at appropriate times and at end but do not impose your own views.
- Try to finish on time - if impossible get agreement to continue but never drift.
- Thank those present for attending.

(iii) *After meeting*

- Have contact memo or minutes prepared by secretary and approved by chairperson - these form the basis of the next meeting.

- Follow up decisions taken.

Practice question 3 *(The answer is in the final chapter of this book)*

Project meeting stages

Required

Outline the stages required to ensure an effective project meeting.

---

4 Roles of participants in meetings

4.1 Chairperson

One person at the meeting will act as chairperson (also called the 'chair'). This person takes responsibility for setting the agenda for discussion and ensuring the orderly and proper conduct of the meeting where all members participate equally and all views are listened to.

The project manager may take on the chairperson's role. Depending on the circumstances, the chairperson of a meeting may take the role of organiser, disciplinarian, arbitrator, antagonist or counsellor.

John Adair suggests several skills that the effective chairperson must learn. These include

- the ability to silence people in a firm and friendly manner;
- the skill of sensing that consensus is near and testing the meeting on that point;
- being alert to non-verbal behaviour;
- the skill of summarising.

When chairing a meeting, it is useful to summarise the objectives of the meeting at the beginning. This will help to focus the attention of the attendees on the job in hand. It may also be necessary to remind the meeting of its objectives at various stages, to stop the meeting drifting out of control.

Other techniques that a chairperson can adopt include asking 'opening questions' to stimulate the thoughts of the group as a whole and asking a specific question to a particular participant to encourage participation and ensure those with specialist knowledge contribute when appropriate.

The chairperson will use summaries to consolidate points agreed on as a basis for moving on. The objective of summarising is to check on the level of understanding and give an opportunity to sort out misunderstandings. There are two different ways of accomplishing this objective:

♦ At intervals in the conversation give a summary of the salient points as you have understood them.

♦ To test understanding by inviting someone else to summarise and check that their summary accords with the one that you would have given at that stage in the proceedings. If a number of people are present, invitations to summarise can be shared around rather than becoming the prerogative of one person. This is a splendid incentive for people to listen hard since they never know when they might be called upon to paraphrase what they have heard.

Summarising reduces ambiguity by pointing things out explicitly and helps to reduce the likelihood that people are agreeing to different things.

4.2   Secretary

The meeting will also require a secretary who is responsible for ensuring that the minutes of the meeting are complete and accurate and providing a copy of them to the team members after the meeting. Prior to the meeting, the project manager should ensure that the secretary has been clearly briefed and has a clear understanding of the purpose and likely content and format of the meeting. The secretary will also deal with correspondence, and advise the chairperson on points of procedure. He or she may also be responsible for fixing the date and time of the meeting and for booking the venue.

4.3   Facilitator

The facilitator is responsible for ensuring that debate keeps moving along, and that experience is brought to the discussion. The project manager should act as facilitator in the team meeting process and take responsibility for setting the agenda for discussion and making sure that the meeting achieves its objective. He or she should give all team members an opportunity to participate.

It is the responsibility of the project manager to make the whole team aware of the overall project objective and the role each member will play in its achievement. If the meeting is designed to solve problems, individual members will be called to offer their own expertise and advice on the situation. An advisor may also be invited to a meeting in order to contribute their specific technical or commercial expertise. The advisor's responsibility is to ensure that all issues are considered, and that conclusions accord with accepted best practice.

In order to stimulate and test new ideas and provide a forum for the exchange of views and feedback, negotiating skills are necessary. Negotiating is an activity that seeks to reach agreement between two or more starting positions. There are behaviours that are typical of successful negotiators and distinguish them from the less successful:

- Attacking the problem not the person - skilled negotiators avoid criticising or attacking the other person and concentrate instead on 'attacking' the problem in a no nonsense but constructive way. Less skilled negotiators are more likely to get locked into an attacking spiral where one side attacks the other, which provokes a counter attack and so on.

- Asking questions - skilled negotiators ask many more questions than the less skilled. The less skilled tend to assume that they understand the other person's point of view and that the other person has the same basic information. This makes asking questions redundant. The skilled negotiator asks questions not only to gain more information and understanding but also as an alternative to disagreeing bluntly and as a means of putting forward suggestions.

- Sticking to the facts - less skilled negotiators are inclined to exaggeration, using expressions such as 'an offer you can't refuse' and 'mutually beneficial', whereas skilled negotiators keep the emotional temperature down by sticking to the facts.

- Being open - the skilled negotiator is more likely to say things that reveal what he or she is thinking, intending and feeling than the less skilled. The less skilled negotiator feels vulnerable to losing the argument and is more likely to 'keep his cards close to his chest'.

- Disagreeing constructively - disagreements are inevitable during the course of a negotiation. Less skilled negotiators disagree first and then go on to give reasons. This often provokes a negative reaction from the other person who bridles at the explicit disagreement and therefore fails to listen to the reasons. The skilled negotiator reverses the order by giving the explanation first and rounds of the explanation by saying that they were in disagreement. This has a more constructive effect because the explanation becomes the focus for the other person's reaction rather than the fact of a disagreement.

- Focusing on interests - one of the problems frequently encountered in negotiating is that sides take up positions which are incompatible. Skilled negotiators concentrate on the interests that lie behind the positions, as they are more likely to provide footholds for finding common ground and moving ahead.

4.4 Antagonists and protagonists

 The team members attending the meeting will adopt various roles, depending on the purpose of the meeting. Some members of the team will be antagonists and possibly disruptive to the team meeting procedures by disagreement and negative attitude to other team members. Antagonists are members of the meeting who continually question the accepted or proposed view. They are responsible for ensuring that alternatives are considered, and that the drawbacks or problems of a proposal are clearly understood.

Protagonists are positive supporters of the issue under discussion. Their responsibility is to ensure that the benefits and advantages of a suggestion are clearly understood. Although positive support is critical for successful project team working, the project manager must be wary and assess the reasons for it, in case it is not beneficial to the project.

5 Presentations

5.1 The pitfalls

Another form of communication is a presentation. Project managers will be familiar with giving presentations to new clients, the project team or to the Board of Directors. However, for a manager who is new to the giving of presentations there are certain pitfalls which should be avoided in order to ensure the success of the presentation.

The following points should be noted in order to avoid failure of a presentation.

♦ Number of people attending - people are often embarrassed by asking questions in front of a large audience. If the presenter is aiming for feedback and participation from the audience which is not forthcoming then the overall effect of the presentation may fail.

♦ People hear what they want and expect to hear - especially when a familiar subject area is being presented; some people may not pay attention. Also, if what the presenter is saying conflicts with set beliefs, instead of hearing what is actually said people often hear what they expect to hear, or interpret what they hear in their own way.

♦ Words are not objective and may be ambiguous - the emphasis placed upon words can alter their meaning and also, many words have more than one meaning. The presenter should choose words with care in order to avoid misinterpretation of the message and should avoid the use of words and phrases that are ambiguous.

♦ Physical factors impede communication – for example, if the room is too cold or too hot or if there is noise from heavy traffic. All of these things will have an effect upon the presentation being given.

♦ Technical noise - can also impede the presentation, for instance if the presenter has a very strong accent which is not perhaps easily understandable by all of the audience.

♦ Emotional factors - can lead to some people not being able to concentrate on the message being said.

♦ Retention - only about 10% of what people hear is retained and the usual attention span is about 20 minutes. It is therefore necessary to alter the delivery of the presentation in order to keep the audience's attention for the majority of the time.

5.2   Producing a presentation

A presentation is a combination of both verbal and visual forms of communication that is used by managers at some meetings, training sessions, lectures and conferences.

 Before any presentation is made it is necessary to establish the objectives of the presentation, why it is being done and what you want it to achieve. Once these things have been identified, the best way to achieve the objectives can be established. Other areas to check prior to the presentation include:

♦ ensuring that all equipment is available and in good working order.

♦ the type of audience in terms of their status, personal preferences, hostilities and likely reactions to what is being said.

♦ whether humour might be injected into the presentation - some audiences would not appreciate an attempt at humour in certain situations.

♦ the venue of the presentation - to ensure that sufficient seating is available and sockets for the overhead projector are within easy reach, etc.

♦ whether notes are to be held on keyword cards or on sheets of paper, the latter offering more room for writing but also being more cumbersome to control.

♦ whether the presenter's voice carries to the farthest corner of the room.

♦ what would be considered suitable dress for the occasion.

 Compiling a presentation that holds the audience's interest and drives the point home with clarity is not as easy as it looks. Some professional presenters advise that you divide your presentation into three sections:

The *introduction* summarises your overall message and should begin with a title slide, or transparency, that succinctly states the purpose of the presentation.

The *main section*, sometimes called the *rationale*, delivers your main points. In general, each point should be made in a simple, powerful text slide and then bolstered with more detail from charts and subsidiary text slides. For some reason, three items of supporting data for each main point seems to work best for most audiences and most arguments.

The *final section* winds up with re-emphasis, starting with a summary, moving on to a *conclusion* and leaving the audience with a message that will persuade them to act - this may be to applaud your department's progress or to buy your scheme. The final line of the presentation must be a definite close.

The presentation must be summarised throughout, because you cannot rely on the audience having read any handouts prior to the presentation.

The audience should be given the opportunity to ask questions and whether this is done at regular intervals or at the end of the presentation will depend upon the topic of the presentation and the audience to which it is addressed.

Platform skills include using your voice and presenting information. When using your voice, the following points should be noted:

♦ Projection - speak louder than usual. Throw your voice to the back of the room
♦ Articulation - do not swallow words
♦ Modulation - vary tone and pitch. Be dramatic
♦ Pronunciation - check difficult words
♦ Enunciation - over emphasise, accentuate syllables
♦ Repetition - repeat key phrases with different vocal emphasis
♦ Speed - speak slower than usual.

There are a number of techniques used for presenting information. When using flip charts:

♦ Lightly pencil in headings in advance when unsure of space

♦ Use the top corner to pencil in your notes for each chart. Write small and no one will notice.

♦ Prepare key charts in advance

Create transparencies, which are simple, concise and expressive:

♦ Project images designed to catch attention - surprise - reasoning - questioning - suspense - humour

♦ Emphasise only major points of your message

♦ Illustrate only one topic per transparency

♦ Limit message to 6-8 lines of six words each.

Graphics, in the form of still or moving pictures, can be a particularly effective method of communication. As is repeatedly quoted in graphic circles

> A picture is worth a thousand words.

Graphics have *advantages* in that they are attention-catching and can have a dramatic impact. They facilitate the understanding of complex material and are comprehensible by those of poor linguistic ability.

The presenter should also be clear about the objectives of the presentation. In order to assess the overall success of a presentation there are a number of factors which can be looked at.

(a) Did the presentation achieve its objectives? Was the system adopted as a result of the presentation?

(b) Did anyone fall asleep during the presentation?

(c) Did anyone leave during the course of the presentation?

(d) Did the presentation run to time?

(e) Were all the questions asked competently answered?

(f) Were there any problems with equipment or material during the course of the presentation?

 Practice question 4 *(The answer is in the final chapter of this book)*

Presentations

Presentations to explain a new computer application are an important aspect of computer systems development.

Required

(a) It may be that such presentations fail to convey to the audience the meaning intended by the presenter (normally a system analyst). Why should this be so?

(b) In the context of the preparation and giving of a presentation, describe:

(i) the aspects which should be taken into account;
(ii) a possible sequence of events which might be gone through.

5.3 Learning outcome

You have now covered the remaining learning outcomes for this chapter.

Evaluate the planning and conduct of a meeting and the roles of the various participants in a typical meeting.

Identify the main problems associated with meetings and recommend how those problems might be avoided or solved.

Recommend changes to the management and conduct of a meeting in order to avoid or solve problems identified.

Produce a presentation on a management accounting topic.

6 Summary

In this chapter we looked at the management of meetings and presentations. Meetings are used in organisations to gather and disseminate information, generate ideas and make decisions. Formal meetings have an agenda, however the formality of the proceedings will depend on the type and purpose of the meeting. A presentation makes something available to an audience. Planning and preparation are essential when producing a presentation.

CHAPTER 5

Components of a computer system

EXAM FOCUS

This chapter deals with the various components of a computer system: input, output and storage devices, as well as the software solutions available to an organisation. The different computer system configurations are also explained. The most examinable areas are the different methods of data input and software solutions.

LEARNING OUTCOMES

This chapter covers the following Learning Outcomes of the CIMA syllabus

Explain the features and operation of commonly-used Information Technology hardware and software

Evaluate the use and relative merits of different hardware and applications architectures

Identify opportunities for the use of Information Technology in organisations, particularly in the implementation and running of the Information System

In order to cover these learning outcomes, the following topics are included

The various types of Information Technology hardware and software in common use in organisations

The different hardware and applications architectures (ie centralised, distributed, client-server) available to organisations

The Information Technology required to operate the applications (eg PCs, servers, networks, peripherals)

---

1 Computer hardware

1.1 The main elements of hardware

 The term 'hardware' is the name given to equipment used in information technology. It includes anything from a small piece of peripheral equipment to a complete computer system. A visual display unit (VDU), a keyboard, a fileserver, a printer and a modem are all examples of computer hardware.

The main elements of computer hardware are shown in the diagram below:

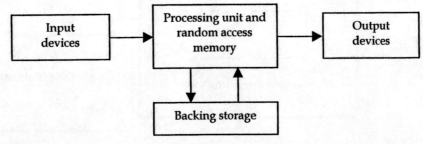

Data is entered through input devices. This data, together with other data held on backing storage, is processed to produce output. Records on the backing store may be updated as part of the process.

1.2 The different sizes of computers

The size of computers can differ greatly from large mainframe computers down to PCs.

Mainframe computers are big and powerful machines found in dedicated data processing (DP) departments. In the old days, mainframes required environmental protection (temperature, humidity, dust, etc). This remains true, but today's models are more robust than their predecessors. To get the best return for large investments, it is necessary to control data processing activities. This usually means setting up a specialised DP department staffed by professionals and with formalised procedures and segregation of duties.

Minicomputers are a halfway house between desktop machines and full mainframe. They are used to provide all computing that is required by a small organisation or dedicated to one particular task in a larger firm. Minicomputers may be staffed by a small number of people who are responsible for data preparation, processing and handling of programs and output (not a fully staffed DP department). They are a relatively quick, easy and cheap way of getting a system up and running. Minicomputers may form part of a network system.

Microcomputers or *PCs* have a means of input (often a keyboard) and can store, manipulate and output data. Their size, storage and processing power may be chosen to suit requirements and the budget of the user. PCs come in both 'notebook' and 'desktop' form. Many people reserve the term 'PC' for a personal computer using the IBM processor specification. (The terms 'IBM compatible' or 'IBM clones' are sometimes used to describe such machines.) The Macintosh computers (Macs) produced by the Apple Corporation run on a different specification, but may still be referred to as personal computers. The microcomputer or PC may be free-standing or part of a network. Some may have only limited capabilities; for example, they may only be able to run a word processing (WP) package, or a spreadsheet package.

The diagram below gives a more detailed idea of the components of a computer system.

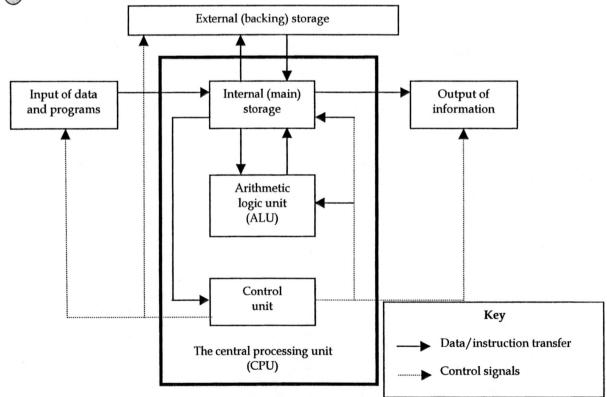

The main components of the central processing unit are described below.

♦ *The control unit* supervises and co-ordinates all processes in accordance with program instructions.

♦ *The arithmetic logic unit* performs the arithmetic operations and logic tests.

♦ *The internal storage (memory)* retains the program and data currently required for processing.

 The functions of the CPU are as follows.

♦ Storage of the program or such part as may then be required
♦ Accepting input data (and retaining it if necessary)
♦ Assembling and communicating output data
♦ Arranging data in store
♦ Carrying out calculations and comparisons
♦ Control of all peripheral devices
♦ Communication with the operator when necessary

2 Data capture

2.1 Introduction

 Data capture is an important subject and refers to the original entry of source data into the computer system. (It does *not* refer to retrieval of information.) The main data capture methods are described below.

2.2 Magnetic ink character recognition (MICR)

 A line of characters in a special font is printed on the source document. The printing ink contains a metallic substance, which enables printed characters to be magnetised. The magnetic image can be sensed by suitable reading equipment and detected characters are converted automatically into code for direct storage within the computer.

This method is used by banks to encode cheques or paying in slips. It is a fast, convenient method, suitable for high volume applications.

2.3 Optical mark reading (OMR)

 This technique depends on assigning values to marks made on a document according to their position. For example, a number (5) may be represented by marking the appropriate box below.

1	2	3	4	5	6	7	8

This type of input method is often used on multiple choice examination answer sheets.

OMR is simple and inexpensive, but it also has some disadvantages.

♦ Special forms are required.

♦ Persons filling in the form may need special training.

♦ Marked forms are not easily understood by people unfamiliar with the techniques.

♦ A lot of space is needed, as each possible character must have a separate position on the form.

2.4 Other methods of direct data capture

♦ *Optical character recognition* (OCR) allows data printed in special characters to be interpreted visually. Ordinary printing ink is used and the shapes of the characters enable them to be converted for input to the computer.

♦ *Kimball tags* are small tickets having numerical information pre-printed and also punched in pin size holes. The tickets are used as identification tags on goods (clothing) and removed at point of sale. A tag can be processed through a special converter of coded information and transferred to punched cards, paper tape or magnetic tape for subsequent input.

♦ *Bar coding* is based on a pattern of black and white strips representing a code. The code is read by a wand or light pen which converts the bar coding into a magnetic form written onto tape for some later input to the computer. It is often used to provide a 'point of sale terminal' (POST). In some shops the code is used to provide continuous stock recording and re-ordering as well as providing the customer with a detailed receipt. A typical bar code is illustrated below.

Example of a barcode

♦ *Scanners* use a beam of light to scan text or an image so that it can be automatically input into the computer. Scanners come in different varieties: they may be hand held, flat bed or overhead.

♦ *Voice recognition* or voice data entry. A microphone is used to input words spoken by the operator or user. This software is becoming more widely available, but it does have problems recognising different accents and ways of speaking.

♦ *Touch screen or light pen*. If these devices are connected to a VDU, then the screen can act as an input device. By touching the screen with the light pen, the user can select a specific application from a menu displayed on the screen.

♦ A *stylus* is often used to input technical drawings and graphic designs. It is a pen with a small bearing in its tip. The operator uses the pen to trace the drawing on a drawing board, with the image being reproduced on the screen.

2.5 Selecting the method of data capture

The main areas to consider are as follows.

♦ Economy – costs must be kept to a minimum.

♦ Accuracy – errors should not be created during the process of data capture.

♦ Time – time spent on data collection should not be excessive in relation to the needs of the system as a whole.

♦ Reliability – the system should be reasonably free from breakdown.

♦ Flexibility – the system should be able to cope with different types of data and with changes in the volume of data.

♦ Volume – the amount of data collected has an important effect on the method selected.

♦ Existing equipment – the use of existing equipment should not be ignored.

Practice question 1 *(The answer is in the final chapter of this book)*

Data capture

Consider the following two separate situations.

(a)   A TV rental company has several thousand customers who are expected to make monthly payments of rent at branch offices of the company. Records of all the customers are kept on a Head Office computer and these records require updating monthly with data relating to customer payments.

(b)   An engineering company manufactures a wide range of standard products in large volumes. Products are made from a variety of components, each of which undergoes a series of manufacturing operations prior to final assembly. For input to computerised work-in-progress, stock control and operator-bonus calculation systems, the company needs to capture data relating to the quantities of components passing through specified operations in the manufacturing departments.

Required

For each of the above systems, describe the method you would propose to capture data. State what you consider to be the main merits of your proposals and briefly mention any possible disadvantages.

Practice question 2 *(The answer is in the final chapter of this book)*

OCR

Required

(a)   Explain the technique of optical character recognition (OCR) as a method of data input.

(b)   List the advantages of this method and briefly describe two different applications in which a systems analyst might recommend its use.

3   Output devices

There is a wide variety of different output devices. The main ones you will meet are described below.

3.1   Printers

Character printers print a single character at a time. This type of printer is found in small business systems where there is no requirement for fast printing speeds. There are two main types of character printers – dot matrix printers and inkjet printers.

Laser printers print whole pages of text or graphics at once, and use techniques developed for photocopying to achieve high speeds.

3.2   Computer output on microfilm (COM)

The output of the system is recorded directly onto microfilm. The film holds a miniature image of what appears to be a printed document, although no original in fact exists.

This method has the following advantages.

♦   Reduced stationery costs
♦   Simple and cheap transport
♦   Ease of retrieval of information
♦   Saving in processor time

Disadvantages are as follows.

♦ Special equipment is needed
♦ COM equipment is expensive

Note also that a VDU is itself an output method in that output can be displayed on screen.

3.3 Selection of output methods

The selection is dependent upon the needs of the user. The following factors should be considered.

In relation to printers:

♦ noise
♦ acceptable print speed
♦ acceptable print face
♦ is it to be used for internal or external purposes?
♦ availability and cost of stationery and consumables
♦ suitability of maintenance contracts

In relation to VDUs:

♦ suitability for long periods of use
♦ flickering of screen
♦ amount that can be displayed on the screen

4 Data storage

The computer memory (inside the computer box) may be split into two different types: RAM and ROM.

RAM stands for *random access memory*. This is a temporary storage facility - any changes made to data loaded into RAM will be lost when the power is switched off unless 'saved' onto a permanent storage device such as the computer's hard disk or a floppy disk.

The operating system (eg Windows) is loaded from the hard disk into RAM when the machine is switched on; applications (eg a word processing package) are then loaded into RAM. RAM is also used to hold data and routine program instructions.

ROM stands for *read only memory*. This too is characterised by a random access facility, but it differs from RAM in that it can only be *read* and cannot be *written to*. In other words the user cannot change what is stored in ROM.

All computers contain some ROM instructions which are 'burned' into the computer at the assembly stage and are programmed to enable the operating system to be loaded. Without instructions in 'ROM' a computer cannot function.

The size of the computer RAM provides a limit on the combined size of programs and data that can be used. If there is not enough memory this will slow down the read or write operation.

The computer memory is measured in 'bytes'. Some of the key terminology for measuring memory size is given below.

Bit	A unit of storage that can hold a single binary value (0 or 1)
Byte	A string of eight bits capable of representing a single character (eg a letter, a digit, a punctuation mark, etc)
Kilobyte (Kb)	A thousand bytes
Megabyte (Mb)	A million bytes
Gigabyte (Gb)	A thousand million bytes

Typical capacities of various storage devices are given below.

Floppy disk	1.44 Mb
RAM in a PC	128 Mb
Hard disk of a PC	30 Gb
File server	75 Gb
Magnetic tape (mainframe)	20 Gb
CD ROM (read only CD)	650 Mb
DVD ROM (read only DVD)	4.7 Gb per side

The computer will have a processor the speed of which measures the number of instructions per second, which it is capable of processing. For example many modern PCs contain processors of 800 MHz (megahertz) and above.

Note that computer terminals may be either 'dumb' or 'smart'.

♦   A dumb terminal is only capable of functioning under the control of the computer to which it is connected. It consists of a screen and keyboard only.

♦   A smart terminal is capable of carrying out some functions (eg validation checks) before transmitting data to the central computer. This is cost effective because the central computer does not need to stay on line waiting for the next input. A smart terminal consists of screen, keyboard and processing unit.

5   Computer software

5.1   The meaning of computer software

Computer software is the term used to describe collections of instructions to the computer hardware.

There are six different categories of software.

♦   Operating systems
♦   Bespoke systems
♦   Off-the-shelf applications
♦   General purpose packages
♦   Utilities packages
♦   Programming tools

Operating systems software is the most important piece of software. It is the software that controls and schedules the interaction of all of the computer functions. The main types of operating software are *command driven* and *menu driven*.

- The disk operating system (DOS) originally used in IBM-type PCs is command driven. Users convey instructions (commands) to the computer by typing characters on their keyboards.

- Apple Macintoshes have always used a menu driven operating system in which users can pull down a variety of menus and select the command they need. This approach is now available on IBM-type PCs running Microsoft Windows software. The acronym WIMP is sometimes used to summarise four key elements in this approach: windows, icons, mouse, pull down menu.

Operating system software allows:

- communication between operator and computer
- control of the processor and storage
- file management
- interaction with peripheral devices (printers, modems etc).

 Bespoke systems are tailor made or purpose written applications to meet the specific needs of the particular organisation in which they are found.

Advantages

- Precisely fits the organisation's information needs.

- The organisation has complete discretion over data structures.

- The system can be integrated with other software applications already in use within the organisation.

- The system can be modified to meet changing needs.

Disadvantages

- Development of the software takes a long time
- It is expensive to develop and test
- There is a greater possibility of bugs within the final system

 Off-the-shelf packages are pieces of software, sometimes termed 'application packages', which have been developed by a software manufacturer, and made available on a commercial basis. They are sold in a form which is ready to install. A wide range of applications is available: spreadsheets, word processing, databases, payroll, accounting and many more.

Advantages

- They are cheaper to buy than bespoke systems are to develop.

- They are available immediately.

- System bugs have been largely eliminated.

- They are available with good training programmes and system documentation.

- New and updated versions of the software are likely to be available on a regular basis.

- The experience of a great number of users has been incorporated within the design of the package.

Disadvantages

♦ The package may not precisely fit the needs of the organisation.

♦ The organisation is dependent upon an outside supplier for the maintenance of the software.

♦ Different packages used by the organisation may have incompatible data structures.

 General purpose packages are packages that can be used for a number of different purposes. For example a database system may be tailored to deal with a wide range of specific problems.

Advantages

♦ Relatively inexpensive when compared to bespoke systems.
♦ Quickly available.
♦ Availability of people with relevant experience of the package.
♦ The package can be used for a number of different applications.
♦ They can be used as a prototype for a bespoke system.

Disadvantages

♦ The package may not fit the exact needs of the organisation as well as bespoke systems.
♦ The organisation will have to adapt itself to the limitations of the package.
♦ The organisation's data must be structured to fit the requirements of the package.

 Utilities packages are software tools designed to improve the way in which the operating system works. Examples include automatic file management back-up systems and anti-virus software.

 Programming tools are the tools that programmers use to designate the way in which the system operates. Such tools include the programming language itself.

 Practice question 3 *(The answer is in the final chapter of this book)*

Applications

Microcomputers used for administrative purposes tend to use packages for spreadsheet, database and word processing applications.

Required

(a) Describe the use of each of these three packages.

(b) What are the advantages and disadvantages of using an integrated package (eg Microsoft Office) which provides all three facilities, compared with using three separate non-related packages?

(c) Discuss some of the factors to be taken into consideration in selecting microcomputer software packages.

 Practice question 4 *(The answer is in the final chapter of this book)*

Software options

A small equipment hire company is considering its information systems strategy. A consultant has produced a comprehensive requirements specification, which is now being used to select appropriate software. Two alternatives are currently being examined.

The first proposal is from a company which has suggested that their software package fulfils 90 per cent of the company's requirements. They have proposed that the company purchases the package and that further work is commissioned to tailor it to the company's specific requirements.

Required

(a)   Briefly explain three advantages of adopting a software package solution.

(b)   Comment on any dangers you can see in accepting the proposal of tailoring the package to the company's specific requirements.

The second alternative is to commission a local software house to build a bespoke or tailored solution. The software will be designed to fulfil the exact needs of the equipment hire company.

Required

(c)   Briefly explain three advantages of adopting such a bespoke or tailored solution to the company's requirements.

Practice question 5 *(The answer is in the final chapter of this book)*

Categories of software

Required

(a)   Briefly describe the major categories of software which may be used on microcomputers.

(b)   Explain the criteria which would be applied, or factors considered, in selecting the software for a large organisation which uses many microcomputers for differing administrative tasks.

5.2   Learning outcome

You have now covered the first learning outcome for this chapter.

Explain the features and operation of commonly-used Information Technology hardware and software.

6   Computer system configurations

6.1   Architectures

The term architecture in IT describes the physical appearance of the system and the way in which its component parts relate to one another, ie the systems configuration. Systems are made up of hardware and software components, but not all systems combine the components in the same way.

The following two sections will explain centralised and distributed architectures, but you should recognise that there are many compromises or hybrids in existence.

6.2   Centralised architecture

A centralised architecture, or centralised processing, is where all the computing of an organisation is concentrated on a single, central processor, usually at the head office. The data for processing centrally might be gathered from a wide area, eg all the local offices, and the output may be sent out over a wide area too. But the actual processing and the 'ownership' of the data files are centralised.

Data might be collected by the central processing system either by physically transporting the records to the central location or electronically, eg from remote terminals linked to the central computer. Output for the local offices might be sent out in a similar fashion. Centralised processing systems are usually used for processing large volumes of data and transactions, as in banks.

 This approach has a number of advantages.

♦ Better controls may be implemented, as the system is centrally managed by expert IT-specialist staff.

♦ The facility to share data will reduce overall storage requirements and lead to consistent decision-making throughout the organisation.

♦ There are economies of scale for large transaction processing systems.

♦ Sharing software should reduce the requirement for training, as all users will use common systems.

♦ Communication is possible between all users, using an in-house electronic mail (e-mail) system.

Disadvantages include:

 ♦ Centralisation does not encourage user independence.

♦ Large centralised systems can be inflexible and changes can take a long time to implement and be disruptive to the organisation.

6.3   Distributed architecture

 An alternative to centralised processing is distributed data processing. As its name suggests, this describes a system where the processing of data is not done at the centre, but is carried out instead at a number of different points away from the centralised location. Each decentralised location could have its own separate data files.

Modern distributed systems use data communications to create and maintain a network of computers that are capable of independent operation and resource sharing as required. Sharing may involve accessing data on remote files or transferring whole files across systems. The responsibility for IT resources has been delegated to individual users and control over processing has been decentralised.

 The advantages of distributed architecture include the following:

♦ Processing on each individual computer may be batch, on-line real time or database but information is passed between various processors as required.

♦ Individual pieces of hardware are available at a low cost, so computers are available within the budgets of individual managers.

♦ Personal computers use user-friendly hardware and software, most of which is available off the shelf.

♦ Users can maintain privacy over their personal data.

♦ Individual computers can be set up with a personal configuration of hardware and software, to perfectly meet the needs of an individual user.

The disadvantages are that it may be costly to maintain and it may result in duplication of effort as end users develop their own systems, which may be similar to other end user systems.

7 Computer networks

7.1 Types of network

A computer network is defined simply as ' computers which are linked together'.

A computer network is merely a method of connecting together two or more computers and a number of devices such as printers. If the network involves modems and telephone lines it is a Wide Area Network (WAN). If it simply involves direct cable links it is a Local Area Network (LAN).

LANs can be made up of several identical computers, often to allow shared access to an expensive piece of equipment, such as a laser printer, or facilities such as disk storage systems, data files, printers, e-mail or fax, to maximise its cost-effectiveness. In some cases several microcomputers provide input to a single mainframe or mini-computer, so that they can be used independently and as intelligent terminals to the central machine.

The wide area network covers distances outside the LAN boundaries, linking organisational units on a national or international basis, usually connecting individual LANs.

7.2 Benefits of networking

The benefits of networking include the following.

♦ Allows staff to share data and programs.

♦ Provides a basis for office management (shared diaries, mail, arrangement of meetings).

♦ Eases the job of maintaining software within the organisation, in that all machines can be simultaneously updated.

♦ Flexible and inexpensive in allowing the sharing of computer resources, eg printers.

♦ Enables regular and frequent back-up copies of files to be automatically made.

♦ The network can be extended as the organisation grows.

♦ If a single machine breaks down, other machines can continue to work.

7.3 Network configurations

There are three main types of network configurations: star, ring and bus.

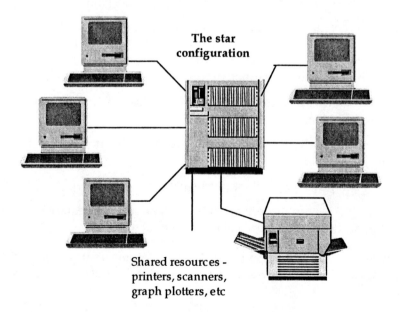

The star configuration

Shared resources -
printers, scanners,
graph plotters, etc

A central computer acts as a controller to the network. The disadvantage of this configuration is that if the central 'fileserver' goes down then the terminals would not be able to communicate.

Each terminal is a 'dumb' terminal, ie it is only a screen and keyboard and does not have its own processing capabilities.

The ring configuration

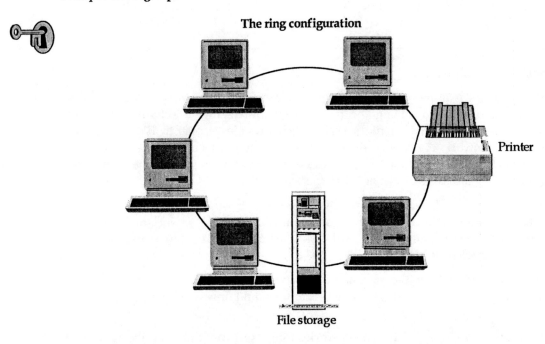

Printer

File storage

In this configuration, there is no central computer, and each of the terminals is capable of processing its own data. The system consists of a cable connected in a continuous loop. Messages are 'packeted' and passed along the loop.

Each terminal would comprise of a screen, keyboard and processing capability, ie an intelligent terminal. If any single computer goes down, then the remaining computers can continue to work and communicate.

The bus configuration

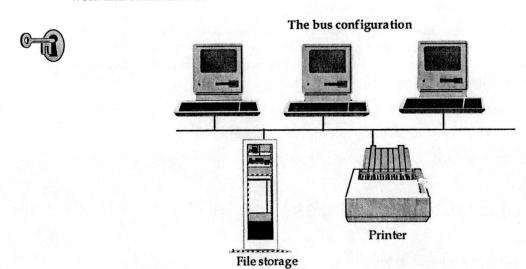

Printer

File storage

A bus configuration is where all the computers are linked as before, but not in a ring. Each terminal is once again capable of processing its own data - it is an intelligent terminal. The cable is a central line, and messages can be processed and transferred by any device.

Practice question 6 *(The answer is in the final chapter of this book)*

Local area network

Required

Define the term 'local area network' and outline the range of structures and technologies used in different types of local area network.

7.4 Client/server architecture

A client/server network is a method of allocating resources in a local area network so that computing power is distributed among the personal computers in the network, but some shared resources are centralised in a file server, which provides access to files for all the workstations in the network. A client could be any workstation attached to the network. A server is another networked computer that provides a specific service, such as managing files (a file server) or routing messages on the network (network server).

In a peer-to-peer network, all workstations are file servers, because each workstation can provide files to other workstations. In the more common client/server network architecture, a single high-powered machine with a large hard disk is set aside to function as the file server for all the workstations (clients) in the network.

The applications carried out by the organisation's users are split between the available hardware, according to how many users need access to them and how much processing power is required.

Client applications - are run on the client workstation, and are those applications that individual users require but which are not shared with other users. In most cases this will include word processing and spreadsheet packages, and any single-user decision support packages.

Departmental applications - are run on the departmental servers, and are available to be shared by users within a user group, office or department. Examples of typical departmental server applications include computer-aided design in a design department, audit software in the finance department, and any shared decision support systems.

Corporate applications - are available to users throughout the organisation and are run on the corporate server. Such applications generally take advantage of the very high processing power of the corporate server, and typically include the major Management Information System applications of the organisation.

7.5 Learning outcome

You have now covered the following learning outcome for this chapter.

> Evaluate the use and relative merits of different hardware and applications architectures.

8 Network enabled technologies

8.1 The Internet

The main features of the Internet are as follows.

- It is a network of networks.
- It exists for mutual benefit.
- It is not sponsored or controlled by Government.
- There are an estimated 300 million users worldwide.
- It provides access to information on a worldwide basis.
- It allows e-mail to take place between computers which would otherwise not be linked.

Electronic mail, electronic conferencing, educational and chat services are all supported across the network, as is the ability to access remote computers and send and retrieve files.

The Internet refers to the physical aspects of the system, such as the communication lines, computers (often known as 'Web servers') and the software required for communication. It is a hierarchical assembly of networks; a network of networks. The term 'world-wide web' (www) refers to the Internet software tool for network navigation.

The www is menu-driven, following hypertext links between related sources rather than files related to one another by server identification. It allows you to pursue the 'strands' of a web of information distributed across the network.

Sending e-mail messages is the most used function on the Internet, together with the sending and receiving of files.

8.2   E-mail

Electronic mail (e-mail) allows messages to be transmitted between users within a single central computer system or around a network without the use of paper or disks as transmission media. The network can be a local area system or a national network using public telecommunication lines. It facilitates the distribution of information to multiple recipients simultaneously.

E-mail messages, instead of being delivered by the post office, are delivered by Internet software through a computer network, right to your computer. Delivery time and costs are far less than other traditional means of sending and receiving mail.

E-mail can also be used to transfer and receive copies of files and documents and to subscribe to electronic discussion groups, electronic journals and electronic newsgroups.

8.3   Teleconferencing

Telephone conferencing is a means of communication that allows participants to hold multiple way communication. Developments in 'video conferencing' via PCs and telecommunication links means that companies can arrange 'electronic meetings' between executives and business partners in different countries. The growing use of video conferencing will reduce dramatically the amount of time and money spent by business executives travelling between subsidiary plants and offices located in different countries and continents.

8.4   Electronic Data Interchange (EDI)

EDI is the electronic transfer of business information, such as customer invoices and purchase orders, with the information being sent in a format that conforms to certain standards. EDI introduces the possibility of 'paperless' trading and promises the end of repetitive form filling, stock orders and other forms of 'paper shifting'. EDI is used predominantly between large business customers and their suppliers.

The advantages of EDI include the following:

♦ speed - transactions are transmitted very quickly, without any delays in printing, posting and re-entering data

♦ reliability - less chance of a transaction being lost in the postal system

♦ accuracy - the possibility for errors is virtually eliminated

♦ labour cost savings from eliminating the need to enter data and handle printed documents

8.5 Teleworking

A combination of communications technology including telephone, fax, e-mail and the Internet has enabled teleworking, with many more people working away from the office environment, changing the entire focus of work.

The virtual organisation allows individuals to work on a project or task and communicate with other members of the team, using e-mail, as though they were sharing an office. It no longer matters where people are located or what time suits them to be working. The Internet allows e-mail messages to be sent anywhere in the world at any time of the day or night for the cost of a telephone call.

The advantages of teleworking include the following:

♦ no travelling time to and from the office
♦ greater flexibility for staff in terms of working hours
♦ lower facilities cost for the organisation

8.6 Learning outcome

You have now covered the final learning outcome for this chapter.

> Identify opportunities for the use of Information Technology in organisations, particularly in the implementation and running of the Information System.

9 Summary

In this chapter we introduced the main elements of computer hardware, software and communications. We examined several different hardware and software system configurations, distinguishing between centralised and distributed processing. It is important to note that distributed systems use a data communications system to create and maintain a network of computers that are equally capable of independent operation and of resource sharing.

The explosion of information and communications technology has led to the emergence of the automated office, teleworking and teleconferencing.

CHAPTER 6

Systems theory

EXAM FOCUS

This topic will regularly appear in the examination, as part of a question. The emphasis in the past has been on defining some of the terms used within the theory, and then applying the theories of open and closed systems, or open loop and closed loop control systems, to practical scenarios.

LEARNING OUTCOMES

This chapter covers the following Learning Outcome of the CIMA syllabus

> Apply General Systems Theory (GST) to the design of Information Systems in organisations

In order to cover this learning outcome, the following topics are included

> System definition
> System components
> System classification
> Coupling and decoupling
> System behaviour - control and feedback
> Entropy - requisite variety

1 Introduction

Both natural and man-made systems can be extremely complex. When looking at an organisation and how it functions, it is useful to be able to analyse what it does and how it behaves in overview terms. In other words, to enable management to structure organisations in an effective way and to make sure that they achieve 'goal congruence', all the constituent parts of the organisation must work together in a unified and consistent manner. The alternative - very undesirable - is a situation where different parts of the organisation are pulling in different directions.

In this chapter we look at systems theory, system concepts, the way systems may be classified, and the questions of control and feedback.

2 Systems theory

2.1 Definition of a system

Systems exist in all aspects of life and in all fields of activity; for example there are solar systems, nervous systems, political systems, communications systems, computer systems, weapons and defence systems, legal systems, planning and control systems and costing systems. All businesses are systems.

One definition of the word system is:

> 'a collection of related activities working together to achieve a common objective'.

What we generally mean when we think of a system is that it is a complex unit formed of many, often diverse, parts subject to a common plan or serving a common purpose. Notice that there are two aspects:

(a) the individual parts of a system are often diverse and may or may not be associated with each other;

(b) the summation or collection of the parts forms a unity, either because the parts are 'subject to a common plan or framework' or because they 'serve a common aim or purpose'.

The elements required for anything to be classified as a system are the following:

♦ component parts, elements or activities
♦ relationships between those parts
♦ an objective or purpose

2.2 Systems concepts

Theoretical approaches to systems have introduced many general principles. Systems theory helps to achieve the objective of goal congruence, and is used to aid an analyst in identifying:

♦ the boundaries of systems
♦ their characteristics
♦ their behaviour patterns.

Goal setting defines exactly what the system is supposed to do. Other principles concern system structures and behaviour, for example the system boundary defines those components which make up the system and those which live outside. Each system is surrounded by a boundary and anything outside the system is known as the environment.

A system can have a range of inputs, eg people, materials, data or money. As a result of receiving the inputs, some form of activity or process occurs, eg storing, calculating, recording or assembling. After the processing is completed, the product or service is transferred to the environment. Typically the output has added value because the system has increased the value of the resources used.

The elements of a system are outlined in the diagram below:

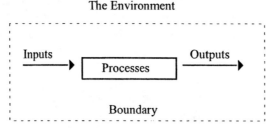

A system can be made up of any number of sub-systems. Each sub-system carries out a part of the system function. Sub-systems can help to handle the system's complexity and improve understanding of the system.

Every system, whatever its nature and purpose (eg central heating system, banking system, payments system), is a way of viewing a group of components or elements and the way in which they interact.

Systems themselves may also be components of larger systems. For example England, Scotland, Wales and Northern Ireland, each of which has its own economic system, social system, legal system, etc, are all part of the UK. The UK itself is a complex system, which is part of the EC. In an organisation, the petty cash system (which is a specific system) is part of the accounting system, which in turn is also part of the overall corporate system for management control.

3   Types of system

3.1   General systems theory (GST)

A successor to the classical and bureaucratic approaches to the structuring of organisations is an influential theory which came to prominence in the 1960s through the writings of E J Miller and A R Rice, and which is known as the systems approach. This model sees businesses as drawing resources - people, finance and so on - from their environment and putting back into that environment the products they produce or the services they offer. In doing so the inputs are converted into the final product or service, hopefully with value being added.

A car manufacturer may buy parts and assemble these into finished vehicles. Depending on a wide variety of factors, not least the efficiency of the assembly, the cars sell for more than the cost of components, labour and overhead. In short, value is added.

GST is used to identify and describe the common properties of systems, and attempts to:

♦   categorise systems into a small number of broad types
♦   describe how systems react to environmental influences
♦   show how systems can be analysed as collections of subsystems.

GST led to the concept of 'synergy' - the idea that a whole can be more effective than the sum of the constituent parts. In commercial terms, we might apply this by asking whether a group of companies, viewed as a single entity, is worth more than the sum of the individual subsidiaries.

3.2   Open, closed and semi-closed systems

GST distinguishes between systems on the basis of whether the environment can cross the boundary and influence the system (an *open system*), or whether the system is completely self-contained and not affected by elements in the external environment (a *closed system*).

An *open system* is interactive with its environment, ie it exchanges material, information and energy with its environment, and continually changes and evolves. This type of system has the ability to adapt to an ever-changing environment. The Management Information System of a business is an open system in that it must react to the changing demands for information. A rise in the price of raw materials obviously affects the information system, as management will find out the full extent of the changes so that they are able to alter their plans and offset any adverse effects to avoid the system becoming disorganised.

A *closed system* is self-contained, ie it does not exchange material, information and energy with its environment. See diagram below:

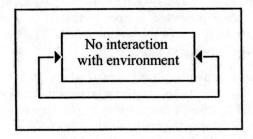

Completely closed systems are not encountered in business; indeed, the category is theoretical in the sense that such a system cannot really exist in practice except, perhaps, as a scientific experiment of some kind. Similarly, not all systems are completely open. Most mechanical systems are termed as semi-closed or relatively closed systems. They interact with their environment in a prescribed and controlled way. Although an organisation is itself an open system, some of its sub-systems may be semi-closed.

3.3 Entropy

Disorganisation in the system (open or semi-closed) is referred to as entropy. If any system is left alone it will tend towards greater disorder. The open system can overcome entropy by amendment (through inputs) and the result is negative entropy (meaning an improved or more complete version). There is a continuous flow of the inputs and so a steady state (homoeostasis) is achieved.

To prevent entropy in an organisation, information must be continually supplied from its environment so that the organisation can keep adapting, eg if a company's computer system did not respond to changes in the price of raw materials, the company would continue to trade for some time, but its decline and fall would be inevitable. Even if no outside change had been imposed, systems can begin to make errors and unless these are detected, more and more meaningless results will be produced.

Dynamic equilibrium means that a system remains static in the sense that it is steered and adjusted to work within desired parameters.

Practice question 1 *(The answer is in the final chapter of this book)*

Entropy

Required

Briefly define and describe the term 'entropy'.

3.4 Adaptive systems

Adaptive systems are open systems which react to changes in the environment. Corporate planners have borrowed this concept of adapting output and behaviour to environmental changes. Essentially they consider all the resources of the business (its strengths and weaknesses) and attempt to develop strategies to overcome the disadvantages of a hostile environment in order to achieve certain corporate goals. This recognition of striving for certain corporate goals is known as the concept of goal congruence and underlies the various systems for planning and control that exist within a business.

3.5 Man/machine systems

The systems operating in business organisations are sometimes referred to as man/machine systems. These are often classified in terms of complexity such as:

♦ Deterministic or mechanistic systems - where the major characteristic is that its output (results) may be accurately predicted assuming that it is operating and is monitored properly, eg a coffee machine in which coins are inserted and which provides coffee with the right mix of sugar and powdered milk.

♦ Probabilistic or stochastic systems - are systems where it is not possible to predict the outcome precisely although we can often give a general indication or set out defined limits. We can, for example, look at past trends, which might give us a good guide to the future. The various techniques of forecasting are useful in this area.

We can classify certain parts of a business system in this way, due to both the internal and external influences. In the case of probabilistic information, it is usual to offer a selection of calculated outcomes, each with its calculated probability (eg, predicted ROI of 12½% in 20X2 with a probability of 0.3, whereas the prediction of 20% ROI would have the associated probability of 0.1).

♦ Cybernetic systems are self-organising - learning as a result of mistakes. In fact such systems are also probabilistic and include living things (animals, plants, humans), social groups and organisations. The problem is that they are very hard to control, compared with deterministic systems.

3.6 The business organisation as a system of sub-systems

A business organisation is an open-ended system with deterministic, probabilistic and cybernetic features. A firm must adapt to the external environment otherwise it will not survive. Within the firm certain aspects can be considered deterministic, such as machines and equipment, and probabilistic, such as policies of stock holding and control. Cybernetic systems may also exist, for example a stock re-ordering system where stock items are replenished automatically and stock levels adjusted in response to changing demands and trends.

Practice question 2 *(The answer is in the final chapter of this book)*

Deterministic or probabilistic

Required

Classify the following as examples of deterministic or probabilistic systems:

(a)   a hamburger bar;

(b)   a computer program;

(c)   a sewing machine in perfect working order;

(d)   an old car not in perfect working order;

(e)   a bank clerk.

Practice question 3 *(The answer is in the final chapter of this book)*

Semi-closed or open

Required

Classify the following as semi-closed or open systems:

(a)   a bank dispenser;

(b)   a space vehicle under ground control;

(c)   a 'fruit' machine in a casino.

---

4   Sub-systems

4.1   Introduction

Most systems can be broken down into sub-systems - the production sub-system and the accounting sub-system of a business, for instance. The systems boundaries may not be easy to determine. The physical boundary may be defined and seen. But to the extent that organisations are systems of people, in other words social systems, the boundaries are much less clear, being formed not by visible structures but rather by relationships.

If we consider a typical business structured on a functional basis, the boundaries of responsibility of the accounting manager may be clear within the accounting function but the boundary of responsibility for co-ordination with other departments may be difficult to define clearly. Even within the organisation the various sub-systems may or may not operate effectively as open systems. A particular function may try to behave as a closed sub-system: a company's production system may focus on producing what the production management wants to produce, irrespective of consumer demand.

4.2 Suboptimisation

An important objective of the organisation is to achieve goal congruence, ie to bring the targets and goals of the different subsystems into harmony. Where the targets of different subsystems conflict this can lead to *suboptimisation*.

 This term refers to a situation in which achieving the goals of one subsystem has a damaging effect on the goals of another subsystem. This often occurs where different departments within an organisation behave as autonomous subsystems of the organisation. As an example, consider a possible conflict between the sales and finance departments in relation to stock levels.

♦ The sales department are anxious to keep stock levels high so that there is no danger of being unable to satisfy customer orders.

♦ The finance department may wish to keep stock levels low, because high stocks lead to higher stockholding costs (storage, handling, insurance, etc).

Suboptimisation can be minimised by effective central management and by careful definition of the objective of each subsystem.

4.3 Coupling and decoupling

 Coupling is the way in which subsystems are linked. Systems that are highly coupled are very closely linked, ie closely coupled, so that the outputs of one system are the immediate inputs of another system. Any delays or problems encountered in one system will immediately create problems in the next system.

As an example, consider a production department split into two subsystems: manufacturing and assembly. Any delay in the delivery of raw materials to manufacturing will inevitably lead to delay in the assembly section.

Another common example of a closely coupled system is the manufacturing supply strategy of JIT (just in time). In this strategy, manufacturers minimise stockholding costs by accepting delivery of raw materials and components only a matter of days or hours before they are required. If the supplier fails to deliver on time the consequences for the manufacturer will be very damaging because there is no buffer stock to keep production moving.

Decoupling means minimising the interdependence between systems. In other words, it is concerned with relaxing the link between subsystems so that they can work independently.

In the above example of the production department, the systems of manufacture and assembly could be decoupled by the use of a stock facility. A certain level of stock would be produced by the manufacturing department and held as a buffer. In that case, a halt in manufacturing (caused, for example, by a supplier's failure to deliver) need not lead to a halt in assembly operations. The use of inventory (stock) control is a mechanism for decoupling processes.

4.4 Benefits of GST

In the systems approach, organisations are systems of inter-related activities. The focus is now on what actually goes on - the activities, including aspects of the technology employed, the people in the company, their relationships and roles, as well as the interaction with the environment. Important elements of the system or sub-systems are the ways the business provides for co-ordination, monitoring and feedback of its activities.

From the viewpoint of an accountant or a manager, GST has the following benefits.

♦ It highlights the existence of subsystems, each of which might have conflicting objectives.

♦ It assists in identifying how the external environment (competitors, customers, government, etc) exerts pressure on the organisation.

♦ It clarifies how the design and implementation of information systems can be to the advantage of the organisation as a whole.

♦ It emphasises that subsystems must be controlled so that they operate towards the good of the organisation as a whole.

♦ It emphasises that organisations must be dynamic (not static) and ready to accept change.

In the past, organisations often suffered from inferior planning activities. Sub-systems were not integrated (coupled) and therefore sub-optimisation occurred. Each sub-system worked towards achieving its own objectives to the detriment of the system as a whole. For example, the production line worked on piecework and therefore produced as much as possible, regardless of whether the product was being sold. This put pressure on the cashflow by increasing payments to the production line, while increasing the costs of product storage.

The aim of this approach is to develop 'team activities' and integrate effort towards the corporate objectives/sub-objectives.

Practice question 4 *(The answer is in the final chapter of this book)*

Systems concept

Required

Describe the concept of *coupling or decoupling* and give an example of how it could be used in the design of a business information system.

Practice question 5 *(The answer is in the final chapter of this book)*

Theory of information systems

Required

Define and distinguish between each of the following terms, and explain their relevance to business information systems, using examples wherever feasible.

(a)   Deterministic and probabilistic systems

(b)   Closed and open systems

(c)   Dynamic equilibrium and entropy

---

5 Control systems

5.1 Elements in a control system

A system must be controlled to keep it in balance; in other words, each system must have its own control system. Without this, the outputs (actual results) of any system may deviate because of unexpected events. A business may have many control systems, such as quality control, stock control and budgetary control. A control system must make certain that a business organisation can cope with unpredictable events, such as competitors' activities, changes in government legislation, non-delivery of raw materials and components, etc.

Control itself comprises three activities:

(a)   establishing performance standards;
(b)   assessing performance and comparing this with the standards;
(c)   correcting deviations from the standard (or plan).

The process of control therefore operates because of feedback. The identified and corrected deviation is fed back into the system in order to bring the system into control, ie to ensure that the target and achievement are in balance. This process of control can be illustrated as follows:

 There are eight common elements of a control system.

+   Input – the inputs from the environment to the system.

+   Process – the way in which the inputs are changed to create an output.

+   Output – the result of the operational process is output to the environment.

+   Standard – the budget or target, eg market share or ROI for an organisation. Other standards relate to quality, quantity, cost (total or unit) and timing.

+   Sensor – a device or function used to measure or record the output, eg the visual check carried out on products in a factory quality control system or complex computer monitoring.

+   Feedback – information about the way in which the system is operating.

+   Comparator – to compare the information or evidence gathered by the sensor with the required output defined by the standard.

+   Effector – the mechanism that changes the inputs to the system, so that the performance of the system can be amended or changed in some way.

 All of this is illustrated in the diagram below:

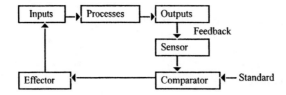

Example

As an example of this, consider the budgetary control system operating in a sales department.

Solution

♦   The *output* of the system is the month's sales.

♦   The *sensor* is the costing system, which records actual sales.

♦   *Feedback* is based on the actual results for the month, collected by the costing system.

♦   The *comparator* is the department's performance report, comparing actual results to budget or standard.

♦   The *effector* is the sales manager, who takes action to minimise adverse variances and maximise favourable variances. The opportunity may also be taken to adjust the standard, as it may be too easily achievable or indeed unachievable.

5.2   Open and closed loop control systems

Feedback is necessary in order to maintain control of a system or business. Managers need to receive information that lets them assess and control the operations of the business activities. To know whether objectives are being achieved, feedback on actual performance is given; this is then compared against expected performance.

 A closed loop control system automatically compares its outputs against the standard previously set; if there are variances, then corrective action is automatically taken, as shown below:

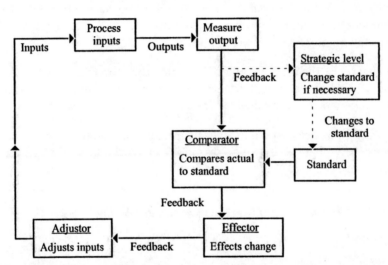

 In an open loop control system corrective action is not automatically taken. Outputs are measured, but environmental factors are also taken into account and internal feedback does not automatically cause adjustment to the inputs, as shown below:

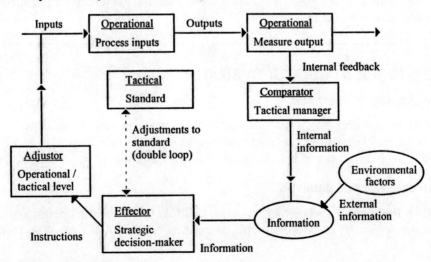

5.3 Example

Consider the example of a sales department budgeting to achieve sales of £100,000 per month.

At the end of Month 7, the output measured by the sensor (the actual sales achieved in Month 7) is only £70,000. The sales manager compares the actual sales to budgeted sales and calculates a shortfall for the month of £30,000.

The sales manager reviews the internal staffing levels of the sales department, and finds that one of his representatives has been absent from the department through sickness. This person normally achieves sales of some £10,000 per month. The sales manager then ascertains the following points from a review of the external system environment.

♦ There has been a delay in the production department, which has resulted in a number of orders achieved in the month not being delivered to customers. This accounts for another £10,000 in sales value.

♦ From one of the call sheets completed by the sales personnel, it had been noted that a number of orders had been cancelled as customers had placed orders with a rival supplier who is currently offering a special promotion.

Armed with this information from both the external and internal environment the sales manager discusses the situation with the sales director. The area covered by the sales person who is currently off sick can be split between the existing sales staff, and the goods not despatched in the month because of problems in the production department will flow through into sales in the following period.

However, with regard to the rival supplier, the sales director then has the opportunity to change the standard, ie to reduce the budgeted level of sales, so that a discount offer can be made to existing customers to nullify the loss of business to the competitor.

Once the sales director has decided the most appropriate strategy, the sales manager and sales staff are advised of any changes in policy or modes of working, so that results in the next period can be improved.

Practice question 6 *(The answer is in the final chapter of this book)*

Open loop and closed loop

Required

(a) Briefly explain the difference between open and closed loop control.

(b) Discuss whether an open or closed loop model would be appropriate for a manufacturing company.

---

6 Feedback in control systems

6.1 The meaning of feedback

In both the open loop and closed loop control systems the concept of feedback is extremely important. The control system will receive feedback in the form of information and the system will respond in such a way as will help to ensure that the objectives of the system are achieved.

Feedback can take two basic forms.

♦ Single loop feedback (associated with normal control systems at the operational or tactical levels of management) is concerned with the routine correction of deviations from a given plan.

♦ Double loop feedback (involving higher, strategic, levels of management) is concerned with comparing results with the long-term plans of the organisation, and as such may result in the organisation adjusting, altering or rethinking the overall organisational plans, budgets and the control systems themselves.

 Feedback control in a debtors system is illustrated below:

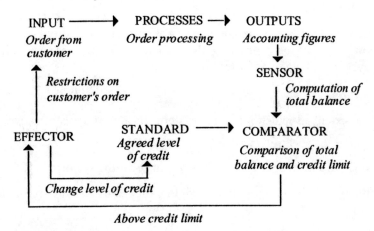

6.2   Negative and positive feedback

Feedback can be classified as either 'negative' or 'positive'.

 Negative feedback is where the response mechanism is designed to *dampen adverse fluctuations* around expected standards. When the system is deviating from the intended path, control action must be taken to reverse the trend, ie to put the system back on course.

A common example comes from a credit control system. If customers are not allowed to exceed a standard credit limit, orders will be restricted if that limit is exceeded. The control system brings the actual activity back towards the planned or budgeted level of activity.

 Positive feedback is where the response mechanism is designed to *increase beneficial fluctuations* around expected standards. This is necessary at times to allow organisational growth.

Again an example can be taken from a credit control system. Positive feedback would be displayed if a customer's credit limit were increased to enable the increase in the value of the customer's orders.

Positive feedback can also occur where there is a feedback loop that has been poorly constructed so that the inputs to a system are modified to achieve further deviations from the required standard. Some examples of this are given below.

♦ The standard set for the system may be inappropriate, eg the sales target may have been set too low. Once the targets have been achieved, the inputs of marketing, advertising, promotion, etc may be reduced, leading to lost opportunities to maximise sales potential.

♦ The actions of the effector may not be understood, with the effect that they do not have the desired effect on the process. With a project that is behind schedule, the action of adding more resources in the hope that this will reverse the trend may actually lead to further delays in the project as a result of the additional management controls required.

♦ The system sensor may be inefficient because it doesn't record information as completely or accurately as required. For example, a video camera in a security system may not be functioning at the time a theft is committed.

6.3 Feedforward control

This is where historical results are used to trigger the control mechanisms. Control is based on trying to anticipate what will happen in the future and bringing into effect the control mechanisms *before* an event occurs, rather than after it. In other words, the mechanism attempts to be 'proactive' rather than merely 'reactive'. This form of control is commonly encountered in budgetary control systems.

A delay in the feedback of information could prevent corrective action being taken in time to have any effect on reversing or promoting the variance. The timeliness of the information produced by the system is therefore of vital importance.

6.4 Control criteria

When assessing the extent to which a control system (of any kind) is effective, we adopt the following criteria:

♦ Inclusivity – It should incorporate all the main aspects of the system.

♦ Comprehensibility – It should be understandable, especially to staff and managers dealing with the system.

♦ Flexibility – It must be possible to amend the system in accordance with relevant changes.

♦ Compatibility – It must 'match' the corporate structure in that authority and responsibility for the system and its results must be granted to specific individuals.

♦ Specificity – Procedures must be oriented to the particular area in which it operates (eg regularity of reporting and the extent of detail in the feedback information).

♦ Punctuality and relevance – It must possess these qualities in relation to its activities.

♦ Cost-effectiveness – The cost of the system must not exceed the total cost of ignoring the deviations and errors controlled.

♦ Participation – The people who are to be controlled should be allowed to take part in determining standards and other aspects of control design.

♦ Control superfluity – It must not include unnecessary controls.

♦ Requisite variety – It must operate in accordance with the law of requisite variety (introduced by WR Ashby in 1956) which declares that 'only variety can absorb variety'; the control system must be able to create as many states as the system that is being controlled.

6.5 Requisite variety

Because this topic is specifically mentioned in the syllabus, you should take the time to make sure that you understand what it means and can give an example to explain it.

A description of requisite variety would be that there must be at least as many different states of control available to be applied as there are ways for the system to get out of control.

If there is variety in the environmental influences on the system, then the system should be varied and have the ability to adapt. The implication of this is that the systems controller must be able to determine variations of the control variables and transmit system change instructions for each change.

Example

Take the example of a stock control system. In a very simple case, all the system has to do is to initiate an order when stocks fall below the reorder level. There is one change (stock below reorder level), and only one response is needed (order stocks).

If we change the variables so that there are two suppliers of stock whose prices vary and the system is to order from the lower cost supplier, it gives us three environmental inputs - stock level and cost of each supplier's goods. The system has to be capable of responding in three ways: no order, order from supplier A or order from supplier B.

As the environmental inputs become more varied and complex, so must any response system. If a manager wishes to control a stock system which has 8,000 different stock items, he or she needs to have access to detailed data on each stock item and to generate a control response for each possible variation in the state of each stock item. This would be impossible for one individual to do in terms of the capacity to receive and transmit data and in terms of processing capacity to generate the necessary variety of control responses. Organisations deal with this by assigning standard control procedures that can be applied to all stock items and providing decision rules to stock-keeping staff for generating the variety of responses required to control the stock system.

Describing all possible responses can only be done in the simplest of systems. Furnishing decision rules is quite effective, but it is difficult to provide rules which cover all eventualities in systems other than machine based ones. This means that where the system to be controlled is other than a purely mechanical one, it is impossible for that process to be controlled by computer. Therefore computers are used to generate and apply all of the decision-based rules and a human generates all control responses for unexpected states.

6.6   Information for control purposes

Information for control purposes must be:

♦ the right information;
♦ delivered to the right person;
♦ at the right time;
♦ for the right cost.

Timing - routine information is produced at regular intervals: daily, weekly and monthly. It is often more convenient to process the information on a regular basis. A system should be reliable and managers should know when to expect information relevant to their jobs, since information is not an end in itself, but merely a step towards action or decision-making. The timing of information is therefore very important. If information is produced more quickly, it invariably costs more to produce and is not necessarily better. This depends on whether it is used to make better decisions.

Accuracy - In designing a system the level of accuracy required depends on the outcome of the action which the information might generate. Various techniques improve accuracy, such as coding systems incorporating self-checking numbers or check-digits. Errors could arise due to

♦ failing to follow set procedures;
♦ using incorrect codes and files;
♦ fraud and irregularities;
♦ loss of data due to breakdowns in the system.

More accurate information is more expensive and takes longer to produce.

Delays - because information is required at different levels in the organisation, the movement through these different levels may often cause delays and introduce errors. If there is an information time lag in our oscillating systems, things could be made worse by accentuating adverse trends at the wrong times. If repeated delays occur, you may find that additional sub-systems have been introduced: these are the unofficial systems.

Practice question 7 *(The answer is in the final chapter of this book)*

Feedback

Required

(a)   Describe what is meant by positive and negative feedback and explain their relevance to business information systems.

(b)   Show diagrammatically the operation of feedback control in a basic accounting system.

Practice question 8 *(The answer is in the final chapter of this book)*

Negative and positive

(a)   Feedback is an important concept in a controlled system. Systems theory defines two types of feedback – negative and positive.

Define the basic components of a controlled system and explain (using an appropriate practical example) the principle of negative feedback.

(b)   Some systems experience positive feedback. Explain what is meant by *positive feedback*. Give one reason (with an example) why it might occur in an apparently controlled system.

6.7   Learning outcome

You have now covered the learning outcome for this chapter.

Apply General Systems Theory (GST) to the design of Information Systems in organisations.

7   Summary

This chapter has introduced the major concepts of systems theory, which is the general theory that applies to all types of system. We can define a system as a set of related parts co-ordinated to achieve a set of goals. An accountant will encounter references to a variety of systems, eg transportation, communication or financial reporting systems, during a normal working day.

Another important aspect of general systems theory is the need for control, which is also a feature of an accountant's daily activities.

A question in your examination may well concentrate on just one aspect of the syllabus. For example, a question on systems theory for 20 marks could be broken down into four requirements. These could be:

♦   the key concepts of systems theory;

♦   the relevance of the key concepts to the design of financial and management accounting systems;

♦   open and closed loop models;

♦   relevance to a type of company.

Within any of the questions you must be prepared to draw diagrams. For systems theory these will be of such things as open and closed loop systems, showing boundaries.

CHAPTER 7

Information systems and decision making

EXAM FOCUS

This chapter deals with the different types of information systems that are available to an organisation, and how these information systems can help the decision making process. This is an area of the syllabus that is regularly examined.

LEARNING OUTCOMES

This chapter covers the following Learning Outcome of the CIMA syllabus

> Recommend how the value of information can be increased by careful design of an organisation's data and information architecture

In order to cover this learning outcome, the following topics are included

> The qualities of information

> Designing data and information architectures to assist and improve planning, decision making and control

> The use of information for decision-making at the various levels of the organisation

> The components of the Information System which can support those decisions (ie transaction processing systems, management information systems, decision support systems, executive information systems, expert systems)

---

1 Information

1.1 Why do managers need information?

 Managers need information for a range of purposes including:

♦ Planning - requires information on available resources, possible timescales for implementation and the likely outcome under different scenarios.

♦ Recording transactions - is necessary for many reasons apart from the legal requirements, eg assessing profitability and materials and labour utilisation, and documentation can be used to answer customer queries and settle disputes.

♦ Performance measurement - information on costs, revenues, volumes, timescale and profitability enables comparisons against budgets or plans to be carried out.

♦ Controlling - information is required to assess whether an activity is proceeding as planned or has deviated from the plan. The information helps management to take some form of corrective action if necessary.

♦ Decision-making - information is needed to help decide what course of action is most likely to bring about the desired objectives.

1.2 Data and information

There is a clear distinction made between data and information. Data can be termed 'raw facts'; information is data that has been processed in some way. Processing may take place by:

♦ adding to the data;
♦ re-forming the data;
♦ adding instructions to the data.

Data does not necessarily need to be electronically processed in order to become information.

An easy way to remember this is: Data + meaning = information

1.3 The qualities of information

Just as raw materials can be processed badly to give a sub-standard product, so raw data can be processed into good or bad information. The information supplied to management must display the following qualities of good information, otherwise it will not be useful.

You can remember these qualities by means of the mnemonic ACCURATE.

♦ A - Accurate. Inaccurate information is of little use for strategic, tactical or operational purposes. The degree of accuracy required will vary. For example, the managing director may be concerned with reporting of profit to the nearest thousand pounds, whereas the sales ledger supervisor will require a high degree of precision in balancing the sales ledger control account.

♦ C - Complete. The more complete information is, the more reliable it will be. However, information should not be more complete than is required. For example, if a company is looking for a new supplier of one of its raw materials, it would be impossible for them to contact all possible UK suppliers; instead a representative sample would be chosen.

♦ C - Cost. The information should not cost more to obtain than the benefit derived from it. Presentation should not require users to waste time working out what it means.

♦ U - Understandable. Information that is understandable is much more readily acted upon. Information presented should not assume that the reader has any prior knowledge or experience.

♦ R - Relevant. The information provided should concentrate on the essentials and ignore trivia. Too much information can hide important issues.

♦ A – Adaptable. Information should be tailored to the needs and level of understanding of its intended recipients. The degree of detail required by the credit controller to monitor the level of debt is different from the level of detail required by the chief executive.

♦ T – Timely. The value of information declines with the length of time that the user has to wait for it. Information that is out-of-date is a waste of time, effort and money.

♦ E – Easy to use. Information should be clearly presented and sent using the right medium and communication channel.

The quality of information is a common component of exam questions. Please note that in an exam you would be expected to give specific examples, drawn from the scenario of the question.

1.4   Information flows

Organisations are dynamic. As they grow larger, their structure automatically changes. The type of structure adopted will influence the type of information system needed by the organisation.

In assessing the information needs of an organisation it is important to establish the way in which information flows through the organisation. Most organisations develop around major functional areas (the functions of production, finance, distribution, etc), and within each area there are additional sub-divisions. In the past managers were usually held responsible for obtaining the information they needed. The manager at the top prescribed such information and his decisions influenced reports at all levels. Statutory reports, such as the annual report and accounts, provided one of the main sources of information.

As organisations grew, more data was required than individual managers could handle and systems and data-processing departments began to develop in order to collect and manipulate data. The information flowed up the channels of management largely by summaries from varying levels of detail.

With the gradual introduction of company-wide systems, many organisations began to recognise the information system's function as being separate from the normal lines of responsibility or authority. For example, basic data gathered by the sales representatives would be useful to the manufacturing staff. Furthermore, improved efficiency and the cost of collecting data often necessitate departmental co-ordination within functions, geographical areas and divisions to improve methods and flows. The information flows from one responsibility unit to another present an information network, which reflects both horizontal and vertical flows.

This assessment of information flows within an organisation will involve addressing the following questions.

♦   Who will require the information – which level of management?

♦   How often is the information required – daily, weekly, monthly, quarterly etc?

♦   What does the organisation want to achieve from the use of IT? Does it want to acquire competitive advantage or reduction in its operating costs?

Practice question 1 *(The answer is in the final chapter of this book)*

Data versus information

Required

(a)   Information may be needed for three levels of management; name them.

(b)   Explain the difference between 'data' and 'information'.

(c)   List, with brief comments, five of the desirable properties of information produced for management.

(d)   Managers need information to enable them to carry out their duties and responsibilities. State, in outline, what you consider these to be.

---

2 Management structure and information requirements

2.1 Management levels

Accountants have a vital role in communicating between the management levels and providing the necessary information for planning and control purposes.

 There are various levels of management that exist within an organisation, and Anthony's Triangle can illustrate these.

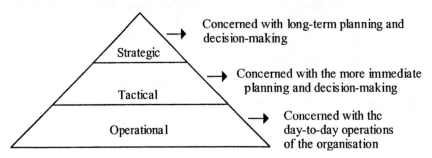

Strategic management (senior management) are managers who are responsible for formulating the organisation's objectives, policies and strategic plans.

Tactical management (middle management) are managers who take the strategic plans and polices and develop tactics to make them work. They are responsible for tactical and operational planning and management control.

Operational management (junior management) are managers who are responsible for routine planning and control.

2.2 Information needs

An organisation's information systems must be organised in such a way as to meet the information needs of the various levels of management.

All levels of management require information. The information required may include any or all of the following.

♦ International information - market conditions, strengths of currencies, political climate.

♦ National information - government policies, trading conditions, impact of new legislation.

♦ Market information - details of competitors, market trends, competitive issues.

♦ Corporate information - business performance and financial results.

♦ Departmental information - comparisons of individual budgets for costs and expenditure.

♦ Individual information - sales made by individual sales persons and remuneration of individuals.

♦ General information - technological developments or environment trends.

 The *strategic level of management* requires information from internal and external sources in order to plan the long-term strategies of the organisation. Internal information is usually supplied in a summarised form.

The *tactical level of management* requires information and instructions from the strategic level of management together with information from the operational level of management. The information would be in a summarised form, but detailed enough to allow tactical planning of resources and manpower.

The *operational level of management* requires information and instructions from the tactical level of management. The operational level is primarily concerned with the day-to-day performance of tasks and most of the information is obtained from internal sources. The information must be detailed and precise.

2.3   Information characteristics

We have looked at the levels of management and the type of information required at each level. The following chart outlines the characteristics of information at each of the levels of management/decision-making in an organisation.

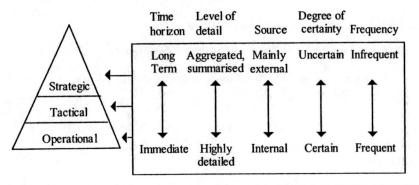

	Time horizon	Level of detail	Source	Degree of certainty	Frequency
Strategic	Long Term	Aggregated, summarised	Mainly external	Uncertain	Infrequent
Tactical					
Operational	Immediate	Highly detailed	Internal	Certain	Frequent

Practice question 2 *(The answer is in the final chapter of this book)*

Information levels

Required

Outline the nature and purpose of information likely to be used at each of the following levels of a business enterprise.

(a)   Top management
(b)   Middle management
(c)   Supervisory management

3   Decision making

3.1   The decision making process

Before we can discuss the various information systems it is necessary to consider the way in which we make decisions. An information system is designed to aid managers in the decision making process. It is therefore necessary to understand how decisions are made before we can begin to discuss different information systems.

The main stages in the decision making process are as follows.

♦   Identify an opportunity to exploit (proactive) or identify a way to solve a problem (reactive).

♦   Conduct a search to establish alternative courses of action.

♦   Gather information about each alternative.

♦   Undertake an analysis of advantages and disadvantages of each alternative.

♦   Rank alternatives in order of preference.

♦   Initiate action to implement decision.

♦   Monitor feedback to ensure response is as expected.

♦   Review outcome and add new knowledge to mental store.

There is no universally accepted model of the decision making process, but Simon's model provides an acceptable basis. The model includes three key elements.

♦ Intelligence – awareness of an opportunity or problem.

♦ Design – formulation of problem and analysis of alternatives of potential applicability.

♦ Choice – the choice of solutions to the problem identified in the intelligence phase, from one of the solutions identified in the design phase.

Once we have made our choice, it must then be implemented.

3.2 Variables in the decision making process

Variables affecting how we make decisions include the following:

(a) The conditions under which decisions are made - a decision can be made under the following three different *conditions*.

  ♦ Certainty - operational managers make decisions based on certainty.
  ♦ Uncertainty - strategic managers make risk decisions.
  ♦ Total uncertainty - use past experience.

(b) The style of decision making - there are two different decision making *styles*.

  ♦ Analytic - the use of set rules. The decision maker would use graphs, probability models, mathematical techniques, etc.

  ♦ Heuristic - the exploration of possibilities. The decision maker would use rule of thumb, gut feeling and experience.

(c) The type of decision - may be categorised into three different *types*.

  ♦ A structured decision. This is where all or most of the variables are known and can be totally programmed. These decisions are routine and require little human judgement (eg setting a credit rating for a new customer).

  ♦ An unstructured decision. These types of decisions are resistant to computerisation and depend mainly on intuition (eg fixing the price of a new product).

  ♦ A semi-structured decision. This type of decision falls between a structured decision and an unstructured decision, in that it is partially programmable but still requires some human judgement (eg adjusting the credit rating of an existing customer).

The relationship between decision types and managerial levels is shown in the diagram below:

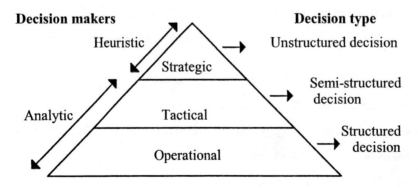

Practice question 3 *(The answer is in the final chapter of this book)*

Decisions and control

Required

(a) Define and distinguish between:

    (i)   structured, semi-structured and unstructured decisions

    (ii)   operational, tactical and strategic control.

(b) Suggest a classification by type of decision and type of control for each of the following information systems.

    (i)   Accounts receivable (ie the debtors ledger)

    (ii)   Warehouse location

    (iii)   Budget preparation

    (iv)   New plant construction

    (v)   Inventory control

    (vi)   Loan approval

    (vii)   Executive recruitment

    (viii) Research and development planning

    (ix)   Short-term forecasting

(c) A decision support system has been implemented by a landscape and garden maintenance company. Part of the system is designed to report on unusual problems reported by the various work crews. Some problems, such as a dying tree, may be important and require attention as soon as possible. This may mean reassignment of crews and extra expenses in terms of equipment, chemicals, etc.

    (i)   Briefly describe the three phases which are commonly considered to make up the decision making process and identify which phase in the part of the decision support system referred to above is being supported.

    (ii)   Explain how the decision support system described might support the two phases of decision making that you did not identify in part (c)(i) above. State any assumptions necessary about the company.

4 Types of information system

4.1 Office automation systems

There are a variety of systems now available to organisations. When recommending a particular system in an exam question, you should justify your choice, and cost should be a major factor.

As the cost of hardware and software packages reduces many people now have computers available at their desks or workplaces. Individuals are allowed to set up their own systems, or to use systems that have been developed centrally.

Office automation is defined as 'the use of computers, microelectronics and telecommunications to help produce, store, obtain and send information in the form of pictures, words or numbers, more reliably, quickly and economically'. Office automation offers the following facilities.

- Videotext
- Electronic mail (e-mail)
- Fax
- Voice recognition systems
- Teleconferencing
- Telecommuting
- Word processing (WP)
- Desktop publishing (DTP)
- Spreadsheets
- Databases

We have already discussed some of these facilities in more detail.

4.2   Transaction processing system (TPS)

This type of system is an operational level system providing day-to-day information about efficiency of operations and activities. It is limited in its support of management decision making.

 The TPS routinely captures, processes, stores and outputs the low-level transaction data. It is normally characterised by the use of one of the following methods of processing.

- Batch processing - eg payroll systems
- On-line processing - sales order entry systems
- Real time processing - stock control systems

Batch processing is a convenient way of dealing with large runs of data to be processed on a regular basis. It is timetabled and leads to economies of scale. Examples include input of invoices, payments of creditors, payment of wages and salaries.

On-line processing is more common nowadays. Its main features are as follows.

- Data is not batched.

- Instead, data is entered by non-computing staff as transactions take place (eg entry of sales order received).

- Each transaction is automatically validated and/or verified as soon as input occurs.

- Mainframe records are updated immediately the data has been verified as being correct. This means that transactions can be entered immediately and duplication is minimised.

- Although users interact directly with the system, records and files are updated only periodically (eg at end of trading for the day). Therefore information is slightly out of date.

Real time processing is a step onwards from on-line processing. Its main features are as follows.

- Transactions are entered as they occur.

- Records are updated immediately.

- It is useful but expensive, since some part of the central computer's resources must be devoted to communicating with remote users and to accessing and updating records. The usual examples are airline reservations and theatre bookings.

4.3   Management information systems (MIS)

 A management information system is defined as 'a system to convert data from internal and external sources into information, and to communicate that information in an appropriate form to managers at all levels and in all areas of the business to enable them to make timely and effective decisions'.

A management information system is usually a single database, which gathers information from the transaction processing system. The resultant information is fed to the user in a predetermined format suitable for his or her use. As this information is for the use of management it must be timely and reliable.

The format of the information supplied is determined by the abilities of the user and by the use that will be made of it.

♦ Strategic management will require information that is broad, aggregated and summarised.

♦ Tactical management requires information that is more detailed and tailored to the user's needs or area of responsibility.

♦ Operational management require very detailed information specific to their responsible area.

The MIS produces reports that are mainly summarised and inflexible, eg scheduled reports, demand reports, exception reports, etc.

 The MIS is usually concerned with the control of activities, although it may in some instances be used for organising and planning. In summary the activities of the MIS consist of:

♦ data capture
♦ data processing
♦ data storage
♦ information retrieval
♦ communication
♦ short-term decision making.

 There are certain problems associated with an MIS.

♦ Information may not be punctually available.

♦ Information may be incorrectly integrated.

♦ Information may be excessive in relation to the need.

♦ Information may be irrelevant.

♦ Information may be presented in an inappropriate format.

♦ Information may be too costly to produce.

♦ Lack of conciseness.

♦ Information overload (far too much information is produced, leading to inefficiency).

♦ Information underload (too little information is produced upon which decisions are to be based).

4.4   Decision support systems (DSS)

 A decision support system is defined as 'a computer based system which enables managers to confront ill-structured problems by direct interaction with data and problem-solving programs'.

They are computer systems which are used as an aid in making decisions when presented with semi-structured or unstructured problems. Their aim is to provide information in a flexible way to aid decision making.

The DSS does not itself make the decision, it merely assists in going through the phases of decision making. The system sets up various scenarios and the computer predicts the result for each scenario by using a process of 'what if?' analysis. A DSS will have the following characteristics.

♦ It provides support for decision making, especially for semi-structured or unstructured decision making.

♦ It provides support for all stages within the decision making process.

♦ It provides support for decisions that are interdependent as well as for those that are independent.

♦ It supports a variety of decision-making processes.

♦ It is user friendly.

A DSS will include the following tools.

♦ Spreadsheets
♦ Expert systems (see below)
♦ Database
♦ Statistical programs

There are three basic elements to the DSS.

♦ A language sub-system, which is likely to be non-procedural (called a structured query language or SQL).

♦ A problem processing sub-system, which includes spreadsheet, graphics, statistical analysis.

♦ A knowledge sub-system, which includes a database function.

A simple DSS task is the analysis of current and historical data to derive strategic information. The system can utilise on-line data retrieval and manipulation to:

♦ analyse data and convert it into a tabular format showing its characteristics;
♦ adopt a criterion and extract specific data from these tables;
♦ integrate the tables;
♦ undertake arithmetic operations on the data items;
♦ sort/merge data from various files to create a report.

4.5   Executive information systems (EIS)

An executive information system is defined as 'a computer based system for total business modelling'. It monitors reality and facilitates actions that improve business results.

An EIS is specially designed for the non-IT executive. Information is provided in a very summarised way. This is the ultimate in information systems. It has the ability to:

♦ call up summary data from an organisation's main systems (eg summary profit and loss account, balance sheet, etc)

♦ analyse the summary data to a more detailed level (eg analysis of the stock figure shown in the balance sheet)

♦ manipulate summary data (eg rearrange its format, make comparisons with similar data)

♦ set up templates so that information from different areas of the business is always summarised in the same format

♦ perform complicated 'what if?' analysis.

The EIS uses built in graphics, charts and other presentational aids. It is also very expensive to develop and run.

4.6   *Expert systems*

An expert system (ES) is defined as 'a computerised system that performs the role of an expert or carries out a task that requires expertise'.

The system holds expert or specialist knowledge and allows non-experts to interrogate a computer for information, advice and recommended decisions. It will modify its knowledge base in accordance with its own results, which therefore means that the system will learn from its experience. An expert system will incorporate the following components.

♦   A knowledge base, which holds the facts and rules.

♦   An inferencing engine. This is the processing software, which applies the knowledge base to the users' problems and produces a proposed solution.

♦   Working memory. This stores all relevant facts and inferences during processing.

♦   An explanation program. This provides an explanation of the reasoning leading to a particular recommendation or decision made by the system.

♦   A knowledge acquisition program. This allows the knowledge bases to be updated, corrected or expanded.

The ES will be used for diagnosing problems, strategic planning, internal control planning and maintaining strategies.

Expert systems can be used at a variety of different levels. At the simplest level they can give factual answers to technical questions. At a more complex level they can make unstructured decisions, offering managers advice and explanations. They can suggest how a decision should be made and recommend a course of action. In this respect they go further than decision support systems.

There are many examples of expert systems in such areas of business as credit control, engineering and recruitment. Even something as simple as the control panel of a photocopier can be considered an expert system, as it allows the operator to diagnose the cause of a machine breakdown and to fix the machine. Expert systems are used widely in the following areas:

♦   law (eg conveyancing)

♦   taxation (eg personal tax)

♦   banking (eg granting credit)

♦   medicine (eg diagnosis of symptoms)

♦   defence (eg aircraft recognition)

♦   training methods (selection and design)

The diagram below provides an overview of the different information systems discussed above.

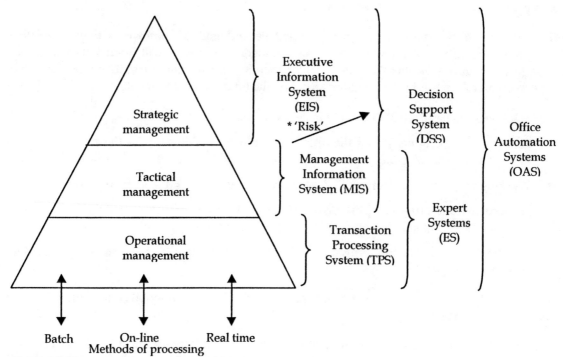

* If the information requirements include a greater element of human judgement and therefore an element of 'risk', a decision support system (DSS) will be more appropriate than a management information system (MIS).

Practice question 4 *(The answer is in the final chapter of this book)*

Information systems

Required

(a)   With the aid of examples, define and distinguish between the following types of information systems.

     (i)   Transaction processing system
     (ii)   Management information system
     (iii)   Decision support system
     (iv)   Office automation system
     (v)   Executive information system

(b)   For each category of information system listed above, give, if seen as appropriate, an example of a task or decision relevant to a company which specialises in organising seminars on management topics, and providing support documentation.

Practice question 5 *(The answer is in the final chapter of this book)*

Management information system (MIS)

A medium sized manufacturer of domestic equipment has a well-established computer based management information system (MIS). Although the hardware and software has been recently upgraded and found to be entirely satisfactory in terms of operational reliability, the design of the MIS has been virtually unchanged for eight years.

As a systems consultant you have been requested to carry out a review of the effectiveness of the MIS with the object of recommending changes where appropriate.

Required

Prepare a briefing paper for the IT manager outlining how you would carry out such a review and to what matters you would direct your attention.

4.7   Learning outcome

You have now covered the learning outcome for this chapter.

> Recommend how the value of information can be increased by careful design of an organisation's data and information architecture.

5   Summary

Important qualities of good information may be memorised by the mnemonic ACCURATE.

Information is used by management at strategic, tactical and operational levels. Their needs, and the characteristics of the information they use, are dictated by their position in the hierarchy of management levels.

To assist managers with practical decision making a large number of computer systems have been developed. These include:

◆   management information systems (MIS)
◆   decision support systems (DSS)
◆   executive information systems (EIS)
◆   expert systems.

We have looked at the different components of the MIS in terms of their role in supporting different types of decision and the typical formats of report that they can produce. The examples given are typical, but in any specific organisation we should expect the Management Information System to be designed to support the decisions made in that organisation.

CHAPTER 8

Communications

EXAM FOCUS

Communication is at the heart of the whole of this syllabus. It is the way that people in an organisation exchange information regarding its operations. It is the interchange of ideas, facts and emotions by two or more persons. To be effective, the manager needs information to carry out management functions and activities. For the examination, you will need a range of communication tools to be able to answer each question.

LEARNING OUTCOMES

This chapter covers the following Learning Outcomes of the CIMA syllabus

> Explain the importance of effective communication and the consequences of failure in the communication process
>
> Analyse communication problems in a range of organisational situations
>
> Recommend changes or actions to avoid or correct communication problems

In order to cover these learning outcomes, the following topics are included

> The purpose and process of communication
>
> Communication problems and solutions
>
> The main communication tools (ie, conversation, meeting, presentation, memorandum, letter, report, telephone, facsimile, electronic mail, video-conference)
>
> Features and limitations of communication tools

---

1 The purpose and process of communication

1.1 Introduction

Communication in business can be defined as 'the transmission of information so that it is received, understood and leads to action'.

 This definition enables us to understand some of the key aspects of business communication:

(a) Information, and not data, should be communicated. Information is active, relevant and prompts action; data, on the other hand, is passive, may be historical or irrelevant and does not lead to action.

(b) Clearly, if information has not been received or is not understandable by the receiver, then communication has not taken place.

(c) The communication should lead to action: this action may take the form of a positive decision or may be a change in attitude. If the communication does not lead to any action then, probably, it ought not to have taken place.

So communication means transmitting messages to people in a manner which stimulates response. In some cases, the response will be direct to the sender, as when two people are engaged in debating the merits and demerits of some proposition. In other cases the response will be indirect as when transfer of the information gives rise to some independent action on the part of the recipient or when he merely stores it for future reference.

1.2　The purpose of communication

Communication is the means whereby people in an organisation exchange information regarding its operations. It is the interchange of ideas, facts and emotions by two or more persons. To be effective, the manager needs information to carry out management functions and activities.

Communication is important in all phases of managing from small businesses to multinationals, and in all functions of management. It is particularly important in the function of leading. It is no exaggeration to say that the communication process is the means of directing, co-ordinating and motivating all levels involved in the organisation's various areas of operations.

This key central role of communication as providing unified activity has been given increased importance by the Systems Theory authors, in particular Chester Barnard. They view communication as the means by which people are linked together in an organisation to achieve a common purpose. This is still the fundamental function of communication; indeed, group activity is impossible without communication because co-ordination and change cannot be effected.

Despite the advance in computer systems and communication technology, most large companies would still cite 'communication problems' as a common, major, area of concern. The need for communication within the organisation arises because of:

♦　day-to-day and periodic control needs;

♦　the incidence of unplanned change;

♦　the introduction of planned change;

♦　the usual interaction in the normal work situation, ie issuing directions and receiving results.

The specific purposes of communication fall generally under the following headings:

♦　to convey information about what is happening internally and externally;

♦　to explain the nature and implications for the business of current and forecast problems;

♦　to establish rules for dealing with different situations;

♦　to stimulate action;

♦　to create relationships between the members of the organisation, and to create, confirm or modify their attitudes towards the corporate entity;

♦　to form collective decisions and render them generally acceptable.

1.3   *Process of communication*

Communication is the process of passing information and understanding from one person to another. It can best be described by way of a diagram.

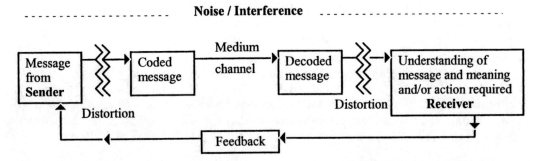

The diagram demonstrates the important elements in the communication process and emphasises that it is a two-way exchange in which the recipient is as important as the transmitter.

The communication process involves six basic elements: sender (encoder), message, channel, receiver (decoder), noise, and feedback. Managers can improve communication skills by becoming aware of these elements and how they contribute to successful communication. Communication can break down at any one of these elements.

The sender initiates the communication process. The code or language of a message may be spoken or written or it may be non-verbal, eg in pictures, numbers or by body language. The medium or channel for communication can be print, mass, electrical and/or digital. The choice depends on a number of factors such as urgency, cost and sensitivity.

Because there may be distortion at the coding or decoding stage, ie the meaning of the message may be lost in handling, feedback is an important way to gauge the receiver's reaction and make sure the message is understood. Within the communication process it is also important to note that the problem of 'noise', ie anything in the environment that impedes the transmission of the message, is significant. Noise can arise from many sources, eg factors as diverse as loud machinery, status differentials between sender and receiver, distractions of pressure at work or emotional upsets. The effective communicator must ensure that noise does not interfere with successful transmission of the message.

2   Communication channels

2.1   *Formal communication channels*

All organisations have formal, acknowledged, and often specified communication channels. There will be lists of people who are to attend briefings or meetings, and distribution lists for minutes of meetings or memos. There will be procedures for telling people of decisions or changes, and for circulating information received from outside the organisation.

Organisational communication establishes a pattern of formal communication channels to carry information vertically and horizontally. (An organisation chart displays these channels). The **channel** is the path a message follows from the sender to the receiver. Managers use *downward* channels to send messages to employees. Employees use *upward* channels to send messages to managers. *Horizontal* channels are used when communicating across departmental lines, with suppliers, or with customers.

Downward communication - instructions relating to the performance of the department and policies for conducting business are conveyed downward from managers to employees. Katz and Kahn (1966) identified five general purposes of superior-subordinate communication:

♦   to give specific task directives about job instructions;
♦   to give information about organisational procedures and practices;
♦   to provide information about the rationale of the job;
♦   to tell subordinates about their performance;
♦   to provide ideological-type information to facilitate the indoctrination of goals.

Such information can help clarify operational goals, provide a sense of direction and give subordinates data related to their performance. It also helps link levels of the hierarchy by providing a basis for co-ordinated activity.

Too much emphasis on downward communication can create problems. People will become reluctant to come forward with their suggestions and problems and may be averse to taking on new responsibilities. There is also a risk of management getting out of touch with their subordinates. For these reasons it is important to stress upward communication.

 Upward communication - creates a channel from which management can gauge organisational climate and deal with problem areas, such as grievances or low productivity, before they become major issues. It also includes the following:

♦   Reports on results achieved - this feedback is absolutely essential to the control of the business against plans, and may lead to further modifications of plans. It is also helpful in the appraisal of a manager's performance.

♦   Suggestions for changes in products, work methods or organisation derived from experience at the operational level.

♦   Information (for example about customer reactions to products, employee morale or developments in other companies) which becomes available through contacts at junior levels.

♦   Requests for consultation on particular working problems.

♦   Itemising of problems encountered (eg shortage of material, equipment difficulties, etc). Failure in this area can be disastrous.

 Lateral or *horizontal communication* channels refer to communication between people or groups at the same level in the organisation. Four of the most important reasons for lateral communication are:

♦   task co-ordination, eg department heads may meet periodically to discuss how each department is contributing to organisational objectives;

♦   problem solving, eg members of a department may meet to discuss how they will handle a threatened budget cut;

♦   information sharing - members of one department may meet with the members of another department to explain some new information or study;

♦   conflict resolution - members of one department may meet to discuss, for example, duplication of activities in the department and some other department.

Co-ordination between departments relies on this form of contact, eg line and staff positions rely heavily on advice passing laterally. Also, managers communicate with sources outside the organisation, such as suppliers and customers.

2.2   Formal and informal communication

Communication can be formal and informal. Upwards and downwards communication tends to be largely formal (ie recognised by the organisation and completed in accordance with a set procedure). Lateral/horizontal communication has a larger informal element. This is partly due to the fact that people are having to operate across departmental boundaries and so personal, informal contact is more successful than structured, formal contact.

3   Barriers and breakdowns in communication

3.1   Barriers

There are many barriers that impede the effective communication of information. They can exist in the sender, in the transmission of the message, in the receiver or in the feedback. They include:

◆ Poorly expressed messages - awkward sentence structure, platitudes, omissions and unnecessary jargon cause lack of clarity and precision that can be avoided through greater care in encoding the message.

◆ Wrong interpretation of message by receiver - is often the case with cultural differences. 'Put a tiger in your tank' was an effective advertising slogan in the US but people in Thailand were offended by it.

◆ Poor retention of message - sometimes it is necessary to repeat the message using several channels, eg in advertising.

◆ Inattention by either party - there are many talkers but few listeners, with people tending to ponder their own problems instead of listening to a conversation.

◆ Assumptions made - these are uncommunicated assumptions that underlie the message, eg a customer may suggest picking up an order from the warehouse (because he will be in the vicinity whilst travelling) and the vendor may have the goods sent to a different warehouse closer to the customer's address (assuming that is where he would want to pick the goods up from).

◆ Mistrust - as well as threat and fear will undermine communication. The message will be viewed with scepticism. A climate of trust that facilitates open and honest communication is needed.

◆ Failure to communicate - may be due to distortion or omission of information by the sender.

◆ Premature evaluation - a common tendency is to approve or disapprove what is being said rather than trying to understand the speaker's frame of reference.

◆ Status barrier - a senior manager's words may be listened to closely, whereas a colleague's advice may be discounted.

3.2   Consequences of poor communication

Poor communication includes a lack of, poor, or inadequate control, as well as faulty co-ordination. Lack of downward communication is likely to result in:

◆ poor awareness of corporate objectives at lower management levels;

◆ poor understanding of working instructions and responsibilities;

◆ poor morale of junior managers because they are not consulted about changes which affect them or their working conditions.

Lack of upward communication, including 'feedback', has the following undesirable consequences for management:

♦ early warning of troubled areas is not received;

♦ benefit of creative ability in subordinates is lost;

♦ participation of subordinates is limited;

♦ need for change is not appreciated because management is isolated from the operation areas;

♦ control becomes difficult;

♦ introduction of change is difficult.

Lack of lateral communication often leads to:

♦ divisions in management teams;
♦ lack of co-ordination;
♦ rivalry between sections and departments;
♦ lack of advice and involvement by staff specialists.

A company's policies, plans, instructions and information are required to be known and comprehended if the corporate plan is to be a success. This communication is only seen by some companies to be necessary from the top echelon downwards to lower ones. It is, however, equally essential, as we saw above, for information, ideas and experiences to flow upwards from the lower levels. If communication is only one way, there is no feedback and this is a severe disadvantage. Apart from anything else, employees will not feel a real part of the company. The management that plans and controls positively, and at the same time pays attention to what people feel and think, will be participative and considerate, and more certain of success.

3.3 Effective communication

Various steps may be taken in order to ensure effective communication within an organisation. These include:

♦ *Adopting feedback* - the 'two-way' nature of communication is ensured, so that the receiver seeks clarity and the sender seeks acknowledgement.

♦ *Using more than one communication network* - sometimes it is possible to use the informal communication network to reinforce the message sent, eg the friendship network.

♦ *Restricting the number of communication 'links in the chain'* - the shorter the distance between sender and recipient of a message, the less the number of potential 'breakdown' points in the communication process. Allowing messages to be conveyed more directly to the recipients encourages this aspect.

♦ *Ensuring clarity* - sensitivity to the needs of the recipient of the message (relating to experience, awareness, intelligence, perception, etc) reinforces the intention to produce a clear message.

In order to overcome the barriers to communication there are a few useful rules to follow.

♦ Communication should be clear and concise
♦ Communication should be supportive and helpful in achieving goals and objectives
♦ Informality can be particularly effective

Practice question 1 *(The answer is in the final chapter of this book)*

Communication skills

Sam Browne is a sole trader. He runs a very profitable newsagents in a leafy town in the English midlands. His shop is very close to the railway station. His customers are the many people who commute daily into Birmingham and the executives who park their cars at the station before catching the early morning express trains to London. Sam is a good salesman, whatever the weather he has a cheery smile for his customers, and he has a shrewd notion of what to stock and the margins available. His weakness is that he can't keep records. His idea of record-keeping is sticking everything into a shoe box.

Not surprisingly, Sam's accounts are in a mess, his tax affairs are getting out of hand and he ignored the need to make a tax return last year. There is a risk that the Revenue will start an investigation and Sam has come to you, as an Accountant in practice, for help. You feel the accounting problems are straightforward if only you can get the full background information from Sam.

You are meeting Sam next Saturday afternoon, when Mrs Browne can look after the shop. First you need to think about how you should approach the meeting.

Required

Draft some notes for the meeting with Sam showing:

(a)   The types of information you require

(b)   How you will manage the communication process

(c)   The skills you will contribute to the process

3.4   Communication via an appropriate channel

There are many different means of communication available.

♦   Conversations
♦   Telephone calls
♦   VDU computer screens
♦   Written reports
♦   Postal communications
♦   Electronic mail
♦   Internet
♦   Fax

The selection of the most appropriate channel will depend on the following factors.

♦   The nature of the information
♦   How quickly the user requires the information
♦   The format required by the user
♦   What channel is likely to motivate the user
♦   Geography – how far the information has to travel
♦   Cost of communication

Practice question 2 *(The answer is in the final chapter of this book)*

Barriers to information flow

Conventional communication theory identifies 'barriers' and other impediments to the smooth flow of information between individuals or within an organisation.

Required

Describe some of these barriers and impediments, and comment on their likely sources.

4 Communication tools

4.1 Methods of communication

In designing the formal system, possible methods of communication can be grouped into classes:

◆ oral methods;
◆ written methods;
◆ visual methods; and
◆ electronic methods

Oral methods - for the rapid interchange of information between people the principal method of communication is the spoken word. Oral communication is preferable for emotive issues and persuasion since it has the advantage of immediate feedback. It is, however, time consuming and, unless recorded, there can be uncertainty about what was said. For many years the telephone has been most important both for internal and external communications. Other examples include face-to-face communication, meetings and tape recordings.

Written methods - of communication of all sorts (letters, memos, bulletins, files, circulars) are the norm in many companies. The dominant characteristic of many managers' working day is paperwork and meetings. Written methods do have the advantage that, being in permanent or hard-copy form, they are less open to misinterpretation. With meetings, for instance, formal minutes may be taken, circulated and agreed to as the definitive written evidence of the meeting. Written methods of communication can be very flexibly used. When trying to reach a number of workers in one place, notice boards are often used, typically to announce current events, meetings and similar matters which are not of crucial significance.

Visual methods - are preferable where it is necessary for the eye to assist the ear; where the message can be made more vivid or where distance, environmental or personal factors preclude the use of speech. Examples include films, videos, graphs, traffic signals and sign language.

Electronic methods - more and more offices are increasingly reliant on a range of electronic communication equipment. Larger businesses link computers through the telephone network using modems leading to the use of electronic mail and computers 'speaking' to each other, some accessing databanks. Personal computers are being arranged in networks; fax machines, e-mail, value added networks (VANs) and dedicated satellite communication systems are becoming commonplace.

A major feature of most electronic methods is their potential low cost coupled with high speed of transmission. It is becoming common for employees to work at home for at least part of their work and to use electronic methods for communication with others in the company. Electronic methods can provide, at an economic cost, information of a scale and promptness which would have been hopelessly uneconomic before their arrival.

The examiner has stated that in the examination 'response will normally be in the form of memorandum, letter, briefing notes, presentation slides or report', so you need to be able to use these formats in your answers. There will commonly be four or five different response formats on each examination paper, and two or three marks will be given in each question for using the required format. You may also get a whole question about a specific aspect of communication, such as meetings or communication problems.

The syllabus identifies a full range of communication tools (conversation, meeting, presentation, memorandum, letter, report, telephone, facsimile, electronic mail, video-conference), some of which have been covered in detail in a previous chapter. We will look at the main advantages and disadvantages of each.

4.2   Oral communications

Method	Advantages	Disadvantages
Conversation	♦ quick, direct and cheap medium with little time lapse between sending and receiving ♦ the meaning can be underlined by using stress, timing and pitch and, with visual contact, facial expressions and gestures ♦ it can be used for the sensitive handling of some communications, eg bad news, reprimand, sympathy, or encouragement ♦ there is instant feedback and messages can be received and acknowledged and misunderstandings sorted out	♦ noise can interfere with the message ♦ little time and preparation may be put into planning ♦ the listener may interpret the facial expression or body language wrongly ♦ some messages may be more memorable if written down ♦ clash of personalities may cause barriers
Telephone	♦ it is fast ♦ it suits situations where a permanent record is not required (or wanted) ♦ allows conversation with people in separate or remote locations ♦ removes the social distractions of face to face communication ♦ status, physical appearance and surroundings are irrelevant ♦ conference calls allow multiple participants	♦ receiver may not be available ♦ non-verbal communication is absent ♦ can be disruptive to receiver if doing another task ♦ easy to become distracted, and do something else at the same time, eg use a PC ♦ no written record gives greater opportunity for misunderstandings
Meetings	♦ allows multiple opinions to be expressed ♦ can discuss a wide range of ideas ♦ can resolve many issues	♦ some personalities may dominate the meeting ♦ can highlight differences and cause conflict ♦ costly in terms of personnel time
Presentations	♦ complex ideas can be communicated ♦ visual aids can be used to help the communication process ♦ good presentations leave a lasting impression	♦ require careful planning and skill ♦ poor presentations lead to audience resentment

4.3 Electronic methods of communication

Method	Advantages	Disadvantages
Electronic mail	◆ quick - regardless of destination ◆ provides a written record ◆ stores messages for a given period after they are received ◆ files may be searched using coded key-words/phrases ◆ can choose to read (automatic filing system) and have attention drawn to priority messages ◆ attachments can be included, eg reports ◆ makes a single message available to many persons	◆ requires some computer literacy ◆ mail may not be checked regularly ◆ lacks privacy and may be forwarded without your knowledge ◆ more than a screenful may not be the best way to communicate ◆ possibility of spreading computer viruses
Video-conference	◆ is a meeting using a computer and video system ◆ in-between a proper meeting and a telephone call ◆ allows non-verbal messages (gestures) to be both sent and received	◆ expensive hardware (compared to telephone) for a high quality system ◆ may be dominated by certain participants ◆ image quality may be poor

 4.4 Written communications

Method	Advantages	Disadvantages
Memorandum	◆ it is brief and only deals with a single topic or a short series of closely-related points (see example below) ◆ provides a permanent record of an internal message ◆ PC template or a memo pad for hand-written messages is often provided	◆ can be perceived as impersonal ◆ if used too often it can be ignored ◆ if the subject matter is too general, people might dismiss it
Letter	◆ provides a permanent record of an external message ◆ adds formality to external communications ◆ it uses a clear simple structure (see example below) ◆ allows personalisation of copies to be sent to a list of people	◆ even if inaccurate or poorly presented, it is a permanent record and can be used to highlight incompetence ◆ may be a long delay between the message being sent and it being received
Facsimile (fax)	◆ allows reports and messages to reach remote locations quickly ◆ it may be cheaper than normal mail ◆ it is more reliable than posting ◆ it often stimulates a faster response than a letter	◆ lacks security because it can be seen by others ◆ fax machine may not be checked for messages ◆ some images do not transmit well
Report	◆ provides a permanent comprehensive written record ◆ uses a clear, simple structure	◆ complex messages or ideas may be misunderstood due to lack of feedback ◆ report result may reflect badly on the author

Practice question 3 *(The answer is in the final chapter of this book)*

Communication and presentation

The new managing director of Hamilton Ellis Ltd, a company that sells specialist computer services, has become increasingly alarmed about the poor quality of the personal communication skills of many of her staff. She knows that, in a highly competitive market, effective communication and presentation skills are essential if the company is to deliver reliable products on time, and win new business. She has asked you to prepare a draft set of management guidelines, which could be issued throughout the company to make both its internal and external communications more effective.

Required

Draw up this set of guidelines, including possible requirements for action.

4.5   Examples of written communications

The **short informal report** - tends to be from and to people who address each other informally when they meet and talk. They are apt to involve a personal investigation and the finished work represents the personal observations, evaluations, and analyses of the writers. The writers are expected to report their work as their own and, as such, the writing style tends to be more personal, using *I, we, you,* rather than a third party approach.

The following example shows the basic structure, which can be adapted to suit different requirements.

REPORT

TO:	Proposer of the report (name and title)
FROM:	Report author (name and title)
DATE:	14th November 200X
SUBJECT:	Layout of short report

1   *Introduction*

   Open with the purpose/terms of reference and name of person requesting the report.

2   *Procedure*

   Outline the methods and techniques used to find the information.

   (a)   Use headings and sub-headings.
   (b)   Use numbers or bullet points to list points.
   (c)   Underline the important text for emphasis.

3   *Findings*

   (a)   Use headings and sub-headings.
   (b)   Use numbers or bullet points to list points.
   (c)   Underline the important text for emphasis.
   (d)   Use relevant charts, graphs, etc as support – use appendix for bulky statistics.
   (e)   Summarise the findings.

4   *Conclusion*

   Suggest deadlines or further action.

   Give opinion and recommendations where appropriate.

Memorandum reports - are also informal and can be any size, from one line to several pages long. For the longer varieties the way the information is organised and displayed should be given consideration. The outline below may be a useful guide:

MEMORANDUM

TO: Jo Parker

FROM: Chris Triggs

DATE: 14th November 200X

SUBJECT: Layout of long memo

BEGINNING

Open with an introduction to the subject and the reason for it. Make references to any earlier discussions, phone calls, meetings, etc.

MIDDLE

The middle section or sections are for the information:

(a)   Use headings and sub-headings.

(b)   Use numbers or bullet points to list points.

(c)   <u>Underline the important text for emphasis.</u>

END

The last section should round off the memo, drawing attention to deadlines or further action which may be required.

Briefing notes - are designed to provide the recipient with a short analysis of a particular situation. A typical briefing note might use the following outline:

BRIEFING NOTES

To:

From:

Date:

Subject:

Background

Key issues

*

*

*

Conclusion

(a)

(b)

(c)

Action required

1

2

Business letters - should be clear, concise and courteous. They should help promote the right image of the organisation. The presentation of business letters depends upon the *house style* of a particular organisation, ie layout, spelling (dispatch *or* despatch) and punctuation (decision making *or* decision-making; Eg. *or* eg.). Although some people prefer one style compared to another, no style can be described as wrong as long as it is *consistent*. The components of the letter are always the same and are always typed on headed paper:

Name and address of organisation	THE TRAINING FIRM 123 Lecturer Row London NW2 4LR Tel: (020) 7323 2147 Fax: (020) 7323 2148	Logo
Our ref	REF NM/WPP	
Their ref	Your ref MK/LM	
Date	25 November 200X	
Recipient's name	Mr S Brown	
Position *Address*	Office Manager 22 Plain Street Swindon S42 7KJ	
Salutation	Dear Mr Brown	
Subject heading	Business letter layout	
Opening paragraph	Acknowledge any previous letter and introduce the subject	
Main body of letter	In a logical manner, give or ask for the required information	
Closing paragraph	Conclude the letter in a suitable manner	
Complimentary close	Yours sincerely	
Name of writer	John Jones	
Designation (position)	Sales Co-ordinator	
Enclosure mark	Enc	

Practice question 4 (The answer is in the final chapter of this book)

Jim Ryan

Jim Ryan is general manager of the CityGo Bus Company. The company is currently one of the subsidiary companies and a regional operating division of a public corporation - the City Bus Corporation. As part of the privatisation strategy of the national government all the operating divisions of the City Bus Corporation have been separately sold by tender-based offer for sale. Some divisions have been acquired by private transport operators while the CityGo division has been acquired through a management buyout (MBO) led by the existing general manager of CityGo, Jim Ryan.

The CityGo Bus Company's computing systems were totally integrated into the City Bus Corporation's own systems and the newly privatised bus company must now implement its own financial systems. The privatisation timetable means that CityGo has only a few months to set up these new computer based systems.

The requirement will be for a project management process which can deal with tight timescales involving a complicated set of interrelated decisions and actions. CityGo management must realise that effective project planning and control needs different management skills from those required to run operational processes.

This is the immediate requirement, but in the longer term CityGo must put in place a strategy for managing information resources in ways which enable it to achieve a competitive advantage or at least competitive parity with other bus operators.

Required

In your role as a management consultant

(a)   Prepare a brief report for Jim Ryan that examines the attributes of a project management process and assesses the range of project management tools and techniques which are available to CityGo to help achieve an effective and efficient changeover to new financial systems.

(b)   Write a memorandum to Jim Ryan, briefly describing five responsibilities of a project manager.

4.6   Learning outcome

You have now covered all the learning outcomes for this chapter.

Explain the importance of effective communication and the consequences of failure in the communication process.

Analyse communication problems in a range of organisational situations.

Recommend changes or actions to avoid or correct communication problems.

5   Summary

Communication establishes relationships and makes organising possible. Every message has a purpose or objective. The sender intends - whether consciously or unconsciously - to accomplish something by communicating. In organisational contexts, messages typically have a definite objective: to motivate, to inform, to teach, to persuade, to entertain, or to inspire.

Organisational communication establishes a pattern of formal communication channels to carry information vertically and horizontally. (The organisation chart displays these channels.) To ensure efficient and effective accomplishment of objectives, information is exchanged. Information is passed *upward* from employees to supervisors and *laterally* to adjacent departments. Instructions relating to the performance of the department and policies for conducting business are conveyed *downward* from supervisors to employees. The organisation carries information from within the department back up to top management.

CHAPTER 9

Systems development lifecycle

EXAM FOCUS

This chapter examines the systems development lifecycle and discusses its role as a framework for the development of information systems. We look at methodologies that have been developed to add discipline to the development process and help the system become more user acceptable. The role of the database administrator and data dictionary, covered later in the chapter, are popular examination topics.

LEARNING OUTCOMES

This chapter covers the following Learning Outcomes of the CIMA syllabus

> Evaluate the operation of the various parts of the Information System of an organisation and the relationships between them
>
> Explain the issues involved in planning and managing an Information Systems project and produce a management plan for such a project
>
> Explain the processes of system design and development and analyse the issues arising at those stages

In order to cover these learning outcomes, the following topics are included

> The concept of the systems development lifecycle when applied to an Information Systems project
>
> The stages in the systems development lifecycle
>
> Databases and database management systems (Note: knowledge of database structures will not be required)
>
> The nature and purpose of data normalisation and Structured English (Note: students will not be expected to apply these techniques)
>
> Performance and technical specification (Note: knowledge of computer programming is not required)
>
> Prototyping, including the use of fourth generation languages to improve productivity

---

1 Development methodologies

1.1 The systems development lifecycle (SDLC)

 The term methodology is used extensively in system development. The British Computer Society's definition is 'a method of developing IS, with identified phases and sub phases, recommended techniques to use and recommendations about planning, management control and evaluation of a development project'.

Methodologies have developed over the years to reflect the increasing complexity of systems and the need to develop useful systems without expensive redesigns at a late stage in production.

The nature of the task and the circumstances within the organisation will determine which stages of any methodology are useful to the analyst and designer.

Changes in an organisation's goals, objectives, products/services and/or structure create a need for modifications to their information systems. The term systems development can be used to describe the steps required to create, design, modify or maintain an organisation's information system. The process is called the systems development lifecycle (SDLC).

1.2 Elements of SDLC

 In the early years of computers, as systems were developed, various factors became apparent to systems developers. The piecemeal development of systems or single programs in response to individual problems should be supplemented by an 'integrated systems approach'. This means that development should proceed with a view to a later period when system elements could be linked together and data from different elements could be shared across the system. The need to foresee this affected developers' approach to the individual elements in the system.

Systems development tended to follow a recognised pattern, subsequently called the *systems development lifecycle*, which included the same stages irrespective of the application. The characteristics of the lifecycle could be exploited by using a systems development methodology to plan and control the project through all its stages.

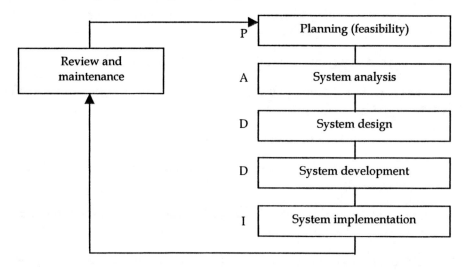

 As indicated in the diagram, the individual steps of the systems development lifecycle can best be remembered by the mnemonic 'PADDI'.

 Planning (P) - will include establishing the terms of reference and a project feasibility study. The *terms of reference* will include details as to what is expected from the project team. The *project feasibility study* is concerned with justifying the system in terms of the benefits it will bring to the organisation. The study will look at the volume and nature of transactions, the operating costs and the availability of alternatives.

 System analysis (A) - this stage will include a detailed investigation of the *existing* system in order to discover the precise nature of the users' needs and the way in which the system currently operates. This will involve fact finding exercises and documentation of the system to enable the production of an outline specification of users' needs.

System design (D) - at this stage all detailed operating characteristics will be designed in terms of inputs, outputs, and files. All processes (manual and computer) will be defined. All controls and security aspects will be agreed.

 System development (D) - will include the acquisition of hardware and software and consideration of whether to develop the system internally or externally.

 System implementation (I) - this stage will include the following steps.

♦ Preparation of the detailed specification used to create computer programs and relevant user documentation (user manuals).

♦ Testing of programs so that master files can be created for extensive field trials.

♦ Planning and execution of changeover procedures.

♦ Validation of the system by parallel running, etc.

♦ System maintenance and review - the system must be regularly reviewed and maintained during its life to ensure that its objectives are being achieved and that performance is satisfactory.

The lifecycle appears linear, moving from one completed phase to the next. In practice, any system development is an iterative process; that is, working by a series of repeated steps towards the solution. For example, design often generates new questions that must be answered by renewed analysis!

1.3   The importance of the systems development lifecycle

 Once a systematic approach to systems development became the norm, substantial improvement was achieved in the quality and efficiency of systems developed.

♦ A feasibility study meant that the new system could be justified in financial and operational terms.

♦ System analysis and design increases the chances that the new system will meet user requirements.

♦ Regular monitoring and review means that systems developers are kept up to date with changing information needs.

However, the lifecycle approach had a number of disadvantages.

♦ It restricted the development of systems.

♦ Most applications comprised straightforward automation of transaction processing systems. This did not exploit the opportunities offered by IT and instead applications largely followed the existing system, with all its shortcomings.

♦ Users were not actively involved in the development of systems.

♦ User requirements were considered to be 'technical' and hence heavy reliance was placed on the abilities of the systems analyst.

 In summary, the use of the lifecycle approach to developing systems led to the following problems.

♦ The information needs of managers being ignored.
♦ Poorly defined user requirements.
♦ Lack of involvement of users in development of systems.
♦ No major rethink of the ways things were done.
♦ Systems were developed independently of one another.

Practice question 1 *(The answer is in the final chapter of this book)*

Systems development lifecycle

Required

Describe the stages and tasks commonly associated with the systems development cycle.

2 Alternatives to the SDLC

2.1 Outsourcing

System development is not always possible (or desirable) within an organisation and may have to be carried out by an external company, sometimes called a facilities management company. This is called outsourcing. However, careful planning and monitoring of the project will be required to ensure that systems development objectives are achieved.

2.2 End-user computing

Instead of being developed by specific development staff, a system may be developed by end users. They may take advantage of Fourth Generation Languages (4GLs), or they might use database software, eg Oracle or Access. Spreadsheet programs such as Excel or Lotus 1-2-3 can also be used to model systems, especially numerical and financial modelling systems.

2.3 Methodologies

Many of the drawbacks of the SDLC have been overcome by the development of structured methodologies. A systems development methodology is a collection of procedures, tools, techniques and documentation aids, which help in the implementation of a new system. Such methodologies have the following advantages.

- They involve users more closely in the design and development process, so avoiding user resentment.

- They analyse the 'needs' of the organisation in a more fundamental way, by looking at the way information is processed at the operational level together with the information needs of managers at the tactical and strategic levels of management.

- They permit flexibility of systems, in that systems can be integrated and can share information.

- They produce easily understood documentation, such as dataflow diagrams, entity relationship models, etc.

- They integrate the development process with the disciplines of project management, to ensure that the system arrives at the correct time and to an agreed level of budget.

Examples of software development methodologies are:

- SSADM (Structured Systems Analysis and Design Methodology);
- JSD (Jackson Structured Design);
- Structured Analysis for real-time Systems (Yourdon).

One single development methodology cannot prescribe how to tackle the great variety of tasks and situations encountered by the systems analyst. Methodologies are constantly changing to accommodate new technological advances and ideas in systems development. The main differences are between process driven, data driven and user driven methodologies.

2.4   *The process driven approach*

Process driven methodologies concentrate on the processes that the system performs. For example, the reason for computerising a manual payroll operation may be to reduce staff costs, as well as to improve the quality and efficiency of the payroll process.

In this example, a shortcoming of this process driven approach is that no attempt is made to consider how the information contained within the payroll system can be harnessed for the benefit of managers at the tactical or strategic levels of management.

The main features of the process driven approach are as follows.

◆   It concentrates on analysing the different activities that form a system.

◆   Each process is analysed in terms of how it converts inputs into outputs.

◆   The emphasis of the system is on the 'activities' or 'functions' carried out in the system and on improving the way information is processed.

◆   An improvement in the way things are done (eg by computerising a manual system) will produce a better and more efficient system.

The process driven approach to developing systems

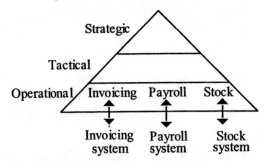

The disadvantages of developing systems based on a process driven approach are as follows.

◆   It leads to an exact duplication of manual activities.

◆   It doesn't force the analyst to critically examine how the organisation operates.

◆   The systems produced are inflexible in the type of information generated, and no attempt is made to link systems (eg a payroll system with a personnel system – common data being employee details).

2.5   *The data driven approach*

Data driven methodologies focus on the data items regardless of the processes they are related to. This is because the type of data an organisation needs is less likely to change than either the processes which operate on it or the output information required of it.

The data driven approach is based on the following considerations.

◆   Data needs are much more stable and constant irrespective of how the information is processed, eg we can change the way sales invoices are processed but a sales report that summarises the sales for the period will still be required.

◆   Systems are designed according to a study of the data in the system, which will lead to more stable and flexible systems.

The data driven approach is often associated with the adoption of a database strategy.

The data driven approach to developing systems

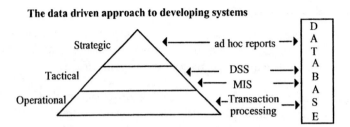

To design a system using this approach the analyst uses tools and techniques that help him understand the ways in which data items relate together (eg entity life histories, entity relationship model, normalisation). These are discussed later.

2.6 The user driven approach

This approach considers the needs of users, as expressed in the outputs or potential outputs required of the system. The users' requirements should determine the type of data collected or captured by the system.

3 Structured systems analysis and design methodology

3.1 Elements of SSADM

Structured systems analysis and design methodology (SSADM) is a hybrid, claiming to combine elements from the following areas.

♦ The process driven approach - documented in SSADM by dataflow diagrams or DFDs.

♦ The data driven approach - to model the entities, relationships and attributes of data (entity models).

♦ The event driven approach - to represent the changes to which entities are subjected by modelling events and states (entity life histories).

♦ The user driven approach – to recognise the importance of user involvement in the development of systems. This approach is based on the use of prototypes - working models of computer systems, which can be developed quickly using fourth generation languages (4GLs - sophisticated, high-level computer languages).

The objective of SSADM is to obtain a true picture of the system under study by viewing it from three perspectives: process, data and events. In other words, it has the following aims:

♦ To represent the various aspects of the system (data, processes and events).

♦ To provide a means of controlling and managing large-scale information system projects.

♦ To be a framework to guide system developers and to be flexible in approach. This flexibility is shown in the fact that the feasibility stage is optional and that there are versions of SSADM for small-scale projects (micro SSADM).

SSADM focuses on the feasibility, analysis and design phases of the SDLC, and represents a detailed and methodical approach often required in large-scale complex projects.

The main components are outlined below:

The component parts of SSADM

Modules and deliverables	Tools and techniques
♦ Feasibility study (optional)	♦ Dataflow diagrams
♦ Requirements analysis	♦ Entity relationship models
♦ Requirements specification	♦ Entity life histories
♦ Logical systems specification	♦ Decision tables
♦ Physical design	♦ Decision trees
	♦ Structured English
	♦ Normalisation (relational data analysis)

3.2   *Features and structure of SSADM*

SSADM can be tailored to suit any systems development and is very flexible. It has precisely defined methods backed up by extensive documentation. SSADM describes precisely how a system is to be developed. The development is divided into clear phases, each phase subsequently defined into stages and each stage broken down into a number of steps which contain activities. There is a progressive increase of detail throughout the phases and subsequent stages. This is shown in the diagram below of the modules and deliverables.

Purpose	Module	Deliverable	Techniques used
To evaluate the project's potential before major expenditure is committed. It defines the objectives of the system and the criteria of success	Feasibility study	Feasibility report	Data flow diagrams Entity models Walkthroughs and documentation
Investigation of the current system and user needs	Requirements analysis	Analysis of requirements	Data flow diagrams Entity models Walkthroughs and documentation
To carry out a detailed analysis of the requirements of the new system	Requirements specification	Requirements specification	Data flow diagrams Walkthroughs and documentation
To produce a detailed spec of the HCI (Human Computer Interface) requirements of proposed system Technical environment for new system described in overview terms	Logical system specification (LSS)	Logical system specification	Normalisation Entity models Walkthroughs and documentation
To turn the LSS into a physical design for the programs and data storage requirements for the chosen system	Physical design	Physical system specification	Physical design controls Walkthroughs and documentation

(**Note:** A walkthrough is a meeting which takes place between all interested parties at which the project is discussed.) Each stage is segmented into steps (assigned names and unique identification numbers) and then into tasks (given numbers relating to the relevant steps).

Practice question 2 *(The answer is in the final chapter of this book)*

Structured approach

Most large organisations use a structured approach in the development of information systems.

Required

Outline the main stages in such an approach.

---

4 CASE tools, prototyping and fourth generation languages

4.1 CASE tools

Computer-Aided Software Engineering (CASE) tools attempt to mechanise some of the more routine tasks in systems and program development. They are used to speed up and make more consistent the systems development process. Major facilities that a CASE tool should offer include:

♦ support for the structured methodology in use
♦ good diagramming facilities
♦ a central data dictionary
♦ access control
♦ consistency checking
♦ prototyping facilities.

There are four basic categories of CASE tools:

♦ integrated project support environment (IPSE)
♦ analyst's workbench
♦ programmer's workbench
♦ individual programs.

The first three categories offer some kind of integrated environment, whereas the fourth category offers individual tools for the analyst or programmer.

Integrated Project Support Environment - the facilities offered by an IPSE might include:

♦ help and advice on how to follow the methodology and how to operate the system

♦ tools to allow the systems designer to develop and draw the various diagrams used in the systems development methodology supported by the IPSE. Diagrams produced may include dataflow or entity relationship diagrams, entity life histories and structure diagrams

♦ project management facilities can allow the systems development team to carry out Critical Path or PERT (Programme Evaluation and Review Technique) analysis, to produce Gantt charts and other control diagrams, to help in allocating resources and estimating costs

♦ form and screen design utilities will allow the analyst to produce the relevant input and output design quickly and effectively. These designs can be used to communicate with users, which can help to improve the standard of system specification

♦ data design tools can be used to help define the different entities, attributes, and relationships and can help in the production of the data dictionary

♦ the IPSE is likely to be run via a menu system, which will allow the systems designer to easily select the required options and to switch between different facilities.

The analyst's workbench is used to help specify the system and programs, and to help produce system documentation. It will incorporate some of the facilities described in the previous section - construction of DFDs, ELH, entity relationship diagrams and structure diagrams; data analysis tools; a screen pointer to help design forms; and screens. It is also likely to be able to perform other important tasks - ensuring that the system conforms to the standards set by the organisation and by the design methodology used.

The programmer's workbench program is to help automate some of the processes involved in turning systems specifications into working programs. Some of the facilities may include:

♦ a menu based method of selecting the different options

♦ help in using the system

♦ a word processor for entry and modification of programs

♦ file and disk utilities

♦ automated compilation and linking of programs

♦ program debuggers and other diagnostic aids. These may allow the testing of individual sections of programs, or the temporary suspension of a program run to assess if the values of variables are as expected

♦ automatic production of program documentation

♦ a library of existing code and subroutines that are often used may be available and capable of being linked in with new programs

♦ code generators may allow the automatic production of programs from Pseudo code, Structured English or Structure Diagrams.

4.2   Prototyping

Prototyping is the production of a working model of a system. Working models are used in many areas of business, from the production of new cars to the training of pilots to fly new aeroplanes. The use of prototypes minimises the risk that the item being designed will not fit the needs of the organisation and allows experimentation without the high cost of failure.

Under the traditional methods of system development, users specified their requirements to the analyst and project team, who then developed the system based on those requirements with little or no further user involvement. Prototyping lets the user 'view' the system during development and make amendments or corrections as required. The usual way of categorising prototyping is as follows:

♦ *Throw-away prototyping* is a basic system produced at an early stage to establish requirements, and then discarded.

♦ *Evolutionary prototyping* creates a basic design as the foundation of future development, which is not 'thrown away'.

♦ *Incremental (staged) prototyping* creates a software system in stages. At each stage it becomes more and more functional and incorporates changes required.

Modern tools used by prototypes include:

♦ integrated data dictionaries

♦ very high level languages (fourth generation languages, 4GLs)

♦ end user query languages

♦ report generators

♦ screen pointers

♦ applications packages - eg spreadsheets - can be used as an inexpensive medium for the speedy development of systems

The advantages of prototyping include:

♦ The final design is highly likely to fit user needs - by having concrete examples it is easier for users to visualise what the computer can do for them and to define their needs fully and precisely.

♦ Employees are involved in the systems development process - this will help to ensure that the system is properly defined, and will reduce the likelihood of dysfunctional behaviour.

♦ Identification of problems - once a full system has been developed, it is very expensive to eradicate any bugs in the programs or difficulties in the way the users relate to the system. With prototyping, the systems analyst or users can identify any problems or omissions and eliminate them. The user-friendliness of the system can be guaranteed.

♦ Code generation - many 4GLs are capable of automatically producing a series of programs written in a third generation language. This makes prototyping a very cost effective way of developing systems.

There are some disadvantages with prototyping:

♦ many 4GLs and other prototyping tools are hungry for computer processing resources and expensive to buy

♦ the development process may become sloppy and unstructured, wasting money and resources and making planning difficult. With suitable controls, this disadvantage can be overcome

♦ prototyping tools often require data to be in a specific format. Existing data files may require conversion before they can be input into the prototype

♦ some prototyping tools are restrictive in the way that systems can be developed, and may not allow hand written codes to be linked in

♦ code produced by code generators may well be less efficient than that produced by an experienced programmer.

4.3 Fourth Generation Languages (4GLs)

A fourth generation language is a programming language that is easier to use than languages such as COBOL, Pascal and C++, which are third generation languages. They are procedural languages meaning that the programmer details each step of a calculation or of how to produce a printout. Well-known examples are Powerhouse and Informix.

Different 4GLs have different facilities, but examples of the kinds of facilities that may be found in a 4GL are listed below:

♦ data dictionary creation and upkeep
♦ screen painter
♦ form designer
♦ report generators
♦ a graphical WIMP (window, icon, mouse, pointer/pull-down menu) interface

Practice question 3 *(The answer is in the final chapter of this book)*

Prototyping

You are a trainee in the accounting department of an organisation that is considering developing a new information system. The management accountant has heard that prototyping is a method of producing application software and has asked you to write a brief report for him.

Required

Write a brief report for the management accountant that:

(a)   explains what is meant by the term *prototyping*.

(b)   gives examples of situations where its use might be appropriate.

5   Databases and database management systems

5.1   Definitions

A database may be defined as a file of data, or files of interrelated data, so held that many applications and programs can use the data and update it.

To appreciate the significance of this definition, it is first necessary to understand that conventional systems tend to organise their files so that there is a separate file for each application or, at most, a few applications. Thus there would be a wages file holding all the data needed to produce each employee's wages and also a personnel file holding the data needed by the personnel department. This means that a substantial number of fields are duplicated in each file causing data divergence.

In a database system, the data in the above two files would all be combined in one file so that many programs could use that file for their own purposes. All communication is handled by a special systems program known as a database management system (DBMS), which may be defined as 'a suite of programs that manages the database'.

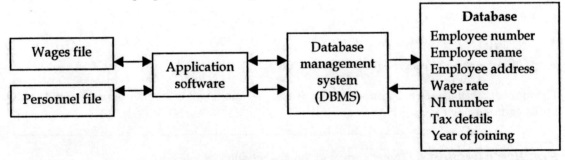

The database management system regulates interactions between the application programs and the information stored in the database. The DBMS also acts as a security barrier, by means of password and security features, to ensure that information accessed by the application programs is only for proper and authorised purposes. The distinguishing feature of a database system is that information need be input only once. For example, if an employee has moved house, the new address could be input via the personnel file, and this information would then be available to the wages file. Without a database system the person operating the wages program and the person operating the personnel program might have to input the change separately.

5.2 Objectives of a database system

The main objectives include:

♦ a database should be shared

♦ it should provide for the needs of different users, who each have their own processing requirements and data access methods

♦ it should be capable of evolving and meeting the future data processing needs of users

5.3 Advantages and disadvantages of a database

A database has the following advantages.

♦ Data is input only once - the repetitive recording of the same information on different files is eliminated. This is known as minimising data redundancy and has the effect of

- saving storage space;

- making updating much easier - only one copy of each field is likely to exist;

- ensuring that the data is equally up-to-date for all purposes;

- ensuring data consistency - all users are accessing the same data and therefore inconsistencies between data cease to exist;

- improving the access to data, thereby allowing for better reporting to management, especially at strategic level, where such reporting would be on an ad hoc basis and might require information from a number of operational departments within the organisation.

♦ It can be used by different users in a variety of different ways - the data is program independent. This means that the physical layout of the database can be altered without the need to alter the programs using the data. The programs access the database management system and the database management system looks after the physical layout of the data.

♦ Storage space is used more efficiently.

♦ Data duplication is minimised.

♦ Data accessibility is maximised.

♦ Flexibility is provided.

♦ Data integrity is preserved (consistency of data).

The main *disadvantage* of a database is its high cost. Tangible and intangible costs are high, both initial and ongoing costs.

Practice question 4 *(The answer is in the final chapter of this book)*

Database

Required

What reasons would you put forward for adopting a database as a basis for an information system?

Practice question 5 *(The answer is in the final chapter of this book)*

DBMS

Required

(a)   Explain what a DBMS is and what it does.

(b)   Describe three advantages of the DBMS approach to data processing.

5.4   Database structures

There are several possible database structures.

♦   Hierarchical structure - where files are linked together using a parent or child structure (one parent - many children). Any one data item can be linked to any number of subsidiary data items, but to only one data item above it in the hierarchy. This structure is sometimes likened to the branches of a tree.

♦   Network structure - this structure is similar to the hierarchical but allows for records to have more than one relationship. Any item of data can be linked with more than one item of data (many-to-many relationships). A network database is expensive to operate and complex for modification to data structures.

♦   Relational structure - this is a more complex structure, which allows one-to-many and many-to-many relationships to occur with a minimum amount of data duplication. Data is split between tables, which are linked together via a set of unique keys. The relationship between the tables is both one-to-many and many-to-many.

♦   Object oriented structure - can store different data types, eg video clips, pictures and sounds, allowing the user to define the data that will be stored rather than having limitations placed on data during database development.

5.5   The database administrator

As the information contained within a database is so important to the organisation, it is normal practice that the database is looked after by a dedicated member of staff, the database administrator.

The database administrator is responsible for controlling and administering the database. A senior experienced person within the organisation, who is familiar with the DBMS and with the organisation itself, normally undertakes this position.

The work of the database administrator is split into two distinct parts.

(i)   **Co-ordinating, analysing and recording all data items**

Tasks under this heading will include the following.

♦   Analysing the data required by each application.
♦   Preparing a data model.
♦   Preparing and maintaining the data dictionary and instructing users on its use.
♦   Recording ownership of all the data.

(ii)   Upkeep and maintenance of the actual database itself

Tasks under this heading will include the following.

- Database design and structure, including the planning of any required changes.
- Planning any necessary hardware changes.
- Evaluating proposals to update or upgrade the database.
- Ensuring data integrity by implementing and controlling database procedures.
- Producing operating manuals.
- Providing training for users on a regular basis.
- Assessing the ongoing performance of the database.

5.6   The data dictionary

The data dictionary is an index of data held within the database that is used to assist in accessing the data. This important design tool records the data, data-flows and all the cross-references needed by the system. It is a standard definition of all the terms the system needs to use, and simple cross-referencing between sections of the system documentation. It facilitates control and uniformity, minimises redundancy of data and promotes improved documentation.

A data dictionary may be kept on paper by the development team, or may be automated and provide checks on, for example, the uniqueness of names. A properly maintained data dictionary ensures that everyone involved on a project is using the same terminology to describe the same object.

Typical data dictionary contents are:

- a list of entity and attribute types;
- a list and set of definitions of all functions and events;
- a list of all functions involving an entity type;
- key-word indices;
- synonyms and homonyms.

An example of a homonym within the business context is an 'order'. This has to be defined further into a sales order, purchase order, maintenance order, etc.

The dictionary records each item of data and stores the following details about each.

- Its characteristics (field width, type of field, etc).

- The origin of the data.

- Possible range of values.

- Validation criteria.

- Ownership of the data.

- Which file it is held in.

- Its position in the file.

- Details of the dialogue used as screen prompts and printout headings.

- Entity life history diagrams.

- A list of all the processes that use data about each entity type.

- The person or department responsible for maintaining the validity of the data and its owner.

A data dictionary helps with:

♦ systems analysis - it helps the analyst organise information about the data elements in the system, where they come from, where they go to and what fields are used.

♦ systems design - it helps the analyst and programmers to ensure that no data elements are missed out. Building the data dictionary is a major part of the process of producing the physical system. Some data dictionaries can generate program code automatically.

♦ systems maintenance - it records the original work and helps to ensure continuity.

Nobody should be allowed to amend the data dictionary without the database administrator's approval. The dictionary is usually stored on computer file referenced by use of a data description language (DDL) thus ensuring that the users adhere rigidly to the standards enforced.

5.7   Structured query language

 Structured query language (SQL) is a data manipulation language used for a relational database. SQL commands are English-like statements, which are used to query, update, insert or manipulate data in the relational database. For example, suppose that we wish to find all orders placed with supplier PG0021. This query would be written in SQL as follows.

Select * from orders where supplier = PG0021.

5.8   Relational data analysis (normalisation)

 For data to be used in a relational database, data items will need to be split into a series of tables each containing a number of unique records. There will be a variety of ways in which data can be split, but the database designer will need to fulfil the following two objectives.

♦ To eliminate any unnecessary duplication of data.
♦ To ensure that each table of data contains a logically distinct set of data.

Achievement of these two objectives will ensure that data storage and access will be efficient and modification to the structure will involve the minimum of difficulty.

 The step-by-step approach of segregating data into tables and fulfilling these criteria is called *normalisation.*

Normalisation removes all items of data which are independent of each other and places them in their own data group. This means that any changes to those items of data would not have unnecessary repercussions throughout the entire database.

The process of normalisation has the following advantages.

♦ There are reduced data storage requirements in the final physical system.

♦ Access paths in the logical system are rationalised, with possible improvements in response times.

♦ Processing (writing, updating and deleting) of data items should have minimum disruption.

When designing the storage of data within the database, it must be possible to link different data items; they must be correctly cross-referenced, and unnecessary duplication of data must be eliminated.

5.9   *Process specifications*

These are sometimes called 'minispecs', and are used in conjunction with dataflow diagrams (which we will look at in the next chapter). The main points to note about minispecs are:

♦ They are written for each activity for which no lower level dataflow diagram exists.

♦ Each process specification describes exactly what must be done in order to transform inputs to outputs.

♦ They must be expressed in an unambiguous form which can be verified by the user and the systems analyst.

♦ They are expressed in a form which includes only information that is not already specified in other documents.

The techniques for process specification include:

♦ Structured English (structured narrative);
♦ Decision tables / trees;
♦ Flowcharts.

Structured English - An example of why natural language process specification is unsatisfactory is given below:

'To be entitled to discount, customers must do £20,000 worth of business per annum and have a good payment history or have been with us for more than five years'.

♦ It is ambiguous - should it be £20,000 and (have a good payment history or five years) or (£20,000 and have a good payment history) or five years?

♦ It is imprecise - what is a good payment history?

♦ It is incomplete - we assume it is £20,000 or more but is this what the specification says?

A structured narrative is essentially a design tool, which presents tasks undertaken by the program in a very detailed format. English is adopted as the language, but the vocabulary is extremely restricted. The approach is intended to pursue the logical program activities and the program layout is followed strictly. It is a subset of English based upon:

♦ sequence
♦ decision   (if...then...else, case...end case)
♦ iteration   (while...do, repeat...until)
♦ nouns that are defined in the data dictionary.

Guidelines for writing Structured English:

♦ use a consistent style;
♦ use layout to reveal structure;
♦ aim to write what must be done, and not how to do it;
♦ avoid adjectives - unless defined in the data dictionary, eg 'good' history;
♦ avoid adverbs - these are expressed in our set of constructs.

Example

if CustBusinessPerAnnum < £20,000
then
      no Discount
else
      if PaymentHistoryStatus = "GoodPaymentHistory"
      then
            give Discount
      else
            if CustTradeRecord >= five years
            then
               give Discount
            else
               no Discount
            end if
      end if
end if

 Decision tables and decision trees – These are a useful method of analysing, and presenting, the logic of a situation, simply because they offer:

- a graphical picture of complex procedures which is easy to comprehend;
- the opportunity of reducing the problem to its simplest level;
- an indication of any omissions or redundancies;
- an efficient method of communicating for analysts, user management and programmers.

Using our previous example the same logic can be presented in the form of a decision tree.

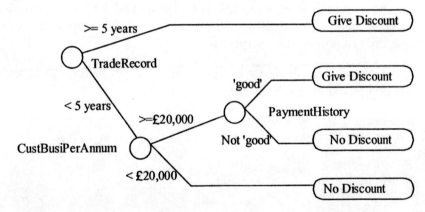

A decision tree lies somewhere between a flow chart and a family tree, and displays the information in a linear fashion. The circles are event forks with each branch terminating in an outcome.

 Flowcharts - The purpose of flowcharting is to reduce a procedure to its basic components and to emphasise their logical relationships, so that a connected pattern of activity can be traced from the beginning to the end. The technique is simple but unfortunately the subject lacks a uniform terminology, both in the descriptions of types of flowchart and in the symbols to be used.

The following illustration is of flowchart symbols:

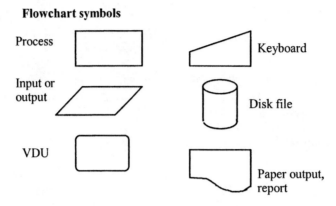

Flowchart symbols

5.10 Learning outcomes

You have now covered the learning outcomes for this chapter.

Evaluate the operation of the various parts of the Information System of an organisation and the relationships between them.

Explain the issues involved in planning and managing an Information Systems project and produce a management plan for such a project.

Explain the processes of system design and development and analyse the issues arising at those stages.

6 Summary

Stages in the systems development lifecycle can be remembered by the mnemonic PADDI: planning, systems analysis, systems design, systems development and systems implementation. This is a process driven approach.

Structured methodologies are data driven approaches. They include structured systems analysis and design methodology (SSADM).

Subsequent chapters will expand upon the principles of the structured methods together with the various graphical techniques, which are utilised to ensure that the final system meets the user's needs.

CHAPTER 10

Systems analysis and design

EXAM FOCUS

This chapter covers several key areas of the syllabus and is of particular relevance to today's accountant, who will often be part of a feasibility study group to assist in the assessment of the viability of a project. Particular attention should be paid to the various fact-finding techniques, together with the graphical techniques of dataflow diagrams, entity relationship models and entity life histories. At least one of these techniques will typically feature in virtually every examination sitting.

LEARNING OUTCOMES

This chapter covers the following Learning Outcome of the CIMA syllabus

> Apply the main tools and techniques used in the gathering, recording and analysis of information relating to an existing Information System

In order to cover this learning outcome, the following topics are included

> Systems evaluation

> Assessing the feasibility of systems projects (ie cost-benefit analysis, technical feasibility, time feasibility)

> Information gathering techniques (ie interviews, questionnaires, observation, simulation, document review)

> Recording and documenting tools used during the analysis and design of systems (ie entity-relationship model, logical data structure, entity life history, dataflow diagram, and decision table)

---

1 Systems analysis

1.1 Model of the analysis stage

We build models of systems, and stages of systems, for three reasons:

♦ to focus on important system features rather than less important features;

♦ to discuss changes and corrections to the user's requirements at a low cost and with minimal risk;

♦ to verify that we understand the user's environment and have documented it in such a way that systems designers and programmers can build the system.

Any tool or model should have the following characteristics:

♦ It should be graphical with supporting textual detail.

♦ It should allow the system to be viewed in a top-down, partitioned fashion (eg maps and atlases down to town plans).

♦ It should have minimal redundancy.

♦ It should help the reader predict the system's behaviour.

♦ It should be transparent to the reader.

 The diagram below is a model of the analysis stage:

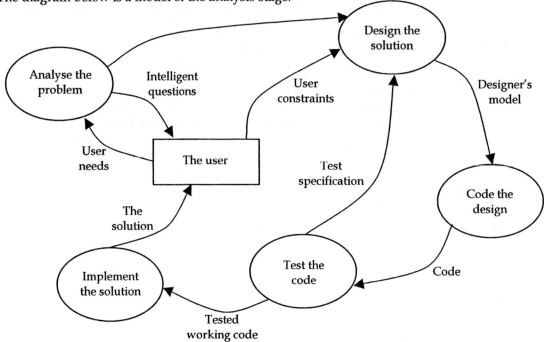

1.2 Steering committee

 A steering committee is formed to monitor and control the feasibility study (although outside consultants may be commissioned) and set its objectives and terms of reference.

This feasibility study is primarily a financial exercise to determine whether the likely benefits will outweigh the likely costs. Management requires as much detailed information as possible to make the correct decision. A computer manufacturer or a management consultant is often asked to carry out a feasibility study, but neither is likely to be familiar with the structure and working of the company.

Therefore a team (the steering committee) composed of people from within the company and those with computer experience could perform the feasibility study and produce a report for senior management.

 This body authorises the project and subsequently monitors its activities. The steering committee's tasks include:

♦ approval or rejection of projects

♦ recommending projects to the board of directors

♦ establishing company guidelines

♦ coordinating and controlling the work of the study groups and project development groups

♦ evaluating feasibility study reports and system specifications. The steering committee must be satisfied that each system has been thoroughly justified

♦ monitoring and reviewing each new system after implementation to check whether the system has met its objectives. If it has not met the objectives, the steering committee will investigate the reasons for the system's failure and take suitable control or remedial actions.

Membership is bound to vary in accordance with the kind of project involved but the steering committee might include the information director or a senior IS staff member, accountants for technical financial advice relating to costs and benefits and a senior user manager.

2   The feasibility study

2.1   Terms of reference

A feasibility study is a formal study to decide what type of system can be developed to meet the needs of the organisation.   The team must be given terms of reference by senior management. These should state:

♦   the scope of the study, which may range from one specific application to examination of the complete organisation; and

♦   the objectives which management wishes to achieve

The steering committee's **terms of reference** for a large project might include the following:

♦   investigate and report on an existing system - its procedures and costs
♦   define systems requirements
♦   establish whether the requirements are being met by the existing system
♦   establish whether the requirements could be met by an alternative system
♦   specify performance criteria for the system
♦   recommend the most suitable system to meet the organisation's objectives
♦   prepare a detailed cost budget within a specified budget limit
♦   prepare a draft plan for implementation within a specified time
♦   establish whether proposed benefits could be realised
♦   establish a detailed design, implementation and operating budget
♦   compare the detailed budget with the costs of the current system

2.2   Justifying the new system

The feasibility study is concerned with the justification of the system: will its introduction result in some advantage to the organisation?

The study will look at the current and future requirements of the system including the following issues.

♦   The volume of transactions
♦   The speed of processing
♦   The methods of processing
♦   Response times
♦   The level of accuracy
♦   Compatibility with other systems
♦   Security
♦   Audit trail
♦   Data inputs
♦   The quality of output
♦   The current hardware and software
♦   The operating costs
♦   The availability of alternatives

The feasibility study will ensure that a true case for computer usage exists. The technical, economic and practical/operational feasibility will be examined:

♦ Technical feasibility - the proposed solution must be capable of being implemented using available hardware, software and other equipment. The types of requirement that might be included in the technical feasibility include:

- Response times
- Capacity to hold files or records of a certain size
- Volume of transactions that can be processed within a given time
- Number of users that can be supported without deterioration in the other criteria

The technical feasibility answers the following types of question:

- can it be done?
- is hardware available which can cope with the work?
- is software available, or capable of being developed?

 ♦ Operational feasibility - if a solution makes technical and economic sense but conflicts with the way the organisation does business, the solution is not feasible. Other questions include: is it really workable? Will the unions accept it? What job changes will the system bring? What organisational structures are disturbed? Is management prepared to accept a redundancy problem? Are the staff concerned capable of adapting to the new system? Is it acceptable to customers and suppliers?

 ♦ Economic feasibility - is it worth doing? Will the application save enough money or generate enough profit to justify itself? The system must be a good investment in that it should be the best option from the projects under consideration and the project selected must compete with other projects in other areas of the business for funds.

The steering committee issues the assignment (project) brief which authorises the feasibility study, culminating in the feasibility report.

2.3 The feasibility report

The results of the feasibility study will then be consolidated within a feasibility report.

 Typically, the feasibility study report would contain:

♦ An introduction, objectives, terms of reference and conclusion.

♦ Expected benefits - these can fall into the following two categories:

(i) *Quantifiable benefits* may arise because the business can manage with fewer accounts staff or fewer temporary staff at busy times.

(ii) *Non-quantifiable benefits* include better customer service, better inventory control and better debt collection. The financial effects of some of these can be measured in retrospect but they may be difficult to forecast. Because there are major unknowns in terms of benefits, even after a careful feasibility study has been carried out, the final decision by management often relies on a belief that computerisation is a good idea. They may also obtain evidence from competitors or customers about their own systems.

♦ The recommended machinery and its operating characteristics, delivery period, installation plan and stand-by arrangements.

♦ All the costs, including capital outlay, leasing and rental options, delivery charges, maintenance charges and conditions of sale and insurance.

♦ Programming (software) support available, standard package programs which may be suitable and their cost.

◆ Equipment maintenance facilities offered by the manufacturer during normal working hours, overtime and night shift operation; availability of spare parts, frequency of both routine maintenance and major overhauls, and the possibility of a permanent on-site engineer.

The importance of good maintenance facilities should not be underestimated. For example, if a company relies on its computer to produce invoices, the effect on cashflow would be serious if the computer broke down and was not operational for some time.

◆ Any special environmental or installation requirements, such as air-conditioning, special power supplies, hollow floors to house electric cables, space required, fire protection systems and safety aspects. With the advent of mini- and microcomputers these aspects are becoming less important for many installations.

◆ Apart from programming assistance, any other support that may be needed. For example, data preparation could be subcontracted.

◆ An initial software system design giving an outline description of how the equipment will be used, the main files required, system input and output, the programs required and time scales involved. None of this will be in great detail at this stage.

◆ Staff training and recruitment details for the computer department and user departments.

◆ Details of other users who have installed similar equipment, particularly for similar applications so that the company can investigate the success, or otherwise, of that system.

 The CBA (cost-benefit analysis) approach is adopted here to assess the overall net gain/loss of adopting the suggested system.

 Practice question 1 *(The answer is in the final chapter of this book)*

Feasibility study

The managing director of a distributor of motor accessories is convinced that the retail outlets to which they sell view them as a 'staid and stodgy' organisation and that new computer systems could help change that image by the production of new look invoices and reports for the outlets. This is despite the fact that there are currently no substantial problems with the existing computer systems. So convinced is he that he calls in the information technology manager and asks him to briefly analyse the situation and report back in person a week later.

The IT manager duly returns as requested to report that most users who have substantial contacts with the computer systems are happy with them. The IT department staff agree that the technology is readily available to update the systems. The IT manager himself is of the opinion that just because it can be done, doesn't mean it should be done.

However, the managing director requests that a feasibility report be produced, and you are asked to carry out the preceding feasibility study.

Required

How would you assess the feasibility of this project?

3 Cost-benefit analysis (CBA)

3.1 Costs

There is no standard approach to systems analysis; CBA is often adopted to assess expected costs and benefits of the design to be recommended. This is an attempt to obtain evidence leading to a positive or negative decision on the system's acceptance. This is also often called a method for 'system justification' (if the system is justified, then it will be recommended).

All costs associated with the new system development should be assessed. The types of cost involved are summarised in the table below.

Type of cost	Examples
Capital costs (eg hardware)	◆ Hardware and software purchases ◆ Desks, chairs ◆ Security systems ◆ Stocks of consumables ◆ Communications equipment
Revenue costs (regular payments, eg for power input, and one-off payments, eg development costs)	◆ File conversion ◆ Staff recruitment fees ◆ Staffing (salaries, staff training and redundancy costs) ◆ Temporary staff costs ◆ Printing of documentation
Ongoing running costs (continuing during the life of the system)	◆ Staff wages and salaries ◆ Stationery and consumables ◆ Insurance ◆ Security and back-up procedures ◆ Training ◆ Recruitment fees ◆ Financing costs ◆ Maintenance of hardware and software
Intangible costs	◆ Low staff morale ◆ Effects of the learning curve on staff efficiency and effectiveness ◆ Opportunity costs ◆ Incompatibility between systems

3.2 Benefits

Similarly, all benefits arising from the new system should be analysed. These include both direct benefits (those that have an immediate effect on cashflow) and indirect benefits (those that affect the long-term profitability of the business). Examples are given in the table below.

Type of benefit	Examples
Direct benefits	◆ Reduced operational costs ◆ Reduced system costs ◆ Greater turnover due to increased sales, as a result of the computerisation of the sales ordering system ◆ Increased output due to automated production facility ◆ Improved working capital management through improved stock levels and debt collection
Indirect benefits	◆ Better decision making, due to a better use of information ◆ Greater control over the operational processes ◆ More freedom to innovate, as much of the routine work is computerised ◆ Improved customer service ◆ Competitive advantage

The return on investment is then calculated. The major motivation for the acceptance of a new system is to achieve a profit, perhaps by raising the profit level through higher turnover and/or reducing costs.

Suppose our present system costs the company £75,000 annually and a new system is recommended to undertake precisely the same activities and provide identical information. The new version will initially cost £250,000 with subsequent annual costs of £35,000. In financial terms, is the new system better?

Two major factors are involved in solving the problem: the time-period and the cost of capital, ie the current rate of (loan) interest.

As well as expected costs, we may consider expected future savings, the returns on expenditure. The net value of a recommended system represents estimated outgoings balanced against returns.

Practice question 2 *(The answer is in the final chapter of this book)*

Cost benefit analysis

You are a project manager charged with the task of carrying out a cost-benefit analysis exercise on a proposed new computer-based application.

Required

What factors would you expect to take into account under each of the following headings?

(a)   The cost of building, installing and operating the system.

(b)   The tactical and strategic benefits which might result from the introduction of the new computer application.

3.3   Methods of investment appraisal

Principal methods of investment appraisal are:

♦   *payback period* (simple to calculate, but a rough measure);

♦   DCF (*discounted cashflow*) approaches including net present value (NPV) and internal rate of return (IRR);

♦   *returns/outlay ratio*, providing a straightforward method of assessment which does not include the timings of savings.

CBA activity is incorporated in the system recommendation in the *feasibility report*. This report (whatever it may be titled in the organisation) is given to the *steering committee*, which has to accept or reject the concept.

4   Systems investigation

4.1   Purpose

The purpose of a systems investigation is to enable the team to understand how the system works. This understanding is done both as an overview and in some considerable detail. It will also be necessary to collect information about volumes of transactions, trends and exceptions. Various techniques are available to the systems analyst so that the analysis of the system is performed efficiently.

The breakdown of decision-making processes in a system is more appropriately dealt with using a decision table, a decision tree or the use of structured text (pseudo code).

The technique of the dataflow diagram is often used to illustrate the information flows in a business at a level which is not concerned with the physical system. The technique of drawing DFDs does not show people or equipment but merely the way in which data is transformed in the system.

In addition to a dataflow diagram it is now regarded as good practice to collect data about data. This is generally a file which lists all data items and explains the properties of each. The analysis of trends is of course useful in judging volumes of transactions and similar. The use of statistical techniques such as graphs or histograms is useful in establishing the future workload of the system. It is useful also to link all parts of a systems investigation together by describing the system in narrative form. Narrative descriptions may also include information obtained at interviews and information obtained by the use of questionnaires.

4.2 Fact-finding techniques

In obtaining the facts there are a number of possible approaches, but any facts obtained must give the answers to the major questions posed, and these are the same irrespective of the functional application of the system concerned. These fundamental questions involve:

♦ the nature of the inputs;
♦ the processing to be undertaken on the inputs;
♦ the output (results) required;
♦ the files utilised.

As far as the sources of these facts are concerned, each investigation is likely to deal with different ones, but, in general terms, we would expect these sources to consist of:

♦ the managers of the user-department;

♦ their staff, including professionals (eg accountants) concerned with the particular functional system;

♦ the current system documentation;

♦ the audit and financial reports relating to the system;

♦ the personnel department.

The fact-finding methods must relate to:

♦ the sources themselves;
♦ the kind of facts sought (an overview? details? highly technical areas?);
♦ the number of interviewees;
♦ resources available (including time and team availability);
♦ the cost of obtaining the facts (degree of cost-effectiveness).

We now look at the various methods available. These are interviewing, questionnaires, observing, measuring and reading.

4.3 Interviewing

Three kinds of interview exist:

♦ *the unstructured interview*, permitting a wide-ranging, though prompted and guided, overview to be provided;

♦ *the structured interview*, including set, established questions designed to satisfy specific information requirements of the 'who?', 'what?', 'where?', 'when?' type (repeated for each interview in the same way);

♦ *the semi-structured interview*, allowing the interviewee to extend and develop answers in accordance with his or her experience, knowledge, etc, at the suggestion of the interviewer.

Interviews can provide excellent results if they are both arranged and conducted properly. In the first place, we have to take into account that there are three organisational levels involved and who will be directly concerned with the system, as follows:

♦ *Senior management* - Interview areas will relate to corporate/functional objectives, strategic (long-term) plans, new products, present and future policies, chief problems and line managers' problems.

♦ *Line management* - Interview areas will relate to tactical (detailed, medium/short-term) plans, suggestions and ideas for system improvements, individual staff responsibilities and the selection of staff to be interviewed individually.

♦ *Operational staff members* - Interview areas will relate to their individual tasks, with demonstration as needed, system problems, and the reason for the new system (or modification) and likely results.

Advantages of the interview approach	*Disadvantages of the interview approach*
♦ A direct relationship is established between the interviewer and the interviewee, and this will usually encourage greater co-operation on the part of the latter.	♦ The approach is very time-consuming and therefore expensive in terms of both the interviewer and the interviewee (the latter, of course, being away from his or her job to attend the interview).
♦ More detail can be provided by the interviewee, and his or her personal experience can contribute to the facts, encouraged by the questioning of the interviewer.	♦ Linked with the previous point raised, this approach is relatively slow (typically, four or five interviews can take place in a working day).
♦ The interviewer is able to adjust and re-orientate the questions in accordance with the perceived experience and abilities of the interviewee, ie the interviewer is not limited by the 'set' questions if he or she feels that modification will produce a better response.	♦ Considerable 'desk research' has to be undertaken to support the interview technique, since both cost and time do establish constraints in respect of its extent.
♦ It is likely that 'passing comments' are able to instigate useful ideas and views and lead to deeper questioning.	
♦ The interviewer is able to answer questions posed by the interviewee to allay any fears concerning the new system or any modification of the existing one.	

4.4   Questionnaires

This technique is often adopted in particular circumstances where relatively few questions need to be answered, responses required are simple and straightforward, the number of respondents is relatively large and they are located over a wide geographical area (eg branches).

In the design of the appropriate questionnaire, there are a number of guidelines to follow:

♦ There must be some form of accompanying communication to establish when the form should be returned, completed, and to explain the reason for the investigation.

♦ Sufficient space must be provided for responses.

♦ Every question must be unambiguous and brief.

♦ The questionnaire must be orientated to the sort of respondent to whom it is addressed.

As far as the questions themselves are concerned, there are various forms adopted:

♦ *control question* (establishing the respondent's identity, in terms of name, job title, grade, work location);

♦ *qualification question* (determining the respondent's competence to respond properly: eg 'are you responsible for the updating of this file?');

♦ *main questions* (obtaining the required facts);

♦ *verification questions* (checking the correctness and the consistency of responses).

Advantages of questionnaires	Disadvantages of questionnaires
♦ The technique is useful in the conditions listed above. ♦ It can be adopted as a preliminary to the actual interview approach. ♦ It may be useful to verify answers provided during an interview.	♦ Individuals providing the responses can be irritated by the restrictive nature of the 'form-filling'. ♦ The response-rate is often relatively low and individuals need to be 'chased' for their completed form. ♦ The questionnaire rarely provides exactly what is wanted, and questions can often be misunderstood. ♦ 'Follow-up' is therefore usually needed for clarification, and there is, by definition, no direct 'eye-to-eye' contact with the advantages this can bring.

4.5 Observing

 This may be undertaken by an individual as the activities/events occur, or by video recording. In either case, the kind of facts which are obtained by this approach include:

♦ methods of working (usually supported by interviewing as well);

♦ the workload (variations, say, in quantities of documents which are processed manually);

♦ the work environment (heating, etc);

♦ office equipment, devices (eg, adequacy and location of the filing cabinet(s));

♦ individual staff interaction (formal and informal);

♦ general office layout;

♦ 'bottlenecks', or locations and/or times at which an increase in the quantity/intensity of work-activity arises and delays occur;

♦ the pace of work.

The advantages here are that this approach offers the opportunity to obtain facts which are not presented in other ways, such as the overall interaction of staff activities and the general working atmosphere (degree of noise, telephone usage, accessibility of equipment, etc).

There are three main disadvantages. Firstly, it is quite time-consuming. Secondly, the situation viewed may, or may not, be untypical while staff are conscious of being observed and lastly, behaviour becomes 'what is expected' rather than 'what really goes on'

4.6   Reviewing procedures manuals

Existing procedural manuals can be reviewed to provide the analyst with an idea as to how the system is intended to operate. But the way the system is supposed to operate may be very different from the way it actually functions, as many an auditor has found!

4.7   Sampling and testing

Sampling is often utilised where it is not possible to interview all of the people involved in the operation of the system. In such a case, samples are selected that are representative of the whole population. Once a sample has been selected, the techniques of interviews, questionnaires, etc can be utilised.

The system can be tested by following information flows or documents to assess its operation. If the system is already computerised, then the systems analyst will conduct a review of existing computerised system documentation including the original specification, dataflow diagrams, project documentation, and any changes that have been made to the original system. It will also include a review of system manuals, for example:

♦   Technical manuals
♦   Procedures manuals
♦   User manuals

4.8   The assembled facts

But what facts do we have when the fact-finding activity is over? We may place these into specific categories, as follows:

Entities - these are 'organisational items', ie anything relating to the corporate body, such as customers, employees, products and so forth. Facts obtained concerning these will relate to:

♦   the nature of the entities;

♦   the entity sub-categories (eg 'customer' could be 'private-sector customer', 'public-sector customer', 'foreign customer' and so on);

♦   the static or dynamic characteristic of the entity (are they likely to change rapidly, slowly?).

Entity description - this shows how the organisation identifies, measures and/or assesses the entities (eg employees are identified by use of a personnel number, name, address).

Data manipulation - how calculations are carried out, such as the adoption of percentages, fractions, decimals, and complications such as the exchange rate.

Quantity of data processed, handled

♦   levels of data input - normal, abnormal;
♦   volume of output;
♦   statistical patterns - trends, cycles, seasonal variations;
♦   changes arising in data-volumes and their reasons.

Documentation flow

♦   description of the flow;
♦   documents originating within the specific system;
♦   the extent of filing;
♦   entries to and extractions from the documents.

Exceptions - these are the non-routine happenings:

♦ special procedures adopted (eg debt collections);
♦ extra work undertaken (eg predictable holiday periods);
♦ error-correction procedures.

Also note that some form of **verification** must be carried out. In other words, just how realistic is the collection of facts which are intended to present a true picture? Responses obtained could divert from the actual facts due to several possibilities, including:

♦ misunderstanding of the question;

♦ a genuine error on the part of the respondent;

♦ unwillingness on the part of the respondent to admit he or she is unaware of the answer, resulting in the substitution of guesswork;

♦ deliberate attempts to conceal the truth for some reason.

Verification will be carried out as a rule by putting the same questions to more than one source and, also, by considering the logic of the situation assembled by the facts.

Practice question 3 *(The answer is in the final chapter of this book)*

Fact finding techniques

Required

Once the feasibility study has been successfully completed and it has been decided to proceed with the development of a new system, discuss the various fact-finding techniques you might make use of to collect all the necessary information about the existing system and the new requirements.

Practice question 4 *(The answer is in the final chapter of this book)*

Collecting information

Required

(a) Describe and evaluate the techniques that are available to the systems analyst to enable collection of information about an existing manual system.

(b) How would the approach of the systems analyst differ if the system under consideration was already computerised?

---

5 Analysis and design methods and techniques

5.1 Systems analysis and systems design

 Systems analysis is the process by which the systems analyst records and evaluates the way in which the system currently functions. The analyst seeks to understand how the system works, and which information flows are crucial to the way in which the organisation functions.

In essence systems analysis involves a detailed fact finding exercise about the areas recommended in the feasibility study. This phase concludes with the construction of dataflow diagrams (see below).

Systems design is a technical phase that addresses inputs, outputs, program design, dialogue design, file design, storage and security. The conclusion of this phase is a detailed specification of the new system.

5.2   Dataflow diagrams

Dataflow diagrams (DFDs) are a means of analysing the data gathered and displaying it in a format which can be easily understood by the user.

The diagram shows how data is moved into, out of and within the system. It maps out the processes that the data goes through and its storage while it is in the system.

Dataflow diagrams are a top-down approach to analysing the flow of data through a system. They are communication devices, which provide a graphical representation of how data is moved through a system.

The examiner may set questions on interpretation of a given diagram, including what is wrong with the diagram in terms of its convention. That is why the understanding of the fundamental concepts and conventions is important.

It is important to note that the dataflow diagram ignores the physical design of the system and analyses the logical design only. This means that the diagram does not show *how* the data is stored or processed, only *what* data is stored and processed. By removing all physical constraints, analysts are better able to view the system and its logical requirements.

The issue of *how* the system should work can be addressed when it is known *what* is required.

5.3   Symbols and notation

There are three common conventions for drawing dataflow diagrams: those of Garne and Sarson, those of Yourdon and those associated with SSADM. The symbols used under each convention are similar, but in this text we use only the SSADM symbols because this is the examiner's preference.

The symbols are explained and illustrated below. They are important not only for drawing diagrams but also for inspecting them.

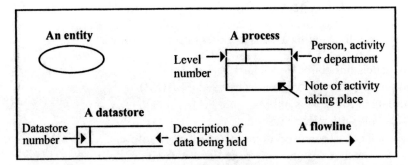

(a)   **Entity** - an entity is something outside the system being analysed, but is relevant because the system interacts with it or holds information about it. An entity can be a department, a customer, a supplier, etc. It is a point at which a dataflow originates (source) or terminates (sink). Because of these terms a dataflow diagram is sometimes referred to as a *source and sink diagram*.

A dataflow diagram can be started or finished using an entity symbol. If the same entity appears on the same diagram more than once, it is noted as follows.

If the same entity appears, say, three times on the diagram, it is not necessary to place three lines down the left hand side of the symbol. Only one is required as this means *appears more than once.*

(b) **Flowline** - this shows the flow of data through the system, and the arrowhead on the end of the flowline indicates the direction of travel or flow of the information. The flowline should always be labelled with the name of the information flowing. This will usually be a document name (payslip, order, invoice, etc).

(c) **Process** - this alters the data in some way. It is a task, activity or operation, which changes or manipulates the data. There must always be an inflow and an outflow of data. A dataflow diagram cannot end on a process box. The explanation in the centre of the process box should always contain a 'verb', a doing word. For example if the process is simply one of checking data, then the data flows in as 'unchecked data', the process is 'check data', and the output is 'checked data'.

The *level number* refers to the level of detail being shown on the diagram. For a high level diagram the level number might be 1, whereas a more detailed diagram may be 2 or 3. Each process box will have a unique level number, so for level 2 process 3, the notation for the level number would be 2.3.

(d) **Datastore** - this shows the type of data held. The method of storage (filing cabinet, microfiche) does not matter; the important thing is *what* is stored. For example if the data stored is payroll records on microfiche, the datastore would be noted as 'payroll records'.

Datastores should usually have a flow of information in and out to the 'closed' end of the symbol. However, they can also be used as alternative methods of finishing a diagram.

Data that flows into a datastore shows information being returned to the store or 'written', whereas data flowing away from a datastore depicts information being taken or 'read' from the datastore.

If the same datastore appears more than once on the same diagram, then (as with the entity symbol) a line is drawn down the left hand side of the datastore.

The general approach to drawing a dataflow diagram is as follows.

♦ Do not mix levels of detail on one chart.
♦ Select and name the set of symbols to be used (SSADM).
♦ Use a template to draw the symbols.
♦ Connect symbols with a flowline.
♦ Place an arrowhead at each end to indicate a two-way flow.
♦ Place an arrowhead at one end only to indicate a one-way flow.
♦ Name and label all symbols.
♦ Place text within each symbol describing the function taking place.
♦ Label flowlines to describe the movement of data taking place.
♦ Check to ensure that each symbol is logically connected to another.
♦ Label the top of each diagram with the system name, date and name of preparer.

The diagram can show up to nine processes at any level, but it is advisable to keep this number down to between four and six where possible.

5.4   *Levels in dataflow diagrams*

The dataflow diagram is drawn at different levels, as follows.

Level 0 diagram = context diagram

This diagram shows the total process in a summary form and helps in the objective setting process, and in communication between management and the analysis team. In other words it gives a general overview of how information flows through the system. This type of diagram would be of use when discussing the system with the strategic level of management. See the example below.

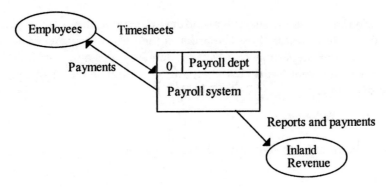

Level 1 diagram = low level DFDs

These allow each subsystem to be examined in isolation from the rest of the system, aiding project management and communication between the users, analysts and software engineers. Again, an example follows.

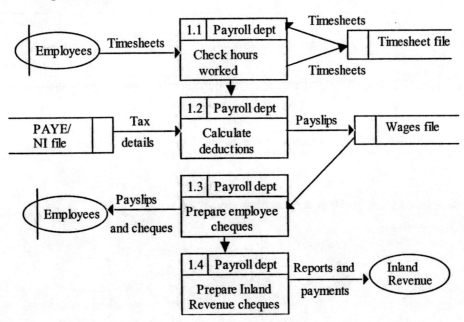

This type of diagram would be of use when discussing the system with the tactical or supervisory level of management.

5.5   *Beginning the diagram*

Before starting to draw a dataflow diagram, it is worth spending a little time finding out what are the entities, processes and datastores that are to form the diagram, and more importantly, the type of system under investigation. This can often be best approached by simply using three headings of entity, process and datastore, and allocating suitable information to each heading from the information in the question.

5.6 Worked example

A small company makes and sells machine tools. The production and accounting systems have been computerised for some time, and a systems analyst is putting together a proposal to computerise the firm's order entry system. The system has been described in narrative form as follows.

The order entry process currently begins when the sales department passes an enquiry from a customer to the order department, which prepares a quotation using the price file and returns the quotation to the sales department. A record of the quoted price is held in the quotation file. The quotation is sent to the customer.

A successful quotation results in the customer sending an order to the order department where the order is matched with the quotation. The order is then given a number and entered onto the order file. The order department uses the details on the order file to create an acknowledgement, which is sent to the customer, and to compile a works order, which is sent to the production department.

Required

Produce a dataflow diagram for the current order entry system.

5.7 Solution

Order entry process – explanation of creation of diagram.

Step 1

Identify the entities, processes and datastores, as well as the system that is under investigation.

Entity	Process	Datastore
Sales department	Prepare a quotation	Price file
Customer		Quotation file
Production department	Match order with quotation and number Create acknowledgement Complete a works order	Order file
System under investigation	Order system	

Step 2

If required construct the level 0 or context diagram.

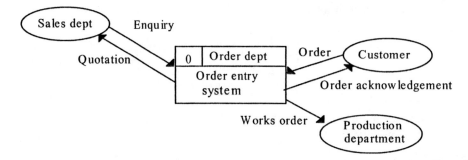

Step 3

Construct the detailed dataflow diagram from the information contained in the question and the details obtained in Step 1.

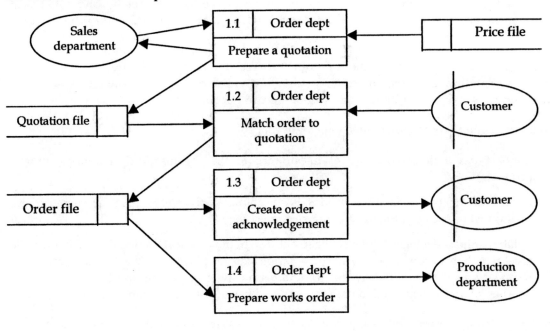

Practice question 5 (The answer is in the final chapter of this book)

Mail order firm

A large mail order firm operates through several thousand local agents, who sell mainly to close friends and relatives. An agent receives a new catalogue every Spring, Summer, Autumn and Winter. Friends select goods from the current catalogue and then pay the agent the appropriate amount, receiving in return a receipt detailing goods ordered and monies paid. The agent adds their order to an order form and pays their money into a separate account used solely for business.

Every Saturday the agent posts the order form (now containing items ordered by a number of people) together with a single cheque drawn on the business account, retaining a copy of the order form, which is kept in a red ring binder.

The company sends items ordered by return of post together with a delivery note. The agent checks the items received against both the delivery note and his or her copy of the order, using telephone calls to resolve any discrepancies. If all is satisfactory, the agent then throws away the order form but retains the delivery note in a blue ring binder.

At the end of every quarter the agent receives, along with the new season's catalogue, a statement of all items ordered in the quarter, together with a commission cheque for 10 per cent of their total value. After checking the details against the delivery notes in the blue ring binder, the agent pays the commission into his or her personal bank account.

Required

(a)   Draw up a dataflow diagram depicting the above procedure.

(b)   Briefly describe *two* graphic tools in common use in structured systems analysis to amplify the logic of the processes identified in a dataflow diagram.

---

6 Entity modelling

6.1 Entity relationship models (ERMs)

Logical data structures (entity models) are used to define the business relationships that exist between the various entities within the system. The entities are detailed within the dataflow diagram.

The dataflow diagram shows 'data in motion' whereas the entity model shows 'data at rest'. As in the dataflow diagram, an entity is something capable of an independent existence or something about which the system will want to record information.

Entity modelling is based upon three important concepts.

♦ Entity types – things that are of importance to the organisation (customers, orders, products).

♦ Attributes – facts or data about entities. For example for the entity 'supplier' the attributes would include name, address, telephone number, etc.

♦ Relationships – the logical links between entities. In the physical model, these will form the access path between data items. For example, an employee is of a certain grade and receives a related level of pay for doing a certain type of job. He or she may also hold another job in the organisation in the future, and has held previous jobs there in the past.

Entity modelling uses the following symbols, which are based on the SSADM convention.

(a)   An entity

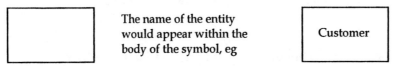

(b)   One to one relationship

This means that one occurrence of a particular entity will have a 'one to one' relationship with another entity. For example, if you consider a husband and wife as entities, it is only lawful in the UK for the entity husband to have one current occurrence of the entity wife and vice versa - this would be depicted as follows:

(This assumes that the database is not being set up to show historical data.)

(c)   One to many relationship ⟵ (Crowsfoot on the 'many' end)

For example, a customer can place one or many orders, but each order relates to only one customer.

(d)   **Many to many relationship**   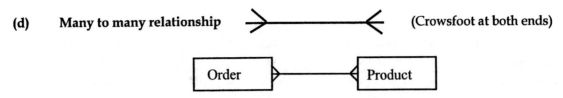   (Crowsfoot at both ends)

An order can be for one or many products, and each product can appear on more than one order.

6.2   *Worked example*

A managing director works for a company that sells many products to many different customers.

Construct a simple entity relationship model.

(1)   A managing director works for a company. Each company has one managing director, who only works for that company.

(2)   A company sells one or many products. Each product relates to only one company.

(3)   Each product can be sold to one or many customers. Each customer can purchase one or many products.

(4)   In summary the relationships are as follows.

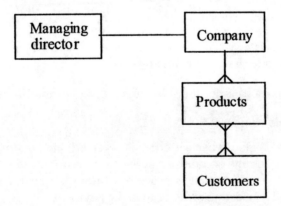

Logical data structures are used to communicate with the users of the system to ensure that correct relationships have been defined. The logical data structure is the beginning of the database design, as the entities become physical files or the database tables.

6.3   *Objectives of entity modelling*

Entity modelling has the following objectives.

- ♦ To identify all relationships between data.
- ♦ To reduce the possibility of misunderstanding the users' database requirements.
- ♦ To optimise shared data usage.
- ♦ To avoid data duplication.

Entity modelling can also be used at the system design stage, as well as in systems analysis, to assist in the design of a database that optimises shared data usage, avoids data duplication, and provides users with the database they require.

Practice question 6 *(The answer is in the final chapter of this book)*

Car agency

AB agency is a vehicle hire and driver hire agency. It has a number of local offices throughout the country. Each local office owns and is responsible for its own vehicles. Customers tend to be regular customers and book vehicles through their local office. Each vehicle is separately booked out and, if required, a suitable driver is then found to take that booking. Customers are invoiced at the end of each quarter for all the bookings falling within the quarter.

Required

Construct an entity model to represent the above relationships.

6.4 Entity life histories (ELHs)

For each entity identified on the entity model, an entity life history is created. The life history deals with the creation, life and demise of the entity. It shows the way in which information is changed over time, and is a diagrammatic representation of the processes and events that affect an entity, tracing the entity from 'womb' to 'tomb'.

An entity life history diagram is interpreted in the following way.

♦ The order of the boxes from left to right shows the time sequence.

♦ Moving from top to bottom in the diagram describes the processes carried out in greater detail.

♦ An asterisk (*) in a box illustrates a repeated process.

♦ A zero (0) in a box shows a choice.

An entity life history allows a system designer to ensure that all events have been considered and the specific business rules have been adhered to.

The ELH may also provide a basis for the subsequent design or modification of the system.

6.5 Worked example

A customer's account is created when an order is received, and removed from the system if there has been no activity on the account for at least two years, or the company has ceased to trade. At present each transaction that is processed through a customer's account can be to order products, to amend an existing order or to make payment.

Required

Construct an entity life history for the above procedure.

6.6   Solution

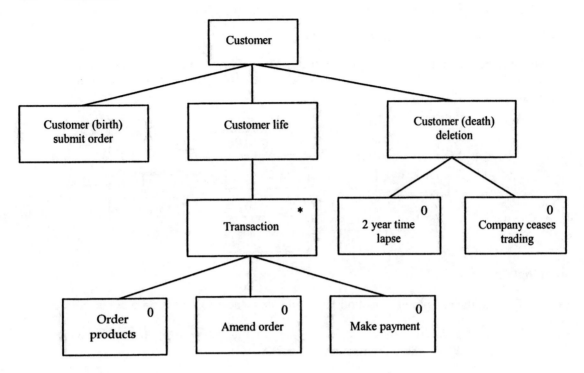

6.7   Advantages of ELH diagrams

An ELH diagram has the following advantages.

♦   It provides a pictorial representation of what happens to an entity.
♦   It provides a way in which the analyst can understand what is likely to happen.
♦   It provides a clear means of communication.
♦   The event drives the process.

It is at the ELH stage that the qualities of information (accuracy, completeness, etc) are incorporated into the system. The mnemonic ACCURATE should remind you of the qualities required for information to be useful.

A   Accurate
C   Complete
C   Cost-effective
U   Understandable
R   Relevant
A   Adaptable
T   Timely
E   Easy to use

The entity life histories can also be used at the systems design stage, because once they have been created for the proposed system they can be passed to the programmer who will use them as the basis for program design.

Practice question 7 *(The answer is in the final chapter of this book)*

Explain in English

The entity-relationship model (or logical data structure) shown in the diagram below has been provided as a part of a functional specification document. The entities in this diagram are shown as rectangular boxes.

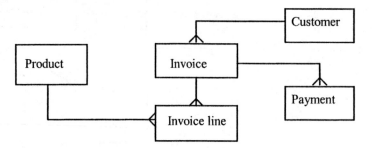

Required

(a)   Explain the meaning of the model shown using a set of English statements.

(b)   The model shown contains a likely flaw in the relationship between invoice and payment. What should the relationship be?

(c)   Many methodologies decompose such relationships. Decompose (or break down), with a brief explanation, the relationship between invoice and payment.

(d)   What data items could be contained in the newly determined entity?

6.8   Learning outcome

You have now covered the learning outcome for this chapter.

Apply the main tools and techniques used in the gathering, recording and analysis of information relating to an existing Information System.

7   Summary

Systems analysis begins with the gathering of information using the following techniques.

♦   Studying documentation
♦   Completing questionnaires
♦   Interviewing
♦   Reviewing procedure manuals
♦   Direct observation
♦   Sampling and testing

In the course of this work the systems analyst will interact with the following categories of users.

♦   Operational users
♦   Supervisory users
♦   Executive users

Dataflow diagrams, entity relationship models and entity life histories are examples of graphical techniques used in the process of systems analysis. All of these graphical techniques are utilised to remove the ambiguities of narrative notes.

CHAPTER 11

Implementation, maintenance and evaluation

EXAM FOCUS

This is an important part of the syllabus, and is often examined in a practical way. It is usually at this part of the systems development lifecycle that the accountant is most heavily involved. If a system is not properly implemented there will be consequential financial effects for the organisation.

As well as implementation, this chapter also deals with the various types of maintenance that are carried out during the life of a computer system and describes the ways in which an existing or new system can be evaluated, together with the evaluation of software solutions.

LEARNING OUTCOMES

This chapter covers the following Learning Outcomes of the CIMA syllabus

> Identify and evaluate the main issues relating to the development of an Information Systems solution, and the risks involved in implementation

> Explain the nature and purpose of systems maintenance and performance evaluation

In order to cover these learning outcomes, the following topics are included

> The features, benefits and drawbacks of structured methodologies (eg SSADM) for the development of Information Systems (Note: detailed knowledge of any specific methodology will not be required)

> The problems associated with the management of in-house and vendor solutions and how they can be avoided or solved

> System testing (ie off-line, on-line and user-acceptance)

> System documentation (ie user and technical manuals)

> Training and user support

> File conversion procedures

> System changeover methods (ie direct, parallel, pilot, phased)

> Maintenance of systems (ie corrective, adaptive, preventive)

1 Preparing for implementation

1.1 The background to systems implementation

Implementation is concerned with putting the systems design into use as smoothly and quickly as possible. Implementation is the most important part in achieving a successful new system that has user confidence. It is the point at which a theoretical model becomes a 'live' system.

Before an implementation strategy can be considered it is imperative that the following matters have been dealt with.

♦ Programs have been stringently tested
♦ Adequate resources are available (people, equipment and finance)
♦ A 'back-up' system has been planned
♦ The system specification is complete

It is often thought that system implementation merely concerns the methods of system changeover, ie the method by which we cease to use the old system and change to use the new system. The methods of changeover - direct changeover, pilot changeover, phased changeover and parallel changeover - are usually well known and understood. However, there are four important stages prior to implementation.

♦ Staff training   (S)
♦ Installation   (I)
♦ File conversion   (F)
♦ Testing   (T)

These four earlier stages of implementation can be remembered by using the mnemonic SIFT.

1.2 Staff training

Training and education are vital elements in the implementation of a new system for the following reasons.

♦ Training – to ensure that people interact effectively and efficiently with the system.

♦ Education – to encourage an atmosphere where the benefits of IT can be properly exploited.

Staff training will ensure that staff can maximise their utilisation of the system, which will in turn maximise the organisation's return on its investment in IT. Training will be needed at different phases during the life of the new system.

♦ When the system is initially introduced.
♦ When there are any major changes to the way in which the system operates.
♦ When there is a change of staff.
♦ When there is a change in a person's job specification.

There is also a need for ongoing training to refresh and remind operators of what they have learned.

Training will be required for members of staff at the operational, tactical and strategic levels of the organisation.

♦ *Operational staff.* These jobs will tend to be mainly repetitive and routine, and will offer very little if any scope for human judgement. The training will therefore be targeted at the specific skills they will need to carry out their role.

◆ *Tactical staff.* These employees will often have to exercise their judgement in response to changing conditions, requiring a more flexible approach to the use of the system. Whilst they will need to know how to operate the basic system, they will also require training on how to use decision support systems, and the spreadsheet and database functions.

◆ *Strategic staff.* These employees will require training in management information systems, decision support systems and executive information systems.

1.3 The training plan

As training is such an important element in a successful organisation, it is essential that a training plan for each member of staff is created. A training plan considers the need for training at three different levels, as shown below:

A training plan

Current organisation needs

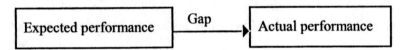

Future organisation needs

Individual development needs

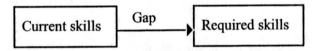

1.4 Key elements of training

There are a number of keys to good training.

◆ Plan the training to take place as close as possible to live usage, so that the staff do not get the chance to forget what they have learned.

◆ Get the design team to produce the user documentation. The documentation will then describe what the users will need to do to perform their various tasks rather than being a technical description of how the system functions.

◆ Select the most appropriate training methods. For off the shelf packages an external computer training specialist may be appropriate. Alternatively for bespoke systems that have been designed in house, it may be more appropriate for the training to be undertaken by the design team, managers, supervisors or external trainers.

When considering training options it is often easier to discuss the options with which you have practical experience.

Practice question 1 *(The answer is in the final chapter of this book)*

Training options

An organisation has decided to purchase a specialist payroll package for use in their business as a supplier of temporary contracts staff. The package is well established with over 500 users in the UK. The changeover is planned for two months time.

The responsibility for the successful implementation of the software package lies with the payroll manager. The payroll manager has attended a standard three-day course to learn how to use and install the package. The course runs once a month at the offices of the software company, with a cost of £750 per delegate.

The training element is an essential part of the implementation process. The payroll manager is currently reviewing four options for the training of her five staff.

(1)   Sending each employee on the standard three-day off-site training course.

(2)   Running the standard three day course at the organisation's own offices and putting all employees on this course. A price of £2,000 per course for a three-day course for up to 12 delegates has been quoted by the software supplier.

(3)   Using the payroll manager to teach other employees on an individual basis, so spreading the payroll manager's knowledge.

(4)   Buying a CBT (Computer Based Training) package available from an independent training company. This package costs £40 for a single user licence and provides training on the facilities and installation of the payroll package.

Required

(a)   Choose three of these training options. For each option chosen, give two advantages and two disadvantages.

(b)   Each of the four training options could be justified for the organisation. Recommend one of these training options, justifying your choice.

1.5   *Installation and file conversion*

With training complete, the time is right to physically install the new system equipment into the organisation's premises. To ensure that this goes to plan a few steps should be taken in advance.

♦   Identify where long lead times may be encountered. For example, it may be necessary to get planning permission for extensions to the business premises. If this is not put in hand well in advance there is a danger of delay.

♦   Ensure that the basic office infrastructure is in place, with enough power points, desk space, filing cabinets, etc.

Once the new system is physically located at the organisation's premises, it is then necessary to load the correct standing data and opening balances onto the new system. This is the process of file conversion. The process must be carefully planned, controlled and resourced.

File conversion is a three-stage process.

♦   Check the closing balances on the old system - here we can utilise some auditing techniques, such as physical stock counts, creditors' reconciliation, debtors circularisation, etc.

♦   Transfer the balances onto the new system. This can usually be completed by a simple interface program. However, if the old and the new systems are incompatible it will be necessary for the balances to be keyed in manually.

♦   Check that the balances have been transferred correctly and in their entirety to the new system – ie one to one checking, checks in total, etc.

Practice question 2 *(The answer is in the final chapter of this book)*

Data conversion

Required

Discuss the issues that arise in data conversion when:

(a)   moving from a current manual system to a computer system;

(b)   moving from a current computer system to a new computer system.

Practice question 3 *(The answer is in the final chapter of this book)*

Payroll system

You are responsible for implementing a payroll system for weekly paid employees, using a bought-in package on a stand-alone microcomputer system. There are 3,000 records (one for each employee) in the current manual system. Each record is held on a card. The information about each employee comprises personal details (personnel number, name, date of birth, grade, section, rate of pay, allowances, deductions from pay, etc), held in the top section of the card. In the body of the card are held a series of line entries, one for each week of the year. As each week is worked the details are entered in the appropriate line: gross pay; tax and national insurance, by reference to the relevant tables; and net pay.

Required

(a)   Fully describe a procedure for transferring data from the manual system to the computer to create the master file prior to going live on the new system.

(b)   Specify the checks and controls to be incorporated into the process to ensure that the computerised master file is accurate, complete, up to date and suitable for running the live system.

1.6   System testing

The system should be tested by its eventual users.

The tests used should meet the following criteria.

♦   They should be realistic, ie they should present the system with a realistic example of the real world environment in which the system is to operate. This will boost confidence among users.

♦   They should be contrived to present the system with as many unusual and unexpected events as possible, with the intention of seeing how the system reacts.

♦   They should present the system with large volumes of transactions to see how the system reacts, particularly in respect of operating and response times.

Testing will take two forms.

♦   Test data will be posted to the new system prior to live use to check for accuracy of processing.

♦   There will then be a period of 'acceptance testing', with careful testing of live transactions in the early periods of use.

Testing is especially important for bespoke systems, and in this case a four-stage approach should be adopted.

♦ Testing the logic of the system and program
♦ Program testing
♦ System testing
♦ Acceptance testing

Each of these is discussed below.

Testing the logic of the system and program is achieved by 'dry running'. The programmer or systems analyst will trace by hand the progress of a number of sets of data through the structure diagrams and program flowcharts. This is equivalent to a manual walkthrough procedure.

Program testing relies on the use of test data. The internal program code is validated. The testing process will be carefully documented: data being tested, expected results, actual results, and any action taken as a result of the test. The test documentation will form part of the overall system documentation. Testing should cover the following items.

♦ Correct batch control totals
♦ Adequacy of interfacing with other programs
♦ Correct output format
♦ Ensuring that the input data is correctly validated

System testing commences once it has been established that the individual programs are working properly. At this stage the system as a whole will be tested and the results documented. It is not just the software that is evaluated; this stage also covers operating procedures, staffing levels, etc. The following matters should be tested.

♦ Audit requirements
♦ Modification of data
♦ Adequacy of information output
♦ Speed of system response

Acceptance testing is organised and performed by the users. The users operate the system using test data, with their use of the system being closely monitored, and they then report their experiences. Testing in this manner allows for gradual user training and gives the user experience of the system prior to implementation.

Practice question 4 *(The answer is in the final chapter of this book)*

Testing

Required

Describe the stages of testing during systems implementation and how each stage of testing should be carried out.

---

2 System changeover

2.1 Possible methods of system changeover

The final stage of implementation is system changeover. There are four changeover options.

♦ Direct changeover
♦ Pilot running
♦ Phased changeover
♦ Parallel running

Direct changeover is the immediate replacement of the old system by the new. This may often be the only choice, because of lack of office space, etc. It is used where the new system is based on an established, off-the-shelf solution. (Without the reassurance that the system is tried and tested this would be a risky option.) Provided that staff have been suitably trained and the system sufficiently tested, a direct method of changeover should work extremely well. As an example, computerisation of a stock system could be completed on a direct changeover basis, as the system could be validated by regular manual stocktakes.

If *pilot changeover* is adopted, a distinct part of the new system is brought into use and, once tested, will be brought into use immediately elsewhere within the organisation. This is useful in distributed systems, where the system can be piloted in one department or office and, when working correctly, brought into use elsewhere. A pilot of the new system could be run in one specified location, and when it has been proved to be correctly working, changeover could commence at remaining locations. This could also be applicable by piloting individual software modules before implementation of all modules.

Another form of pilot changeover is known as *restricted data running*. This is where just some transactions are run on the new system to begin with. Once everything is functioning properly all other transactions are processed on the new system. As an example, in a sales ledger system transactions with selected customers (say those with initials A–F) could be used to pilot the system.

In effect, pilot implementation allows the selection of a typical part of the organisation for testing with live data, rather than test data.

Phased changeover is a more popular method than either direct changeover or pilot changeover, but is very time consuming. Here, distinct parts of the system are gradually phased into use, first the personnel module (say), then the stock module and so on. An advantage of this method is that the cost of implementation can be spread out over the phases. However, the organisation may encounter disruption as different parts of the organisation will be using different, and possibly incompatible, systems until changeover is complete.

With *parallel changeover* the old and the new system are run in parallel for a predetermined period to ensure that the new system is functioning correctly. In this situation there is a direct comparison of information between the old and the new system. It is very expensive and time consuming, especially in terms of staff resources. This form of changeover should only be used for systems critical to the business where the cost of failure would be high.

Practice question 5 *(The answer is in the final chapter of this book)*

System changeover

A small chain of four department stores is located in and around a major metropolitan area. It is about to implement, in all stores, a point of sale system with linkages to a central computer. The stores all currently use conventional cash registers. You have been asked to assist in the conversion to the new system.

Required

(a)   An evaluation of the various approaches to the system changeover.

(b)   A checklist, in sequence, of the activities likely to be carried out during implementation.

(c)   Suggestions as to how the new system might be evaluated after three months of operational running.

2.2 Learning outcome

You have now covered the first learning outcome for this chapter.

> Identify and evaluate the main issues relating to the development of an Information System solution, and the risks involved in implementation.

3 Systems maintenance

3.1 The meaning of systems maintenance

Once developed and implemented, an information system is likely to remain in use for a long time. Those involved in the original development may leave the organisation or move on to other areas of activity. Despite this, the system itself must be maintained and perhaps enhanced in order to meet changing requirements.

Where changes are proposed it is important to consider the impact on the systems specification. Any change must be illustrated, documented and verified with the user by making appropriate changes in the system model. Any such changes require expert management and control.

The costs involved in systems maintenance are considerable, and may amount to a significant proportion of the total development costs. The need for maintenance arises very early: indeed, by the time the system is handed over for implementation there may already be a need for amendments. Once the system is operational, further improvements and adaptations will be required to meet changed circumstances.

 From this discussion it should be clear that systems maintenance is not simply the process of keeping the system working in its original form. On the contrary, maintenance in this context implies development as well. In this respect the analogy of, say, motor car maintenance would be misleading. We maintain our motor cars to preserve their original level of functionality as long as possible, not to enhance or adapt them. With computer systems, enhancement and adaptation are part of the maintenance process.

3.2 Classifying maintenance work

 Systems maintenance may be classified into different types based upon the 'trigger' that sets the maintenance work in progress. There are four main types of maintenance.

- Corrective maintenance
- Perfective maintenance
- Adaptive maintenance
- Preventive maintenance

 Corrective maintenance is the elimination of system bugs, which are usually identified during the operation of the system. This type of maintenance is expensive. An important objective during the design and implementation stages should be to minimise the need for corrective maintenance by getting the system as near as possible perfect to begin with.

Despite all efforts to achieve this, however, there will always be a need for at least some corrective maintenance. The need may arise from any of the following sources.

- Human error
- Poor documentation
- Physical faults in the computer hardware
- Poor training of users
- Inadequate supervision
- Unexpected interactions with other systems
- Malicious damage to programs and data

Perfective maintenance is work undertaken to improve the efficiency or effectiveness of the system. It may be prompted by the availability of new technology or the development of new techniques. Alternatively it may arise because a user requests an enhancement to the original design.

 Adaptive maintenance arises from changes in the organisational environment or changes in the information required by users. It may also be triggered by changes in organisational structure, or by external developments such as a change in the legislation relating to data protection.

♦ User requirements may have changed or may have been ill defined when the system was being designed.

♦ The system environment may have significantly changed.

♦ The system may have grown beyond the limits that were originally envisaged for it.

 Preventive maintenance is based upon regular routine servicing to keep equipment in good working order.

The various 'triggers' giving rise to maintenance operations are summarised in the diagram below:

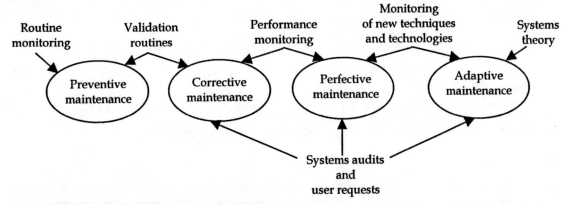

3.3 Software maintenance contracts

(Don't get this confused with a 'hardware' maintenance contract.)

If software has been purchased from an external supplier there will usually be some form of support or maintenance contract. Normally the purchaser will have to pay an additional cost for this facility but it may well be advantageous to do so. It is common to find a price quoted for a support package extending over a defined period of time. Once this has elapsed, it is open to the purchaser to pay an additional fee to extend the period of cover.

 Typical features of a software maintenance contract are listed below.

♦ The supplier provides technical support through a telephone helpline.

♦ The supplier provides software upgrades to rectify identified faults.

♦ The supplier provides software revisions that allow the user to comply with changes in government regulations. A good example of this is a payroll package: this must be amended regularly to cope with changes in tax bands/rates.

♦ The purchaser benefits from discounted prices on major upgrades of the software package.

♦ The purchaser receives regular newsletters or factsheets providing information about new products or new uses of the package.

Obviously the maintenance contract is a legal document. Amongst other things it sets out the obligations of the purchaser, particularly in relation to restrictions on use of the package. For example, the document will invariably set out rules on using multiple copies of the package on a network. Although such usage is permitted, there will be an additional charge.

Other details in the agreement will cover the supplier's liability in relation to consequential damage caused by failure of the software. There will also be details of procedures and restrictions relating to termination and assignment.

3.4 User groups

 Many software suppliers set up user groups to provide help and advice to users of certain application packages. Such groups are another possible source of maintenance operations.

Although a user group is usually initiated by the software supplier, it will be run by a committee of users. At periodic intervals users will meet to discuss system performance and problems, and to arrange presentations of new software applications.

There are a number of benefits from joining a user group.

♦   Helps with solving technical issues.

♦   Relatively inexpensive to set up and run.

♦   Places pressure on manufacturers to amend and upgrade system applications.

♦   Provides access to other users who may utilise the software in different and more effective ways.

Practice question 6 *(The answer is in the final chapter of this book)*

Maintenance

(a)   A manufacturing company is about to implement a bespoke inventory control system. The implementation team is keen to collect data that measures the quality of the delivered system. A Help desk has been set up to support the users of the software.

Required

Define and show the difference between *corrective* and *adaptive* maintenance.

(b)   The implementation team wishes to monitor the user-friendliness and frequency of use of the system. They want to ensure that users find the software easy to use and that managers extensively use the enquiry and reporting facilities.

Required

Suggest a total of *three* appropriate measures of user-friendliness and frequency of use and describe how such data might be collected, interpreted and acted upon.

---

4   Systems evaluation

4.1 Measuring success

 Once a system has been implemented it is important to review its operation. The idea is to ensure that the original objectives of the system, as measured by defined performance criteria, have been met, and to deal effectively and efficiently with all unforeseen problems. This continual evaluation will identify various requirements for maintenance.

The success of system implementation can be measured in four ways.

♦ The extent to which the features of the system are accepted by users.

♦ Whether the functioning system meets the objectives set for it during the feasibility study stage. Greater than expected running costs, or less than expected benefits, are obviously bad news.

♦ Whether the performance of the new system is adequate for the users' needs (response times, ability to log in simultaneously, system reliability, etc).

♦ The operational integrity of the system (completeness and accuracy of processing, ease of recovery from system crashes and losses of data).

To identify the anticipated system improvements it will be necessary to make direct comparison between the new and the old system. The timing of this comparison is crucial: if it is completed too soon after implementation then the results may be distorted by teething problems. The following areas should be considered.

♦ Perceived value - the willingness of user departments to contribute time and money from budgeted resources to system upgrades.

♦ User satisfaction - users are asked to comment on essential aspects of the system, eg response times, output quality, reliability, etc.

♦ System logs - the amount of times a system is used will act as a good indicator as to how well it has been adopted by users.

♦ Significance and task relevance - ie how effective the system has been in improving the information flow within an organisation.

4.2 Cost benefit analysis

The techniques of cost benefit analysis can also be used as a quantitative method of system evaluation. The main techniques include the following, which have already been discussed in a previous chapter.

♦ Payback period
♦ Return on investment
♦ Discounted cashflow (internal rate of return, net present value)

4.3 System performance

The system should be evaluated to measure the extent to which resources are being utilised. Areas of under-utilisation could point to potential improvements in efficiency. The success of the system could be measured by considering (*inter alia*):

♦ efficiency and effectiveness
♦ delays or response times
♦ capacity
♦ reliability
♦ complexity
♦ frequency of operator errors
♦ compatibility
♦ controllability and adaptability
♦ acceptability and usability
♦ security.

4.4 Post-implementation evaluation

Once the new system is fully operative there is a need for two different systems evaluations: the **initial audit** and the **periodic review** (perhaps an annual review).

The initial audit is held approximately six months after initial implementation. Its aims are as follows.

♦ To assess the system's operational performance
♦ To verify system objectives and assess how realistic they are
♦ To compare planned performance with actual performance
♦ To establish the extent to which the agreed objectives have been achieved

The aspects that are assessed and measured are as follows.

♦ Error reports created by the system
♦ Performance characteristics
♦ Turnaround and response time
♦ Machine usage
♦ Data input volumes and paper handling
♦ Output reports (accuracy, timeliness, etc)

The audit refers to the costs and benefits expected and achieved and is undertaken by staff of the IT department, user management and other relevant staff.

The periodic (annual) review aims to establish the optimum system in relation to the current environment. Aspects examined are as follows.

♦ Divergences from expected standards
♦ The state of the hardware
♦ The level of user satisfaction with reports and other outputs
♦ Possibilities of improvement
♦ The need to redesign input, forms, etc

This evaluation will result in the need to carry out 'adaptive maintenance'.

Practice question 7 *(The answer is in the final chapter of this book)*

Performance criteria

Required

A new computer system must be evaluated in terms of its performance. What performance criteria must it satisfy?

---

5 Performance monitoring

5.1 Areas to monitor

Performance monitoring is vital when acquiring new equipment and software to improve performance of an existing system, and when acquiring additional equipment or streamlining existing equipment.

The main areas to consider include the following.

- Processing delays
- Efficiency of security procedures
- Levels of error rates (if these are high, reasons should be identified)
- User feedback
- Assessment of usage of system output – is all of it used?
- Manual procedures should be assessed and compared with estimated requirements
- File sizes and growth in transaction processing
- Review of operating costs, in total and by individual process

5.2 Improving system performance

The two areas to focus on are system inputs and system outputs.

With regard to *system inputs* we can look at operator efficiency, storage capacity, software upgrades and data validation checks.

- Operator efficiency – if a stand-alone system is operated, the introduction of a multi-user system would improve operator efficiency, since this will allow multiple access to the same files. This will allow flexibility in use of operators' time, in that under-utilised operators can assist operators with heavy workloads.

- Storage capacity – this can be increased to improve the system response rates.

- Software upgrades – new features included in upgrades may improve efficiency.

- Data validation checks on input may reduce input errors and delays.

The *system output* can be improved by simply:

- processing more transactions
- producing more management information
- increasing accessibility of information
- improved databases, spreadsheet facilities.

To some extent the monitoring process can itself be incorporated within the computer system. The main computer based monitoring methods are described below.

Hardware monitors. The purpose is to measure electrical signals in specific circuits of the computer hardware in order to identify and report periods of idle time or inactivity. This allows inefficiency in performance to be highlighted.

Software monitors. This is a computer-based program, which identifies excessive delays during the execution of the program.

System logs. An automatically produced system log records various aspects of system performance.

6 Software options

6.1 Bespoke or off-the-shelf?

The following factors should be considered in evaluating whether to write a bespoke package or purchase a supplier's program package.

- Availability of hardware and software in-house which could be used or modified
- Comparative costs
- Comparative implementation periods
- Functions provided and significance of any shortfall against requirements
- Use of analysts and programmers to better purposes on other projects

6.2 Evaluating off-the-shelf packages

A procedure to evaluate packages should incorporate the following steps.

♦ Establish the objectives and characteristics of the applications for which the package is to be used.

♦ Establish the characteristics of the existing system in terms of equipment, staff, degree of flexibility (present and future).

♦ Identify suppliers of suitable packages and establish their capability in terms of staff, programming language, sales and company status.

♦ Evaluate each package for performance claims, sales history, price structure, installation assistance and maintenance. Establish whether any required functions will attract an increased cost, and how far the package can be modified.

♦ Establish communication with other users of the package.

♦ Determine input and output requirements, language used, run-times, minimum equipment required and whether it accords with the long-term equipment and system plans for the installation.

♦ Determine what facilities are offered by the operating system and whether housekeeping routines are available to re-sort files and for sundry routine tasks.

♦ Calculate the cost of the new system in terms of processing equipment, forms, additional supplies, program modifications and education.

♦ Define conversion costs of files and records, additional programs, clerical and operations staff effort.

♦ Evaluate the documentation provided.

♦ Examine the contract for restriction on use and sale, termination and penalty clauses, title and common law rights.

♦ Inform other interested users within the organisation in order to avoid duplication of effort.

A scoring system is often used to evaluate software packages. Weightings are applied to each feature required by users: say a weighting of 1 for a feature of little importance, up to a maximum weighting of 5 for features of critical importance. For each requirement present in the software package an amount equal to the weight is added to the package's score. The package with the highest score can be regarded as the best fit with user requirements.

Practice question 8 (The answer is in the final chapter of this book)

Software selection

A manufacturing company has issued an invitation to tender requesting proposals for a replacement to its current inventory control software. The hardware is not being replaced. Three proposals have been received offering competing software package solutions. The manufacturing company wishes to compare the three solutions to decide which (if any) they should buy.

Required

(a) Describe five issues that will have to be considered in evaluating each proposal. Briefly explain why each issue is relevant and must be included in the evaluation.

(b) Initial evaluation suggests that none of the proposals provides the perfect solution. What methods can the company use to assess the strengths and weaknesses of each proposal and hence choose the most effective solution?

6.3 Learning outcome

You have now covered the final learning outcome for this chapter.

Explain the nature and purpose of systems maintenance and performance evaluation.

7 Summary

The five stages of systems implementation are as follows.

- ◆ Staff training
- ◆ Installation
- ◆ File conversion
- ◆ System testing
- ◆ Changeover

The four stages prior to changeover are easily remembered by the mnemonic SIFT.

The need for systems maintenance arises from a variety of causes. In general, it is possible to classify maintenance operations in one or other of the following categories.

- ◆ Corrective maintenance
- ◆ Perfective maintenance
- ◆ Adaptive maintenance
- ◆ Preventive maintenance

Once implemented, a new system must be evaluated in use. Techniques of cost benefit analysis are useful here. It is common to perform both an initial audit (perhaps six months after implementation) and a periodic review, perhaps annual.

Regular monitoring should also be a feature of systems evaluation. To some extent monitoring activities can themselves be built into the computer system.

When choosing software, adopt a systematic approach both to the decision between bespoke and off-the-shelf solutions and to the evaluation of application packages themselves.

CHAPTER 12

Control of activities and resources

EXAM FOCUS

This chapter introduces the key concepts of control from a theoretical perspective. Control is often difficult to explain or define clearly and achieving control can involve quite complex systems and procedures. An examination scenario is likely to give an illustration of an organisational control system, such as standard costing or variance analysis and ask questions about the feedback mechanism.

LEARNING OUTCOMES

This chapter covers the following Learning Outcomes of the CIMA syllabus

> Evaluate and recommend appropriate control systems for the management of organisations
>
> Evaluate the control of activities and resources within the organisation
>
> Recommend ways in which the problems associated with control systems could be avoided or solved

In order to cover these learning outcomes, the following topics are included

> The application of control systems and related theory to the design of management accounting systems and information systems in general (ie control system components, primary and secondary feedback, positive and negative feedback, open and closed-loop control)
>
> The views of classical and contemporary management writers relating to control
>
> The way in which systems are used to achieve control within the framework of the organisation (eg contracts of employment, policies and procedures, discipline and reward, reporting structures, performance appraisal and feedback)

---

1 Organisational control

1.1 What is control?

Control is an integral part of management. It is a general concept that is applied to both organisational performance and individual behaviour.

Organisation implies control. A social organisation is an ordered arrangement of individual human interactions. It is the purpose of control to bring about conformance to the requirements of the organisation and to the achievement of the goals.

 Control is primarily a process for motivating and inspiring people to perform organisational activities that will further the organisation's goals. It is also a process for detecting and correcting unintentional performance errors and intentional irregularities such as misuse of resources or theft.

Most people are of two minds towards control. Whilst they may not like controls being applied to their own performance, they recognise the need for and usefulness of control systems for:

♦   giving feedback about task performance

♦   providing some degree of structure to tasks, defining how tasks are to be carried out and specifying how performance will be measured

♦   rewarding people, eg pay based on performance

1.2   *Organisational performance*

At the organisational level, management need to exercise control over the behaviour and actions of employees to ensure a satisfactory level of performance. Managerial control systems are a way of checking progress to determine whether the objectives of the organisation are being achieved. They also enable an organisation to adapt to a changing environment by changing the work activities of its employees to meet operational objectives.

 Whatever the nature of control, there are five elements to a control system, shown in the diagram below:

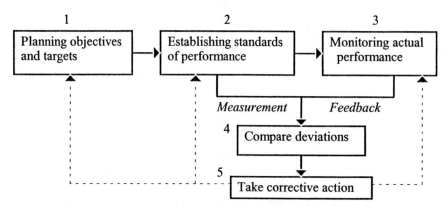

♦   Planning - involves clarification of the goals to be achieved. People need to know exactly what should happen and what is required of them. Objectives and targets should be specified clearly. Planning is the framework for control.

♦   Establishing standards of performance against which the level of success can be measured - requires realistic measurements, preferably in quantitative terms. Planning and measurement are prerequisites of control.

♦   Monitoring actual performance - requires feedback and a system of reporting information that is accurate, relevant and timely and in a form that enables management to highlight deviations from the planned standard of performance. Feedback also provides the basis for decisions to adjust the control system, eg to revise the original plan. Feedback should relate to the desired end results and also the means designed to achieve them.

♦   Comparing actual performance against planned targets - requires a means of interpreting and evaluating information to give details of progress, reveal deviations and identify possible problems.

♦   Taking corrective action - requires consideration of what can be done to improve performance. It requires authority to take appropriate action to correct the situation, to review the operation of the control system and to make any adjustments to objectives, targets or standards of performance.

1.3   Application to an accounting system - budgetary control

In a budgetary control system the financial performance of a department is compared with the budget. Action is then taken to improve the department's performance if possible.

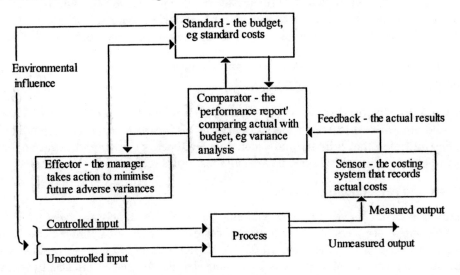

The opportunity may also be taken to adjust the standard (ie, the budget) if it is seen to be too easy or too difficult to achieve.

A number of complications have been included in the budgetary control system illustrated:

♦   the impact of the environment on the system, eg prices of raw materials may rise uncontrollably or interest rates may increase;

♦   differences between actual and budgeted results may not be controllable directly by the departmental manager, eg rises in certain input costs may be caused by another department;

♦   the accounting system cannot measure all the output of the department, hence feedback may be incomplete, eg an investment for longer term profits may have been made at the expense of short-term cost control.

Control is maintained through a network of information flow, which is the means of control. When such information is not fed back it is of no value to the system. This process of routing back into parts of the system is known as 'feedback'. It is a fundamental aspect of any control system.

 Feedback control is the measurement of differences between planned outputs and outputs achieved, and the modification of subsequent action and/or plans to achieve future required results (CIMA Official Terminology). The effector responds to the information received from the comparator and initiates corrective action. In order to take any action, the effector, eg a manager, must consider:

♦   the accuracy of the information fed back (the feedback);

♦   the significance of the variation from standard or norm;

♦   what inputs are required to restore the system to an acceptable standard or a reasonable degree of stability.

 Feedback control is concerned with past events being compared with targets or standards. However, systems can be made more adaptive if an attempt is made to anticipate future events in the light of the latest information. This is known as **feedforward control**.

Feedforward should be used extensively in budgetary control systems. For example, if in January there is a shortfall of sales against target, this information is used to take whatever corrective action is possible. However, it may be that what is being indicated by the January results is a longer-term effect, which will impact on the results for the whole year. These effects should be predicted and used to revise the sales forecast for the whole year, because many decisions (production, distribution, etc) will depend on the forecasts being realistic.

Similar feedforward techniques can be used for all the cost elements of the budget and also for the cash budget, where it is especially important.

 Although we have already discussed this topic in a previous chapter (Systems Theory), we need to elaborate further to stress the information and control aspects of feedback. The examiner has indicated that primary and secondary feedback, positive and negative feedback, and open and closed loop control systems are syllabus topics requiring specific study.

1.4 Open and closed loop systems

The systems described above, and any systems involving feedback are called closed loop systems. Associated terms are feedback loop and control cycle. Feedback makes the difference between open and closed loop systems. In CIMA's official terminology, feedback is described as 'modification or control of a process or system by its results or effects, by measuring differences between desired and actual results'. Feedback is an element in a feedback system and forms the link between planning and control.

 CIMA define a closed loop system as 'a control system, which includes a provision for corrective action, taken on either a feedforward or a feedback basis'.

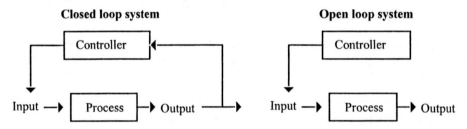

Control systems which do not involve feeding back output information are called open loop systems. Open loop control is described by CIMA as 'a control system, which includes no provision for corrective action to be applied to the sequence of activities'. An open loop system operates independently; it is not provided for within the system. Control must be exercised by external intervention.

 The term open loop implies there is a break in the feedback loop. This may arise either because feedback is not produced or because it is not used. For example, in some accounting systems useful cost information is collected but it is not reported to the right people. In other systems the report is given to the right person but it is not read. Both would be examples of open loop systems.

1.5 Primary and secondary feedback

 Primary feedback is often called single loop feedback. It is feedback that is based on past performance and which is gathered to govern future performance. Single loop feedback has a narrow focus and is mainly concerned with task control.

Secondary feedback or double loop feedback is control information that indicates differences between actual and planned results allowing for control adjustments to be made to the plan itself. Double loop feedback gathers information from both the system output and the environment. This control information is used by a higher level of management in the system.

The diagram below shows the production system of an organisation seen as a double loop feedback control system

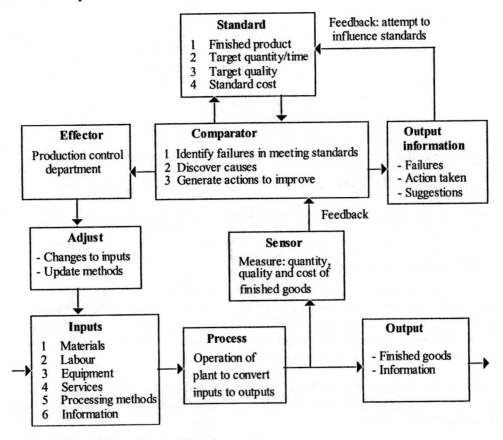

1.6   *Negative and positive feedback*

Positive feedback results in deviations from the plan being continued or increased, which can cause the system to repeat or further intensify the particular condition being considered. You may have heard the term 'vicious circles' where a chain of effects circulates in an ever-increasing manner; this is a form of positive feedback. It may well be that a favourable deviation has occurred and the organisation may want to increase this. For example, where sales orders are higher than expected, the firm takes action to maintain, or preferably increase, these by boosting advertising. In some respects it could be said that the whole idea of growth is a form of positive feedback where, arising from an initial small start, things just get bigger and bigger. They also tend to be more unstable and things get out of control more quickly.

Negative feedback is information which shows that the system is deviating from its planned course in a way that is detrimental to its operation. Action is needed to return the system to its original course. This is the most common kind of feedback, which arises when action is taken in the opposite direction to offset the variance. In other words, the control activity reverses the direction of the tendency which will bring the system back to its intended course. A typical example is where a thermostat controls a central heating system. Defined limits are set on the required room temperatures and if it becomes too warm, then the thermostat records this and, in effect, adjusts the heating system, usually by switching it off temporarily. We sometimes use the term 'self-regulating' to describe such systems. Negative feedback systems are on the whole more stable and likely to conform to accepted standards and norms.

Practice question 1 *(The answer is in the final chapter of this book)*

Feedback control loops

A feature of general systems theory and of all managerial control systems is the existence of feedback control loops. The normal feedback loop, sometimes termed single loop feedback, is the most formalised; yet, from a system's viewpoint, higher level feedback, sometimes termed double loop feedback, can be said to be of equal importance.

Required

(a)   describe a single loop feedback control cycle, identifying each element in the loop;

(b)   discuss the importance of feedback in the control of systems;

(c)   describe the role of double loop feedback.

1.7   Cybernetic control models

Cybernetic control is a more sophisticated control mechanism that relies on feedforward controls. Under this approach, the objective is compared with predicted outcomes. This enables anticipatory control actions to be taken to reduce any deviation. It is a superior control mechanism, as errors (and the cost of errors) do not occur. However, it does require an adequate predictive model to enable the forecasts to be made.

Cybernetics is the study of how systems regulate themselves, reproduce themselves, evolve and learn. The basic cybernetic control models consist of analysing a simple input-process-output control loop as shown below:

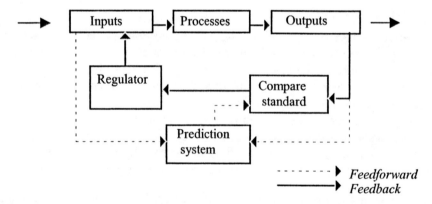

This shows how controls are needed to keep a system operating within present guidelines. They must be there to overcome the potential reasons for being out of control (or risks) that a system faces. This model may be adequate to explain simple controls, but more complex models indicate a wider range of control functions and are more appropriate for some systems.

The cybernetic model is expanded using a theory put forward by Emmanuel C R, Otley D, and Merchant K, in *Accounting for management control*, Chapman and Hall, 2nd ed, 1990. The expanded model demonstrates that the control process is more than a simple process within a self-contained organisation.

The diagram below highlights the conditions necessary for a controlled process.

Emmanuel and Otley argue that for control to exist, certain conditions must be met and the absence of any one of these conditions implies a lack of control:

♦ Objectives must exist. If there are no objectives, control has no meaning.

♦ Output must be measurable in the terms of the objectives as stated. Objectives will take time to be met and may not be fully met at all. Thus the output of the process must be measurable relative to the objective.

♦ There must be a predictive model of the process being controlled. Causes for the non-attainment of objectives can then be determined.

♦ It must be possible to take action so as to achieve the objectives more closely.

They suggest that control goes beyond the basic feedback and feedforward control into changing the process, the objectives and the predictive model of the system as appropriate. This wider framework of control includes several actions that can be taken:

♦ Change inputs - this is a first order control
♦ Amend objectives - a second order control
♦ Change the process – this is systematic learning
♦ Amend the model of the process – this is internal learning

Although this framework is more realistic than the basic model, it still falls short of the complexity of the real world situation.

Practice question 2 *(The answer is in the final chapter of this book)*

Open systems

Required

Explain:

(a)   the concept of open systems;

(b)   how the concept is used in organisation theory

---

2 Classical and contemporary control theories

2.1 Forms of control

Control can serve a number of functions and can be manifested in many different forms:

♦ Control can be involved in general results or with specific actions.

♦ Controls can be connected with the measurement and performance of day-to-day operational activities - calling for more specific standards of performance and speedy corrective action.

♦ Controls can be concerned with an evaluation of overall performance of the whole organisation or with major parts of it - this requires broadly based standards of performance and remedies for corrective action. Total quality management programmes are used for all areas of the organisation.

♦ Control systems can focus on the measurement of inputs, outputs, processes and/or the behaviour of people.

2.2 Strategies of control

Choosing a control strategy depends on the variables that affect the organisations, such as:

♦ stability of the external market;
♦ number of competitors;
♦ size of the organisation;
♦ nature of input variables;
♦ how measurable outputs are;
♦ nature of the business.

These variables will vary from organisation to organisation. For example in a consumer goods company in a stable market, controls will focus on quality and cost of input and output variables. Also control will focus on consumer market research information in order that consumer responses to product and marketing changes can be understood.

Where the environment is unstable, the organisation is small and dependent on technology and R&D, for example growing software companies, then control is based on expertise, and recruitment and training will therefore be key.

Four particularly significant strategies are explained by Child (Child J, *Organisation: a guide to problems and practice*, Paul Chapman, 2nd ed, 1988):

♦ personal centralised control - is an approach often found in small owner-managed organisations. The approach is characterised by centralised decision-making and initiative around a leadership figure.

♦ bureaucratic control - is an approach often found in large organisations. It is based on the specification of how members should behave and carry out their work. Tasks are broken down into easily definable elements and standard methods for their performance are specified. Reward and punishment systems can be designed to reinforce this control strategy.

♦ output control - relies on the ability to identify tasks having a measurable output or criterion of overall achievement. Once these have been identified, management can specify output standards and targets. Rewards and sanctions can be related to performance levels expressed in output terms.

♦ cultural control - tends to be exemplified by organisations offering professional services and staffed by professional people. It is based on the acceptance and willing compliance with the requirements of management, eg through strong professional identification and acceptance of the values and beliefs of the organisation.

2.3 Scientific management

 This approach is very much associated with the management theorist, F W Taylor. It centres on the concept of optimal ways of performing tasks by changing the production process from one controlled by craftsmen to one where management control the production process and determine the inputs.

Taylor's main contributions include the following:

♦ time study to establish the optimum production methods and rate

♦ scientific selection of labour to perform the task: Taylor's work was concentrated on the Bethlehem Steel Works and he used workers who were physically strong and motivated to learn how to earn more money by their efforts

♦ division of labour

♦ close supervision to motivate labour

♦ incentive payments and targeting systems

 Industrial psychology is another control theory that is related to scientific management, but is an attempt to apply psychology to analysing how people behave in business organisations. Again the objective is to find a best way to organise and motivate employees.

2.4 Administrative theory

The work of Fayol and Weber influenced this control theory. It was an attempt to apply Taylor's approach by developing general rules for effective management practice. The general assumption both of this approach and of Taylor's is that there is always one best way of carrying out a task, which, once discovered, can be applied universally. Weber regarded an organisation as an authority structure. He identified three grounds for supporting legitimate authority - charismatic leadership, traditional or patriarchal leadership, and bureaucracy. He saw the role of technical knowledge in bureaucratic administration as the primary source of superiority.

 The main elements of administrative theory are:

♦ division of tasks by function (specialisation)
♦ systems and procedures to deal with all tasks
♦ an accepted hierarchy of authority
♦ rules to specify tasks and duties
♦ selection or promotion based on technical competence
♦ an impersonal approach to interpersonal relationships

The control is based on the fact that people should behave as robots. It is an entirely inward-looking structure with no built-in provisions to adjust to changes in the environment.

2.5 Systems theory

 The systems approach studies the organisation in the wider context of the environment in which it operates and recognises that the work situation involves both social and technical factors, which interact with each other. Systems theory is basically concerned with problems of relationships, of structures, and of interdependence.

Systems can be described as closed or open. Emery and Trist suggest that a closed system allows most of its problems to be analysed with reference to its internal structure and without reference to its external environment. Closed systems focus on internal components such as variables of size, technology, location, ownership, managerial strategies, and leadership style. Thus, this approach can be applied at the technical level of the organisation because it is necessary to reduce uncertainty. However, complex systems in the world are not closed systems, but open systems that react with other systems.

The salient characteristics of an open system are a self-maintenance based on a process of resources from the environment and interaction with the environment. Katz and Kahn summarise the essential characteristics of an open system as follows. 'The open system approach begins by identifying and mapping the repeated cycles of inputs, transformation, output and renewed inputs which comprise the organisational patterns. Organisations as a special class of open systems have properties of their own, but they share other properties in common with all open systems. These include the importation of energy from the environment, the throughput or transformation of the imported energy into some product form, the exporting of that product into the environment, and the re-energising of the system from sources in the environment.'

 Open systems also share the characteristics of negative entropy, feedback, homeostasis, differentiation, and equifinality. The law of negative entropy states that systems survive and maintain their characteristic internal order only so long as they import from the environment more energy than they expend in the process of transformation and exportation.

Economist Kenneth Boulding, one of the founders of The Society for General Systems Theory, classified various systems by their level of complexity as follows:

1 Frameworks: systems comprising static structures, such as the arrangements of atoms in a crystal or the anatomy of an animal.

2 Clockworks: simple dynamic systems with predetermined motions, such as the clock and the solar system.

3 Cybernetic systems: systems capable of self-regulation in terms of some externally prescribed target or criterion, such as a thermostat.

4 Open systems: systems capable of self-maintenance based on a throughput of resources from its environment, such as a living cell.

5 Blueprinted-growth systems: systems that reproduce not by duplication but by the production of seeds or eggs containing preprogrammed instructions for development, such as the acorn-oak system or the egg-chicken system.

6 Internal-image systems: systems capable of a detailed awareness of the environment in which information is received and organised into an image or knowledge structure of the environment as a whole, a level at which animals function.

7 Symbol-processing systems: systems that possess self-consciousness and so are capable of using language. Humans function at this level.

8 Social systems: multi-peopled systems comprising actors functioning at level 7 who share a common social order and culture. Social organisations operate at this level.

9 Transcendental systems: systems composed of the 'absolutes and the inescapable unknowables'.

(Boulding, *The World as a Total System*, Sage, 1985)

It could be argued that a business organisation is a social system, and therefore at Level 8. However, the working of such systems is imperfectly understood. The business organisation is in some ways simpler, having many of the characteristics of a primitive cybernetic system - with output being measured, compared with a standard by a comparator and the effector taking action to adjust the input or process. Emmanuel and Otley (1985) argue that, at the least, valuable insights into the control of business organisations can be obtained by treating them as being at Levels 3 or 4.

2.6 Contingency theory

 Contingency theories see the organisation as existing within a given environment, affected by both internal and external forces (history, market, technology, employees, etc). In this situation there are no universally valid rules of management.

There are three types of contingent factor:

♦ **Environment** - this will affect the control system according to the degree of predictability (control systems are more helpful to management where the organisation operates in a relatively stable environment), the degree of competition in the market place and the number of different products/markets. A competitive market will require more sophisticated systems of control.

♦ **Organisational structure** - includes size and the degree of decentralisation. As the organisation gets bigger it will tend to require more formal controls.

♦ **Technology** factors include the degree of mechanisation of the production process and the length of the production run. Organisations with large batch and mass production may require a very formal control system.

2.7 Contemporary control theories

 Further developments in the thinking on organisations and control are still in progress. Most of them are a continuation of one of the classical theories. Recent theories include:

♦ Radical structuralist - based on the work of Braverman (Braverman H, *Labour and Monopoly Capital – The Degradation of Work in the Twentieth Century*, New York: Monthly Review Press, 1974)

♦ Structuration - based on the work of Giddens

Braverman - several themes underlie the main directions of the labour process debates. The first theme, which drew the most attention at the outset, was the argument that capitalism contains a logic of de-skilling manifested in Taylorism. The economic history of the consequences of de-skilling are very profound. Where once workers could control days and hours of work, manner and pace of construction and even, in some cases, what to make and its shape and decoration, these areas of idiosyncrasy, skill, pride and creativity were progressively removed by capitalist manufacture. He argues that the more work is centralised, the more items are mass-produced, and the more science and technology get built into the machines and procedures, the more interchangeable workers become and the less control they have. De-skilling makes wage labour more efficient, transfers work knowledge from workers to the owners of capital and any managers employed by them, separates knowledge of how to do a job as a whole from its performance and passes all control to the owners of the capital.

The second theme was control. The initial step of taking the tool from the worker's hand and fitting it to a mechanism is part of a continuous historical evolution, which has led by stages to a complete rehash of the work process and control. Braverman was particularly interested in the use of technology to transfer control over the labour process from workers to management.

Finally, Braverman explored the implications of scientific management for class structure, leading to an exploration of labour markets. His analysis is based on traditional Marxist categories of a reserve army of labour, productive and unproductive labour, and class fractions.

 Structuration - the concepts can be used to develop a theory of control systems that has the advantage of allowing for individual action as well as the constraints of social forces and systems. Structuration distinguishes between the system, the structure and the interaction of agents.

- Agents - all human beings are knowledgeable agents. That is to say, they know a great deal about the conditions and consequences of what they do in their day-to-day lives. Agents are also ordinarily able discursively to describe what they do and their reasons for doing it. However, for the most part these faculties are geared to the flow of day-to-day conduct. The rationalisation of conduct becomes the discursive offering of reasons only if individuals are asked by others why they acted as they did. Such questions are normally posed, of course, only if the activity concerned is in some way puzzling - if it appears either to flout convention or to depart from the habitual modes of conduct of a particular person.

- System - the social grouping under consideration.

- Structures - social identities, and the position-practice relations associated with them, are 'markers' in the virtual time-space of structure. They are associated with normative rights, obligations and sanctions that, within specific collectivities, form roles. The use of standardised markers, especially to do with the attributes of age and gender, is fundamental in all societies, notwithstanding large cross-cultural variations, which can be noted.

Among the structural properties of social systems, structural principles are particularly important, since they specify overall types of society. It is one of the main emphases of structuration theory that the degree of closure of societal totalities - and of social systems in general - is widely variable.

This theory - sometimes called interactionism - is an attempt to achieve order from the interactions of social agents. It emphasises people, the compromises they negotiate and the instability and changeability of all structures.

3 Systems and control

3.1 Control mechanisms

 In order to measure efficiency, some performance measure is required. Classical economics theory assumes the primary objective of any business organisation is profit maximisation. Even accountants have moved away from this, and at different times use at least four distinct performance measures: profit, return on capital invested, cash flow, and discounted values of cash flows.

These are all financial indicators, and companies undoubtedly also use non-financial performance indicators, eg growth, market share, etc. Various studies have been carried out to try to identify the key performance indicators used by business organisations, but they have failed to come up with a list that can be universally applied.

Financial controls are concerned with the flow of money and other liquid assets, to make sure that these are properly utilised, and to ensure that funds are available when required. Organisational control, on the other hand, has a wider meaning, and is primarily concerned with the integration of the various business activities. Clearly the information required for organisation control will be more extensive than for financial control.

 In order to ensure the organisation is operating in line with its agreed strategy, control mechanisms need to be developed to provide data that allows the organisation's activities to be monitored. These can take a variety of forms depending on the emphasis of the organisation's activities. Johnson and Scholes have detailed examples of various analyses that can be carried out.

Type of analysis	Control
1 Financial analysis	Measure the extent of variance from financial plans
♦ ratio analysis ♦ variance analysis ♦ cash budgeting ♦ capital budgeting	♦ elements of profitability ♦ cash flow ♦ investment
2 Market analysis	Measure the extent to which strategic plans are achieving improved competitive standing
♦ demand analysis ♦ market share analysis	♦ changes in demand ♦ market share
3 Sales and distribution analysis	Monitors the extent to which sales budgets or distribution levels are being achieved
♦ sales budgets ♦ distribution analysis	
4 Physical resource analysis	Monitors plant, and materials utilisation
♦ capacity fill ♦ yield ♦ product inspection	
5 Human resource analysis	Monitors productivity, capabilities and stability of the workforce
♦ work measurement ♦ labour turnover ♦ training needs	

3.2   Ouchi's three types of control

Control systems should be understandable and economical, be related to decision centres, register variations quickly, be selective, remain flexible and point to corrective action.

A variety of control strategies exist. Outlined below is a model developed by William Ouchi (Ouchi WG & Maguire MA, Organisational Control: Two Functions, *Administrative Science Quarterly*, 20, 559-569, 1975). This model outlines three types of control.

♦ Market control - this type of control is based on using pricing to control organisational behaviour from both an internal and external perspective. This approach can only be used where it is possible to price the output in line with the organisation's needs and customer demand, taking into account competitors' pricing strategies.

In this situation it would be helpful for organisations to produce contribution margin statements. These statements are based on defining the difference between the sales price of one unit and its total variable costs (manufacturing, selling and administrative). The contribution margin is the difference between the two. This margin represents the rate at which the product contributes to the organisation's fixed costs and profits. An income statement prepared in a contribution margin format is one that groups costs according to behaviour - variable versus fixed.

The Ouchi model would suggest that if internal costs were then found to be high, the organisation's control strategy may consist of contracting out services, eg public sector introducing competitive tendering; transfer pricing review, eg Hoover's closure of French plant and concentration on Scottish plant to encourage efficient use of internally generated economies; or a relaunch of the product into a higher price bracket.

- Bureaucratic control - this form of control was particularly popular in the 1970s when organisations went through rapid growth. This approach represents a formal approach to control consisting of policies, procedures, hierarchies of authority, specialists and defined roles which govern all that the organisation does. This type of organisation is described by Handy as a role culture.

  The strength of the organisation lies in its specialisation or functions, whose work is controlled by policies and procedures covering such matters as job descriptions, communication procedures, working practices, procedures and rules for settling disputes. All major activities are co-ordinated by senior management; the ultimate result/output is as planned. Power is based on the position one holds in the hierarchy and therefore control is by means of senior management decision-making and rules and regulations.

  Bureaucratic control works well in stable environments, but as this type of formal control system is relatively inflexible and slow to change it does not suit unstable environments.

- Clan control - this approach is based on corporate culture, where control is based on a group of related people (the clan) behaving in a commonly agreed way due to shared values, beliefs and traditions. Child noted that effective control can only really take place in organisations if there is positive commitment from employees. Clan control would state that to obtain this commitment there must be:

    - shared values, beliefs and traditions, which means that similar types of people are recruited;

    - a common understanding and acceptance of the organisation's vision and mission;

    - a common set of standards in terms of acceptable and 'rewardable' behaviour;

    - respect for the 'head' of the 'clan'.

3.3 Behavioural control and output control

Ouchi and Maguire suggest that the study of control in organisations includes selection and training, socialisation processes, bureaucracy, formalisation and the measurement of outputs. They refer to two independent forms of control - behavioural control and output control - that serve different functions.

Behavioural control - is based on personal supervision. It is responsive to the particular needs of the tasks, the abilities of the manager and the norms of the organisation. This method of control ensures that activities are closely supervised. In this way the organisation can ensure employees are keeping to procedures, working towards targets and keeping in line with their job descriptions.

A dilemma many managers are faced with is whether they emphasise productivity or their concern for the employees. Often employees are more productive when managers are seen to be fair and concerned with employees' problems. Often safe working can be in direct conflict with achieving production targets; the element that is emphasised by the supervisor will depend on the culture of the organisation, the pressures it is facing and the style of the supervisor.

Output control - a different approach to supervisory control is to focus not on the behaviour of employees (ie the extent to which they are complying with laid-down procedures) but on their outputs. Under this approach the emphasis is on the measurement of outputs and results achieved; within limits (imposed by general notions of responsible behaviour and by organisational culture) the means used to achieve the results are less important. It serves the needs of the organisation as a whole and is used because of a demand for a quantifiable, simple measure of organisational performance.

Both types of control are not mutually exclusive. If controls over behaviour are applied without adequate attention to output controls, this can lead to increased bureaucracy. An over-emphasis on formal rules and procedures may lead to people following the rules and regulations but overlooking important goals such as providing effective customer service.

3.4   Behavioural control

Although behavioural control is based on supervision, there are other aspects to be considered. The organisation will have laid down procedures and policies that set down standards for many aspects of work, and document the accepted methodology of activity in the organisation. These include:

♦   Contracts of employment - these form the most basic control tool for the relationship between employer and employee. They contain, often in great detail, standards of behaviour and expected performance required of the employee, and the duties and responsibilities of the organisation. In the case of disciplinary proceedings, the contract (and any accompanying code of conduct) can be used as a basis for corrective action.

♦   Reward systems - there are many examples of reward systems being used as an incentive to give credit to good performance. Salary may be linked to clear performance criteria, or a bonus may be paid for exceptional work. Once again, the terms of such reward schemes must be clearly expressed, and the employees must be confident that the reward will be received if they perform accordingly. For project-based work, project team members may be paid a bonus on completion that is linked to cost, time or quality criteria.

♦   Appraisals - as well as the informal day-to-day contact between managers and their subordinates, there is still a role for the formal performance appraisal system. A periodic process of performance review and objective setting allows career planning and is very motivating for staff. The appraisal is also an opportunity to identify training and career development needs.

3.5   Organisational structure

We have already discussed the division of work as a control mechanism but not explained how it is implemented. Once this division of work has been established, three essential factors appear, which illustrate the different management structure necessary, namely:

♦   responsibility (levels and reporting relationships are defined);
♦   control (systems);
♦   delegation and forms of authority (tend to be formalised).

Organisational structure has been defined by Kast and Rosenzweig as 'the established pattern of relationships among the components or parts of the organisation'.

As organisations grow, there is a need to establish a hierarchy and set up various departments. This process is called differentiation. Without this type of structure there is no way of achieving unity of effort - integration - among the various subsystems in the accomplishment of the organisational tasks. Integration is essential for utility of direction - towards the common goal.

The hierarchy is called vertical differentiation, and departmentalisation is called horizontal differentiation. The hierarchy is structured (eg in the form of an organisation chart) so that interrelationships and the progression to the common objective are apparent. This allows for a clear line of authority and accountability (scalar chain) to be positively identified, each subordinate having only one immediate superior.

Authority can be regarded as the right or power to delegate responsibility and it emanates from the shareholders to the board of directors and down through the scalar chain. Responsibility is an obligation to use authority to see duties are performed.

Span of control can be defined as 'the number of subordinates over whom a given superior exercises direct authority' (Graicunas). There is no universally correct size for the span of control. It will depend on:

♦ the nature of work: the more repetitive the work, the greater the number that can be controlled (Urwick);

♦ the ability and training of subordinates and supervisors;

♦ the degree of delegation exercised;

♦ the effectiveness of communications, and also physical proximity;

♦ the personality of the manager.

The width of the span of control and the length of the scalar chain clearly have implications for the shape of the organisation. Depending on the number of managerial levels, organisations can have a tall or flat structure. Both are shown below:

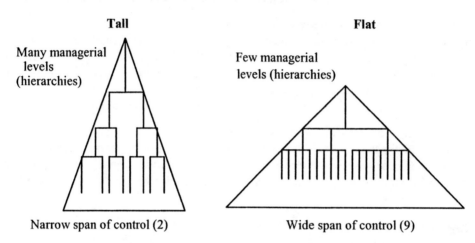

Urwick favoured structures with wide spans of control and few hierarchical levels because this encouraged delegation and the exercise of meaningful responsibility.

Flat organisations have many advantages:

♦ a wide span of control encourages delegation and motivation through job enrichment;
♦ lower management overhead costs;
♦ communications tend to be better as horizontal and lateral communication is encouraged;
♦ promotions are real and meaningful;
♦ closer contact between top management and lower levels.

Generally, classical theorists believed that flat organisation structures were more efficient in terms of cost, communications and motivation. Tall organisations tended to encourage bureaucracy and slow market response.

Practice question 3 *(The answer is in the final chapter of this book)*

Control

Required

Discuss the statement 'control is the essence of management'.

3.6 *Learning outcomes*

You have now covered all the learning outcomes for this chapter.

Evaluate and recommend appropriate control systems for the management of organisations.

Evaluate the control of activities and resources within the organisation.

Recommend ways in which the problems associated with control systems could be avoided or solved.

4 Summary

This chapter has introduced the key concepts of control from a theoretical perspective. Basic control models consist of analysing a simple input-process-output control loop where controls are necessary to keep a system operating within present tolerances. The basic model explains the use of feedback and feedforward controls.

Most management accounting controls are based on the cybernetic control model but even this model is limited in its ability to cope with real world dynamic organisations.

We looked at some classical theories of control and also noted how they have affected the modern day thinking on control.

CHAPTER 13

Internal audit and control

EXAM FOCUS

An understanding of internal control and how it functions is an essential pre-requisite to understanding the internal audit process. The role of internal audit has undergone significant changes in recent years. This chapter deals with the process of the audit and the tools available to assist in the review. You should expect to see at least one part of a question on accounting systems and internal controls in each exam.

LEARNING OUTCOMES

This chapter covers the following Learning Outcomes of the CIMA syllabus

> Explain the process of internal audit

> Produce a plan for the audit of various organisational activities including management, accounting and information systems

> Analyse problems associated with the audit of activities and systems, and recommend action to avoid or solve those problems

> Recommend action to improve the efficiency, effectiveness and control of activities.

In order to cover these learning outcomes, the following topics are included

> The process of review and audit of internal controls

> The major tools available to assist with such a review (eg audit planning, documenting systems, internal control questionnaires, sampling and testing)

> The role of the internal auditor and the relationship between the internal auditor and external audit

1 Review and audit of internal controls

1.1 Internal control

 The Auditing Practices Board defines an internal control system in their Glossary of Terms as including 'all the policies and procedures (internal controls) adopted by the directors and management of an entity to assist in achieving their objective of ensuring, as far as practicable, the orderly and efficient conduct of its business, including adherence to internal policies, the safeguarding of assets, the prevention and detection of fraud and error, the accuracy and completeness of the accounting records, and the timely preparation of reliable financial information. Internal controls may be incorporated within computerised accounting systems. However, the internal control system extends beyond those matters which relate directly to the accounting system'.

It is for management to determine the extent to which internal controls are to be applied within the organisation. There are numerous factors to be considered, eg:

♦ the nature, size and volume of transactions;
♦ the geographical distribution of the enterprise;
♦ the controls exercised personally by individual members of management;
♦ the cost of setting up controls and the benefits obtained thereby.

 A previous Auditing Guideline on internal control put forward eight features of systems on which an auditor may place reliance. These controls are applicable to both computerised and non-computerised environments.

(i) *Organisation* - there must be a well-defined organisational structure showing how responsibility and authority are delegated.

(ii) *Segregation of duties* - a fundamental form of control in any enterprise is the separation of responsibilities so that no one person can fully record and process a transaction. This can be achieved by ensuring that the custodial function, the authorisation function, the recording function and the execution function are kept separate (CARE).

(iii) *Physical controls* - these are concerned with the custody of assets and records, and also with ensuring that access to assets and records is only permitted to authorised personnel.

(iv) *Authorisation and approval* - all transactions require authorisation or approval by a responsible person. Limits on authorisations should be set down in writing.

(v) *Arithmetical and accounting* - these controls include those that check the arithmetical accuracy of records such as control accounts, cross totals, reconciliations and sequential controls over documents.

(vi) *Personnel* - the proper functioning of the system depends upon the employment of well-motivated, competent personnel who possess the necessary integrity for their tasks.

(vii) *Supervision* - an important aspect of any control system is the existence of supervisory procedures by the management.

(viii) *Management* - these are controls exercised by the management outside the day-to-day routine of the system. Examples are the use of monitoring procedures through the use of budgetary control and other management accounting techniques as well as the provision of internal audit procedures.

 CIPFA classify and describe the controls that are specific to computer systems. These are outlined below:

♦ Organisational controls
♦ Operational controls
♦ File and software controls
♦ Terminal controls
♦ Environmental controls

1.2 Internal check

 Internal check can be described as one of the features of internal control. The essence of internal check is to ensure that no one person carries too much responsibility and each person's work is reviewed or checked by another. This is achieved by a division of responsibilities. The absence of internal check leads to errors remaining undiscovered and can also lead to fraudulent acts, which are committed because the executant feels free of any form of supervision.

Practice question 1 *(The answer is in the final chapter of this book)*

Highland Manufacturing Co

The Highland Manufacturing Co Ltd has recently introduced a new range of products, which require components that are extremely expensive and would be easily saleable if stolen. The materials and components store has previously been operated with little control, as the items stored were inexpensive with a rapid turnover. The management are now concerned that procedures should be introduced for these new components to ensure that too large a stock is not carried and that control is exercised throughout all the stages, from receipt to use of the items.

Required

As the management consultant to the company, write a report advising the management on suitable procedures to ensure the control they are seeking.

2 Internal audit

2.1 Internal and external audit

The internal audit is an independent appraisal function carried out by specially assigned staff. The Glossary of Terms issued by the APB defines internal audit as 'an appraisal or monitoring activity established by management and the directors for the review of the accounting and internal control systems as a service to the entity. It functions by, amongst other things, examining, evaluating and reporting to management and the directors on the adequacy and effectiveness of components of the accounting and internal control systems'. Internal audit may also be viewed as having a problem-solving function whereby impartial advice is given to management on all aspects of policy.

The Institute of Internal Auditors (IIA) state that internal audit 'assists members of the organisation in the effective carrying out of their responsibilities. To this end, internal auditing furnishes them with appraisals, recommendations, counsel and information'.

The external audit is carried out by independent accountants. Their duties are imposed by statute and cannot be limited, either by the directors or by members of the company. The external auditor reports to the shareholders on the truth and fairness of the financial statements. The external auditor therefore does *not* have responsibility for:

♦   preparing accounts;
♦   setting up control systems;
♦   evaluating the efficiency of systems and procedures;
♦   reporting on compliance with management policies;
♦   detecting all fraud and error.

2.2 Role of internal auditor

Internal auditors are employed by the enterprise. Their role depends on the responsibilities assigned to them by the management, their skills and experience, and the size and structure of the enterprise. One or more of the following areas may be covered:

♦   review of accounting systems and related internal controls;

♦   examination of financial and operating information for management, including detailed testing of transactions and balances;

♦   review of the economy, efficiency and effectiveness of operations and of the functioning of non-financial controls;

♦ review of the implementation of corporate policies, plans and procedures;

♦ special investigations.

2.3 Relationship between internal and external auditors

The internal auditor is a servant of general management. The scope of his duties can be extended or reduced accordingly. The external auditor is independent. He has a statutory responsibility to report on the truth and fairness of the financial statements prepared by the enterprise, giving an account of management's stewardship. The existence of an internal audit function may reduce the amount of detailed checking carried out by the external auditor but the responsibility for the report upon the financial statements of the enterprise belongs to the external auditor alone.

2.4 Functions associated with internal audit

The tasks carried out by internal audit staff vary widely from business to business. The following activities are usually regarded as being within the province of the internal auditor:

♦ reviewing systems and controls, financial or otherwise - establishing adequate accounting and internal control systems is a responsibility of the directors and/or senior management. Internal audit is often assigned responsibility for reviewing the design of systems and processes, monitoring their operation and recommending improvements.

♦ special investigations, and the prevention and detection of errors and fraud.

♦ examination of financial and operating data, and testing transactions and balances - this may include a review of the means used to identify, measure, classify and report information as well as specific enquiry into individual items including detailed testing of transactions, balances and procedures.

♦ review of the operation of non-financial controls and the efficiency of business systems - the effectiveness of operations.

♦ review of implementation of corporate policies, plans and procedures - complying with laws, regulations and other external requirements.

2.5 Features of internal audit

There are many features and considerations of internal audit.

Independence - is achieved through the organisational status of internal audit and the objectivity of internal auditors. The status of internal audit should enable it to function effectively although the support of management is essential. Internal audit should be involved in the determination of its own priorities, in consultation with management. Accordingly the head of internal audit should have direct access to, and freedom to report to, all senior management including the chief executive, board of directors and, where one exists, the audit committee.

Each internal auditor should have an objective attitude of mind and be in a sufficiently independent position to be able to exercise judgement, express opinions and present recommendations with impartiality. Even though the internal auditor is employed by the organisation, he or she should be free from any conflict of interest arising either from professional or personal relationships or from pecuniary or other interests in an organisation or activity which is subject to audit.

Appraisal - of the work done and systems used in the organisation is the concern of internal audit. Auditors do not do the work that is being audited.

Staffing - the internal audit unit should be managed by a head of internal audit who should be suitably qualified and possess wide experience of internal audit and of its management. He or she should plan, direct, control and motivate the resources available to ensure that the responsibilities of the internal audit unit are met and should participate in the recruitment and selection of new staff. To satisfy the requirements of each internal audit task, staff with varying types and levels of skills, qualifications and experience should be employed. The full range of duties may require internal audit staff to be drawn from a variety of disciplines. The effectiveness of internal audit may be enhanced by the use of specialist staff particularly in the internal audit of activities of a technical nature. New entrants to internal audit work should have time to familiarise themselves with the activities of the internal audit unit and the organisation, and to demonstrate their suitability for audit work.

 Training - the organisation has a responsibility to ensure that the internal auditor receives the training necessary for the performance of the full range of duties. Training should be tailored to the needs of the individual. It should include both the theoretical knowledge and its practical application under the supervision of suitably competent and experienced internal auditors.

 Relationships - in order that the internal auditor may properly perform all his tasks, it is necessary for all those with whom he has contact to have confidence in him. Constructive working relationships make it more likely that internal audit work will be accepted and acted upon, but the internal auditor should not allow his objectivity to be impaired.

Since internal audit evaluates an organisation's internal control system the external auditor may need to be satisfied that the internal audit function is being planned and performed effectively. This review needs to be seen by both parties as a necessary part of the working relationship.

Regular meetings should be held between internal and external auditors at which joint audit planning, priorities, scope and audit findings are discussed and information exchanged. The benefits of joint training programmes and joint audit work should also be considered.

 Due care - the internal auditor cannot be expected to give total assurance that control weaknesses or irregularities do not exist. In order to demonstrate that due care has been exercised the internal auditor should be able to show that the work has been performed in a way which is consistent with this principle. The internal auditor should possess a thorough knowledge of the aims of the organisation and the internal control system. He or she should also be aware of the relevant law and the requirements of relevant professional and regulatory bodies.

 Ethical standards - the ethical statements issued by the accountancy bodies are relevant to the work of internal auditors. The internal auditor must be impartial in discharging all responsibilities; bias, prejudice or undue influence must not be allowed to limit or override objectivity. At all times, the integrity and conduct of each internal auditor must be above reproach and information obtained during the course of his work should not be improperly disclosed. He should not place himself in a position where responsibilities and private interests conflict and any personal interest should be declared. Gifts or other rewards should not be accepted.

Quality of internal audit performance - the head of internal audit should promote and maintain adequate quality standards in the internal audit unit. He should establish methods of evaluating the work of his staff to ensure that the internal audit unit fulfils its responsibilities.

 Planning, controlling and recording - internal audit work should be planned, controlled and recorded in order to determine priorities, establish and achieve objectives, and ensure the effective and efficient use of audit resources.

2.6   *Reliance on internal audit*

Before an external auditor can place reliance on the internal audit function it is necessary to evaluate its effectiveness by considering the following points.

♦   *How independent is the internal auditor?* - while *reporting* independence is to a certain extent limited, the internal auditor should possess investigative independence if his function is to be effective.

♦   *The scope and objectives of the internal auditor's function* - the external auditor will be interested in those activities which have an important bearing on the reliability of financial statements.

♦   *Due professional care* - this would be evidenced by audit manuals, internal audit plans and procedures for reviewing work in hand.

♦   *Technical competence* - the internal audit function should only employ staff who are adequately trained and proficient.

♦   *Reports* - the quality of the internal auditor's reports and their impact on management should be noted.

If, after such an evaluation, the external auditor decides to place reliance on the internal audit function he should consider the following:

♦   the materiality of the items to be tested or of the information so obtained;
♦   the audit risk inherent in those areas to be tested;
♦   the level of judgement required;
♦   the availability of complementary evidence;
♦   the internal auditor's specialist skills.

Practice question 2 (The answer is in the final chapter of this book)

Internal audit tasks

'The tasks carried out by internal audit staff vary widely from business to business.'

Required

(a)   In general, what activities would you regard as being within the province of the internal auditor?

(b)   Explain the particular features of an internal control system upon which an investigator is likely to place reliance.

(c)   How might these features be applied in an investigation of the procedure for receiving cheques from customers, their recording and subsequent banking?

2.7   *Learning outcome*

You have now covered the first learning outcome for this chapter.

>   Explain the process of internal audit.

3   Audit planning

3.1   Audit work plans

 Because the internal audit is in a key position to act as guardian of the internal control system, its management is very important. As with many functions, planning forms the initial step of internal audit. The internal auditor should prepare strategic, periodic and operational work plans.

The **strategic plan** should usually cover a period of between two to five years during which all major systems and areas of activity will be audited. It should set out the audit objectives, audit areas, type of activity and frequency of audit, and an assessment of resources to be applied.

The **periodic plan**, typically for a financial or calendar year, translates the strategic plan into a schedule of audit assignments to be carried out in the ensuing period. It should define the purpose and duration of each audit assignment and allocate staff and other resources accordingly and should be formally approved by management.

Operational work plans should be prepared for each audit assignment as it is arranged covering:

♦ objectives and scope of the audit;

♦ time budget and staff allocation; and

♦ methods, procedures and reporting arrangements, including supervision and allocation of responsibilities.

All internal audit plans should be sufficiently flexible to respond to changing priorities.

3.2   The purposes and benefits of planning

Audit planning involves balancing the work to be done against the resources available; effective and efficient audit is more likely to be achieved if operations are planned in advance and committed to paper. This planning involves consideration of all possible areas of audit operation and evaluation of changes which have either taken place or are expected to take place - changes in both priorities and objectives. The need to determine audit priorities arises because of the infinite variety of work available for audit in contrast to the limited audit staff.

 The main purposes of internal audit planning are:

♦ to determine priorities and to establish the most cost-effective means of achieving audit objectives;

♦ to assist in the direction and control of audit work;

♦ to help ensure that attention is devoted to critical aspects of audit work; and

♦ to help ensure that work is completed in accordance with pre-determined targets.

The benefits of audit plans include the effective use of audit staff and the determination of priorities. An audit plan does, however, confer other benefits; the more important ones being:

♦ sets a performance target and a basis for control;

♦ provides a medium whereby aims and achievements can be communicated to the Chief Financial Officer, external audit, management services, etc;

♦ provides a means whereby unjustified criticism of audit activity can be resisted;

♦ highlights areas of exclusion from the audit plan.

3.3 Stages of internal audit planning

The stages of internal audit planning are:

♦ to identify the objectives of the organisation;

♦ to define internal audit objectives;

♦ to take account of relevant changes in legislation and other external factors;

♦ to obtain a comprehensive understanding of the organisation's systems, structure, and operations;

♦ to identify, evaluate and rank risks to which the organisation is exposed;

♦ to take account of changes in structures or major systems in the organisation;

♦ to take account of known strengths and weaknesses in the internal control system;

♦ to take account of management concerns and expectations;

♦ to identify audit areas by service, functions and major systems;

♦ to determine the type of audit, eg systems, verification or value for money;

♦ to take account of the plans of external audit and other review agencies; and

♦ to assess staff resources required, and match with resources available.

3.4 Control of the internal audit

Controlling the internal audit unit and individual assignments is needed to ensure that internal audit objectives are achieved and work is performed effectively. The most important elements of control are the direction and supervision of the internal audit staff and review of their work. This will be assisted by an established audit approach and standard documentation. The degree of control and supervision required depends on the complexity of assignments and the experience and proficiency of the internal audit staff.

The head of internal audit should establish arrangements:

♦ to allocate internal audit assignments according to the seniority and proficiency of internal audit staff;

♦ to ensure that internal auditors clearly understand the responsibilities and internal audit objectives;

♦ to communicate the scope of work to be performed and agree the programme of work with each internal auditor;

♦ to provide and document evidence of adequate supervision, review and guidance during the internal audit assignment;

♦ to ensure that adequate working papers are being prepared to support internal audit findings and conclusions; and

♦ to ensure that internal audit's performance is in accordance with the internal audit plan or that any significant variations have been explained.

The head of internal audit should establish arrangements to evaluate the performance of the internal audit unit. He may also prepare an annual report to management on the activities of the internal audit unit in which he gives an assessment of how effectively the objectives of the function have been met.

Practice question 3 *(The answer is in the final chapter of this book)*

Internal audits

'Internal audit and internal checks are different internal controls. However, the nature of the work of internal auditors will depend on the nature and range of internal checks in existence.'

Required

(a)   Define, and differentiate between, internal audit, internal check and internal controls.

(b)   Outline the types of control which may exist in an organisation.

(c)   Briefly explain how you would expect these controls to be applied to a wages system.

4   Types of internal audit

4.1   Introduction

Internal audit is broader in scope than the investigation of financial systems and records. The internal audit department might be asked to look into any aspect of the organisation.

In this section, we will examine the main types of audit:

♦ Systems audit
♦ Value for money (VFM) audit
♦ Management audit
♦ Social audit

4.2   Systems audit

The systems audit is generally considered to be the key auditing role of concern and is where the auditors examine and test the business accounting and other control systems to see whether or not they constitute a reliable basis for the preparation of the accounts.

The systems audit will determine:

♦ Whether the internal controls are working satisfactorily

♦ Whether there are any weaknesses in the system of internal controls

♦ Whether management can place reliance on the internal controls for ensuring that resources of the organisation are being managed effectively and information being produced by the system is accurate.

A typical approach to a systems audit can be illustrated by a diagram:

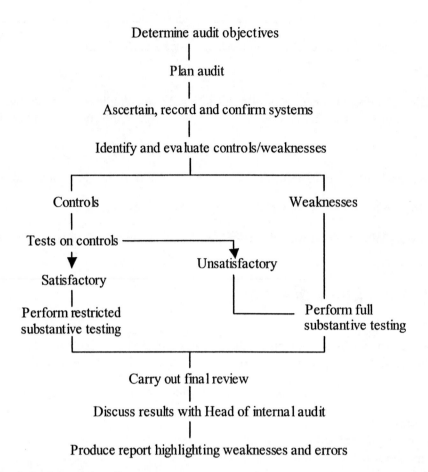

Determine audit objectives

Plan audit

Ascertain, record and confirm systems

Identify and evaluate controls/weaknesses

Controls | Weaknesses

Tests on controls ──── Unsatisfactory

Satisfactory

Perform restricted
substantive testing

Perform full
substantive testing

Carry out final review

Discuss results with Head of internal audit

Produce report highlighting weaknesses and errors

4.3 Explanation of the diagram

The internal auditor must decide at the outset on the objectives that need to be fulfilled. These may range from a limited review of part of the business systems, or may focus on the entire range of accounting systems.

♦ Planning - the auditor must plan and control the audit work if the work is to be done to a high standard of skill and care.

♦ Ascertainment of systems - the auditor must enquire into and ascertain the system of accounting and internal control in order to understand how the system works and to gain an impression as to whether systems are reliable.

♦ The auditor should test the controls and evidence needs to be obtained to decide whether they are reliable.

♦ The auditor then reviews the results and discusses them with the head of internal audit.

♦ A report will be produced detailing the auditor's findings.

4.4 Value for money audit (VFM)

A **value for money** audit (sometimes called **operational audit** or **efficiency audit**) is often associated with a type of internal audit in the public sector.

The concept of value for money has been defined by CIPFA in 1986 as the 'pursuit of economy, efficiency and effectiveness in the use of resources' (the three Es). Basically the concept relates to obtaining the maximum benefit or output for every pound spent by an organisation without any reduction in the quality of the product it supplies or the level of service or the services it provides.

Management will identify areas for audit as part of their ongoing duty to ensure that the organisation is operating in accordance with the three Es. If they find part of the organisation is not apparently economic, efficient or effective, then a value for money audit may be commissioned. The audit will then either confirm that there are changes to be made to the organisation, or alternatively provide assurances that the three Es are, in fact, being met.

 The main purposes of a VFM audit will be to:

♦ investigate a system or activity in the organisation

♦ judge whether the objectives of the system are being achieved - is the system working effectively?

♦ judge whether the resources (money, manpower, equipment and machinery) of the organisation are being used efficiently in achieving the objectives

♦ judge whether the system is being operated economically, eg is there unnecessary overspending?

The technique involves two separate concepts:

♦ calculating and evaluating value for money for any particular activity system
♦ auditing this value for money calculation

 The basic approach to the audit involves identifying and measuring four aspects of performance:

♦ money spent
♦ inputs purchased
♦ outputs achieved
♦ outcomes achieved

The relationship between money spent and inputs purchased gives a measure of economy. Inputs compared to outputs gives a measure of efficiency and outcomes compared with outputs identifies effectiveness.

The report to management in a VFM audit should provide management with constructive advice so that any necessary action can be taken as quickly as possible. As a general rule the report should contain the following information:

♦ statement of the agreed objectives of the audit;

♦ summary of the important facts relating to the area or activity audited;

♦ an explanation of any performance indicator used during the audit;

♦ the findings of the auditor, possibly set out as mentioned above (summary of recommendations plus an appendix with the detailed findings).

Finally, the auditor may request a further meeting with management a few months after the report is submitted. The purpose of this meeting will be to assess how far management has implemented the auditor's recommendations, and whether additional assistance is required in this area.

4.5   Management audit

According to the CIMA official terminology, a management audit is 'an objective and independent appraisal of the effectiveness of managers and the corporate structure in the achievements of entity policies and procedures'.

Many of the principles of VFM audits can be applied to management audits. In so far as there is a distinction, VFM auditing is primarily concerned with the quality of operations while management auditing is concerned with the quality of management.

 The aim of management audits is to identify existing and potential management weaknesses and recommend ways to rectify them. Unlike financial auditing, management auditing is primarily concerned with the future - how efficiently management plans and executes the company's activities.

A management audit will also involve the three Es:

♦ An investigation into the effectiveness of managers and the corporate structure.

♦ A judgement about whether managers are effective - are management objectives being achieved?

♦ A judgement on whether the organisation's management structure is efficient - does it facilitate effective management activity?

♦ A judgement on whether the organisation is being managed economically - is there an unnecessary layer of management?

 The main benefits of management audits are their ability to predict problems and their solution and the way in which they help the business achieve its objectives. Business failure is generally caused by poor management and, by analysing the quality of management, the management audit provides the opportunity to identify the ways in which management may be improved. Also, the management audit provides an objective appraisal of managers. This may be preferable to an informal system, which could be too dependent on the 'impression' created by individual managers.

The following stages provide a framework for understanding the process of management audit:

♦ Identify the objectives of the organisation.

♦ Establish detailed plans to achieve the objectives.

♦ Review the organisational structure to assess whether it can effectively execute plans and achieve objectives.

♦ Examine the performance of each part of the business (preferably on the basis of responsibility). This should be in quantitative terms, and be compared with any standards or outside statistics that are available.

♦ Report and make recommendations.

4.6 Management auditing problems

 There are several problems with management audits:

♦ Reluctance to actually implement changes agreed. Even though the manager may have initially been persuaded by the management auditor's arguments, people are resistant to change. For this reason, there is a need for continued involvement by the management auditing team.

♦ The problem of incompetent managers. Such managers need to be removed from their positions, yet there is a reluctance to dismiss senior staff. Other possibilities may include a sideways move into a harmless role.

♦ Obtaining sufficient time during the audit to interview senior managers. This problem can be overcome only by a commitment to the audit from the most senior management level.

4.7 Benchmarking

In the context of internal audit, the technique of benchmarking against similar organisations could be used to expose areas of inefficiency, especially in relation to value for money audits and management audits.

However, it is vital to select an organisation that is similar, or to adjust the measures to allow for differences in circumstances, otherwise the comparisons will be invalid.

We will be discussing the different types of benchmarks and their advantages and disadvantages in the chapter on quality.

4.8 Social audit

A **social audit** is an evaluation of the organisation's impact on society, particularly in terms of the impact on the environment, employees and in ethical areas. Examples of a social audit include a cultural audit, a pollution/wastage audit, a safety audit or an equal opportunities audit.

Despite the difficulty of identifying a socially responsible decision, managers must always consider the effects of their decisions upon profits. One argument is that by pursuing socially orientated activities the management may in the long run increase their profits. As concern over the social behaviour of management grows, there has developed a need to find new methods to measure the performance of management with regard to various social activities.

Many organisations have developed specific assessment procedures that review management's actions in respect of social issues. Several approaches have developed which can be grouped under the heading of a 'social audit'. Four of the most popular activities are described below:

♦ *Inventory approach* - this lists the organisation's social activities that have occurred during a specific period of time. This approach provides little or no data on the extent of involvement or the effectiveness of the programme.

♦ *Cost approach* - in addition to a list of activities, an account of the amount spent, in terms of financial outlay, resource used, etc. Once again results are not recorded so no indication of the effectiveness of the activities is given.

♦ *Activity management approach* - along with a list of activities and costs, this approach also requires a statement concerning whether the organisation has met its goals with respect to each activity. A criticism of this approach is that many of the stated goals cannot be measured quantitatively.

♦ *Cost-benefit analysis* - this incorporates the features of the other three approaches, but attempts to quantify both the costs and values of each activity. As before, the problem of quantifying the benefits and then comparing them with actual costs remains an unresolved issue.

4.9 Learning outcomes

You have now covered the following learning outcomes for this chapter.

> Produce a plan for the audit of various organisational activities including management, accounting and information systems.

> Recommend action to improve the efficiency, effectiveness and control of activities.

5 Audit tools and techniques

5.1 Analytical review

Analytical review is 'the examination of ratios, trends and changes in balances from one period to the next, to obtain a broad understanding of the financial position and results of operations and to identify any items requiring further investigation' (CIMA official terminology).

It can be used as a source of audit evidence by checking whether the information in accounting records is consistent with the auditor's prior expectations. In deciding the extent of use of analytical review, the auditor should consider the cost and level of assurance connected with each form of testing. In most cases, analytical review procedures will be used in conjunction with other tests.

The term 'analytical review' is used to describe a variety of procedures, and encompasses the following

♦ an analysis of the relationship between items of financial data (eg between sales and cost of sales), or between financial and non-financial information (eg between payroll costs and the size of the workforce)

♦ a comparison of actual data with predictions derived from the analysis of known or expected relationships between items of data

♦ a comparison of information for the latest period with corresponding information for earlier periods, other comparable enterprises or industry averages

♦ an investigation of unexpected variations which are identified by such analysis and comparison

♦ an evaluation of the results of such analysis, comparison and investigation in the light of other audit evidence obtained to support the auditor's opinion on the financial statements

The aim is to ensure that the various items making up the financial statements are consistent with the auditor's knowledge of the business, consistent with each other (eg the relationship between purchases and creditors) and also with known trends (eg inflation).

The main methods of analytical review include ratio analysis using normal ratios, and trend analysis - explicit comparison with previous years with expectation of change.

5.2 Goal analysis

Goal analysis is an extension of analytical review into the area of organisational goals and the extent to which they have been achieved. The organisation's goals, identified in its corporate plan and incorporated into its departmental objectives, should form the basis for the internal auditor's investigations into its operations, and should contribute to the external auditor's pursuit of the statutory audit objectives. Goal analysis is most useful when objectives are unclear or there are multiple objectives.

In some public sector organisations, goal analysis is useful in the area of value for money audits. Many of the goals will be imposed by statute and their identification and assessment will be an explicit part of the auditor's responsibilities. Even for private sector companies the statutory framework will be of relevance in goal analysis, although in a more general sense.

5.3   Audit tests

There are two types of test that are used in systems audits:

♦   *Compliance tests* - are tests of controls and provide evidence as to whether or not the controls on which the auditor wishes to rely were functioning adequately during the period under review. They check the functioning of a control, not the transaction itself. For that reason all exceptions revealed by the compliance testing should be thoroughly investigated irrespective of the amount involved in the particular transaction which is being used as the medium for carrying out the test.

Compliance tests are required to be performed only on those controls on which the auditor wishes to rely in considering his future audit work. If a control is irrelevant, there is no need to test it. In practice, if a control is irrelevant it may be that the company could save costs by eliminating it.

♦   *Substantive procedures* (or substantive tests) - are those tests of transactions, account balances and the existence of assets and liabilities and their valuation, eg stocks, fixed assets and debtors and other procedures such as analytical review which seek to provide audit evidence as to the completeness, accuracy and validity of the information contained in the accounting records or in the financial statements.

The term 'substantive' implies testing for reassurance on money values (substance). It is therefore necessary to clarify what these objectives are. In this context the objectives might be to ensure that expenditure is correctly recorded and represents value received by the business and that liabilities are completely and accurately recorded and properly disclosed in the financial statements. The philosophy used by certain practices adopts a general approach based on testing purchases and expenses for overstatement and testing liabilities for understatement.

Where the preliminary evaluation indicates that suitable internal controls exist, the auditor can proceed to design and carry out compliance tests. Where the preliminary evaluation discloses weaknesses or the absence of controls, the auditor can proceed to design and carry out substantive tests. Note that the preliminary evaluation and some part of the compliance testing should be carried out before the substantive testing. This is because the auditor's opinion of the effectiveness of the internal controls will directly affect the nature, extent and timing of the substantive testing.

The nature, extent and timing of substantive tests are a matter of judgement for the auditor. Where the auditor places reliance upon internal control, and his evaluation of internal control and compliance tests provide assurance that the controls are working adequately, he will limit the substantive tests to be carried out.

Where weaknesses in (or absences of) internal control arise, the auditor will need sufficient evidence that material errors or omissions have not occurred in the financial statements. In this situation substantive tests should not be limited.

5.4   Testing methods

Whichever method is chosen for testing, it should be used correctly, consistently and methodically with the results clearly recorded in working papers. Tests provide evidence for opinions in reports and their conclusion must be justifiable.

Testing methods include:

♦   Physical measurement, eg quantities in inventory
♦   Interviews
♦   Questionnaires, eg internal control questionnaires
♦   Observation, especially where control produces no hard copy
♦   Checking of written documents
♦   Test data sets, especially in computer environments
♦   Walkthrough tests

5.5 Recording of information

One of the important methods of working for internal auditors is to record the operation of various systems and sub-systems within the organisation. The tools and techniques to do this include working papers, flowcharts and questionnaires.

Working papers - internal audit work should be properly recorded because:

♦ the head of internal audit needs to be able to ensure that work delegated to staff has been properly performed - he can generally do this only by reference to detailed working papers prepared by the internal audit staff who performed the work;

♦ working papers provide, for future reference, evidence of work performed, details of problems encountered and conclusions drawn; and

♦ the preparation of working papers encourages each internal auditor to adopt a methodical approach to his work.

The head of internal audit should specify the required standard of internal audit documentation and working papers and ensure that those standards are maintained.

Internal audit working papers should always be sufficiently complete and detailed to enable an experienced internal auditor with no previous connection with the internal audit assignment subsequently to ascertain from them what work was performed and to support the conclusions reached.

Venables and Impey (Venables J S R and Impey KW, *Internal Audit*, 3rd ed, Butterworth, 1991) outline the possible contents of working papers. The list includes the following:

♦ the objectives of the investigation

♦ details of past work completed in this area and review of previous work

♦ the methods used in the investigation, along with a timetable and details of actions to be taken (if possible)

♦ details of the investigators involved

♦ evidence collected, eg management statements and memos, copies of correspondence, statistical data and accounts and internal control information

♦ general conclusions and interpretations of evidence collected

♦ action proposed, along with reasons

♦ conclusions and final report

Flowcharts – are diagrammatical representations of the flow of something: information, data, document, function or activity and the sequence of operations in a system or process. Examples of flowcharts are dataflow diagrams, procedure flowcharts and program flowcharts. They are used to analyse, describe or criticise an existing system or to organise the design of a new system. Their advantages include the following:

♦ They portray the flow of documents through the system and enable the auditor to relate those movements with procedures and checks carried out as part of that system.

♦ They show the movement of documents in such a way that, when properly prepared, the sources and destinations of all documents will be clear.

♦ They help to highlight weaknesses in the control of the business.

♦ They enable audit tests to be clearly related to weaknesses in the accounting system.

Symbols are used to represent documents, operations and checks carried out.

It is unlikely that you will be asked to draw audit flowcharts for examinations, but you will need to know of their usefulness to internal auditors. You could be expected to comment on a system described by a flowchart or to give reasons for their use.

Internal control questionnaires (ICQs) - are usually regarded as documents for *evaluating* rather than *recording*. However the various questions making up the ICQs can be constructed in such a way as to require answers in the form of descriptive notes on the system. They are basically detailed checklists of specific internal control techniques that should be present in a system for good internal control.

The questions are framed so as to discover any situation where there is no subdivision of duties between essential functions, where controls do not exist, or where the aspects of managerial supervision that are so essential to efficient operations are deficient.

An important feature of the ICQ is the way in which questions are phrased; an affirmative answer indicates a strength and a negative answer a weakness. An identified weakness in an ICQ can be cross-referenced to the part of the audit programme concerned with evaluating that particular aspect of the system. A drawback of the conventional ICQ is that it is too long and too passive in determining key areas of audit risk.

An **internal control evaluation summary (ICE)** - may be used in conjunction with ICQs or in substitution for them. The principal difference between an ICQ and an ICE is that the latter concentrates on the most serious weaknesses that could occur within a system through the use of 'key' questions. The answer to the key question depends upon an evaluation of desirable features of the system, which are set out in a number of 'follow up' questions.

For example, the answer to a key question such as 'can liabilities be set up for goods or services which are either not authorised or received?' depends upon satisfactory answers to various follow up questions, some of which are exemplified below:

♦ is there adequate segregation of duties between authorising, recording, custodial functions and execution?

♦ is the issue and authorisation of purchase orders controlled?

♦ are goods inspected and are pre-numbered goods received notes prepared?

Practice question 4 *(The answer is in the final chapter of this book)*

Internal control

Required

In relation to internal control, explain what you understand by the following terms:

(a)   Substantive testing;

(b)   Analytical review;

(c)   Compliance testing.

---

6   Assessing and managing risk

6.1   *Managing risk*

In general terms, risk would be taken as meaning anything that could cause the organisation to make a financial loss. It can be defined as the 'chance of bad consequences'. The types of risk include disasters outside the control of the organisation, poor trading, mismanagement, errors because of human or machine problems, and misappropriation of resources, physical assets or intangible assets.

Internal auditors must understand the concept of risk and how it may be assessed in the planning of controls within an organisation.

The following step-by-step process is a useful framework for the risk assessment.

- ◆ Identify risks
- ◆ Quantify risks
- ◆ Identify counter-measures (some of the possibilities are listed below)
- ◆ Cost counter-measures
- ◆ Choose which counter-measures are required
- ◆ Draw up contingency plans
- ◆ Implement the plan to manage the risk
- ◆ Monitor, review and update the plan
- ◆ Constantly watch for new risks

The counter-measures that an organisation can adopt include the following possibilities.

- ◆ Transfer the risks (by means of an insurance policy). Limited liability is another way of transferring risk.

- ◆ Ignore the risks, if the counter-measures cannot be justified.

- ◆ Modify a system so as to eliminate the risks.

- ◆ Reduce the probability of risk by introducing controls, eg two signatures on payments.

- ◆ Reduce the exposure to risk by removing the organisation from risky situations.

- ◆ Adopt measures that reduce the cost associated with a risk (eg by ensuring an adequate back-up system).

- ◆ Enable recovery by implementing recovery procedures appropriate to the situation, eg relocation plans and computer disaster recovery plans.

6.2   Audit risk

In the context of internal audit, audit risk could be defined as the risk that the auditor(s) will issue an inaccurate statement, or fail to identify a material mis-statement in the financial systems or accounts, on a matter that is in their area of responsibility. Some level of audit risk will have to be accepted. In practice organisations will quantify their acceptable level of audit risk.

Total audit risk (AR) is determined by three individual factors:

- ◆ inherent risk (or IR) - this is the risk that we have been discussing up to now, along with the counter-measures. As we noted, this risk will be affected by various conditions existing within the organisation as well as conditions outside the organisation, eg how much the company is subject to market forces, the cash situation of the company, the trading history of the company, and the nature and incidence of unusual transactions.

- ◆ control risk (or CR) - the risk that a material error will be neither prevented nor detected by the internal control system of the business.

- ◆ detection risk (or DR) - refers to the risk of something adverse or irregular not being noticed or the chance the auditor does not detect risks through substantive tests. In internal audit, this could be an inefficient and risky procedure not being challenged.

These three risks multiplied together give total audit risk, ie $AR = IR \times CR \times DR$

6.3   *Assessing the risk*

Inherent risk - in the absence of knowledge or information to enable the auditors to make an assessment of inherent risk for a specific material account balance or class of transactions, the auditors should assume that inherent risk is high.

To assess inherent risk, the auditors should use their experience of the organisation together with professional judgement to evaluate numerous factors, examples of which are:

♦   the integrity of management

♦   management experience and knowledge and changes in management during the period, for example the inexperience of management may affect the running of the company

♦   unusual pressures on management, for example circumstances that might predispose management to mis-state the financial statements, such as the industry experiencing a large number of business failures or an entity that lacks sufficient capital to continue operations

♦   the nature of the entity's business, for example the potential for technological obsolescence of its products and services, the complexity of its capital structure, the significance of related parties and the number of locations and geographical spread of its production facilities

♦   financial statement accounts likely to be susceptible to mis-statement, for example accounts which required adjustment in the previous period or which involve a high degree of estimation

♦   the complexity of underlying transactions and other events which might require the use of the work of an expert

♦   the degree of judgement involved in determining account balances

♦   susceptibility of assets to loss or misappropriation, for example assets which are highly desirable and movable such as cash

♦   transactions not subjected to ordinary processing

Control risk - in order to assess control risk, the auditors need to obtain an understanding of the accounting system and the control environment, ie:

♦   the main classes of transactions in the entity's operations and how they are initiated

♦   significant accounting records, supporting documents and accounts in the financial statements

♦   the accounting and financial reporting process, from the initiation of significant transactions and other events to their inclusion in the financial statements.

An understanding of the control environment enables the auditors to assess the likely effectiveness of control procedures. A strong control environment, for example one with strong budgetary controls, increases the effectiveness of control procedures.

The preliminary assessment of control risk is the process of evaluating the likely effectiveness of an entity's accounting and internal control systems in preventing and correcting material mis-statements. There is always some control risk because of the inherent limitations of any internal control system. The more effective the entity's accounting and internal control systems are assessed to be, the lower the auditors' assessment of control risk. Where the auditors obtain satisfactory audit evidence from tests of control as to the effectiveness of the accounting and internal control systems, the extent of substantive procedures may be reduced.

Detection risk – the size of the detection risk is up to the auditor, and his decision as to how much work to do on a particular area. If he plans detailed audit testing, then detection risk is low. If he plans very limited audit testing, then detection risk is high. The auditor will generally decide on the level of detection risk in the light of his assessment of inherent risk and control risk. If they are both assessed to be significant, then the auditor will decide to carry out detailed testing to ensure that the overall audit risk remains acceptable.

6.4 Learning outcome

You have now covered the final learning outcome for this chapter.

> Analyse problems associated with the audit of activities and systems, and recommend action to avoid or solve these problems.

7 Summary

This chapter has defined the term 'internal control' and outlined the function of internal audit. It also examined the tools and techniques used by internal auditors for both analysing and recording of organisational systems.

CHAPTER 14

System controls and audit

EXAM FOCUS

This chapter covers the controls that should be built into a system to satisfy both internal and external audit requirements. The growth of computerisation within organisations has resulted in the need for a re-think about the tools and techniques that auditors use as part of their auditing responsibilities. It is also important to recognise the additional problems and issues that new technology causes for control. This topic could quite easily form the basis of a practical or case study question in the examination. The way in which the external auditor can use computer assisted audit techniques to audit through the computer, instead of auditing around the computer, is also discussed.

LEARNING OUTCOMES

This chapter covers the following Learning Outcomes of the CIMA syllabus

Evaluate and recommend improvements to the control of Information Systems including those using Information Technology

Evaluate specific problems associated with the audit of systems which use Information Technology

In order to cover these learning outcomes, the following topics are included

The controls which can be designed into an information system, particularly ones using Information Technology (eg security, integrity and contingency controls)

The identification and prevention of fraud

The techniques available to assist audit in a computerised environment

The use of Information Technology to assist the audit process (ie CAATs)

---

1 Information systems control

1.1 Introduction

Once the system prototype has been accepted, consultation with the auditor can begin as to the controls considered necessary for the system.

 The external auditor must ensure that the system produces a true and fair view of the organisation's activities. He will be concerned with reviewing and evaluating the controls in the following areas.

- ♦ Controls within the computer system
- ♦ Controls over the system development
- ♦ Controls within the operating environment
- ♦ Controls over the acquisition of computing facilities
- ♦ Controls over the use of resources.

The situation of the internal auditors is different. They are employed to ensure that organisational procedures are followed accurately and according to management requirements. The internal auditor will be concerned with ensuring that controls are exercised over the system environment, systems development and information processing. Controls in these areas can be classified as *general controls* or *application controls*. If these controls are in place then the external audit function can check them, to assist in their assessment of the true and fair view given by the financial statements of the organisation.

1.2   General controls

General controls relate to the environment within which computer-based systems are developed, maintained and operated, and are generally applicable to all the applications running on the system. General controls can be conveniently split into three distinct areas.

◆ Controls over the system environment
◆ Controls over system development
◆ Controls over the system operation

Controls over the system environment are designed to ensure that the system operates smoothly within a secure environment. Such controls may include the following.

◆ Personnel recruitment policies to ensure honesty and competence.

◆ Segregation of duties between different types of job, to minimise tampering with programs and or data.

◆ Proper training programmes for new staff and for new systems developments.

◆ Physical security of hardware and software against accidental or malicious damage.

Controls over systems development are designed to ensure that systems are developed on a planned and financially viable basis. Such controls may include the following.

◆ Authorisation procedures for project development (steering committee or senior management).

◆ Proper system justification in terms of cost and systems operation (feasibility study and cost benefit analysis).

◆ Proper control over the actual process of system development (project management techniques).

◆ Regular review of work completed – the use of structured walkthrough techniques.

◆ Use of a systems development methodology (such as SSADM – structured systems analysis and design methodology) to provide uniformity of documents, and to ensure that user requirements are specified in detail in advance, and agreed by the users.

◆ Controls to ensure that all systems are fully tested before being implemented.

◆ Controls to ensure that all changes to the original system are correctly documented and approved.

Controls over system operation may include the following.

◆ Controls to ensure regular reviews of system performance, correction of system bugs, etc.
◆ Authorisation procedures for program amendments and testing.
◆ Basic physical security against natural disasters or thefts.
◆ Back-up procedures (maintaining copies of files off-site, back-up facilities).
◆ Access controls.
◆ Hardware controls (anti-virus checkers).
◆ Controls over access to data files (locks, passwords).

- Segregation of program files and data files.
- Controlled humidity and temperature.
- Measures to ensure the system is not accessed during data transmission (hacking).
- Controls to ensure that the computing resources are used efficiently.
- Security of confidential data against loss and unauthorised access.
- Adequate supervision of staff.
- Good working conditions for staff.

Practice question 1 *(The answer is in the final chapter of this book)*

Internal audit interest

Required

Describe the most likely main areas of interest for an internal audit function assigned the task of reviewing an organisation's computer-based systems.

2   Security controls

2.1   Risks to information systems

The British Computer Society defines security as 'the establishment and application of safeguards to protect data, software and computer hardware from accidental or malicious modification, destruction or disclosure'. Security is the protection of the system from harm. It relates to all elements of the system, including hardware, software, data and the system users themselves.

There are three basic concerns relevant to the computerised information system. Security should maintain:

- the availability of the computerised service itself;
- the integrity of the data that it processes and stores; and
- the confidentiality of the data before, during and after processing.

Controls are procedures or system features that help to ensure that the system operates in accordance with the requirements of the organisation and the user. The issue of the information system's security is based on the following three elements:

- physical - the operation of computer equipment can be severely impaired where it is subject to events such as fire, flooding and improper environmental conditions, eg heat;

- people as a threat; and

- the data/information that might be lost or damaged.

The security measures adopted should perform the following functions:

- the avoidance or prevention of loss;
- the deterrence of as many threats as possible;
- easy recovery after any loss;
- identification of the cause of any loss after the event; and
- the correction of vulnerable areas to reduce the risk of repeated loss.

2.2 Data security

A critical element of effective data protection is the need for security. There is a range of issues which should be considered:

- the nature of the personal data and the harm that would result from access, alteration, disclosure, loss or destruction;

- the place where the personal data is stored;

- reliability of staff having access to the data.

Security measures involve different aspects:

- physical security, such as the security of disk storage facilities, from flood as well as unauthorised access;

- software security, such as maintaining a log of all failed access requests; and

- operational security, with regard to such things as work data being taken home by employees, and periodic data protection audits of the computer systems.

Under the terms of the 1998 Data Protection Act, the need for privacy is recognised by the requirement that all data should be held for clearly designated purposes; accuracy and integrity must be maintained and data must be open to inspection; only legitimate parties can access data and information must be secured against alteration, accidental loss or deliberate damage. Furthermore, the Act states that data must be obtained fairly, to precise specifications and must not be kept for longer than required.

2.3 Physical security

Computer systems consist of a mixture of electronic and mechanical devices that can be severely impaired when they are subject to events such as fire, flooding, and improper environmental conditions. As well as covering these threats, physical security also covers the prevention of theft and accidental or malicious damage caused by external parties or internal staff.

The organisation must assess the physical risks applicable to them, and put in place appropriate controls. These controls sometimes detect the risk and sometimes prevent it, and might include the following.

- *Fire systems and procedures* - systems of fire alarms, heat and smoke detectors can alert staff to the risk or presence of fire in time for preventive action to be taken. The fire control system might also trigger automatic fire extinguishing equipment, though the use of water sprinkler systems in offices with computer hardware is inappropriate due to the damage they can cause to electrical equipment.

- *Location of hardware away from sources of risk* - the siting of computer facilities away from areas susceptible to flooding or natural disasters is common sense, but there are other controls that may be less obvious, eg locating equipment where it cannot be seen through windows from a public area may reduce the risk of theft.

- *Regular building maintenance* - attention to roofs, windows and doors will reduce the risk of water penetration and make forcible entry more difficult.

- *Training* - staff should be given copies of relevant policies and procedures, and trained in the implementation of them. Specific training should cover evacuation drills, fire control and fighting, safe behaviour, first aid, how to deal with a bomb threat and general risk identification and management.

♦   *Physical access controls* - there are a number of steps that can be taken to prevent the access of unauthorised persons to computer facilities. Examples include:

-   Employing security guards to check identification and authorisation
-   Issuing badges to staff
-   Using badge readers or coded locks on access doors from public areas
-   Bars on windows overlooking public spaces
-   Closed-circuit television systems
-   Automatic door closing and locking
-   Electronic tagging of hardware, as is common in retail outlets

2.4   Controlling environmental risks

 Environmental threats can come from extremes of temperature, excessive humidity and interruptions or inconsistencies in the power supply.

The best way to control these risks is to isolate the computer system from the outside world by placing it in a specially designed computer room or building. Obviously this is possible for a large central computer, but not for personal computers. The mechanisms that can be used to control the computer environment include the following.

♦   *Heating and air-conditioning systems* - although not possible for portable hardware, computer equipment should be stored and used in an environment protected from extremes and changes of temperature and humidity.

♦   *Smoothed power supplies* - equipment can be purchased to smooth out any variations in voltage and current from the power supply. Such problems arise as a result of poor quality electricity supply, or the use of other equipment that draws a lot of power (such as heating) or introduces sharp 'spikes' to the supply (such as a kettle switching on or off).

♦   *Uninterruptable power supplies (UPS)* - the risk of losing power due to failures or disaster can be eliminated by the purchase of UPS equipment. This is a storage battery that automatically takes over when the mains power fails, giving the user sufficient time to save their work and exit the system. An auxiliary generator can be connected to the power supply, for use in cases when the mains power fails.

 Some buildings with a lot of computer equipment have a dedicated power circuit for its use, often identified by coloured sockets or different plug shapes. Commonly, this circuit will be protected by a sophisticated UPS with smoothing and a backup generator.

 ### Practice question 2 *(The answer is in the final chapter of this book)*

Security

You are a trainee management accountant in a small manufacturing company. Your head of department is going to a meeting and has asked you to provide some information for him.

Required

Write a briefing report for the head of department which:

(a)   Examines the factors which you consider most affect the security of an organisation's computer systems;

(b)   Identifies ways in which the risks associated with computer security might be successfully managed.

2.5   Individual staff controls

No matter what the size of organisation, or the type of hardware involved, where activities are undertaken that are important to the commercial fabric of the organisation, individual staff functions must be specifically defined and documented where they involve data processing in any form.

This is vital, as it may be the only control in smaller organisations that will prevent, minimise or lead to the detection of fraudulent manipulation of data during processing, destruction of data, accidental, incorrect processing of data and unauthorised access to personal or confidential data that may be in contravention of the Data Protection Act 1998, or may be otherwise unlawful.

It is necessary to restrict access to the system, to protect the confidentiality of the software and data. Access must be limited to those with the proper authority, and a number of controls are available. These include the physical access controls that we have already outlined as well as the following:

♦ Logical access system - unauthorised people can get around physical access controls and gain access to data and program files unless different controls are used to deter them. Measures such as identification of the user, authentication of user identity and checks on user authority are alternative ways of achieving control.

♦ Personal identification - the most common form of personal identification is the PIN (personal identification number), which acts as a form of password. Users should be required to log in to the system using a unique user name and a password that is kept secret and changed frequently. Users should be persuaded to use passwords that are not just personal details or the name of their dog or cat. Passwords should not be written down, and never taped to the edge of the screen of the PC!

Other, more sophisticated personal identification techniques that are coming into use include fingerprint recognition where the user's fingerprint is recorded using an optical scanner and this is compared with the user's every time access is requested. Eye retina 'prints' and voice 'prints' are being investigated and it is likely that by the end of the decade, if not before, these forms of checking will be the normal security control mechanism in addition to or in place of password control.

♦ Usage logs - the system should be designed to automatically record the log-in and log-off times of each user, and the applications accessed. Periodic checks should be made for unusual patterns, such as a day-shift worker accessing the system at night.

♦ Storage of diskettes and tapes in secure locations - given that one of the risks that the organisation is trying to counteract is the physical destruction of the installation, it is sensible to put in place controls to ensure that back-up data is stored in a fire-proof environment on-site, and occasionally some form of master back-up is removed from the installation site completely.

3   Integrity controls

3.1   Data integrity

Data integrity means completeness and accuracy of data. For decisions to be made consistently throughout the organisation, it is necessary for the system to contain controls over the input, processing and output of data to maintain its integrity.

While computer systems are made up of physical items, the input of data and the output of information is designed for the benefit of human beings and is subject to their interpretation. Security risks arise where input and output occurs. The risks may arise due to innocent events such as running the wrong program, or inadvertently deleting data that is still of value to the organisation. More importantly, as more and more systems consist of networks of computers either in the form of Local Area Networks and/or Wide Area Networks, the risks of unauthorised users getting access to those systems increases significantly. This type of activity is referred to as 'hacking' and encompasses anything from the unauthorised accessing of personnel information to the manipulation of important accounting or other financial information.

Many of the security controls described in the previous section will have some effect on data integrity.

 Data controls - should ensure that data is:

♦ collected in full and with accuracy;
♦ generated at the appropriate times;
♦ kept up-to-date and accurate on file; and
♦ processed properly and accurately to provide meaningful and useful output.

Information can only be reliable if the underlying data is also reliable. Controls should be exercised to ensure that data could only be derived in the first instance from properly identified and responsible data providers. In order to remain reliable, such data must subsequently be processed and maintained in an adequately controlled environment.

Input data can get lost or it might contain errors. Human error is usually the biggest security weakness in the system. Controls ought to be applied to reduce the risk. The extensiveness of the input controls will depend on the method used to process the input data and the cost of making an error. If the consequences of input errors would be costly, the system should include more extensive controls than it would if the cost of making an error was insignificant.

 Input controls - will be designed with completeness, authorisation, accuracy and compliance with audit needs. The controls will use the following techniques:

♦ **Verification** - determines whether the data has been properly conveyed to the system from the source (unlike validation which is concerned with whether the data is correct or not). This procedure is normally carried out by a system user to check the completeness and accuracy of data. The main types of error found in data verification are copying errors and transposition errors, eg where a value £369,500 might have been entered as £365,900. Similarly, transposition errors in the text might be found where a customer's name might have been entered wrongly (Smtih instead of Smith). Various checks are used including:

- Type checks – every entry must comply with the prescribed format, eg dates may be defined as consisting of 2 digits, 3 alphabetic characters and 2 further digits such as 04DEC00. Any other form of input will result in an error.

- Non-existence checks - data fields requiring entry may have a separate validation table behind them such that the data being input must exist on that table, eg a supplier account number must exist already before the system will accept that number on an invoice.

- Checks for consistency - where data is originally entered and does not require on-going maintenance, the fact that it is still consistent with the original data input should be checked within an appropriate time-scale, eg batch totals should not be altered once input, payee codes for suppliers paid by BACS should be confirmed by print-out against source data on a half-yearly basis.

- Duplication/repetition checks - the system may check, for example, that only this invoice has been received from a supplier with the supplier's invoice number currently being input.

- Range checks - a minimum and maximum value could be established against which input can be checked.

- Input comparison between document and screen.

- Checking batch and hash totals.

- One-for-one checks between data lists.

♦ **Validation** is the application, normally by the computer software, of a series of rules or tests designed to check the reasonableness of the data. Computers are unable to check the completeness and accuracy of data, as they are unable to see or read the source data. Instead, they must be programmed with rules and tests to apply to data to check its reasonableness. Techniques used in validation include:

- Comparison of totals, eg checking that the total of debits equals the total of credits on a journal voucher.

- Comparison of data sets, eg a one-for-one check between two computerised files of data to identify and reject any differences.

- Check digits - are commonly used in supplier, customer and account numbers. The computer would perform the calculation on the code input, and compare the digit calculated with the check digit input.

- Sequence numbers - often documents such as invoices, orders and credit notes have sequential numbers to avoid omission of a document. The software can be programmed to reject any document that is out of order, or to periodically report any missing documents.

- Range checks - the computer might be programmed with an acceptable range for each piece of data, eg if products are priced between £3.49 and £12.99, the sales system might be told to reject unit prices lower than £3.00 and higher than £20.00.

- Format checks - the software might be programmed to expect certain data to be alphabetic, numeric or a combination of the two. A numeric field would then reject the letter O being input instead of the number 0, or the letter l (lower case L) instead of the number 1.

♦ Approval - controls acceptance of the input for further processing after entry.

♦ Authorisation - limits the input activity to selected individuals.

♦ Passwords and badge readers - control access authorisation to data input areas using a recognised code.

 File controls - should be applied to make sure that:

♦ Correct data files are used for processing
♦ Whole files or data on a file are not lost or corrupted
♦ Unauthorised access to data on files is prevented
♦ If data is lost or corrupted, it can be re-created.

 Processing controls - should ensure the accuracy and completeness of processing. Data processing errors can arise due to programming error, system design and/or data corruption on the system itself. Because these errors are likely to occur throughout the life of a system, with varying degrees of seriousness, specific measures should be taken to identify when they occur and to ensure that corrections are made to the data, either before or after processing has occurred.

Programs should be subject to development controls and to rigorous testing. Periodic running of test data is also recommended. Other processing controls include the following:

♦ Standardisation - structured procedures for processing activities
♦ Batch control documents - information about the batch that is entered prior to processing
♦ Double processing - repeat of processing with comparison of individual reports

Data communication/transmission control - if a system operates over a WAN, then the original input at the terminal/PC may become corrupted during transmission, either during on-line processing or where the information is stored in a batch file and transmitted over the WAN later for processing. Similar issues need to be considered for LANs but far fewer problems arise due to the greater level of resilience inherent in LANs.

Controls are necessary where data is transmitted in any form. The less sophisticated the techniques used for transmitting data, the higher the level of separate controls that need to be designed to identify errors and ensure that incorrect data is not processed.

 Output controls - these are controls to ensure that the produced output is checked against the input controls to ensure completeness and accuracy of processing. The system output, particularly in hard copy form, must be controlled so that the recipient receives complete and accurate information. There are a number of features that can be built into each report to ensure this.

♦   Batch control totals – the totals of accepted and rejected data.

♦   Exception reports – reporting abnormal transactions that may require further investigation (eg a report of all employees paid more than £3,000 in a particular payroll run).

♦   Start of report/page number/end of report markers - it should be impossible for a user to receive a report with pages missing without realising immediately. This is often used in error reports, where careless staff might 'lose' some pages from a report of the errors they have made.

♦   Nil return reports - if there is nothing to report, a report should be produced that says so. This is particularly important for error, exception and security control reports. A person committing a fraud might steal the report that showed evidence of their action, then claim there was no report produced because there were no items to report.

♦   Distribution lists - the header of each report should show the distribution list for the report, the number of copies, the copy number and the planned recipient of the report.

 Applications controls - can be incorporated in the software of the system to ensure that applications preserve the integrity of data. These controls include the following:

♦   *Passwords* - are a set of characters that may be allocated to a person, a terminal or a room which have to be keyed into the system before access is permitted. They may be built in to the system to allow individual users access to certain parts of the system but not to others. This will prevent accidental or deliberate changes to data.

♦   *Authorisation levels* - certain actions may require a user to have authorisation attached to their user-name. This type of control is commonly used for the production of cheques. Authorisation is also often necessary when rolling forward the system defaults at the end of a month or year, due to the complicated nature of correcting such a move when it is done in error.

♦   *Training and supervision* - staff should receive adequate training to prevent them from making the most common mistakes. They should also be made aware of any tasks that they should not attempt.

♦   *Audit trails* - software should be written in such a way that a clear logic exists in the sequence of tasks it performs, and data at different stages of processing is kept rather than being over-written. In this way the sequence of events can be evidenced for the benefit of any observer trying to check that the system works correctly.

Practice question 3 *(The answer is in the final chapter of this book)*

Control guidelines

Controls are invariably incorporated into the input, processing and output stages of a computer-based system.

Required

(a)   State the guidelines which should normally be followed in determining what controls should be built into a system.

(b)   Identify and briefly describe one type of control which might be used to detect each of the following input data errors.

> (i)   Errors of transcription resulting in an incorrect customer account code.
>
> (ii)   Quantity of raw material normally written in pounds weight but entered in error as tons.
>
> (iii)   Entry on a despatch note for a product to be despatched from a warehouse which does not stock that particular product.
>
> (iv)   A five-digit product code used instead of a six-digit salesman code.
>
> (v)   Invalid expenditure code entered on an invoice.

3.2   Systems integrity

Systems integrity relates to the controlling and monitoring of the system in order to ensure that it does exactly what it was designed to do. Factors include:

- project management;
- operations management;
- systems design;
- personnel;
- procedure control;
- hardware configuration.

These factors are all relevant to the system achieving what it was designed to do.

Some of the controls that we have already discussed in earlier chapters are applicable to the integrity of the system. There is an overlap with control measures that apply to security of the system and to system integrity because, obviously, the loss of security to a system will result in the loss of integrity of the system also.

Administrative controls - relate to personnel and support functions. For some positions, segregation of duties is a security requirement involving division of responsibility into separate roles. The selection process for personnel (both recruitment for new staff and movement within an organisation) should reflect the nature of the work. If sensitive information is handled, positive vetting might be applied. Staff should all have detailed job descriptions, with those responsible for control clearly identifiable. Other controls include job rotation, enforced vacations, system logs and supervision.

Administrative procedures should be clearly documented and adhered to. These include health and safety procedures, especially fire drills, the operation of a 'clean desk' policy, logging document movements and the filing or shredding of documents.

The physical security of the site is vital; it is now common for computer installations to be in unmarked buildings, with a single entry point, and staff carrying identification. Visitors need to be authorised and accompanied whilst in the building. Access to more sensitive facilities can be controlled by devices such as magnetic swipe cards. Siting of hardware should ensure that the screens and documents are not visible to the 'passer by'. Access to specific terminals can be restricted by the use of devices such as passwords.

Procedures to be followed in the event of interruptions to processing should be documented and observed. Computer-based information should be backed up frequently, with the copies stored in separate locations, in fire-proof safes. Recovery plans should identify procedures for all eventualities from the retrieval of a corrupt file through to complete system failure due to, for example, fire. These plans should clearly identify the people responsible to effect the procedures.

 On-line and real time systems - in this kind of processing, transactions are input as and when they arise. There is no attempt to accumulate and batch similar transactions. This gives rise to particular control problems. Traditional batch controls are not normally applicable, while the number of people inputting transactions from widely scattered terminals makes security difficult to ensure.

The following controls may be used in on-line and real time systems.

♦ Using passwords with a logical access system.

♦ Transaction log – the totals of data on the transaction log (which may be a daily or weekly log) can be matched to movements on master file control accounts.

♦ Supervisory controls, ie regular physical supervision by management. This is particularly important for situations where there is a lack of segregation of computer operator duties.

♦ Physical restriction of access to terminals – terminals may be kept in separate locked buildings or offices. The terminals themselves may require a key to be inserted before the terminal can be used.

♦ Documentation of transactions. All transaction or input documents should be recorded and signed or initialled by appropriate personnel within the user department. Pre-numbering of documents is also important so that sequence checks can be performed, and reports of duplicated or missing data can be produced.

♦ Matching transactions to master file data. An on-line system enables full matching of transaction data to master file data.

 Systems integrity in a network environment - The complexity of local and wide area networks allows for many more breaches of security than a single computer, and each breach can, of course, affect many computers. The main risks on a networked system are:

♦ hardware/software disruption or malfunction.

♦ computer viruses - usually unwittingly distributed on floppy disks or by an e-mail attachment sent over the network. Once the virus comes into contact with a system it replicates itself onto the system and lies dormant until either the use of the system, some defined event or transaction, or a certain date activates it. The replication of the virus makes it almost impossible to find its original source.

- unauthorised access to the system - hacking is usually associated with people who are not employees of the organisation, but who gain access to an organisation's data for mischievous or malicious intent. However, in its widest term – a person who gains access to a computer without permission – it can also be applied to company employees themselves. Hacking has been made possible by organisations using open telecommunications networks which are accessible to the hacker via powerful workstations and modems.

- electronic eavesdropping.

Possible controls include many that we have already discussed and some that are specific for the risks outlined above. They include:

- Physical access controls - the use of strict controls over the locking of the rooms in which the computers are located and the distribution of keys to authorised personnel only. This is vital where the computers are used either to access sensitive data files or to alter or develop programs. In addition, machine access - the restriction of access to and use of computers by keys, cards and badges – should be controlled.

- User identification - this includes the positive confirmation of the identity of the user and the proof of his or her identification (authentication). The former includes the input of the name, employee number and account number. The latter includes the input of something that is known (eg passwords, question-and-answer sequences), something that is possessed (badges, cards), or something personal to the user (eg finger print, hand or voice features, signature).

- Data and program access authorisation - after identification of the user, the type of privileges are checked to ensure that the user has the necessary authority. Privileges cover the type of files and programs that can be accessed, and the activities allowed during access. The user is denied access if he or she is not specifically authorised.

- Program integrity controls - ensure that unauthorised access and alterations cannot be made to programs.

- Database integrity controls - controls and audit techniques that protect database management systems software and data against unauthorised access, modification, disclosure and destruction.

- Anti-virus software (regularly updated with new releases) - detects known viruses and destroys them. Any common virus will be known and identifiable by the anti-virus software. However, it must be recognised that such software only protects against known viruses. All external disks and e-mail attachments should be checked before they can be used internally. Most organisations implement stringent internal procedures to make sure that unauthorised disks and programs are not used within the organisation. Failure to comply with these requirements usually leads to disciplinary action, including dismissal.

- Surveillance - the detection of security violations by direct observation, by review of computer logs or by use of the operator's console to display current program and data usage.

- Communication lines safeguards - while impossible to fully protect communication lines, controls such as encryption, phone tap and bug checks should go a long way to prevent penetration of the system via the communication lines.

- Encryption - is a control to translate a message into coded form using a code key that is only known to the sender and recipient of the message. This is a useful control for preventing eavesdropping.

- Firewalls - are security devices that effectively isolate the sensitive parts of an organisation's system from those areas available to external users.

♦   Administrative considerations - procedures that ensure that controls and safeguards are effective in preventing, deterring and detecting unauthorised or fraudulent systems data and program access and modification.

3.3   Contingency controls

Contingency controls are those which correct the consequences of a risk occurring, rather than preventing or reducing the risk. It is the process of planning for catastrophes, and in the computing environment this usually means the breakdown of the computer system.   For organisations that rely upon their computer systems to carry on their business the loss of those systems, even for a short period, can be disastrous, therefore good contingency plans should be put in place. The greater the effort invested in the preparation of a contingency plan, the more effectively the organisation will be able to mitigate the effects of a disaster.

The plan should include:

♦   Standby procedures - so that essential operations can be performed while normal services are disrupted.

♦   Recovery procedures - to return to normal working once the breakdown is fixed.

♦   Management policies - to ensure that the plan is implemented.

A number of standby plans merit consideration and are discussed below. The final selection would be dependent upon the estimated time that the concern would function adequately without computing facilities.

♦   Reciprocal agreement with another company. Although a popular option, few companies can guarantee free capacity, or continuing capability, which attaches a high risk to this option.

♦   A more expensive, but lower risk, version of the above is the commercial computer bureau. This solution entails entering into a formal agreement which entitles the customer to a selection of services.

♦   Empty rooms or equipped rooms. The former allows the organisation access to install a back-up system, which increases the recovery time but reduces the cost. The latter can be costly, so sharing this facility is a consideration.

♦   Relocatable computer centres. This solution involves a delay while the facility is erected and assembled, and also larger computers cannot usually be accommodated.

The effectiveness of the contingency plan is dependent on comprehensive back-up procedures for both data and software. The contingency plan must identify initial responses and clearly delineate responsibility at each stage of the exercise - from damage limitation through to full recovery.

Data back-up - where the data is maintained by batch processing, the Grandfather/Father/Son method of backing-up should be used. The principle of this method is that at any point in time the last two back-ups made should be available plus all of the batches that have been processed since the older of the back-ups was made. These would be in the form of master and data tapes that would be separately labelled and stored. Once the Grandfather tape becomes older than that, it can be re-used as the latest tape for back-up purposes and becomes the Son.

More likely, where the data is maintained on-line, data will be backed-up each day, so that if the normal storage medium fails, the information is available for the system to be restored to the last point of data entry prior to the back-up being taken. Copies of all data files should be taken on a frequent and regular basis and kept off-site or in a fireproof safe. The data can then be restored in case of data loss or corruption.

Software back-up - copies of system software and applications should also be taken and stored off-site. Thus the computer system can be re-created on new hardware in case the building is damaged or destroyed. Software can also be restored in case it becomes corrupted or accidentally deleted.

 Practice question 4 *(The answer is in the final chapter of this book)*

Food wholesaler (I)

You have been appointed as head of a newly created internal audit section within the computer department of a large food wholesaler. The department has a number of operational systems, some on line and some batch processing, and a central corporate database. A significant effort is currently being devoted to a new systems development.

Required

Your first task is to review the various types of controls which exist in the department and its computer systems. Describe what you are looking for in your review.

 Practice question 5 *(The answer is in the final chapter of this book)*

Multi-user system control

Required

List and give a brief explanation of the control techniques and safeguards to protect a system where multiple users have access to centralised data through terminal devices at remote locations linked to a central computer system via telephone lines or other communication links.

3.4 Learning outcome

You have now covered the first learning outcome for this chapter.

> Evaluate and recommend improvements to the control of Information Systems including those using Information Technology.

4 Audit implications of computer based records

4.1 Introduction

The auditor's choice of strategy and the techniques he employs must be chosen to provide the necessary reassurance and to overcome the problems that he may encounter.

4.2 Around the computer and through the computer

 From an audit point of view, the computer can be viewed as a mysterious 'black box'. Information is input (and this can be physically audited), the computer system does something with it, resulting in some sort of output (and this too can be physically audited). This has led to the concept of auditing 'around the computer': in other words, checking inputs, checking outputs, but ignoring what is happening during processing.

However, this approach to auditing is no longer regarded as satisfactory because auditors have a duty to take account of the possibility of material mis-statement arising as a result of computer errors. They are obliged to assess what is happening during computer processing, and this approach is often referred to as auditing 'through the computer'.

4.3   The particular audit problems with computer systems

Auditors face the same problems in auditing computerised systems as in manual systems. In addition, however, there are some particular difficulties that do not arise in manual systems.

◆   *Lack of visible audit trail.* It is difficult for the auditor to trace an individual transaction through the system, from the originating document to the financial statements or vice versa. This is because most systems are designed to minimise the volume of printed data and reports: control is implemented by the principle of exception reporting, so that the detailed printouts of stored data are not available.

◆   *Lack of primary records,* especially where input is scanned in, or where information is electronically sent between departments or organisations (eg electronic just in time ordering systems).

◆   *Data needed for audit purposes may be overwritten.* Data stored on disk will eventually be overwritten by new data. For this reason the auditor will need to plan the audit testing to ensure that the appropriate data is available at the time of his audit. It may even be necessary to make frequent visits to the organisation to ensure that an adequate sample of transactions has been tested.

◆   *The need for specialist expertise and assistance.* The auditor may need to utilise the services of a computer specialist. If so this will need to be programmed within the auditing plan, and the auditor must ensure that he has taken adequate steps to justify his reliance on the information generated by the specialist.

◆   *Centralisation.* In a centralised information system, all procedures and resources are located in a single department. Such a system has particular weaknesses, in terms of inadvertent or deliberate corruption of data, and potentially a lack of an adequate system of segregation of duties. It is therefore important, at the planning stage of the audit, that the auditor identifies and evaluates the extent of the controls adopted by the organisation, to assess whether reliance can be placed on their operation.

5   Computer assisted audit techniques

5.1   Introduction

As computer systems are becoming an increasing part of today's accounting function, the problem of the 'loss of audit trail' is becoming more common. To overcome this problem the auditor may use CAATs (computer assisted audit techniques). These are techniques that use the power of the computer to perform audit work; in other words it is auditing 'through the computer', rather than 'around the computer'.

There are two main groups of CAATs: audit packages (or audit software) and test packs (audit test data).

5.2   Audit packages

These are computer programs used for audit purposes to examine the contents of the organisation's computer files; in other words, an inbuilt audit trail. This is a relatively common technique, which is suitable for substantiating the records of a client.

Audit software may either be provided by the existing programs, or by specialised audit software (embedded audit software modules). If, for example, audit software is used to interrogate a purchase master file, it could select at random accounts for detailed checking, print out balances over a pre-determined level, etc.

The software may also provide assistance in the following areas.

♦ Detecting unreasonable rules – eg a check to ensure that no sales ledger balance is greater than the total sales made to that customer

♦ Detecting violation of system rules – eg a check on all sales ledger accounts to ensure that no account is above the specified credit limit

♦ Calculation checks – eg a check which adds the value of open items on a file to ensure that they agree with control records

♦ Statistical analysis – identifying doubtful debts, obsolete stock, etc

♦ Completeness checks – eg checking the sequence of sales invoice numbers to ensure that they have all been utilised

♦ Sample selection – the computer is used to select a sample of transactions data, based upon predetermined criteria established by the auditor. The computer could also be used to generate a set of random numbers for checking.

5.3 Problems with using audit software

The problems associated with the use of audit software include the following.

♦ Cost – initial set-up costs will be high, because the client's procedures and files need to be investigated in detail prior to identifying audit tests. The use of a specially written program will also be expensive.

♦ Small computer systems – the costs of use may outweigh the benefits.

♦ System changes – a change to the client system can mean expensive alterations to the audit software programs.

♦ Output quantities – the program may produce large amounts of paper-based information, which may be as a result of the program being badly designed. To avoid this problem, some programs can be set to terminate after a given number of items have been included within the count.

However, there are a number of spin-off benefits that arise from the use of audit software.

♦ Time management – project management software can be used to control the work of the audit.

♦ Data transfer – data can be transferred from the organisation's systems to the auditor's PC for analysis and checking.

♦ Data analysis – the auditor makes use of spreadsheet programs or statistical analysis programs to examine data produced by the client.

♦ Graphics – software packages are available that aid flowcharting and documenting systems.

♦ Word processing – WP software can be used to prepare and process audit programs.

♦ Risk analysis – this is a program that enables the auditor to key in the estimated material error in an account. From this, the program would automatically generate the sample size to be tested.

5.4 Test packs

These are used by the auditor for computer processing to test the operation of the organisation's computer programs. The test packs will check the computer programs with the data that is tested but they cannot guarantee to discover all errors. Effectively, the test pack is re-performing day-to-day transactions. The data processed in this manner is specially prepared by the auditor, and so will be designed to contain errors to ensure that the client's programs reject such errors. The auditor will also be able to test the computer treatment of the test data with the expected result gained from processing data manually, to ensure that the data is being processed correctly. Particular care must be taken not to process the test data on the 'live' system - the processing of the auditor's test data would cause severe embarrassment.

There are three main approaches to the use of test data.

♦ *Using live data.* The auditor uses real data that has been processed and which takes in the controls he wishes to test. The auditor then determines in advance the anticipated results. The processed data is then checked against the expected result and any differences are investigated. It is unlikely that this method would be used, because the chances of the live data containing all of the normal, exceptional and absurd data required by the auditor to test the controls are slight.

♦ *Using dummy data in a normal transaction run.* The auditor constructs a series of dummy transactions which contain the required conditions. These transactions are then processed together with the normal data, and actual results are compared with predicted results. This method has the advantage of producing a realistic test environment, in that the system's actual programs and data files are being used in the test. However, care must be taken to reverse the transactions to eliminate the effects of the test data on the organisation's actual data.

♦ *Setting up a special run containing dummy data.* The auditor creates special data and uses it within copies of the client's data files, thus eliminating the dangers associated with 'live testing'.

5.5   Problems associated with using audit test data

♦ *Objectives of the tests* - test data is likely to be confined to pure compliance testing, and may therefore be less valuable in audit terms than using audit software.

♦ *Recording* - the use of test data does not necessarily provide visible evidence of audit work performed. Full details should be contained within the auditor's working papers.

♦ *Live testing* - careful planning and control is required to remove all test data from the organisation's system.

♦ *Special run* - care must be taken to ensure that the 'normal' programs and files have been used.

♦ *Costs* - considerable costs may be involved in ascertaining the relevant controls and in constructing original test data.

5.6   The advantages of using CAATs

 The auditor will enjoy many benefits from the use of CAATs.

♦ A much larger number of items can be tested quickly and accurately.

♦ The accounting system and its records (tapes and disk files) can be tested, rather than relying on testing printouts, which are copies of the underlying records.

♦ After overcoming the initial set-up costs, in the long run CAATs will prove a cost effective method of obtaining audit evidence.

♦ The large volume of transactions processed by a computer system will force the auditor to rely upon programmed controls. CAATs are likely to be the only effective way of testing programmed controls.

Practice question 6 *(The answer is in the final chapter of this book)*

Food wholesaler (II)

Refer back to Practice Question 4. To perform an audit of the computer department described there you might well have to make use of computer assisted audit techniques.

Required

What types of computer software might be used by auditors in the course of their audit?

5.7 Learning outcome

You have now covered the final learning outcome for this chapter.

> Evaluate specific problems associated with the audit of systems which use information technology.

6 Summary

Controls in a computer system may be classified as application controls (relating to a particular application program, and covering input, processing, output and data) and general controls (relating to the system environment, systems development and systems operation).

Batch processing is a traditional method of handling transactions and lends itself to a number of particular controls, essentially based on comparing manual calculations with computerised calculations. Alternative processing methods - on-line and real time processing - cause additional control problems.

Particular problems arise in the audit of computerised systems: lack of visible audit trail, lack of primary records, overwriting of essential data, and the need for specialist assistance. To some extent it may be possible to use computer based auditing methods to overcome these problems.

CHAPTER 15

Management of quality

EXAM FOCUS

'Quality' and 'quality management' are widely used business terms, which can be interpreted in different ways. The terms could mean that the organisation operates a formal and comprehensive quality control system, or they may merely signify that the aim of the organisation is to produce quality products or services without any formal method or process to achieve it.

One of the problems with the term 'quality' is that it is a relative measure and often difficult to quantify; one person's judgement of quality is very unlikely to be exactly the same as another person's. This chapter introduces the concept of quality and discusses the different aspects of Total Quality Management. Because TQM has been studied by several management gurus and is also associated with other management tools such as benchmarking and business process re-engineering, it is a very rich area for an examiner to choose from.

LEARNING OUTCOMES

This chapter covers the following Learning Outcomes of the CIMA syllabus

> Analyse problems with the management of quality in an organisation

> Evaluate the features, benefits and drawbacks of contemporary approaches to the management of quality

> Produce and communicate a plan for the implementation of a quality improvement programme

In order to cover these learning outcomes, the following topics are included

> The concept of quality and how the quality of products, services and activities can be assessed, measured and improved

> Quality circles

> The different types of benchmarking, their uses and limitations

> The use of benchmarking in quality measurement and improvement

> The various approaches to the management of quality (ie, quality inspection, quality control, quality assurance, total quality)

> External quality standards (eg the various ISO standards appropriate to products and organisations)

> Contemporary developments in the management of quality

1 The concept of quality

1.1 Definition of quality

For an organisation, quality means satisfying the customers' needs and expectations. There are many definitions of quality, from the simple and easy to remember 'fitness for use' (Dr J Juran, 1988) and 'conformance to requirements' (Dr P Crosby, 1979) to the longer definition given by ISO 8402 (ISO, 1986) - 'the totality of features and characteristics of a product or service that bears on its ability to meet a stated or implied need'.

In 1992 Crosby broadened his definition for quality: 'Quality means getting everyone to do what they have agreed to do; and to do it right the first time is the skeletal structure of an organisation, finance is the nourishment, and relationships are the soul'. Japanese companies found the old definition of quality 'the degree of conformance to a standard' too narrow and consequently have started to use a new definition of quality as 'user satisfaction' or 'providing extraordinary customer satisfaction' (Wayne, 1983).

In all of these definitions, the customers' expectations and specific requests are the main factors. Therefore it is important for an organisation to identify such needs early in the product/service development cycle. The ability to define accurately the needs related to design, performance, price, safety, delivery, and other business activities and processes will place an organisation ahead of its competitors in the market.

The table below defines quality from the viewpoint of different Quality professionals. It is separated into three sections: customer based definitions, manufacturing and service based definitions and value based definitions.

 Customer based quality definitions

Edwards (1968)	Quality consists of the capacity to satisfy wants
Gilmore (1974)	Quality is the degree to which a specific product satisfies the wants of a specific consumer
Kuehn & Day (1962)	In the final analysis of the marketplace, the quality of a product depends on how well it fits patterns of consumer preferences
Juran (1988)	Quality is fitness for use
Oakland (1989)	The core of a total quality approach is to identify and meet the requirements of both internal and external customers

 Manufacturing and Service based quality definitions

Crosby (1979)	Quality (means) conformance to requirements
Gilmore (1974)	Quality is the degree to which a specific product satisfies the wants of a specific consumer

 Value based quality definitions

Broh (1982)	Quality is the degree of excellence at an acceptable price and the control of variability at an acceptable cost
Newell & Dale (1991)	Quality must be achieved in five basic areas: people, equipment, methods, materials and the environment to ensure customers' needs are met
Kanji (1990)	Quality is to satisfy customers' requirements continually; TQM is to achieve quality at low cost by involving everyone's daily commitment

In recent times a great deal of attention has been devoted to quality issues in the UK. Although there has always been a general awareness of the need to ensure the satisfaction of the customer, it is the worldwide nature of competition that has focused attention on the need to act.

Competitive pressure has often come from the Japanese, whose basic premise is that poor quality is not acceptable. A story often quoted (which may or may not be true) concerns a UK manufacturer who wanted to set a tough standard to its new Japanese component supplier - defects should be no more than two per 1,000.

The components were delivered with a separate package containing two defective components and a note - 'We do not know why you want defects but here they are anyway'.

Before various approaches are considered to improve quality, it is useful to consider the extent of *quality related costs*. Such costs exist because resources are wasted as a result of errors, poor workmanship, poor systems and poor communication.

1.2   Quality related costs

CIMA's official terminology defines quality related costs as

'the expenditure incurred in defect prevention and appraisal activities and the losses due to internal and external failure of a product or service, through failure to meet agreed specification'. Quality costs are classified as

♦ **prevention costs** are the cost of any action taken to investigate, prevent or reduce defects and failures. They include those of the following functions: quality engineering, design and development of quality control and measurement equipment, quality planning activities by functions other than quality assurance, calibration and maintenance of production equipment used to evaluate quality, the maintenance and calibration of test and inspection equipment used in control of quality, supplier assurance, quality training and the administration and audit of quality.

♦ **appraisal costs** are the costs of assessing quality achieved. They include those of the following functions: laboratory acceptance testing, inspection and test (including goods inwards), in-process inspection, set-up for inspection and test, inspection and test materials, product quality audits, review of test and inspection data, field (on-site) performance testing, internal testing and release, evaluation of site materials and spare parts, and data processing of inspection and test reports.

♦ **internal failure costs** are costs arising within the organisation of failure to achieve the quality specified. In a manufacturing company these may include defect and failure analysis, re-inspection and testing, the losses incurred due to the failure of purchased items to meet specification, reviewing product designs and specifications, and losses due to non-conformance leading to reduced selling prices.

♦ **external failure costs** are costs arising outside the manufacturing organisation of failure to achieve specified quality (after transfer of ownership to the customer). The costs include: complaints administration, product or customer service including product liability costs, the costs of handling and accounting for rejected products including recall and refit costs, the costs of analysing and repairing materials returned by customers, warranty replacement, the costs arising from replacing products due to marketing errors, design and specification errors and factory or installation errors.

A company should aim to quantify the costs of poor quality. This will enable it to focus on the benefits of improvements. Such a performance indicator can be used to motivate staff, change culture, change management attitudes, etc.

Current thinking is that it is more expensive to develop new customers than to retain existing customers. Poor quality can drive away existing customers, eventually leading to lower prices. Money spent on improving quality may pay for itself if it retains customers.

Service companies face a particular problem. They are much more likely to have external than internal failure costs, as it is often not possible to go back and rework the service: the customer has already received it.

You must know the four categories of quality cost and be able to give examples of each that are relevant to the scenario setting in the exam.

Practice question 1 *(The answer is in the final chapter of this book)*

Quality costs

Required

Briefly describe *four* types of quality cost and give *four* examples of each.

1.3 Conditions for quality

There are four pre-conditions for quality to be fully accepted and absorbed into an organisation. They are commitment, competence, communication and continuous improvement (Kaizen).

Commitment - senior management must be committed to the quality philosophy so that their enthusiasm reflects on the workforce and makes it more likely that the customer requirements of quality will be met.

Competence - is gained with continual training and development of skills and experience. Without competence it would be very difficult to create quality in a product or service.

Communication - the quality message must be communicated throughout the organisation - operational to strategic levels. Communication improves the understanding of the purpose and benefits associated with the quality programme, and ensures that all members of the organisation understand the concept of quality and its importance to the organisation as well as the individual.

Continuous improvement (Kaizen) - Kaizen is a Japanese word meaning gradual and orderly, continuous improvement. As originally described in the book *Kaizen, the Key to Japan's Competitive Success*, Masaaki Imai stresses that Kaizen means continuing improvement in personal life, home life, social life, and working life. When applied to the workplace it means continuing improvement involving everyone - managers and workers alike. It involves the continual analysis of organisational processes to obtain continued improvement in performance and quality.

There are two parts that make up Kaizen: improvement/change for the better and ongoing continuity. Lacking one of those elements would not be considered Kaizen. For instance, the expression of 'business as usual' suggests continuity without improvement. On the other hand, the expression of 'breakthrough' contains the element of change and/or improvement without continuity. Kaizen should contain both elements.

1.4 Writers on quality management

Deming's work *Out of Crisis* on quality management outlined areas where managers could improve quality:

♦ All waste should be eliminated

♦ The systems for production and service delivery should be improved to reduce waste and enhance quality by ensuring the production system works optimally

♦   Training staff helps them do their job better

♦   Quality and reliability are as important as price when considering alternative suppliers

♦   Mass quality inspection should not be depended on as it ties up resources and working capital in stock

Crosby is another theorist on quality. He is so prominent in America that General Motors bought a 10% stake in his firm. His thinking is based on his background working on the Pershing missile programme, where the main objective was zero defects. The zero defects concept and his assertion that a product should not have to be corrected once it is built (right first time) are embodied in his four standards.

♦   Quality is defined as conformance to requirements, not as 'goodness' or 'elegance'.
♦   Prevention is the system for advancing quality, not appraisal.
♦   The performance standard must be Zero Defects, not 'that's close enough'.
♦   The importance of quality is measured by the cost of not having quality.

The problem for Crosby's standards is that quality must be judged from the customer's point of view. He asserts that his process is customer-oriented but companies such as IBM in the USA, after pounding away at quality for many years, have found that a second revolution is required - to become more responsive to customers. Crosby firmly believes that quality is not comparative, it either conforms to customer requirements or it is unacceptable. It is the role of management to make sure that the customer's needs are reflected in the specifications set within the organisation. Quality is, therefore, an attribute and not a variable.

Juran defines quality as 'fitness for purpose'. This can be described loosely as 'that which relates to the evaluation of a product or service for its ability to satisfy a given need'. The elements of this theory are:

♦   quality of design, which can include customer satisfaction which is built into the product;
♦   quality of conformance, or a lack of defects;
♦   abilities; and
♦   field service.

Because customers incorporate such things as 'value for money' in their 'fitness for purpose' equation, Juran's theory is looking at quality from the point of view of the customer and is a more practical concept.

1.5   Learning outcome

You have now covered the first learning outcome for this chapter.

Analyse problems with the management of quality in an organisation.

2   Total quality management (TQM)

2.1   What is TQM?

CIMA defines Total Quality Management (TQM) as 'the continuous improvement in quality, productivity and effectiveness obtained by establishing management responsibility for processes as well as outputs. In this, every process has an identified process owner and every person in an entity operates within a process and contributes to its improvement'.

The development of TQM can be traced to several consultants including Deming, Juran and Crosby. Total quality management is a concept which recognises the vital importance of quality to the successful business and requires a company to have a culture and philosophy that puts quality as the key priority at all levels and in every part of a company's operation. If we break it down into its constituent parts:

- *Total* - means that everyone in the value chain is involved in the process, including employees, customers and suppliers.

- *Quality* - must conform to the customers' requirements.

- *Management* - must be fully committed and encourage everyone else to become quality conscious.

TQM is an extension of quality assurance and aims to ensure that goods produced are of the highest quality. It is particularly suitable for use in a service industry, since the emphasis is on eliminating all possibility of an error before the customer receives the service.

The most important areas of business affected are as follows.

- Everyone in the organisation has well-developed customers (most of whom will be internal).

- TQM is only as strong as its weakest link, ie it only takes one person in the chain to produce work which is below the quality required for the whole chain to be broken. Therefore everybody is important.

    For example, imagine a high price, high quality hotel. Everyone employed by the hotel should appreciate the quality of service expected by the customers. A customer is likely to remember the poor quality areas rather than actions performed well. The cleanliness of rooms, helpfulness of reception staff and response time in dealing with problems are all likely to influence the customers' perception of whether the hotel is providing a quality service.

- Quality must be actively managed; it does not occur by itself. Tom Peters argues in his book *Thriving on Chaos* that many quality programmes fail because companies have a passion for improving quality without having a control system to support it or they have the controls without the passion. TQM is something with which all staff in an organisation are involved and it must be led from the top.

2.2 The purpose of total quality management

In many manufacturing industries, quality standards can be necessary at four levels.

(i) At **policy levels** it is necessary to determine the desired market level of quality. An interesting example is the food supermarket chains. Typically, as an industry becomes more mature, so customers respond to higher quality rather than a cheap pricing policy. Tesco, in the last five years, has actively pursued a policy of higher quality of goods and higher standards in stores and service - this supersedes the previous Cohen philosophy of 'pile it high and sell it cheap'.

(ii) Quality standards must be determined and specified at the **design stage** to meet the market level of quality. This is an area where Japanese companies concentrate a great deal of quality effort. Japanese companies are rarely trailblazers in introducing new products. They prefer to wait until the design is perfected so that quality can be guaranteed. Japan has not been a major inventor in compact disc equipment, video recorders or camera/photography industries, yet Japanese companies dominate all these areas.

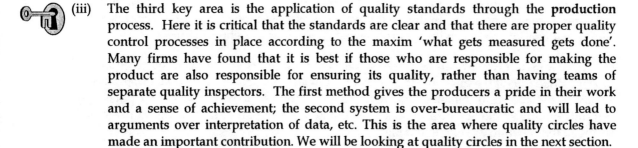

(iii) The third key area is the application of quality standards through the **production** process. Here it is critical that the standards are clear and that there are proper quality control processes in place according to the maxim 'what gets measured gets done'. Many firms have found that it is best if those who are responsible for making the product are also responsible for ensuring its quality, rather than having teams of separate quality inspectors. The first method gives the producers a pride in their work and a sense of achievement; the second system is over-bureaucratic and will lead to arguments over interpretation of data, etc. This is the area where quality circles have made an important contribution. We will be looking at quality circles in the next section.

(iv)   Finally, the quality has got to get to the **customer**. The product must be installed properly, its uses must be explained easily and after-sales service must be of the highest quality. At the end of the day, it is the customer who will determine whether his or her requirement for quality has been satisfied. This stage would include training of client's staff, format of instruction manuals, availability of after-sales service, etc.

The concept of total quality management embraces all four of these levels. It is an integrated view of the quality function that emphasises the need for high quality and nil defects in all areas.

Total quality management seeks to define the best available practice and quality in every aspect of the company's operations and creates an employee philosophy that expects high quality throughout.

2.3   TQM - a plan for quality

The organisation's policy for quality culture requires it to:

♦   establish an organisation which is 'for quality'
♦   identify the customers' needs
♦   ensure that the organisation has the ability to meet these needs economically
♦   ensure that all bought-in goods and services meet the quality needs
♦   promote a philosophy of prevention rather than detection
♦   provide education and training for continuous quality improvement
♦   hold regular reviews of quality management systems to ensure continual improvement.

TQM recognises that change requires management action. Education is the process of providing all employees with the common language of quality, helping them to understand what their role is in the quality improvement process, as well as helping them to develop a knowledge base for preventing problems. Implementation of TQM consists of the development of a plan, the assignment of resources, and the support of an environment consistent with a quality improvement philosophy. In this phase, management must lead by example and provide follow-up education.

To Crosby, (Crosby P B, *Quality Without Tears: The Art of Hassle-Free Management*, McGraw-Hill, 1984) education is a multi-stage process that every organisation must go through, a process he calls the Six Cs.

♦   Comprehension - the first stage, or C, addresses the importance of understanding what is meant by quality. Comprehension must begin at the top and eventually include all employees. Without comprehension, quality improvement will not occur.

♦   Commitment - also must begin at the top and represents the stage when managers establish a quality policy.

♦   Competence - developing an education and training plan during this stage is critical to implementing the quality improvement process in a methodical way.

♦   Communication - all efforts must be documented and success stories published so that complete understanding of quality by all people in the corporate culture is achieved.

♦   Correction - focuses on prevention and performance.

♦   Continuance - emphasises that the process must become a way of life in the organisation. Continuance is based on the fact that it is never cheaper or quicker to do anything right the second time, so quality must be integrated into all day-to-day operations.

There are three basic principles in the TQM approach for the continual improvement of quality:

♦ focus on the customer
♦ understand the process
♦ involve people.

2.4 Features of TQM

The philosophy of TQM is based on the idea of a series of quality chains, which may be broken at any point by one person or service not meeting the requirements of the customer. The key to TQM is for everyone in the organisation to have well-defined customers - an extension of the word, beyond the external customers of the company, to anyone to whom an individual provides a service. Thus the 'Paint shop' staff would be customers of the 'Assembly shop' staff who would themselves be the customers of the 'Machine shop' staff.

The idea is that the supplier-customer relationships should form a chain extending from the company's original suppliers through to its ultimate consumers. Areas of responsibility need to be identified and a manager allocated to each, and then the customer/supplier chain established. True to the principle outlined above the quality requirements of each 'customer' within the chain would be assessed, and meeting these would then become the responsibility of the 'suppliers' who form the preceding link in the chain.

Quality has to be managed - it will not just happen. To meet the requirements of TQM a company will probably need to recruit more staff and may also need to change the level of services on offer to its customers, which includes 'internal' customers. This would probably entail costs in terms of the redesign of systems, recruitment and training of staff, and the purchase of appropriate equipment.

Thackray (Thackray J, *Fads, Fixes & Fictions*, Management Today, June 1993, 40-42) indicated the following features of companies which follow TQM.

♦ There is absolute commitment by the chief executive and all senior managers to doing what is needed to change the culture.

♦ People willing to try new ideas. This again has implications for the culture and structure of the organisation. If staff are expected to try new ideas, there needs to be a positive attitude within the company.

♦ Strong communication both up and down the company. Senior management will want to communicate their enthusiasm downwards; employees will want to discuss ideas with those higher in the organisation.

♦ Activities are divided into those that add value to the business (the core activities) and those that support the core activities. Support activities should not take over the organisation.

♦ There is a real commitment to continuous improvement in all processes.

♦ Attention is focused first on the process and second on the results.

♦ There is an absence of strict control systems.

The last two points appear to go against the central thrust of UK management accounting. The point being made is that concentrating on getting a process right will result in an improved result. A process is a detailed step in the overall system of producing and delivering goods to a customer. Improving a process without worrying about the short-term effects will encourage the search for improvement to take place, the improvement will more likely be permanent, and will lead to further improvements. A concentration on results and control generally means attaching blame to someone if things go wrong. Therefore employees would not have an incentive to pick up and correct errors but rather would be encouraged to try to conceal them.

2.5 Problems implementing TQM

Common reasons why TQM may not be implemented successfully include the following.

♦ Lack of support from top management: they may not even recognise there is a quality problem.

♦ Lack of communication and motivation. Workers are expected to take more responsibility under TQM. They need to be motivated to do this and know why they are doing it.

♦ Emphasis remains on punishing mistakes, so employees will not try any new ideas.

♦ High staff turnover leading to lack of continuity and higher training costs.

♦ Lack of funds. The problem with initiating any kind of quality programme is that there are considerable initial costs, such as training. The benefits do not come until later, when the goods are sold.

TQM is most suitable for the kind of industry in which it is easy for a customer to change supplier. In the example of the hotel chain earlier, many guests may not complain about the hotel, they will just go elsewhere next time.

The most important point for the examination is to be able to give practical advice.

♦ What is the company's current attitude towards quality?

♦ What are the likely costs of improving quality?

♦ What will be the likely benefits?

♦ Are there any specific areas of the business that would benefit from increased quality, and how could this be achieved?

Practice question 2 *(The answer is in the final chapter of this book)*

Total quality

Required

(a) What is meant by 'total quality'?

(b) Explain the conditions and requirements of total quality within organisations.

---

3 Quality circles

3.1 Installation of quality circles (QC)

A QC is a small group, usually five to eight employees, who come from the same work area and voluntarily meet on a regular basis to identify, investigate, analyse and solve their work-related problems.

The decision to install a QC must come from top management, who will allocate finance to it, consider the cost of installing the system, train people to make an adequate contribution, launch the scheme, appoint leaders, etc.

Wherever it is employed, QC requires both the individual and the organisation to be motivated to improve quality by error reduction, material utilisation, machine operation, productivity, etc. The procedure is designed to supplement the conventional quality control procedures. However, the objectives extend beyond the essential problems of quality. General productivity is considered as well as methods to reduce frustration and grievances, reduce labour turnover, and push power down the echelons of the organisation (albeit within the parameters of Japanese traditions of responsibility).

It has been the Japanese experience that 95% of the problems in the workplace can be solved with simple quality control methods such as the seven quality control tools (Ishikawa, 1986). These are Pareto diagrams, cause-and-effect diagrams, stratification, check sheets, histograms, scatter diagrams, and graphs & control charts. These tools will help QCs to brain-storm systematically and to analyse the problems critically. Then, through logical thinking and experience, most problems can be solved.

 P W Betts, in his *Supervisory Studies*, advocates the following structured approach to the successful implementation of QC in a western organisation:

♦ Allow members to select the problem possibly using a brain-storming technique.

♦ Draw up a list and vote on the priorities for selecting the problem.

♦ Gather data and analyse.

♦ Establish solutions and determine the most suitable one, possibly setting a target and a time scale for achievement.

♦ Obtain the essential agreement from management.

♦ Implement the proposal.

♦ Check periodically and revise if necessary.

In addition, Crosby (another advocate of QC) suggests the team should exclude specialist problem solvers and that the members should be of similar status. He sees the leader's role as being a quiet co-ordinator.

3.2   Benefits of quality circles

 The benefits arising from the use of quality circles are substantial:

♦ improved quality leading to greater customer satisfaction;

♦ greater motivation of employees;

♦ improved productivity;

♦ shop floor understand and share management/customer problems;

♦ a spirit of seeking improvements is generated;

♦ staff become more aware of opportunities for improvement because of training, in areas outside quality circles;

♦ improved two-way communication;

♦ customer confidence established;

♦ financial benefits considerably exceed the costs.

 Practice question 3 *(The answer is in the final chapter of this book)*

Quality circle

Required

(a)   What is a quality circle?

(b)   What benefits can a quality circle bring to an organisation?

(c)   Why, if they are beneficial, are they relatively uncommon in the UK?

4 Benchmarking

4.1 Introduction

Benchmarking is the process of determining who is the very best, who sets the standard, and what that standard is. Through benchmarking, organisations learn about their own business practices and the best practices of others. Benchmarking enables them to identify where they fall short of current best practice and determine action programmes to help them match and surpass it.

Benchmarking often occurs as one component of a more extensive cost assessment or cost reduction effort, a total quality management (TQM) programme, or a strategic planning effort.

4.2 Benchmarking activities

Any activity that can be measured can be benchmarked. However, it is impracticable to benchmark every process and organisations should concentrate on areas that:

♦ tie up most cash;
♦ significantly improve the relationship with customers; and
♦ impact on the final results of the business.

The choice of the activity to be benchmarked will determine the approach that needs to be taken. Types of benchmarks that can be used include:

♦ **Internal benchmarks** - one internal unit learns from another. They assume there are differences in the work processes of an organisation as a result of geographical differences, local organisational history, customs, differences among business units, and relationships among managers and employees.

♦ **Competitive benchmarks** - are direct comparisons with competitors. They identify specific information about a competitor's products, processes, and business results and then make comparisons with their own organisation. Where information may be commercially sensitive an appropriate third party can be used. Some competitive benchmarking is yielding some seemingly unusual alliances. For example, several semiconductor manufacturers, including Intel, Motorola, Digital Equipment Corp, and Hewlett-Packard, have agreed to share information in the area of total quality management programmes, even though they are competitors. They are banding together, some experts pointed out, so that the US semiconductor industry can compete more effectively against its Japanese counterpart.

♦ **Process or activity benchmarks** - makes comparisons with organisations in different, non-competing product/service sectors but with similar core operations. They involve the identification of state-of-the-art products, services, or processes of an organisation that may or may not be a company's direct competitor. The objective of this type of benchmarking is to identify best practices in any type of organisation that has established a reputation for excellence in specific business activities such as manufacturing, marketing, engineering, warehousing, fleet management, or human resources.

There are six basic steps to process benchmarking:

(i) *Plan:* Understand and measure critical success factors
(ii) *Search:* Research appropriate organisations for process comparison
(iii) *Observe:* Monitor process performance and analyse performance gaps
(iv) *Analyse:* Determine the root cause of the performance gap
(v) *Adapt:* Select best practices and modify for company environment
(vi) *Improve:* Enhance and integrate business process improvements.

♦ **Generic benchmarks** - compare identical business functions, irrespective of the business

♦ **Customer benchmarks** - compare performances with customer expectations.

4.3   Reasons to benchmark

It is only natural for managers to compare the performance in their organisation with that of competitors and other types of organisation. They will want to know:

♦   Who has the best sales organisation?

♦   The most responsive customer service department?

♦   The leanest manufacturing operation?

♦   How do we quantify that standard?

Once the management decides what to benchmark, and how to measure it, the object is to decide how the winner got to be the best and to determine what to do to get there. Without knowing what the standard is you cannot compare yourself against it. If a customer asks 'What is the Mean Time Between Failures on your widget?' it is not enough to know that it is 120 hours on your standard widget and 150 for your deluxe widget. You also have to know where your competitors stand. If the company against whom you are competing for this order has a mean time of 100 hours you are probably safe. However, if it is 10,000 hours, who do you think will get the order?

The reasons to benchmark include the following:

♦   learn best practice from any industry to improve internal processes

♦   learn from other organisations' successes

♦   improve understanding of environment: customers, competitors, products and processes

♦   minimise complacency - if a company is complacent, its urge to achieve satisfaction is likely to entice it to set goals that are too easy to reach. In the absence of objective measures and external comparisons, lack of performance may not be noticed until it is too late to recover. Complacency is a potential problem at all levels of management. Every manager should be asking the question 'how high can I realistically set goals for those people directly reporting to me?'

♦   helps to assess job performance and to set performance goals

♦   encourages continuous improvement. It supports answering questions such as 'what functions are most in need of improvement?' and 'how are others doing the same thing better?'. The hallmark of a good manager is a healthy level of dissatisfaction with the status quo. Benchmarking enables this dissatisfaction to be channelled into productive change.

5   Approaches to the management of quality

5.1   Managing quality

There is part of a question in the pilot paper covering this topic.

Quality management suggests a concern that the organisation's products or services meet their planned level of quality and perform to specifications. By developing the right approach to quality, organisations can benefit by 'getting it right first time' and avoiding the problems which faulty goods and dissatisfied customers can bring.

There are two main approaches to quality management.

♦   Quality appraisal

♦   Quality assurance

Quality appraisal - concentrates on monitoring levels of quality at the end of a process. Any products not up to a required standard will not be delivered to customers.

The management role in quality appraisal is to:

♦ set standards for the quality of the finished product

♦ plan how to meet these standards through training, reorganisation, etc

♦ record quality achieved (note that this has implications for the accountant who may have to set up information systems to monitor)

♦ take remedial action if necessary.

An examination question is most likely to focus on the first of these. When setting standards, management should consider:

♦ what level of quality is expected by the company's customers
♦ the costs and benefits of differing levels of quality
♦ the impact of different levels of quality on employees and the organisation.

For example, a software company is launching a new product that will have some technical support. The company needs to consider the following issues.

♦ Is there a certain minimum level of support that customers will expect, such as a user-friendly manual?

♦ The company could have telephone support available during office hours or 24 hours a day. Obviously the 24 hour service costs more but may be profitable if customers are prepared to pay a higher price for it.

♦ Organisational issues, such as the fact that a 24 hour telephone support line requires trained staff, access to the office on a 24 hour basis, and sufficient telephone lines to handle calls.

An example of the above considerations occurs in car manufacture. Quality appraisal would involve waiting until the car is finished and then checking it thoroughly. Any areas not meeting the required standard would be rectified before the car was allowed to be sold. A record would be kept of what defects were being found to see if there were any problem areas on the production line. Staff would aim to meet particular quality targets, which would be raised over time.

Quality appraisal has the advantage that it is reasonably quick and cheap to implement, and it will not involve changing the working practices of the employees.

Quality assurance - echoes the ideas of the writers Armand Feigenbaum and Phil Crosby. Feigenbaum argues that prevention is better than cure. He emphasises the role of systems design to eliminate errors. Similarly, Crosby argues that companies should operate a *right first time* process, ie that the goal should be zero defects.

Quality assurance is about designing a process of which the end result is guaranteed to be of an acceptable standard, because of the checks that have been made along the way.

Quality assurance could also be used in the car manufacturing industry. This would mean the workers involved in each process of manufacture checking that their work was up to required standards before passing the car to the next stage in the production process.

Quality assurance often looks at 'internal customers'. Workers are asked to develop internal customers and treat them as they would any external customers. The goods they supply to their internal customers should be of an acceptable standard. In the car manufacturing example, these internal customers would be the workers at the next stage of the production process. The theory is that having internal customers focuses all employees on the importance of their work towards the goal of having a zero defect product.

Quality assurance requires employees to be more responsible for their work, which means that changes in attitude and management style may be required. This, and the length of time it takes to implement, will deter some firms.

5.2 Quality control function

 Quality control is the title given to the more traditional view of quality. It may be defined as the process of:

♦ establishing standards of quality for a product or service;

♦ establishing procedures or production methods which ought to ensure that these required standards of quality are met in a suitably high proportion of cases;

♦ monitoring actual quality;

♦ taking control action when actual quality falls below standard.

Quality control is concerned with maintaining quality standards. There are usually procedures to check quality of bought-in materials, work-in-progress and finished goods. Sometimes one or all of these functions is the responsibility of the research and development department on the premise that production should not self-regulate its own quality.

Statistical quality control through sampling techniques is commonly used to reduce costs and production interruptions. On some occasions, customers have the contractual right to visit a manufacturer unannounced and carry out quality checks. This is normal practice with Sainsbury's and Tesco's contracts with manufacturers producing 'own label' goods.

In the past, failure to screen quality successfully has resulted in rejections, re-work and scrap, all of which add to manufacturing costs. Modern trends in industry of competition, mass production and increasing standards of quality requirements have resulted in a thorough reappraisal of the problem and two important points have emerged:

♦ It is necessary to single out and remove the causes for poor quality goods before production instead of waiting for the end result. Many companies have instigated 'zero defects' programmes following the Japanese practice of eradicating poor quality as early in the chain as possible and insisting on strict quality adherence at every stage - as Crosby points out in his book *Quality is Free*, this is cost effective since customer complaints, etc reduce dramatically.

♦ The co-ordination of all activities from the preparation of the specification, through to the purchasing and inspection functions and right up to the function of delivery of the finished product is essential.

It is accepted that it is not possible to achieve perfection in products because of the variations in raw material quality, operating skills, different types of machines used, wear and tear, etc but quality control attempts to ascertain the amount of variation from perfect that can be expected in any operation. If this variation is acceptable according to engineering requirements, then production must be established within controlled limits, and if the variation is more than the acceptable one then corrective action must be taken to bring the variation within acceptable limits.

 Overall quality control may be looked at under the following five headings:

♦ *Setting standards* - Sometimes called 'new design control' this function involves the preparatory work necessary before production commences. It includes the location of possible sources of manufacturing troubles from trial runs, preparing inspection specifications after sampling, and planning the production and inspection functions based on the results of these preliminary activities.

♦ *Incoming material control* - This ensures the availability of the necessary material of the required quality standards during production. Close quality contacts must be made with the supplier to establish quality control at the source. The first deliveries received are subjected to 100% inspection to establish the supplier's level of quality. Information is given to the supplier to allow him to take remedial action if necessary. When the required quality level has been reached, other deliveries are subjected to sampling tests only.

♦ *Product control* - This involves the control of processed parts at the production sources so that most differences from quality specifications that may have arisen are put right before any defective parts are produced. The three aspects of product control are:

(i) quality mindedness of the operatives and to this end extensive training programmes in quality control are arranged;

(ii) inspectors and testers with good training and experience help line supervisors to pinpoint potential causes of defects by showing them how to apply control techniques;

(iii) applying sampling checks to the finished product before delivery.

♦ *Special purpose studies* - This is the investigation of the causes of defective products and looking for ways of improving elements of production quality.

♦ *Appraisal* - This is critical appraisal of the overall results obtained from the programme and consideration of ways to deal with changing conditions.

Practice question 4 *(The answer is in the final chapter of this book)*

Quality control

Required

Describe and comment on some of the techniques of quality control used within manufacturing or service industries.

5.3   Quality control audit

Apart from receiving reports, management may also commission a quality control audit to find answers to the following questions:

♦ What is the actual level of rejects?

♦ Are the standards fairly set?

♦ Are the standards achieved at the expense of excessive costs?

♦ What is the number of customer complaints?

♦ Has the quality control system been modified in accordance with changes in processing policies, materials and products?

♦ What are the costs of quality control?

♦ What is done to improve performance by eliminating causes of poor performance?

♦ Should a personnel audit on efficiency and knowledge be carried out?

6 External quality standards

6.1 The role of standards

The British Standards Institution, through its Certification and Assessment Services, provides industry with first class product certification and company quality assessment schemes. Most of the BS quality standards apply to specific products, but BS 5750 was developed to apply to the organisation as a certificate of achievement in total quality management.

When an organisation operates to the quality standard BS 5750 it is a way of demonstrating that the organisation is committed to quality and has been assessed accordingly.

There are three parts to the BS 5750 standard:

(a)   specification for design;
(b)   specification for manufacture and installation;
(c)   specification for final inspection and test.

The ISO 9000 series is a family of quality management and quality assurance standards developed by the International Organisation for Standardisation (ISO), based in Geneva, Switzerland. You may wish to visit the ISO's website at **www.iso.ch** to learn more about the organisation.

The ISO 9000 standards were revised in 2000; the revised standards have '2000' in their name, but it may be a little while before the old names are no longer used, so both are referred to here. The ISO 9000 standards currently comprise:

♦ ISO 9000 : 2000 'Quality management systems – fundamentals and vocabulary'. This defines the fundamental terms and definitions used in the ISO 9000 family.

♦ ISO 9001 : 2000 'Quality management systems – requirements'. This integrates the previous three standards ISO 9001, ISO 9002 and ISO 9003. The new ISO 9001 : 2000 specifies the requirements that an organisation's quality management system must demonstrate to consistently provide product that meets customer and applicable regulatory requirements and aims to enhance customer satisfaction. The new ISO 9001 is now the only standard in the ISO 9000 family against which third-party certification can be carried.

♦ ISO 9004 : 2000 'Quality management systems – Guidelines for performance improvements' offers guidance on continual improvement of the quality management system.

♦ Ten further guidelines within the ISO 9000 family offer guidance on specific topics (eg ISO 10006 offers guidelines in project management to help ensure the quality of both the project processes and the project products).

The old ISO 9001 to 9003 were so important before the 2000 revisions that you may still hear references to them today. They covered the topics explained below.

ISO 9001 was the Quality Systems Model for quality assurance in design, development, production, installation and servicing.

As quoted from the Scope of ISO 9001:1994, this International Standard specifies quality system requirements for use where a supplier's capability to design and supply conforming product needs to be demonstrated. The requirements specified are aimed primarily at achieving customer satisfaction by preventing nonconformity at all stages from design through to servicing. This International Standard is applicable in situations when design is required and the product requirements are stated principally in performance terms, or they need to be established; and confidence in product conformance can be attained by adequate demonstration of a supplier's capabilities in design, development, production, installation and servicing.

ISO 9002, the *Specification for Production and Installation,* concerned organisations with product and service quality in production and installation only.

ISO 9003 was the *Specification for Final Inspection and Test.* This was for activities which can only be quality assured at final inspection and test.

6.2 Why is ISO certification useful?

Irvine (1991) points out that many companies are now seeking certification to quality standard ISO 9000 to demonstrate that they are in control of their business, and have proved it to a certification body. ISO 9000 certification is a good way of measuring progress and monitoring maintenance of the standard. It brings marketing benefits, but should be regarded as the beginning of a continuous improvement process rather than the end.

The EC Council Resolution on a global approach to conformity assessment (DTI, 1990) provides three reasons why companies should implement a quality system based on ISO 9000.

♦   To improve awareness of quality and have the standard for UK products,

♦   To reduce the need for customer supplier demonstration of quality assurance procedures by introducing a third party Quality Assurance certificate,

♦   To open markets outside the UK by ensuring that ISO 9000 is compatible with EC and USA quality procedures.

Whittington (1988) in his study to assess the interest for organisations in implementing ISO 9000 and the difficulties they faced, discovered four different reasons for implementing the standard.

♦   Due to pressure from large customers,
♦   To maintain contracts with existing customers,
♦   To use the constraints of the standard to prevent scrap,
♦   To reduce auditing of the quality system by customers.

Failure to implement the standard for the right reason may prevent companies from gaining the potential benefits from the system. Two of the companies studied by Whittington claimed that ISO 9000 costs a lot of money to implement and maintain, and that their product quality is no better than before the system was implemented. He also found that there was no reduction in assessment and auditing as claimed by much of the literature. Inappropriate reasons for implementing the standard, according to Whittington, are:

♦   To make reference to the standard on company letter-head paper,
♦   To get the kitemark symbol on the company's product,
♦   To enforce discipline on employees,
♦   To retain existing customers.

Besides the right reasons, the degree of commitment by top management will determine the success of the system. Top management needs to generate a favourable environment to enhance the development of the system. This can be achieved by developing a company quality policy and objectives. This will enable all the employees to work towards the same quality goal.

7 Contemporary developments in quality management

7.1 TQMEX

In the 21st century, the creation of the global market, international orientation of management that crosses national boundaries, introduction of new technologies, and shift towards customer-focused strategies make the competition stronger than ever. The criteria for success in this global, internationally oriented market have been changing rapidly. In order to expand business, enter new markets, and set realistic, competitive long-term objectives, excellence became an imperative. Management's effort has been directed towards discovering what makes a company excellent.

The TQM EXcellence Model, outlined by Samuel K M Ho in his book *TQM: An integrated approach*, advocates an integrated approach in order to support the transition to systems management which is an ongoing process of continuous improvement that begins when the company commits itself to managing by quality. The Model, shown below, illuminates the elements that form a base to the understanding of TQM philosophy and implementation of the process company-wide.

One of the learning outcomes for this chapter is to be able to produce and communicate a quality plan for the implementation of a quality improvement programme. We have already discussed the stages of a TQM plan and the TQMEX extends this but could be used as an illustration of a quality programme.

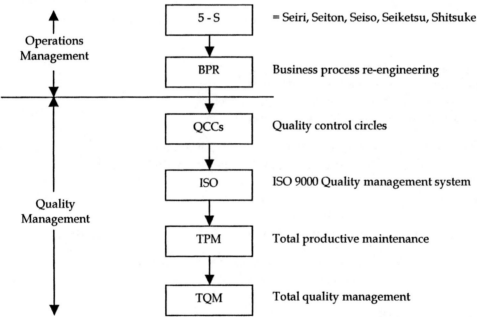

The TQMEX Model

7.2 The steps involved in TQMEX

In order to have a systematic approach to TQM, it is necessary to develop a conceptual model. Generally, a model is a sequence of steps arranged logically to serve as a guideline for implementation of a process in order to achieve the ultimate goal. The model should be simple, logical and yet comprehensive enough for TQM implementation. It also has to sustain the changes in business environment of the new era. The TQMEX Model also reflects teachings of the contemporary quality gurus. The idea was to develop a universally applicable step-by-step guideline by including recognised practices in TQM:

♦ Japanese 5-S Practice (5-S) - as Osada pointed out, 5-S is the key to total quality environment. Therefore, it should be the first step

♦ Business Process Re-engineering (BPR) - is concerned with re-defining and designing your business process in order to meet the needs of your customers effectively. It is more concerned with the business objectives and systems, and should follow as Step 2

♦ Quality Control Circles (QCCs) - are concerned with encouraging the employees to participate in continuous improvement and guide them through. They improve human resources capability to achieve the business objectives. Therefore, this should be Step 3.

♦ ISO 9000 Quality Management System (ISO) - ISO 9000 is designed to develop a quality management system based on the good practices in the previous three steps

♦ Total Productive Maintenance (TPM) - is a result of applying 5-S to equipment based on a sound quality management system. In fact ISO 9001 requires procedures for process control and inspection and testing equipment, which are part of TPM. Therefore TPM should be implemented in Step 5.

 If the above five steps have been implemented successfully, the organisation is already very close towards achieving TQM.

TQM EXcellence is a sequential model, which is easy to remember and simple to implement. This is in line with the quality principle of Keep It Short and Simple (KISS). Companies starting to implement TQM should follow TQMEX step-by-step.

Dr Deming used to say 'TQM will last forever'. Therefore it is important to understand that the TQMEX implementation should not be a programme in its own right. It should be a continuous process, subject to an improvement cycle. The Deming Cycle should be followed at each stage of the TQMEX implementation. There should also be measurable inputs and outputs, so that the changes can be identified for further improvement.

 The following steps serve as the guidelines:

♦ Establish appropriate measures
♦ Define measurable inputs and outputs
♦ Define and document current procedures and working practice
♦ Identify problems that cause errors and reduce productivity
♦ Develop and implement corrective actions.
♦ Standardise the procedure
♦ Repeat activities for continuous improvement

7.3 Introduction to 5-S

The 5-S practice is a technique used to establish and maintain a quality environment in an organisation. The name stands for five Japanese words: Seiri, Seiton, Seiso, Seiketsu and Shitsuke (Osada, 1991). The English equivalent, their meanings and typical examples are shown in the following table:

Japanese	English	Meaning	Explanation
Seiri	Structurise	Organisation	Throw away rubbish. Know what to discard, what to save, and how to save things so that they can be accessed later
Seiton	Systemise	Neatness	It is a question of how quickly you can get the things you need and how quickly you can put them away, eg 30-second retrieval of a document
Seiso	Sanitise	Cleaning	Individual cleaning responsibility from the managing director to the cleaner
Seiketsu	Standardise	Standardisation	Innovation and total visual management are used to attain and maintain standardised conditions so that you can always act quickly
Shitsuke	Self-discipline	Discipline	The emphasis here is on creating a workplace with good habits

The 5-S technique has been widely practised in Japan. Most Japanese 5-S practitioners consider 5-S useful not just for improving their physical environment, but also for improving their thinking processes too. Apparently many of the everyday problems could be solved through adoption of this practice.

7.4 How to implement the 5-S

5-S implementation requires commitment from both the top management and everyone in the organisation. It is also important to have a 5-S Champion to lead the whole organisation towards 5-S implementation step-by-step. If you decide to be the 5-S Champion of your organisation, the following steps will help you to achieve success.

♦ **Get Top Management Commitment and be Prepared** - sell the idea of the 5-S to the most senior executive of your organisation.

♦ **Draw up a Promotional Campaign** - the first thing to do for a promotion campaign is to set up a timetable.

♦ **Keeping Records** - it is important to keep records not only of decisions made but also of the problems encountered, actions taken and results achieved.

♦ **5-S Training** - it is essential in the 5-S activities that you train people to be able to devise and implement their own solutions. Progress that is not self-sustaining (progress that always has to rely upon outside help) is not real progress. Training should also include section-wide or company-wide meetings where people can announce their results. Not only does this provide incentive, but also the exchange of ideas and information is often just what you need to keep everybody fresh.

♦ **Evaluation** - workplace evaluations and other means are needed to keep everyone abreast of what is happening and to spot problems before they develop into major complications. In essence, you need to devise ways that will get everybody competing in a friendly but no less intense manner. Your evaluation tools are the key and it is as simple as using the 5-S Audit Worksheet as your evaluation criteria.

7.5 Business process re-engineering (BPR)

The pioneers of BPR are generally acknowledged as Hammer and Champy (Hammer M and Champy J, *Re-engineering the Corporation: a manifesto for business revolution*, Brealey, 1993). They define it as 'the fundamental re-thinking and rational re-design of the business processes to achieve dramatic improvements in critical contemporary measures of performance such as cost, quality, service and speed'.

Business process re-engineering is usually carried out as part of an overall strategic review of the organisation. Often management want to use the process to achieve a number of objectives in addition to the establishment of user requirements. These include:

♦ The introduction of Total Quality Management

♦ To create focus within the organisation upon the processes which create value

♦ To identify internal barriers to serving the customer

♦ To create a set of benchmarks against which the organisation's processes can be measured against its competitors

BPR is a management process used to re-define the mission statement, analyse the critical success factors, re-design the organisational structure and re-engineer the critical processes in order to improve customer satisfaction. BPR challenges managers to rethink their traditional methods of doing work and commit themselves to a customer-focused process.

The approach is based upon the concept that business processes are the most important activities of the organisation and so information systems should be focused upon supporting these processes. Business processes are those processes by which the organisation carries out its primary and supporting functions.

Primary functions are those by which inputs in the form of materials, know how, staff's time and other scarce economic resources are transformed into something of value to the customer. **Supporting processes** are those processes which enable the primary process; examples of these would be the:

♦ Personnel system
♦ Information system
♦ Research and development.

These business processes remain fairly constant over time and so the requirements derived from these needs can form the basis of a system which will serve the organisation's needs for some time.

7.6   Total productive maintenance (TPM)

TPM is a system of maintenance covering the entire life of the equipment in every division including planning, manufacturing, and maintenance.

The goal of TPM is to increase the productivity of plant and equipment by improving and maintaining equipment at optimal levels to reduce its lifecycle cost. Because of its targeted achievement to increase productivity out of the equipment, the term TPM is sometimes known as Total Productivity Management.

If the organisation is able to eliminate the causes of the 'six big losses' that reduce equipment effectiveness, they will achieve cost-effectiveness. These losses are:

♦ Reduced yield (from start-up to stable production)
♦ Process defects
♦ Reduced speed
♦ Idling and minor stoppages
♦ Set-up and adjustment
♦ Equipment failure

Implementation plans for TPM vary from company to company depending on the level of maintenance and particular plant requirements. TPM consists of six major activities:

♦ Elimination of the 'six big losses' based on project teams organised by the production, maintenance, and plant engineering departments

♦ Planned maintenance carried out by the maintenance department

♦ Autonomous maintenance carried out by the production department

♦ Preventive engineering carried out mainly by the plant engineering department

♦ Easy-to-manufacture product design carried out mainly by the product design department

♦ Education and training to support the above activities

TPM can be successful in achieving significant results only with universal co-operation among all constituents involved with the six activities listed above. Once a decision has been made to initiate TPM, company and factory leadership should promote all six of these activities despite excuses that may come from various quarters.

7.7 The Quality Management Principles

With growing global competition, quality management is becoming increasingly important to the leadership and management of all organisations. The standard of Quality Management Principles is another contemporary approach to the management of quality.

 It can be defined as 'a comprehensive and fundamental rule or belief, for leading and operating an organisation, aimed at continually improving performance over the long term by focusing on customers while addressing the needs of all stakeholders'.

This standard was developed by using the ISO TC176 on Quality Management and Quality Assurance consensus process (Source document: ISO TC176/SC2/WG15/N131, Quality Management Principles and Guidelines on their Application, May 29, 1997). It provides a clear statement of the eight Quality Management Principles and places them in a business environment/framework. It also provides executive management with an understanding of the benefits for their organisation when using the Quality Management Principles.

 By applying the following eight Quality Management Principles, organisations will produce benefits for customers, owners, suppliers and society at large.

(i)   **Customer-focused organisation** - organisations depend on their customers and therefore should understand current and future customer needs, meet customer requirements, and strive to exceed customer expectations.

Customer satisfaction is the result of the number of positive and negative factors which are experienced by the customer. The more satisfier factors present, the higher customer satisfaction. Eliminating dissatisfiers alone (by improving processes) will not result in increased satisfaction level. It will only result in fewer dissatisfiers. A 'delighter' factor is very positive to the customer when experienced, but not expected. For continued survival, the attention and commitment of very few dissatisfiers and more satisfiers and delighters than the competitors is necessary for achieving business success. A customer-driven organisation is directed towards the marketplace, as shown in the following diagram:

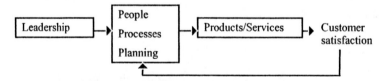

(ii)   **Leadership** - leaders establish unity of purpose and direction of an organisation. They should create and maintain the internal environment in which people can become fully involved in achieving the organisation's objectives. The stronger culture/values towards the market place, the less need for policy, instructions, organisational charts, etc. Leaders empower and involve people to achieve the organisation's objectives.

(iii) **Involvement of people** - people at all levels are the essence of an organisation and their full involvement enables their abilities to be used for the organisation's benefit. Proactive people will actively seek opportunities and make things happen; they will be innovative and creative in furthering the organisation's objectives. It is beneficial for the organisation when people are satisfied with their job and are actively involved in their personal growth and development. Quality happens through people, not by the system itself. Satisfied customers are created by people, not by the product itself.

(iv)   **Process approach** - leads to better use of resources, shorter cycle times and lower costs. Processes should be managed to meet the requirements and needs of both internal and external customers.

(v)   **System approach to management** - identifying, understanding, and managing a system of interrelated processes for a given objective improves the organisation's effectiveness and efficiency. Work Flows is a tool which illustrates the interdependencies among the processes.

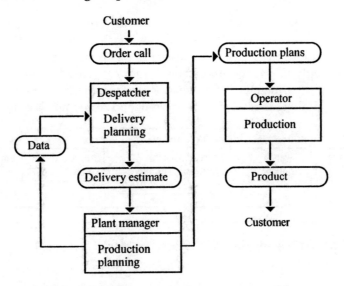

(vi)   **Continual improvement** - continual improvement should be a permanent objective of the organisation aiming for ever-higher process effectiveness and efficiency. These activities often require new values and behaviour focusing on measuring and reviewing performance and acting on results. The Plan-Do-Check-Act cycle of Dr Deming is commonly used when describing continual quality improvement. Essentially the cycle goes through the following stages:

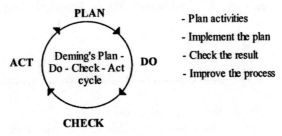

The cycle was first developed by Dr Walter A Shewhart, and later introduced by Dr Edward Deming in Japan.

The ISO 9004 Quality Improvement standard describes the methodology in 8 steps:

1   Involving the whole organisation
2   Initiating quality improvement projects or activities
3   Investigating possible causes
4   Establishing cause-and-effect relationships
5   Taking preventive or corrective actions
6   Confirming the improvement
7   Sustaining the gains
8   Continuing the improvement

Tools and techniques for quality improvements are Brain-storming, Affinity diagram, Benchmarking, Cause-and-effect diagram, Flowchart, Control chart, Histogram, Pareto diagram, Scatter diagram, etc.

(vii)   **Factual approach to decision making** - effective decisions and actions are based on the analysis of data and information. Management by fact is one of many management concepts to teach managers to prevent management by opinion. The analysis of relevant data allows informed decisions to be made and significantly reduces the risk of decisions based on opinion. Performance and data are often viewed as just numbers. However, performance can be improved by using data. Decisions and actions should be based on the analysis of data and information to improve results.

(viii)   **Mutually beneficial supplier relationships** - an organisation and its suppliers are independent, and a mutually beneficial relationship enhances the ability to create value.   Continuous feedback on customer needs and requirements will ensure continuous supply of quality products and services. Based on mutual trust and open communication, partnerships for quality are established with selected primary suppliers for jointly understanding the current and future needs of the end-customers.

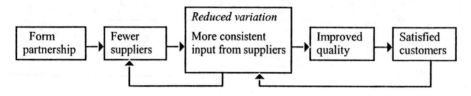

Practice question 5 *(The answer is in the final chapter of this book)*

Quality assurance

As senior product management accountant you have been informed by the MD that 'something drastic has to be done about quality'. In his view, quality is the responsibility of your department and he has suggested that you take a tougher line with those responsible for quality problems, raise quality standards, increase inspection rates, and give greater authority to quality control inspectors.

Some of the senior members in your department have expressed their anxiety and need to know where they stand.

Required

Write a memo to the senior staff who are worried:

(a)   evaluating the suggestions made by the MD;
(b)   stating what additional or alternative proposals you would offer.

7.8   Learning outcomes

You have now covered the final learning outcomes for this syllabus.

Evaluate the features, benefits and drawbacks of contemporary approaches to the management of quality.

Produce and communicate a plan for the implementation of a quality improvement programme.

8   Summary

Quality is a vital issue in modern approaches to strategic management. Although significant costs are associated with improving quality, the costs of not doing so may be even heavier. This is sometimes summarised in the phrase 'Quality is free', in the sense that financial benefits outweigh financial costs.

For many years the main approach to quality, at least in the UK, has been quality appraisal - sometimes referred to as *'inspecting* quality into the product'. By contrast, modern approaches emphasise quality assurance: *'designing* quality into the product'.

CHAPTER 16

Solutions to practice questions

Chapter 1

1 Project

Examples of projects include:

- arranging a dinner party
- organising a holiday
- hosting a conference
- designing and producing a brochure for publicity
- building an extension to a house
- modernising a factory
- designing and implementing a computer system
- re-building a city after a tornado

2 Project lifecycle

- **Identify the need** - you have been working hard and feel a holiday will make you feel better. A friend has suggested visiting a place that is very interesting archeologically.

- **Develop a proposed solution** - pick up brochures from the travel agents, look on Teletext and sites on the Internet to find a suitable venue. Check that the prices, times, modes of travel, health and political restrictions are all favourable. Buy a travel guide and note the places of interest. Check that the holiday chosen fulfils all the objectives and then book it at the best price available. Start planning the other aspects of the holiday - the clothes, passport, excursions and luggage.

- **Project performance** (including the monitoring and control) - go on holiday and, whilst enjoying yourself, make sure that the travel arrangements and accommodation are as expected and all the planned trips can be achieved within budget.

- **Project closure** - return home, evaluate and appraise the holiday and get back to work to pay for the next trip.

3 Project objectives

A project is an undertaking to accomplish a specific objective or goal, through a unique set of inter-related tasks and activities, whilst utilising resources effectively. The project objective is the anticipated result or final outcome.

The project objective is to be completed to the customer's satisfaction and quality expectations. It is usually defined in terms of scope, timescales and cost.

Examples of projects and project objectives could include:

- Re-organising a factory layout with the objective of improving productivity

- Going on holiday to Tanzania with the objective of climbing Kilimanjaro

- Organising a dinner party with the objective of getting some friends together and having a good time

4   Project feasibility

(a)   Project feasibility is a term used to describe how achievable various project options are. The feasibility is normally established using a feasibility study, which may be carried out on a number of potential strategies. It will determine whether the project outcome will achieve some form of advantage, either in terms of cost reduction or competitive advantage, for the organisation.

(b)   The feasibility of the project can be assessed from four different perspectives.

- ◆   Technical feasibility
- ◆   Economic feasibility
- ◆   Social feasibility
- ◆   Ecological feasibility

Technical feasibility is the matching of the project requirements to the performance that can be achieved from currently available technology, materials and processes. For example the technical feasibility will be assessed in terms of how easily the resources can be upgraded and whether the organisation currently employs staff that are sufficiently technically qualified or experienced to deal with the new system.

Technically the project is feasible if the employees have the expertise and the project can meet the new requirements envisaged by the customer.

Economic feasibility is the consideration of the various costs that will be incurred in the development and implementation of the new project, together with an assessment of the on-going running costs of its development. It will also consider the various financial and non-financial benefits that the new project should provide once all of these costs and benefits have been established. They will be included within a full-scale cost/benefit analysis exercise - utilising the various project appraisal techniques of:

- ◆   cashflow analysis
- ◆   payback
- ◆   return on investment
- ◆   discounted cashflow
- ◆   net present value.

Social feasibility - concerns assessing the impact of the new project on the organisation image, and on individuals both inside and outside the organisation. If a solution makes technical sense but conflicts with the way the organisation does business, the solution is not feasible. A project may be rejected because it forces a change in management responsibilities and chains of command or because the costs of redundancies, retraining and reorganisation are considered too high.

Ecological feasibility - concerns the effects on the environment and on the health and safety of the people involved. When considering the raw material input, the processes and the disposal of waste products at the end of the project or lifecycle, an organisation must take into account the environmental considerations.

5 **Feasibility report**

(a) The main sections to be included in a feasibility report will include the following.

- Introduction and objective - what the report sets out to achieve.

- Terms of reference - the areas to be considered and the limits within which the report has been prepared.

- Review of the existing system - brief details of the way in which the current system operates, together with details of the limitations in the current system.

- System requirements - a statement of the requirements of the new system and how the system will work in conjunction with other systems within the company.

- Proposed system - details of the proposed system, its functions and component parts.

- Alternatives considered - the nature and extent of other systems that were considered before the recommended solution was put forward.

- Costs and benefits - a summary of the key costs and benefits of the proposed system.

- Development plan - proposals for how the system is to be developed.

- Staff and training requirements - details of the changes in staff requirements and any resultant training needs that will be identified as a result of the new system.

- Implementation timetable - the way in which the system is to be implemented, addressing issues such as file conversion, system installation, testing and changeover procedures.

- Conclusions - a recommendation to proceed or otherwise with the proposed system.

- Appendices - to include detailed calculation of the project appraisal techniques utilised in the assessment of the costs and benefits of the proposed system. Also include any items where full details have not been given in the main body of the report, eg system flowcharts, etc.

(b) The assessment of system costs can be considered under the following headings.

- Development costs
- Operating costs

Development costs will include the measuring costs of the existing system and the cost of estimating the proposed system.

- Systems design and development

  A cost on a full cost basis from the start of the feasibility study until the system is handed over for maintenance. This heading includes all programming and testing.

- Installation costs

  Preparation costs of the site, delivery charges and other costs arising from any new equipment or computers required.

- Capital costs

  Computers and equipment required for the application.

- Launching costs. These include staff training, file conversions, systems testing and parallel running or other changeover costs.

♦ Policy costs

Unrecovered costs of incremental capacity increases.

♦ Cost benefits

Value of equipment no longer required.

Operating costs are the marginal cost of current operations that would be displaced by the proposal.

♦ Staff costs
♦ Supplies – stationery, etc
♦ Outside services
♦ Space costs
♦ Other

The marginal costs of operations under the envisaged system include the following items.

♦ Computer costs
♦ Staff costs
♦ Supplies – stationery, etc
♦ System maintenance
♦ Other

Chapter 2

1 Steering committee

(a) Management requires as much detailed information as possible to make the correct decision. A computer manufacturer or a management consultant is often asked to carry out a feasibility study, but neither is likely to be familiar with the structure and working of the company.

Therefore a team (the steering committee) composed of people from within the company and those with computer experience could perform the feasibility study and produce a report for senior management. Generally, this is a standing committee, whose membership reflects the project being dealt with. For this type of project, the members are likely to comprise:

(i) the director of finance (or perhaps the deputy chief executive) as chairperson;

(ii) the director of management services;

(iii) the head of the IT department;

(iv) the chief analyst;

(v) the chief programmer;

(vi) the management representatives of the user department(s);

(vii) external consultants (if utilised).

Membership is bound to vary in accordance with the kind of project involved. Some members may only attend meetings relevant to their specialist areas, eg the chief programmer may only attend meetings where programming aspects will be considered. The project leader will also attend to report progress.

(b) The committee's terms of reference usually incorporate:

(i) granting (or refusing to grant) approval for a given project, approving its budget and according priorities;

(ii) making recommendations concerning projects to the board of directors (or the most senior body in the private or public sector organisation);

(iii) granting permission for the next stage in the project to be undertaken;

(iv) monitoring and controlling projects;

(v) reporting project progress to the board, or other body.

The steering committee issues the assignment (project) brief which authorises the feasibility study, culminating in the feasibility report.

2 Project manager

Six illustrative responsibilities are:

Agree the terms of reference of the project

Every project should start with Terms of Reference describing the objectives, scope, constraints, resources and project sponsor or client. It is the responsibility of the project manager to compile and agree these Terms of Reference. In particular he or she must be confident that the project can meet its objectives within the time agreed (a constraint) with the resources available. The Terms of Reference may be expanded into a Project Quality Plan, which will describe such issues as quality procedures, standards and a risk assessment. Producing the Project Quality Plan will also be the project manager's responsibility.

Plan the project

The agreed project will have to be broken down into lower level tasks and activities, each of which will be given a time estimate. A precedence (which tasks must be completed before others can start) will also be agreed. The project task breakdown, hierarchy of tasks, and task estimates will form the basis of the project plan. This will allow the project manager to determine the critical path and hence the elapsed time of the project. The project manager will also be able to see more clearly the resource requirements of the project. The project manager usually has the responsibility to produce and interpret the project plan, often using a computerised tool.

Monitor the project

During the project the project manager must ensure that the overall project remains on target. Hence he or she will monitor the progress of tasks and record their completion on the project plan. Some of these tasks will over-run their original estimates and the consequences of this have to be carefully monitored and managed. The project will also be affected by new user requirements, staff illness and holidays and other external factors that cannot be predicted at the start of the project. The project manager has to reflect all these in the project plan and produce revised versions showing the effect of these changes.

Report on project progress

It is usually the responsibility of the project manager to report project progress both upwards (to the project sponsor or client) and downwards (to the rest of the project team). Progress reports usually specify what tasks have been completed in the last period, what tasks have been started but not completed (with perhaps an estimate to completion) and what tasks are scheduled to start in the next period. Reports should also highlight problems and changes, showing the effect of these on the project plan and suggesting a course of action. The project sponsor can then decide whether such changes are implemented in the project or left until a later phase of the development. Project reports may also contain important cost and time information showing the overall cost of the project to date.

Undertake post-project reviews

A post-project review usually takes place at the end of the project and it will be the responsibility of the project manager to organise and chair this review and report on its conclusions and recommendations. The post-project reviews will consider both the products of the project (such as the robustness of the software, the satisfaction of users, etc) and the organisation of the project itself. It may review the estimates of project cost and duration and compare these with actual costs and duration. Large variances will be discussed and analysed and any lessons learnt recorded and fed back into the project management method.

Motivate the project team

Most projects are undertaken by a multi-disciplinary team brought together for the purpose of undertaking the project. Once the project is complete the team will probably be disbanded. During the project it is the responsibility of the project manager to motivate team members so that the tasks they are assigned are completed on time and to the required quality. Project managers have direct influence over the work that is assigned to the team members, the amount of responsibility individual team members are given and the recognition they are accorded on completion of their work. How the project manager goes about these management tasks will critically affect the morale and motivation of the team members.

3   Project management

Project management differs from functional management in that it is the management of resources which are attempting to achieve specific objectives within set timescales and budgets. Functional management, on the other hand, is concerned with providing an on-going service.

A project has boundaries and it is one of the activities of the project management team to set and keep the project within those boundaries.

A project will be initiated to develop or try something new, and accurate costs are therefore difficult to estimate. It is also difficult to estimate benefits or eventual outcome and projects must therefore be carefully controlled and monitored.

The project management team would need, first of all, to identify the standards for:

(i)   the organisation of the project, including any user involvement;

(ii)   estimating, resourcing and scheduling the project including drawing up a project plan;

(iii)   quality control;

(iv)   the activities performed and their assessments;

(v)   the end product produced or developed.

Each project will be different, but it is still necessary to identify suitable technical standards relating to what is being developed.

The development of a computerised administrative system is used to illustrate an approach to project management. The stages are as detailed below.

Organisation

Creating a project board who will be responsible for the project and who will have authority over it. The board will be responsible for:

(i)   approving plans;
(ii)   monitoring progress;
(iii)   allocating resources;
(iv)   assessing results; and
(v)   recommending continuance or termination.

A project manager will be in charge of the project itself and he will report back to the project board.

The project manager is responsible for:

(i)   defining individual responsibilities;
(ii)   preparing state or phase plans;
(iii)   setting objectives;
(iv)   collating information from project teams;
(v)   controlling team activities; and
(vi)   reporting to the project board.

The project manager would have a number of project teams with team leaders reporting back to him.

Planning

At the beginning of a project outline technical plans will be needed to identify the major technical activities. When the technical plans have been produced, identification of required resources can then take place. These resources include 'expert' staff, who may be required at particular times or for particular activities.

The project itself will be broken down into a number of stages, with each stage being monitored and then assessed at its completion. In this way identification of deviances from the expected plan can be fully analysed.

Controls

At the end of each stage the project manager will report to the project board, and they will compare the actual achievements against the expected achievements.

These comparisons will allow the project board to estimate the likelihood of the project being successful, completed within the specified timescale, and completed within the specified budget.

Activities/end products

The activities of the project should result in the end project being quality assured, as each activity is fully monitored throughout.

A quality assurance test would be performed before each stage or before the final project was deemed to be completed.

Review

At the completion of the project the management of that project would be reviewed. Although no two projects are the same, experience gained throughout the course of the project should be fully assessed and documented in order that similar types of projects may benefit in future.

4   Project processes

The conditions that are necessary to manage a successful information system project include:

Well defined objectives - The overall aims of the project are well defined, have been agreed by all who have an interest in them and have been tested throughout the relevant parts of the organisation.

Proper resourcing - There has been a proper analysis of the resources required to make the project a success. Resources include money, personnel, equipment, software, office space and other support resources. The resources have been fully discussed and full agreement to allocate the resources has been gained from those who control them.

Senior management support - Senior management have given their support to the project, do so very publicly, and their reasons for giving their support are sustainable such that the support will continue throughout the life of the system.

Application of project management techniques - All those involved with the project should be familiar with project management techniques and these should be appropriately applied to the project.

Capable project manager - There needs to be a single person who is in operational control of the project. This person should be experienced in the management of projects of the nature of the one to be carried out.

Correct balance of project team members - The project team should consist of individuals who have the necessary range of technical skills and organisational knowledge. In addition enough of the team members should have experience of projects of this nature to ensure the success of the project. Finally there needs to be a balance of personalities within the team to ensure that the team functions well as a group.

Communication strategy - There is an explicit strategy to communicate the project's:

- ◆ Objectives
- ◆ Current state of progress
- ◆ Revisions from the original plan
- ◆ Methods of integrating the various needs of different groups

This implies that there will be clear lines of communication between all concerned parties and there will be a general communications system to the wider organisation. Existing communications channels may be utilised or it may be necessary to set up communications systems specifically for the project.

Feedback channels - There should be properly established methods of gaining feedback from those that are affected by the project and whose commitment is needed to make the project a success.

Client focus - The project team need to ensure that they remain focused upon meeting the needs of the people that the project is intended to serve. This may well mean revising aspects of the project part way through.

5   Effective teamwork

(a)   Some of the characteristics of effective project teams include:

- ◆ they all understand the project objectives
- ◆ there is a clear understanding of each team member's role in the project and their individual activities and responsibilities
- ◆ there is a focus on the project results
- ◆ they have a high degree of team working and team spirit
- ◆ there is a high level of co-operation
- ◆ they share trust and commitment

(b)   The barriers to effective teamwork include:

- ◆ unclear project objectives or a lack of understanding of the objectives
- ◆ unclear definition of responsibilities and role in the project
- ◆ poor communication between team members
- ◆ lack of co-ordination
- ◆ poor project leadership
- ◆ high turnover of team members

An effective project manager, who can foster team spirit, communication and co-operation by strong leadership and delegation, can overcome many of these barriers.

Chapter 3

1 Project planning

Project planning is the arrangement of the activities required to achieve the project objective. The first part of this stage is the establishment and agreement of the project objectives. This means determining exactly what the project aims to achieve. The next stage is to determine what activities or tasks need to be undertaken to achieve the objective.

The project plan articulates exactly what needs to be achieved, how it is to be achieved, by whom and at what time in the project's life. It is a benchmark against which actual project results can be compared and monitored. If the comparison of actual versus plan indicates a deviation, then corrective action needs to be taken.

It is important that the planning stage involves the members of staff who will be working on the project. These people will be in the best position to know what activities will be needed, how they will be performed and how long they will take. In addition, by encouraging team participation in planning, it is more likely that they will become committed to achieving their activity targets.

2 Feasibility

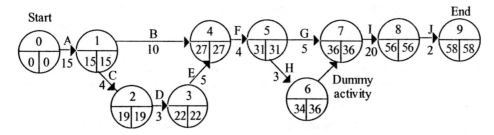

The network of the activities listed shows the overall project duration is 58 days, and that activities A, C, D, E, F, G, I and J form the critical path. Any delay in their completion is likely to extend the overall duration of the project unless measures can be taken to reduce the duration of other activities on the critical path.

The computer manager is right to feel concerned about the probability of getting the project completed smoothly and on time, for several reasons.

♦ There is already pressure because he was late starting his employment. This can easily lead to hasty decisions and increases the temptation to skimp on activities like testing.

♦ Activity B, 'modify software', is not on the critical path – there is two days' slack compared with the other path through the network (CDE) that must be completed before installation and testing of the software. However, software development or modification needs to be carefully planned and controlled and it is often difficult to monitor its real progress until some actual results are generated by it. If problems show up at this late stage then it will be difficult to correct them without significantly extending the activity and disrupting the overall project.

♦ In addition, it is not clear whether or not the four days' allocation to Activity F, 'installing and testing the software', includes any provision for fixing any problems that are shown up by the testing – and this activity is on the critical path.

♦ Since the software modification is not under the computer manager's direct control, he may not be able to allocate extra resources to the activity in order to speed it up.

♦ The critical path actually involves all but two of the activities, and one of them, 'modify software', is liable to delays. So delay in almost any activity is likely to extend the project's duration.

3   Order entry system

(a)   The network diagram is as follows.

Critical path is B, D, E.

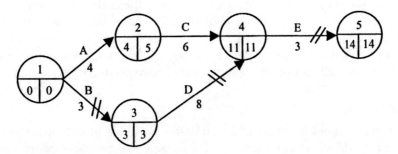

(b)   A Gantt chart is a straightforward method of scheduling tasks; it is essentially a chart on which bars represent each task or activity. The length of each bar represents the relative length of the task. Its advantages lie in its simplicity, the ready acceptance of it by users, and the fact that the bars are drawn to scale.

In this context, before a Gantt chart can be used, estimates must be made of the resources required for each of the various activities - in terms perhaps of training personnel, or equipment requirements. Once the chart is constructed, it will at once become apparent where there are shortfalls or excess of those resources.

4   Network

(a)   The network diagram is as follows.

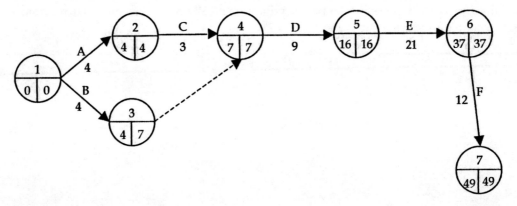

(b)   Critical path = ACDEF

Estimated project duration is 47 days. (There is float of three days on activity B).

5   Project software

Planning

Project management software can be used to enter activities, estimates, precedents and resources to automatically produce a network diagram (showing the critical path) and a Gantt chart (showing resource use). These diagrams are difficult to produce and maintain manually, and the software also allows for simple 'what if?' experiments (adding resources, changing estimates, re-setting precedents) with the objective of meeting the required delivery date. Resource profiles can be printed off as a planning tool for staff used on the project.

Estimating

Project management software allows the entry of actual data – the hours or days actually taken to complete a particular task. Many of these tasks are the same in systems development across different projects (for example, interview users, construct a logical data structure), and so a considerable amount of information can be collected about the time taken to complete common tasks. This can be used to improve future estimates. A computer may also be used to support the actual estimating model itself.

Monitoring

Project management software allows the entry of actual data, which can be used to monitor the progress of the project and to re-plan the rest of the work. During re-planning the critical path may change, and it is important to know this.

Reporting

Most project management software packages have comprehensive reporting requirements, which allow managers to print out the progress and status of the project. This means that standard progress reports can be produced automatically and so ensure that precious time is not wasted in producing such reports.

Chapter 4

1 Communication

A business organisation needs communication for a variety of reasons:

(a)   for day-to-day and periodic control;

(b)   to cope with the impact of unplanned changes in circumstances;

(c)   to permit the introduction of planned change;

(d)   because the normal working environment simply necessitates communication;

(e)   to create and maintain good staff morale.

These points give rise to a number of very important aspects of business communication.

Firstly, communication exists to convey information about what is happening both inside and outside the organisation. Secondly, explanations are needed about the nature and the implications of the current (and the forecast) problems. Thirdly, rules have to be laid down about specific situations - the 'manuals' have to be written, among other things. Fourthly, communication stimulates action. Fifthly, there cannot be relationships of any kind within a firm unless there is communication. On a more technical level, communication creates, conforms or modifies the attitudes of the members of the organisation towards the corporate identity. Lastly, communication enables collective decisions to be formed and renders them generally acceptable.

It is not merely that communication is necessary; the right kind is essential. The wrong kind (poor communication) results in lack of co-ordination, poor control and possibly eventually no control at all.

Downward communication allows subordinates to be aware of company objectives, direction, changes which could affect them directly and so on. Upward communication (this includes the all-important concept of 'feedback') gives early warning of problem areas; provides the benefit of the creative ability of subordinates; gives the opportunity of adding cohesion to the management team and co-ordination between divisions and sections; and enables real problems to be identified.

Broadly speaking, a business organisation's policies, plans, instructions and information need to be known and understood by everybody if the company's corporate plan is to be a success. Some companies regard downward communication as the only important kind. This means, however, lack of feedback. The two-way (plus lateral) communication system is best. In this connection, one may note the contemporary move towards employee participation and disclosure.

Certain rules may be laid down and one approach is to state that company communication has to be:

(a)   necessary and appropriate (to justify expenditure of time and funds on it);

(b)   relevant - the sender has to know what the message is, who for, and what the intended effect is;

(c)   complete (and accurate) - all facts which are necessary must be given;

(d)   understandable - the language must be clearly understood;

(e)   brief - unnecessary padding (as with too many communications) makes readers less liable to take the message seriously.

These are very basic rules, but they serve as guidelines and help to avoid the major errors.

2   Project meeting agenda

A typical agenda might look like this:

Project status review meeting agenda

Date and time of meeting
Details of the venue location

1	Welcome and apologies for absence
2	Minutes of the last meeting
3	Matters arising from the last meeting
4	Achievements since last meeting
5	Current status of project - scope, time and cost
6	Forecasts for scope, time and cost of project
7	Variances in scope, time and cost of project
8	Corrective action plan
9	Assignment of action plan tasks with deadlines
10	Date and time of next meeting to be agreed
11	Meeting close (expected time)

---

3   Project meeting stages

To ensure an effective project team meeting, the following steps might be taken:

♦ Start on time.

♦ Have contact memo or minutes prepared by secretary to distribute to all team members and all staff affected by the outcomes of the meeting. This forms the basis of the next meeting.

♦ Put members at their ease and focus minds on purpose of meeting.

♦ Review agenda to ensure that all relevant issues are to be addressed.

♦ The project manager's role is to ensure that all the agenda issues are addressed and that all the relevant points are discussed within the given time.

♦ The project manager should act as facilitator and encourage team members to participate.

♦ The project manager should ensure fair play - link speakers and control interruptions and side issues.

♦ All points must be clarified and recorded.

♦ Summarise at appropriate times, and at the end of the meeting the main points and action tasks need to be summarised and agreed by team members.

♦ Try to finish on time - if impossible get agreement to continue but never drift.

4   Presentations

(a)   It is often difficult to convey to an audience exactly what is meant. When giving a presentation regarding a new computer application the analyst must beware and overcome the barriers to communication, which include the following.

Preconceived ideas: Most people hear what they expect to hear, and their expectations are based upon their previous experiences.

Cognitive filters: People will hear what they want to hear, and will filter out ideas that conflict with their beliefs.

Misinterpretation: Ideas that conflict with beliefs or expectations may be interpreted in such a way to fit in with an expected view.

Mistrust: Unless the analyst gets the audience upon his side, the audience may well mistrust the information he is presenting. They may stereotype the analyst in some way and this may influence their receptiveness to his ideas.

Subjectivity: The analyst must choose his words with care as many words have a number of different meanings and this can lead the audience into misunderstanding the concepts.

Incorrect coding: Hopefully, being an analyst, the presenter would have good communication skills, but where a presenter is not very experienced, he may not be good at actually coding his thoughts.

Noise: There are all sorts of 'noise' in communication: bad accents, the use of slang and the use of technical terminology could all be construed as noise.

Physical environment: The environment in which the audience is located could become a barrier to communication if it is either too cold or too hot. If either of these is the case then the audience quickly loses concentration. The analyst should therefore attempt to vary his presentation by changing styles in order to keep the attention of the audience.

Retention: Research has shown that most people only take in approximately 10% of what they hear; it is therefore necessary for the presenter to build redundancy into his communication.

Feedback: If there is a large audience it is unlikely that the audience will participate and produce feedback for the presenter; it may be necessary to change the style of presentation in accordance with the number of people in the audience. The presenter should therefore enquire of the number of people who will be attending the presentation.

(b)   (i)   Before making a presentation, the presenter should be sure of the objectives of the presentation, and what should be achieved.

The success of a presentation can be judged in a number of ways:

♦   the attentiveness of the audience;
♦   running to time;
♦   competent answering of questions;
♦   operation and convenience of all equipment and material;
♦   achieving the objective of the presentation.

Before starting the presentation it is wise to check that all the equipment is working properly. The room should be viewed with the number of the audience in mind to ensure that seating arrangements are adequate and everyone can view the board/screen/flipchart.

It is also necessary prior to the presentation to check the adequacy of the room if such things as plug sockets are required.

If the presenter can get some idea of the type of audience he is catering for, then their interests, personal preferences, hostilities and likely reactions can be assessed.

Inexperienced presenters should take the opportunity to rehearse in front of colleagues before the actual presentation itself.

Consideration should also be given to the style of dress of the presenter. If the presentation is formal then the presenter should be suitably dressed for the occasion; if, however, the presentation is to employees on the factory floor then the presenter should consider modifying his style of dress.

The form in which the presenter's notes should be held must also be considered. Some presenters prefer cards with key words while others prefer sheets of paper. The presenter may however choose to use an overhead projector and slides on which to keep and display his key words.

(ii)   The sequence of events which might be gone through is as follows:

♦ check all equipment;

♦ greet the audience;

♦ inform the audience of the objectives and content of the presentation;

♦ give out any handouts (allowing sufficient time for the audience to read them);

♦ make the presentation;

♦ ask if the audience has any questions (this may be done at intervals throughout the presentation or it could be left to the end of the presentation);

♦ summarise at regular intervals throughout the presentation, and summarise again at the end of the presentation;

♦ thank the audience for their time.

While it is very rare that any presentation is 'mistake free', good preparation will minimise the likelihood of mistakes. If a mistake occurs it will depend upon the atmosphere at the time and the personality of the presenter as to how it is handled. Humour is often the best approach but on no account should the presenter try to ignore the mistake and pretend it did not happen.

Chapter 5

1   Data capture

(a)   *TV rental company*

Each customer is equipped with a rent book with vouchers. Each voucher has the customer's account number, branch number, and monthly rental encoded in an OCR typeface. When the customer visits the shop the voucher is torn out of the book and processed by a document reader, which encodes the data onto magnetic tape. The tape can be read off, and the data transmitted to the Head Office computer by means of a terminal link at weekly intervals. The customer's record consists of a voucher stub, which can be stamped by the branch staff.

Advantages

♦   The human effort of keying-in and verifying data is eliminated as the source document is machine-sensible.

♦   Errors at source are eliminated as the amount and key code numbers are pre-printed.

Disadvantages

♦   Customers may lose their rent books or forget to present vouchers when making payments, creating additional work in preparing source documents.

♦   The costs of specialist form design may be prohibitive if rentals are subject to regular review.

(b)   *Factory costing system*

The method of data capture is as follows. Terminals are sited at strategic points in the factory. There is a terminal with a full QWERTY keyboard and VDU in the works office.

Materials

A parts list and progress card are prepared by the works office. One part of the parts list is used to draw out materials or components, and returned to the works office who match it with its counterpart. (No entries are made through the terminal until this matching is done.)

The data keyed in by the terminal operator is as follows.

♦   Job number
♦   Product number
♦   Number of units
♦   Stages in production

As the components are assembled, they are accompanied by the progress card.

Labour

The terminals used for recording labour are badge readers, equipped with a numeric keyboard and certain control keys. Each operator has a plastic badge where the following details are encoded.

♦   Operator number
♦   Department number

As each batch of components reaches each operator, the following tasks are performed.

- The operator inserts the plastic badge and encodes the job number using the terminal keyboard.

- The task is then carried out.

- On completion the operator depresses a key to retrieve the card.

The system is linked to a real-time clock which records the start and finish times of each operator. The job number keyed in must match with the job number on the work-in-progress file.

Advantages

- The recording of material usage is integrated with stock recording, so that one operation in the works office 'sets up' the job on the work-in-progress file and records the issue of materials.

- The system for recording labour times reduces the errors associated with clerical methods.

Disadvantages

- The cost of specialised equipment may not be matched by the benefits.

- Errors by operators may result in poor quality input.

- Breakdowns (such as computer failures) may cause considerable disruption to operators.

2 OCR

(a) Optical character recognition (OCR) is a data capture technique which enables a computer to read printed or written documents directly. This eliminates the need to key in data, so saving time and reducing the likelihood of error. Until recently special fonts normally had to be used for the documents. Although these are still readable by the staff operating the system, they embody special exaggerations of shape for each of the characters to facilitate machine reading.

These special shapes make handwritten documents difficult to produce effectively, and they would probably be restricted to a very small part of the character set. More commonly, OCR systems use information pre-printed by computer, specialised typewriter or letterpress, which can be circulated for normal use by staff within a section of the information system and subsequently used to input data directly into the computer.

Modern hardware and software can recognise a wide range of printed fonts.

(b) The main advantages associated with the use of OCR are as follows.

- The ability to combine computer readable and human readable data can greatly enhance the efficiency of the system and facilitate the use of 'turnaround' documents for data capture.

- The elimination of the normal data entry routines of keying and verification saves time and reduces the scope for error.

- The reading equipment can be easily operated by relatively unskilled staff and reading and rejection rates compare favourably with other forms of input.

Relevant areas for the application of OCR are those that feature documents containing a large amount of data which is fixed at the start of a transaction, together with a small amount of extra data which is added as the transaction proceeds. OCR can be used to input the fixed portion of the data.

Two possible examples are the tickets used in a periodic physical stocktake to record quantities of items in stock or quantities and conditions of work-in-progress, and job control documents. In the case of the stocktake the background information relating to the stock items can be pre-printed in OCR font and quantities and other stocktake data added by hand. If only numerical digits are needed it may be possible to do this in a form which the computer can read directly. Similarly, job control forms can contain the job identification data in OCR font and be completed with details of actual time taken, actual quantities of materials used, etc by the employee involved.

In both these examples processing time should be saved and the scope for error reduced by the direct input of at least part of the data used by the system.

3   Applications

(a)   Most small businesses make use of microcomputers and application packages to support their administrative requirements. The most popular of these packages are spreadsheets, databases and word processing packages.

A *spreadsheet* is an array of rows and columns forming a grid of 'cells'. Spreadsheets are normally used to create a model of a business situation (eg a cashflow forecast) by defining formulaic relationships between the variables concerned. The user can then perform 'what if?' analyses on the variable data, eg by asking 'what if we increase our selling prices by 5 per cent?'. The popular uses are cashflow forecasts, breakeven analyses and profit forecasts.

Formula fields are entered into the spreadsheet, thus making calculations automatic. When the variable data is altered the automatic calculations are performed throughout the spreadsheet model. This enables managers to view the effect of price or product increases over a lengthy period of time. The spreadsheet is known to be one of the major tools of decision support systems.

A *database* is a collection of data. This could refer to a manual collection of data, such as an address book or card index file. Nowadays, however, the term invariably refers to the computerisation and computer storage of data.

A database package should more accurately be referred to as a *database management system* (DBMS). It is a suite of programs that allow for the manipulation, storage, processing and sorting of data.

Data should be stored independently of the applications that use it; this feature is referred to as 'data independence'. However, a definition of their relationships with other data items needs to be held.

Word processing packages allow for the input, storage, manipulation, editing, formatting and printing of text. The word processing package is one of the most popular packages in use within the business environment.

Letters and reports can be stored on disk, retrieved, edited and printed, before again being stored, in their new format, on disk. This allows for a number of standard letters, reports, documents etc, to be stored ready for use.

(b)   An integrated package consists of a number of modules, which either act independently or can be 'integrated' together, to perform joint functions. Examples of integrated packages include the following.

  ♦ Microsoft Office
  ♦ Lotus SmartSuite
  ♦ Corel WordPerfect Office
  ♦ Ability Office
  ♦ Star Office
  ♦ Appleworks
  ♦ Microsoft Works

The advantages of an integrated package include the following.

  ♦ One set of instructions for the user to learn. For example, all the modules would use the 'F' keys (function keys) in the same way.

  ♦ Mailmerge between database files and word processing files is made easier. Spreadsheets or parts of spreadsheets can be incorporated into word processing files.

  ♦ Cheaper to buy, because one package only is being bought instead of a number of specific packages.

  ♦ Less program storage required, also less data storage required.

  ♦ Faster processing of data because there is no need to convert data to ASCII in order to transfer it from one package to another.

  ♦ More resilient as there are no interface problems to be overcome.

The possible disadvantages of an integrated package are as follows.

  ♦ Each module might not have available all the facilities that could be found in a dedicated package. Compromise may be necessary.

  ♦ Dedicated packages are more likely to be updated at a faster rate than integrated packages.

(c)   There are many different application packages on the market and this presents a difficulty for anyone wishing to purchase an application package. Unless the user is aware of his detailed requirements he may end up purchasing a package that is either too sophisticated for his use, or one that is inadequate for his use. In order to purchase a software package a user must be fully aware of its intended use. Also the user must be aware of the capacity of the machine on which the software package will run. Some of the main factors to be taken into account in the purchase of a software package are as follows.

  ♦ How user friendly is it? Is it menu driven or command driven?

  ♦ How much RAM is required in order to run the package?

  ♦ How much does it cost? Is the value of the software to the company greater than its cost?

  ♦ How secure is the package? Does it have password facilities in order to prevent unauthorised use?

  ♦ Is it able to run on a variety of different machines?

  ♦ What are its additional features that make it different from other packages?

♦ How often is it upgraded? Will the upgraded version always be compatible with all earlier versions?

♦ Is there any maintenance or service cover provided?

♦ How reputable is the dealer?

♦ How reputable is the manufacturer of the software?

4   Software options

(a)   Advantages of a software package solution include the following.

♦ Early delivery. The package is ready to use. With a bespoke system, there is a delay while the system is designed, written and tested.

♦ Proven product. The package is a tested proven product. Earlier users have found the bugs and the problems. Bespoke systems are usually affected by program errors in their first few months of operation.

♦ Cheaper price. The package has been developed on the principle that its development cost will be recouped over a number of sales achieved over time. With a bespoke solution, the complete cost falls upon the commissioning company and so it is unlikely to be as cheap.

♦ Quality documentation. Packages are usually accompanied by high quality documentation and training. This documentation can be assessed before the product is purchased.

(b)   Problems with package solutions

♦ The cost of fulfilling all the local requirements may be very costly and may therefore reduce the cost advantage of buying a packaged solution. The advantage of early delivery may also be lost.

♦ The software house will have to ensure that future upgrades take into account the tailored requirements. Failure to do so may lead to unpredictable side effects. Recognition of the need to take into account such requirements may also be reflected in higher maintenance charges.

(c)   Advantages of a bespoke solution include the following.

♦ Complete fulfilment of the company's requirements. The software will fulfil all the needs listed in the requirements specification.

♦ Ownership of the software. The software belongs to the organisation.

♦ Changes to requirements can be accommodated. The future direction of the company may be unpredictable. It may develop into areas not supported by enhancements to the software package.

♦ Competitive edge. All the companies that use a particular software package are unlikely to have any information systems competitive edge. Organisations that choose a bespoke solution may be able to offer a service that few of their competitors can match.

5   Categories of software

(a)   The major categories of software which may be used with microcomputers are as follows.

♦   Operating systems. Every computer must have an operating system working all the time the computer is in use. An operating system is a program or set of programs which provide a 'bridge' between applications software and the computer hardware – in fact, it is the operating system which makes the computer work as we expect a computer to work.

There are a number of operating systems available for microcomputers. The one used on most personal computers is Microsoft Windows but other systems providing other features or more stability are becoming more popular.

♦   Applications software. Applications packages are ready-made programs designed to carry out particular tasks eg stock accounting, payroll, project planning. Nowadays there is a tendency to include general purpose software such as word processors, spreadsheets and database programs under the heading of applications packages.

♦   Utilities programs. Utilities programs are often included with the other computer operating system program(s). Utilities are generally 'tool-box' type programs providing facilities which may be used by a number of other programs or in a number of circumstances, eg a file sorting utility, a file copying utility or a disk formatting program.

(b)   The criteria which would be applied and factors considered when selecting microcomputer software for a large organisation's administrative tasks are as follows.

♦   Functionality. A check must be made that the software provides all of the functions and features to satisfy the system's requirements. If it does not conform exactly, then the choice is to accept the software as it is, choose different software, or modify the organisation's working practices or the software.

♦   Flexibility. Does the software, in the main, satisfy the requirements of different users to whom it will be made available? Does the software cater for the needs and way of working of both experienced and inexperienced users?

♦   Maintainability. It should be checked that the software is written in such a way that modifications can be made, not necessarily by the user or purchaser, if errors are found or changes are needed by amendments to legislation or the computer operating system.

In some cases the supplier may be able to modify (or have modified) the software to accommodate user requirements.

♦   Supplier support and viability. Are the supplier and the producer of the software likely to remain in business during the life of the software in the organisation? Will the supplier supply upgrades or enhancements to the software as these become available or necessary? Will the supplier provide training courses for organisation staff? Is the support local to the organisation?

♦   Ease of use. A check should be made that the software is not difficult to use by the type of users to which the software will be made available. Some software is regarded as being 'intuitive', ie it is generally obvious without resorting to manuals what the user must do and what facilities the user can draw upon. However, a check must be made that the documentation provided with the software is comprehensive and easy to understand.

Some software provides 'in-built' help facilities and these should also be checked.

♦ Portability. Once an organisation has taken on a piece of software for general use there will be a large investment in both the software and user training. Software which can be used on a number of different computers, ie is portable, is an attractive proposition. However, suppliers' claims of complete portability between machines and operating systems should be carefully checked and proved.

♦ Availability of a site licence. Software which must be bought as individually numbered packages is difficult for a large organisation to manage. It would be preferable for the organisation to buy one copy which is then customised for the organisation (eg the name of the organisation is made to appear as the software owner on the opening title screen), and then the package is copied and used everywhere within the organisation.

With a site licence, the organisation is allowed to make more copies of the software if copies are corrupted or deleted by users.

♦ Market share. Software which has a large market share in the total market for commonly used microcomputer software may be more attractive because it should be less expensive, and it should be error free, well tested and flexible.

♦ User groups. User groups exist for certain software packages as well as for hardware. These groups are useful both for the mutual support between members and for the pressure they can bring in order to have errors corrected and enhancements made. It would be useful to know if a user group exists for a package and if so, for the organisation to join it, perhaps in the person of a representative of the main user department.

6 Local area network

The term 'local area network' is used to describe any collection of computer devices such as computers, word processors, printers, facsimile machines and workstations which are connected together in close geographical proximity.

LANs are an important development in information technology because they gather various types of technique such as data transmission, word processing and computing. A typical LAN may cover a factory, a warehouse, an office complex or an educational establishment such as a college. Devices are connected by plugging them into the system in the same way as an electrical appliance in the home can be plugged into the ring main circuit. LANs are high-speed transmission devices with speeds quoted at over 10 million bits per second. They use the concept of formatting data into 'packets', which are then circulated through the network. There are various forms of LAN structure.

Ring structure

The 'ring' can be depicted diagrammatically as follows:

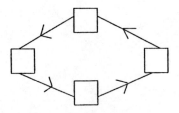

The ring consists of a cable connected in a continuous loop. Messages are 'packeted' and passed along the loop. Each packet has a unique code or protocol which enables the receiving device to obtain the message.

Bus structure

The 'bus' structure is illustrated diagrammatically as follows:

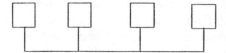

A message can be transmitted by any device. The unique protocol attached to the message enables devices to identify messages related to them.

Star structure

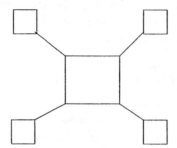

A star structure LAN has a major device, such as a microcomputer, which controls the process and passes messages to and from the various points of the star.

Various manufacturers have attempted to develop standard communications systems for particular types of equipment, in the absence of an all-embracing industry standard. Such systems are marketed under various proprietary names such as Ethernet (Xerox Corporation), and IBM's Token Ring.

Chapter 6

1   Entropy

Entropy means the tendency for a system to become more and more disorganised over a period of time. Closed business systems can become increasingly disorganised over time, since by their very nature they fail to take into account relevant information from the environment. An open business system overcomes this condition, by receiving inputs from the outside environment to take into account new information and conditions. In this way the system can become even more organised, displaying 'negative entropy'.

2   Deterministic or probabilistic

(a)	A hamburger bar	Probabilistic
(b)	A computer program	Deterministic
(c)	A sewing machine in perfect working order	Deterministic
(d)	An old car, not in perfect working order	Probabilistic
(e)	A bank clerk	Probabilistic

3   Semi-closed or open

(a)	A bank dispenser	Semi-closed
(b)	A space vehicle under ground control	Open
(c)	A 'fruit' machine	Semi-closed

4   Systems concept

Coupling refers to linkage between subsystems. Highly coupled subsystems are closely linked, so that problems or delays in one subsystem will lead to difficulties with the next. For example, a failure to deliver raw materials of a product will lead to production disruption. Decoupling means relaxing the link between the two subsystems so that they can work independently.

The principle of coupling and decoupling can be used in the design of a production system. One of the subsystems may be concerned with the production of components which are subsequently used by another subsystem in the assembly of a final product. If the system is highly coupled then assembly can be disrupted by problems in production. The subsystems can be decoupled by the production system producing stock, which is subsequently used by the assembly subsystem. Stock or inventory control is essentially a mechanism for decoupling processes.

5   Theory of information systems

(a)   A *deterministic system* operates according to a predetermined set of rules. Its future behaviour can therefore be predicted if its present state and operating characteristics are accurately known. A computer program is a deterministic system, but business systems are not deterministic because they interface with a number of indeterminate factors. A *probabilistic* system is governed by chance events and its future behaviour is a matter of probability rather than certainty. Business systems are probabilistic; information systems are deterministic in the sense that given inputs result in known type and content of information.

(b)   A *closed system* is one that does not interact with its environment, ie it has no input or output. It is completely self-contained and can continue in a state of equilibrium throughout its existence. This concept is more relevant to scientific systems; examples in the business context are rare. An *open system* does interact with its environment; this interaction may be in the transfer (to or from) of materials or information. Most business systems are open systems, and the ability of a business system to adapt to an ever-changing environment is a significant factor in its success. Obvious examples are sales, purchases, stock control, etc.

(c)   *Dynamic equilibrium* is a steady state condition in which the system readily adapts to environmental factors by reorganising itself. In a manufacturing company, this might be material purchase and product manufacture or marketing. *Entropy* is a measure of disorganisation; open systems tend to increase their entropy unless they receive 'negative entropy' in the form of information from their environment, eg increased material costs.

6   Open loop and closed loop

(a)   *Open loop control system*

An open loop control system is one which has interfaces with its environment and is able to adapt its behaviour to accommodate changes in this environment. The changes which are discerned act as triggers for feedback control which in turn acts on the processes of the system and changes the output(s). This is illustrated in the following diagram.

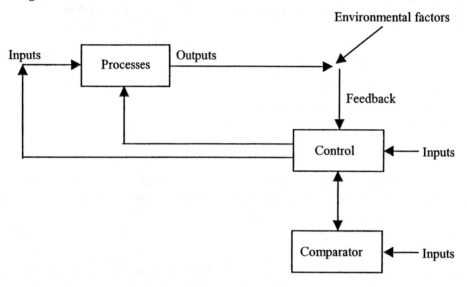

Closed loop control system

A closed loop control system is one which has no direct interaction with its environment for control purposes, although environmental interaction may be facilitated through the feedback loop comparator.

Closed loop control systems are generally mechanistic in nature such as the thermostatic control on a central heating water boiler or the speed governor on an engine. In the case of the boiler, the control is only concerned with maintaining the water temperature at a particular value. However, the house temperature affects another thermostat, which causes hot water to be drawn from the boiler and cold water to be returned, which in turn affects the boiler thermostat. An example is shown in the diagram

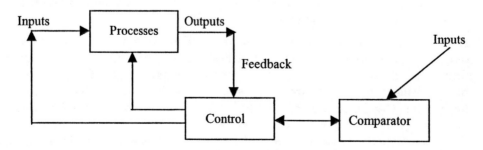

(b)   For a manufacturing company, the total organisation must be able to interact with the environment: for example, the production must be geared to market demand which is affected by the market forces of supply and demand, legislation, fashion, changing technology, competition, interest rates, etc. In addition they must react to information from or about their customers with regard to credit worthiness and debt.

In the short to medium term, the company needs to determine the demand for particular products and what are the trends in demand. These short to medium-term considerations will influence the manufacture of products, the amount of labour and materials required and the cashflow needed to support this.

The information fed back to the company will relate to its own product sales in particular areas and markets, etc plus information about the sales of products from its competitors.

In the longer term, the company will need information to enable it to assess the future demand pattern. This information will affect long-term planning on capital investment, recruitment, training, research and development, etc. This information, along with estimates of the future economic state and potential legislation, can only come from outside the organisation; thus the company will need to have an open loop control system responding to and anticipating demand.

A mechanised manufacturing unit within the company may be able to exist as a closed loop control system. Certain performance criteria will be set for it in terms of product output, labour and materials input, and the unit will then attempt to control its working to keep close to these targets. The working which must be controlled will relate to production rates, the proportion of rejected products, the number of stoppages of production, etc.

A closed loop is suitable for this area of control because complete knowledge of output requirements is available at all times and the unit can function mechanistically. Environmental interaction is brought about by adjustment of the comparator; that is, by changing the required production rates, level of quality etc but it is likely that this will only be done occasionally when compared with the production cycle.

7   Feedback

(a)   Feedback is when the system output is sampled, measured and fed back to the input with subsequent modification, if necessary, to the output. The type and amount of feedback is important to system stability and equilibrium. The process by which a system is regulated is called *negative feedback*; without negative feedback, a system would become increasingly disorganised. For example, in an accounting system debts would increase and more bad debts would be incurred. *Positive feedback* is where the control signal tends to increase the difference between output and standard (eg an increase in bad debts as more customers are permitted to exceed their credit limit).

(b)   Feedback control in a basic accounting system

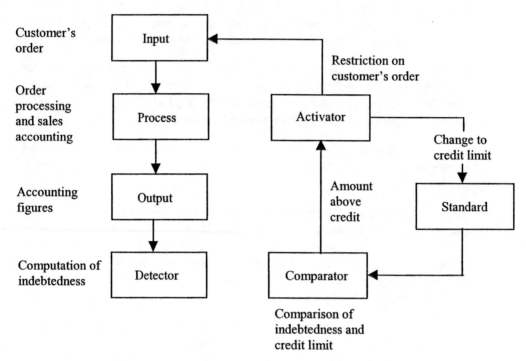

8   **Negative and positive**

(a)   A system is established to achieve defined objectives, for example a stores system has to maintain a minimum stock level. These objectives define the *standard* which the system is aiming for.

Each system attempts to reach these defined objectives by a *process* of some kind that takes in inputs and turns them into outputs. The values of the outputs are measured by a *sensor*, which passes this information to a *comparator* that evaluates the values of the system against the *standard* required. If the values do not conform to the standards required then the inputs of the system are changed by an *effector*. This alters the input so that the process can produce outputs of the required value.

These terms are illustrated below in the context of a stock control system.

Standard	Target stock value
Input	Order goods
Process	Purchase order system
Output	Stock level
Sensor	Daily stock level report
Comparator	Purchasing manager
Effector	Purchasing clerk

In a controlled system there is a feedback loop that monitors the outputs of the process and, if the output does not meet the standard, changes the input values to allow the process to produce the outputs required. This is an example of negative feedback: the system has recognised that it will not meet its targets and so has applied changes to allow it to meet its original objectives.

In the stock level maintenance system all goods below the re-order stock value will be reported on the daily stock level report. Re-ordering is authorised by the purchasing manager and actioned by the purchasing clerk. The received goods will bring the system back to its desired standard.

(b)   *Positive feedback* will take place when there is a poorly constructed feedback loop which modifies the inputs to a system so that its performance deviates even further from its required standard.

The fault could be anywhere in the feedback loop. For example:

♦ The sensor may measure the wrong output. The output selected to monitor performance may be inappropriate.

♦ The standard set for the system may be inappropriate. For example, the target set for sales in an organisation may be too low and so exceeding sales targets may lead to a reduction in inputs (reduce marketing spend, sales commissions) because the targets have been met, so losing opportunities for further growth.

♦ The performance of the effector may be misunderstood so that it does not have the required effect on the process. For example, many projects are monitored against a required project plan. Failure to be on schedule leads to organisations adding extra resources and staff to the project in the hope that this will bring the project back on time. However, there is considerable evidence to suggest that adding resources to certain types of project (such as software development projects) and at certain stages in the project lifecycle actually leads to additional project delays and so the project slips further behind schedule.

Chapter 7

1   Data versus information

(a)   Strategic, tactical and operational

(b)   'Data' is the noun used to describe the raw material of a management information system, namely the masses of facts and figures before they have been collated, edited, summarised or organised in any way. The end product of any such process is known as 'information'. Raw data needs to be processed to produce information so that management can more easily interpret the results without having to perform tedious calculations or sift through irrelevant figures.

The details on a customer's order, a time-sheet or a bin card constitute data. Once processed to give invoices, payroll analysis or current stock levels the details become meaningful management information.

(c)   The following are desirable properties of information:

(i)   *Accurate.*   The repercussions of inaccurate information could be serious, although it must be noted that there is no point in calculating sales figures to the nearest penny for the sales manager - the nearest £100, £1,000 or £10,000 would probably be sufficient, depending on the size of the business.

(ii)   *On time.*   However correct and accurate the information may be, it will be of little use if it is produced too slowly to be acted upon. Out-of-date information is relatively useless except for historic records but there is always a conflict between timeliness and accuracy.

(iii)   *Complete.*   The information must present management with the full picture. Overall summaries should be supported by more detailed analyses so that total sales can be broken down by product, for example, and management can see that an overall rise in sales is disguising a dramatic fall in the sales of one particular product. If too few facts are presented, management may have to resort to guess-work and hence may make a wrong decision.

(iv)   *Relevant and concise.*   A common fault with information produced by computer systems is that far too many figures are produced. It is costly and time-consuming for managers to sift through masses of figures and extract only the relevant parts. For this reason exception reporting, where deviations from the forecast results are highlighted, is thought to be a more economical method of informing management.

(v)   *Well presented.*   Many computer printouts are badly designed and difficult to follow. They should be laid out in such a way that the information can be readily assimilated by the user.

(d)   The four most important managerial functions are planning, organising, directing and controlling.

♦   Planning consists of identification of objectives and the selection of policies and methods necessary to achieve these objectives.

♦   Organising is the process of setting up and maintaining a formal organisation structure so as to define activities and relationships in a fixed framework.

♦   Directing involves guiding and supervising the work of subordinates towards the objectives laid down.

♦   Controlling is concerned with checking actual progress towards objectives and applying necessary correction.   It requires that standards (eg budgets) be established and actual results compared with the standards.

2   Information levels

Two examples of top management (strategic) information:

♦   Communication of corporate objectives to the management of the business expressed in terms of profit targets and measures of wealth such as earnings per share.

♦   Communicating information on strategy for future acquisitions of companies in different fields as a hedge against risk.

Two examples of middle management (tactical) information:

♦   A twelve-month budget of sales analysed by product group.
♦   A manufacturing plan for the next twelve months.

Two examples of supervisory management (operational) information:

♦   An 'aged' analysis of debts showing all customers whose deliveries have been stopped pending settlement of overdue balance.

♦   A list of all purchase orders outstanding with the financial evaluation of total purchase order commitment.

3   Decisions and control

(a)   (i)   *Structured decisions* - this is where all or most of the variables that affect a decision are known, decision making is programmable, outcomes are known. These types of decisions are routine and require little human judgement to be exercised.

Unstructured decisions - this type of decision is least served by computerisation. It requires a high degree of human judgement to be exercised. Decisions are made in conditions of uncertainty and complexity. Intuition will feature highly in areas of unstructured decision-making.

Semi-structured decisions - this type of decision will fall somewhere between the two previous types. Some aspects of the decision will benefit from use of information provided by computer systems, and this is where a decision support system assists. However, with semi-structured decisions a degree of human judgement will need to be exercised.

(ii)   *Operational control* - this is concerned with the efficient and effective execution of specific tasks. One of the tasks of operational managers is to oversee the operating details of the organisation. Operating managers will make decisions using set rules, which have been predetermined, and correct implementation will result in a predictable outcome.

Tactical control - middle managers are usually associated with tactical control and this relates to the implementation of the short-term planning decisions. Examples of tactical control are allocation of budgets and ensuring sufficient resources are at hand to meet the organisational objectives. The decision making falls between operational and strategic, with constant fluctuations.

Strategic control - this is concerned with the long-term objectives and the formulation of strategic plans. The decisions made at this level will impact down upon the other levels of management control. Because the decisions are concerned with the future and the future is unpredictable, strategic managers are operating in conditions of risk and uncertainty.

(b)   The answer is best illustrated in a tabular format.

Type of decision	Type of control		
	Operational control	*Tactical control*	*Strategic control*
Structured	Accounts receivable	Short-term forecasting	Warehouse location
Semi-structured	Inventory control	Budget preparation	Building new plant
Unstructured	Loan approval	Executive recruitment	R&D planning

(c)   (i)   According to Simon the three phases of the decision-making process are as follows.

Intelligence	This is the awareness of a problem situation that will have to be addressed, or an opportunity that exists which could be exploited.
Design	The decision maker will formulate a number of alternatives to the problem or opportunity situation.
Choice	The decision maker will choose one of the alternatives from the design phase to solve the problem or exploit the opportunity highlighted in the intelligence phase.

The phase being supported in the scenario is the intelligence phase where information about a problem situation is brought to the attention of the decision maker.

(ii)   *Design phase* - the decision support system would enable the company to consider and develop a number of alternatives for reassignment of crews. It would also provide the means to analyse the additional costs that would be incurred by the company in terms of chemicals, equipment, etc.

Choice phase - the decision support system would help the company to choose the best alternative, based upon the whereabouts of crews and the additional costs that would be incurred. Assistance could also be provided in the reassignment and rescheduling of the crews once the decision has been made.

4   Information systems

(a)   (i)   *Transaction processing systems (TPS)*

These systems carry out the day-to-day operations, such as order-entry, payroll, etc. They were one of the earliest developments, having been originally developed in the 1950s.

TPS are not strictly decision-making systems but the information provided from them is used to support the decision-making systems.

TPS are mainly concerned with structured situations, at the operational level of decision making.

TPS can be divided into two main groups: batch, and on-line.

(ii)   *Management information systems (MIS)*

An MIS will support decision-making by the production of routine structured reports. The MIS is usually concerned with the control of activities, although it can be used for organising and planning.

The output of an MIS is information for management. The information provided should be timely and reliable.

The limitations of the MIS appear in unstructured situations.

(iii)   *Decision support systems (DSS)*

These are interactive systems, which provide assistance to managers in an environment where decision-making is less structured.

Over the last decade there has been an increasing awareness of the need for DSS – this has been mainly due to the recognition of the importance of the corporate database as a strategic resource which can be used to provide fast and flexible information, thereby giving the organisation a competitive advantage.

(iv)   *Office automation systems (OAS)*

These are the systems that create, store, modify, display and communicate the correspondence of the business. Communication can be written, verbal, facsimile or in video form.

Now that most computers are networked there is the ability to share computer files and send messages to one another via the communications network. This service is provided by electronic mail systems and electronic bulletin boards. The electronic bulletin boards are a public service whereby public messages can be posted.

OAS also includes voice mail systems, image processing systems, collaborative writing systems, and video conferencing facilities.

(v)   *Executive information systems (EIS)*

These systems have been developed for use by senior executives. They provide summarised data at the highest level of aggregation. Sophisticated graphic techniques will be used in the presentation of the information.

An EIS must be easy to use, but must be able to obtain data from numerous external sources and integrate that data together in order to give a comprehensive picture of the real-world situation.

EIS provide facilities for 'drilling down' to more detailed levels of information should the need arise.

(b)   The above systems could be used as follows.

(i)   *TPS*

Provide information concerning the number of orders received in a day and the levels of stock available.

(ii)   *MIS*

Provision of information concerning the overall profits for the last month and highlighting the most profitable lines.

(iii) *DSS*

Information concerning the most likely location for opening a new sales centre and whether there is availability of expertise in the relevant area. Possible impact of re-deployment of staff to the new area.

(iv)   *OAS*

Communication facilities to enable exchange of information to take place via the computer terminals (e-mail).

(v)   *EIS*

Information for chief executive officers of parent company concerning the operations markets of all of its strategic business units.

5   Management information system (MIS)

Briefing paper on the design of the management information system

To:	IT manager
From:	Consultant
Date:	5th November 20X0

Review of the effectiveness of a management information system

The aim of a management information system is to give all levels of management the information they need in order to plan and control the activities for which they are responsible. To be effective, the information provided should be suitable for its purpose, sufficiently complete and accurate, produced on time and delivered to the appropriate person. Overall, the value of the system should be greater than its cost.

A review of the system should cover the following aspects:

♦   examine all the outputs of the existing MIS (ie the reports produced) in order to become familiar with the information that is currently produced.

♦   talk to representatives from different levels of management in every department of the firm to establish the effectiveness of the system.

♦   discuss solutions with key staff after suggesting alternative formats for the information, based on previous experience with other companies.

The questions raised will include the following:

(i)   Are the reports understandable? Are they used or ignored?

(ii)   Is there time to read all the reports that are produced? Is there too much detail or too little information?

(iii)   Is the information produced on time to be of use?

(iv)   Is the information summarised in a form that is directly relevant to the decisions which have to be made or, for example, do two or three reports have to be combined to obtain the key information?

(v)   Is the type of information produced relevant to the firm's current methods of operating, or does it reflect out-of-date systems?

(vi)   Can the system respond quickly to additional information requirements or changes to the required format?

(vii)   Do the managers make use of additional information obtained informally from outside the MIS? Have managers developed their own information systems? What useful ideas are contained within these systems?

Most managers will be pre-occupied with their present information requirements. However the consultant's role is to encourage management to be forward thinking and consider the firm's future requirements.

When the information needs of managers are assessed and compared with the capabilities of modern hardware and software, the next step will be to take a view as to whether the MIS needs completely redesigning or whether the existing system can be easily adapted.

To do this the relevant capital and running costs of both alternatives, compared with the values of the benefits provided, needs to be considered. The information needs of management will need to be ranked in order of the extent to which their value to the organisation exceeds the cost of production. In this type of analysis, establishing the value of each type of information is the most difficult task, and is clearly subjective.

When examining the extent to which the existing system can be adapted or changed the following factors, amongst others, should be considered:

(i)   Are there simple alternative ways of achieving the same result?

(ii)   Are there inefficiencies in the production of information, including unnecessary duplication of data and procedures, or bottle-necks?

(iii)   Can some centralised activities be decentralised to end-users?

(iv)   Is all relevant data collected from both inside and outside the firm?

(v)   Do hard-copy reports have to be produced so frequently? Can the users interrogate the system for the information they need?

(vi)   How feasible is it to add management's existing information requirements to the existing system?

It is likely, however, that technological changes in the last eight years have made available completely new methods of solution to the firm's information requirements, and that, although the new computer system is found to be perfectly reliable, management are not exploiting its capabilities.

The most likely advantages to come from the design of a totally new information system are related to the development of a single system using database files. Not only will this be more efficient to run (ie it will operate more quickly and will minimise duplication of data), but it will also greatly increase management's ability to interrogate the system for their exact information needs and their ability to vary report requirements to adapt to changing circumstances. However, the implications of a systems change of this magnitude must be pointed out to the firm's directors. There may be necessary changes to organisation structure, which must be handled very carefully.

Chapter 8

1   Communication skills

(a)   Types of information required

There is a substantial amount of information that can be gathered before the meeting. Sam Browne's business is hardly unique; a firm of accountants which deals with sole traders could provide services to a number of newsagents. The accountant visiting Sam should already be aware of the nature of Sam's business, the types of supplier, the likely turnover and the expected profit margins on newspapers and journals, sweets and cigarettes.

The types of information which must be solicited at the meeting could be divided into:

◆   hard information, dealing with facts and documents, which will all be necessary to put Sam's chaotic affairs to rights, especially in relation to tax;

◆   soft information, such as feelings, point of view and morale. This information could include finding out about Sam's attitudes to the record keeping process, as this will affect the reliability of any additional information which he gives. If Sam is merely incompetent at keeping records, simpler procedures might help him overcome his problems. He might regard an accountant's presence there as an unnecessary waste of time, and this might attract some of the force of his resentment which would be more appropriately directed at the tax authorities.

(b)   The communication process

Communication is a way by which information is exchanged, which is the purpose of the meeting with Sam Browne. It can also involve instruction, encouragement or persuasion. Because his co-operation is required the purpose of the meeting will also be to establish a relationship with Sam, building trust and understanding, so that he responds with useful information. The communication model shown below demonstrates the elements in the process, emphasising that it is a two-way exchange in which the recipient is as important as the transmitter.

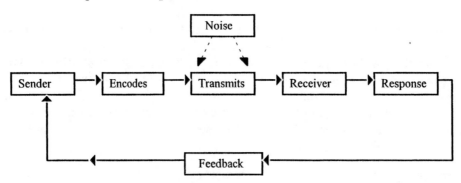

The hurdles to communication (in this case it may be Sam's attitude) may be overcome if:

◆   the communication is planned effectively. Prior knowledge of similar businesses will be of assistance here;

◆   direct, simple language is used;

◆   maximum feedback is obtained. This includes the acknowledgement that both the message and the response are understood, the proposal and clarification of ideas, checking up on any misunderstanding and further questioning and response to avoid confusion.

(c)   The skills contributed to the process

While giving the appearance of a friendly chat rather than an inquisition, interviewing skills must be used to put Sam at ease so that the two-way process of communication can go as planned.

Information given by Sam should be written down. A pre-planned sheet of questions and the types of response required would make this task easier and ensure that nothing is missed. Unless a tape recorder is used as a method of recording the information, skills in note taking and summarising will be used in the recording process and include the following:

(i)   noting key facts, perhaps using a mind map;
(ii)   questioning areas of uncertainty;
(iii)   noting any follow-up questions.

If the summary is to be communicated to someone else then an assessment of Sam's approach to the record-keeping problem should also be made.

The main skills required will be in effective listening to elicit the maximum information from the meeting. These include:

(i)   being prepared to listen, not just simulating attention;

(ii)   keeping an open mind and not assuming the expected;

(iii)   providing Sam with feedback;

(iv)   trying to grasp the gist of the matter rather than getting bogged down with Sam's problems.

A low level of interest and other worries about the situation can impede effective listening. Even worse, fixed ideas of what Sam is expected to say may prevent appreciation of the full situation. Effective listening will also help to reveal any gaps in Sam's logic.

2   Barriers to information flow

These can be identified as message-related, personal, group and organisational in their source. All will have something of the characteristics of noise, filtering and distortion.

Message-related - this depends upon whether the message is clear and perceived as meaningful. This will depend upon:

♦   how immediate the message is;
♦   what the message contains;
♦   how it is presented;
♦   how frequent the type of message is;
♦   if it is on time.

A simple weekly cost control report, presented in a clear readily understandable way on the Monday morning following the week's operations, will have much to commend it. By contrast, a detailed report, eloquently testifying to the management accountant's technical ability and presented on Thursday or Friday of that following week, will be of little value and held in very low regard.

Personal - there are four causes of barriers under this heading.

(a) The perception of the sender in the eyes of the recipient. If there is no regard for the sender, then his message will go unheeded, or at least be relegated in priority. Conversely, if there is high regard, then action will be precipitated.

(b) There is always the two-fold problem of capacity, both to receive and to absorb. First a recipient who is overloaded with paper and messages will give no message the regard it should have, but rather concentrate on merely clearing his desk. Secondly, capacity will also relate to the ability to understand the message and that could mean complete misunderstanding of what is expressed and what is being communicated.

(c) The existence of information overload. The worst example of this is the American style management reporting pack, which is usually circulated around to senior executives on a monthly basis. While the technical quality of the highly detailed information is frequently superb, there is often too much because it takes the form of a mobile database. The end result is that the recipient will look at only the bits that are relevant to him, or only look very superficially at what is sent.

(d) Perception of need is very much a production approach to the problem. A barrier develops simply by misinterpreting the needs of the user of the message. It can arise from the relative positions in an organisational hierarchy, status within that hierarchy, levels of trust and influence, and the presence of any bias within the message. It is to resolve problems in this area that much of the work on reporting of financial data in both the UK and the United States has been directed.

The impact of a group - they can exert influences over the individuals to distort the perception of a message.

Organisational - in many respects this can be the biggest area of difficulty. The areas where there may be potential barriers to effective communication are as follows:

(i) The mode of communication, which in turn will affect its timeliness.

(ii) The distance it has to travel. Where this is far, the perception is that 'they' are too remote, and hence do not understand 'our' problems. Worse still, this can develop into a cavalier attitude so that communication will be ignored if it suits the local purpose.

This can be alleviated by divisionalisation, decentralisation and effective delegation but with strong local management.

(iii) The nature of the recipient. Certain functions within an organisation will feel that because of job security or technical security, they can adopt an autonomous approach and ignore communications if they choose, preparing to take the consequences of their actions.

Other areas for generating potential barriers are:

♦ the number of hierarchical levels which can cause distortion;
♦ the existence of a 'one-way' communication system;
♦ deliberate distortion because of perceived preferences and loyalties;
♦ possible translation of language;
♦ inadequate feedback procedures;
♦ the style of the management.

This latter point is really whether or not communication is encouraged. The manager who opts for 'open door' management must be prepared to be available to his subordinates, and must make it possible for them to get in to see him. If the open door is seen to be either ineffective, or just not operated, then a situation will develop where subordinates will feel reluctant to communicate. The worst possible result of this could be the escalation of a problem, which if discussed at an earlier stage might not have deteriorated into the potential conflict or alienation situation that ultimately develops.

3   Communication and presentation

Management guidelines on making internal and external communication more effective

(a)   **The importance of communication**

Effective communication is important for managers for two reasons.

(i)   Communication is the process by which managers accomplish the functions of planning, organising, leading and controlling.

(ii)   Communication is the activity to which managers devote an overwhelming proportion of their time. Rarely are managers alone at their desks thinking, planning or contemplating alternatives. In fact, managerial time is spent largely in some form of communication with subordinates, peers, supervisors, suppliers, or customers. When not conferring with others in person or on the telephone, managers may be writing or dictating memos, letters, or reports - or perhaps reading memos, letters or reports sent to them.

(b)   **The communication process**

Communication can be defined as a process consisting of a sender transmitting a message through a medium to a receiver who responds.

Elements of the proposed model of communication include the sender, encoding, message, channel, receiver, decoding, noise and feedback. Encoding is the process by which the sender converts the information to be transmitted into the appropriate symbols or gestures. Decoding is the process by which the receiver interprets the message. If the decoding matches the sender's encoding, the communication has been effective.

Noise is that which interferes with the communication. Types of noise include distractions and environmental noise. Feedback is the receiver's reaction to the sender's message; thus, it repeats the communication process, with the sender and the receiver roles reversed.

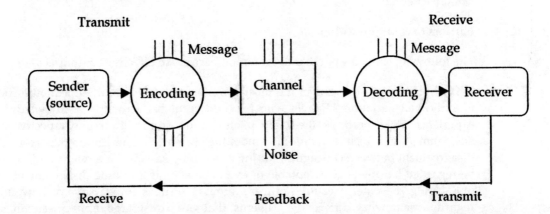

(c)   **Methods of communication**

Communication may be 'one-way' or 'two-way'. In one-way communication the sender communicates without expecting or getting feedback from the receiver. For example, policy statements from top managers are one-way communication. Two-way communication exists when the receiver provides feedback to the sender. For example, making a suggestion to a subordinate and receiving a question or counter-suggestion is a two-way communication.

Research has shown the following.

(i)   One-way communication is less time consuming than two-way communication.

(ii)   Two-way communication is more accurate than one-way communication. Feedback allows the sender to refine his or her communication for the receivers so that it becomes more precise and accurate.

(iii)   Receivers are more sure of themselves and of their judgements when two-way communication is used. In addition they can use questions to clarify any doubts they may have.

(iv)   Senders can easily feel attacked when two-way communication is used, because receivers will call attention to the sender's ambiguities and mistakes.

(v)   Although it is less accurate, one-way communication appears much more orderly than two-way communication, which often appears noisy and chaotic.

If communication must be fast (and accuracy is easy to achieve) one-way communication is both more economical and more efficient. If orderliness is considered vital - as in a large public meeting - one-way communication might also be more appropriate.

Where accuracy of communication is important, however, the two-way method is almost essential. Without feedback from the receiver, the sender has little basis for judging the accuracy of the communication or the degree of understanding and comprehension experienced by the receiver.

In most situations, managers will have to create the most efficient mix of one-way and two-way communication. Some categories of managerial communications, such as straightforward statements of company rules and policies, require little or no feedback to assure clarity. In many other cases, such as the formulation of organisational objectives or the implementation of a new sales strategy, two-way communication is usually essential.

(d)   **Barriers to communication**

The following are some of the most common barriers to effective communication.

Differing perceptions - one of the most common sources of communication difficulty is individual variation. People who have different backgrounds of knowledge and experience often perceive the same phenomenon from different perspectives. The environment in which it occurs influences the way a communication is perceived. A disagreement between colleagues, during a planning session for a major project, might be regarded by others as acceptable or even healthy. If the same disagreement broke out during the chief executive officer's annual address to employees, it would be regarded somewhat differently. Events that are considered appropriate in some circumstances are inappropriate in others.

Language differences - are often closely related to differences in individual perceptions. For a message to be properly communicated, the words used must mean the same thing to sender and receiver. The same symbolic meaning must be shared.

Further barriers to communication may result from the use of jargon. Sometimes people use jargon to exclude others or to create an impression of superiority; both of which make communication difficult. Finally, the contemporary globalisation of industry brings to light the problem of language barriers - a problem which although not insoluble cannot be ignored.

Emotional reactions - anger, love, defensiveness, hate, jealousy, fear, embarrassment all influence how we understand the messages of others and how we influence others with our own messages. If, for example, we are in an atmosphere where we feel threatened with loss of power or prestige, we may lose the ability to gauge the meanings of the messages we receive and will respond defensively or aggressively.

Inconsistent verbal and non-verbal communication - we think of language as the primary medium of communication, but the messages we send and receive are strongly influenced by such non-verbal factors as body movements, clothing, the distance we stand from the person we are talking to, our posture, gestures, facial expression, eye movements and body contact.

Distrust - the credibility of a message is, to a large extent, a function of the credibility of the sender in the mind of the receiver. A sender's credibility is, in turn, determined by a variety of factors. In some cases the fact that a message comes from a manager will enhance its credibility, but it can also have the opposite effect.

(e)   **Overcoming barriers to communication**

Overcoming barriers is a two-step process:

(i)   one must learn to recognise the various types of barriers which can occur; and

(ii)   one must act to overcome the barriers.

Overcoming different perceptions - the message should be explained so that it can be understood by those with different views and experiences. Whenever possible, we should learn about the background of those with whom we will be communicating. Empathising and seeing the situation from the other person's point of view and delaying actions until the relevant information is weighed helps to reduce ambiguous messages. When the subject is unclear, asking questions is critical.

Overcoming differences in language - the meanings of unconventional or technical terms should be explained. Simple, direct, natural language should be used. It is also helpful to remain sensitive to the various alternative interpretations possible for a message. Messages can often be restated in different terms. Sometimes even a minor change can have beneficial effects. If, for example, we are replacing an unpopular sales quota system with a new system in which reaching sales objectives is only one measure of productivity, we might do well to avoid the word 'quota' entirely because of its negative association with the old system.

Overcoming emotionality - the best approach to emotions is to accept them as part of the communication process and to understand them when they cause problems. If subordinates are behaving aggressively, try to empathise. Get them to talk about their concerns, and pay careful attention to what they say. Once you understand their reactions you may be able to improve the atmosphere by changing your own behaviour. Before a crisis, try to understand your subordinates' emotional reactions and prepare yourself to deal with them.

Overcoming inconsistent verbal/non-verbal communication - the keys to eliminating inconsistencies in communication are being aware of them and not attempting to send false messages. Gestures, clothes, posture, facial expression and other powerful non-verbal communications should concur with the message.

Overcoming distrust - credibility is the result of a long-term process in which a person's honesty, fair-mindedness and good intentions are recognised by others. There are few shortcuts to creating a trusting atmosphere; a good rapport with the people with whom one communicates can only be developed through consistent performance.

(f)   **Communication in competitive markets**

The development of effective communication and presentation skills are essential if Hamilton Ellis Ltd is to succeed in the highly competitive market of computer services. These skills encompass image projection, negotiating, selling and managing the customer relationship.

Maintaining good customer relationships requires speedy and accurate communication whenever necessary in response to complaints, competitors' actions/reactions and product/service development.

Such communications need to be consistent with the company's mission statement and strategies.

(g)   **Action consequences**

The need to improve personal communication and presentation skills will have consequences for the following.

(i)   Recruitment and induction programmes for staff - ensuring that all new recruits have the necessary skills required.

(ii)   Staff appraisal processes - ensuring that existing staff are made aware of the new skills required and enabling them to attain such skills.

(iii)   Marketing programmes - ensuring that all sales staff are able to communicate and present information effectively.

(iv)   Introduction of training programmes - ensuring that tailor-made courses cover areas such as writing skills and visual presentation skills, telephone techniques and interpersonal interaction including body language.

4   Jim Ryan

Part (a)

To: Jim Ryan - CityGo Bus Company

From: Management consultant

Date: XX October 200X

Subject: Project management process and project management tools and techniques

A one-off project such as the new system changeover at CityGo will give rise to a number of different implementation problems. These can conveniently be examined under the headings of scope, time, cost, quality and risk.

Scope - this is where the project's objectives and boundaries are defined. Its relationship with other activities must be established so that no disruption is caused. The operational financial systems are clear and well understood at CityGo, so the requirements will be easy to define.

Time - a time constraint is a usual feature of project management because each project will have a start and completion date defined. This particular project at CityGo has time as its key constraint.

Cost - consideration needs to be given to both revenue expenditure and capital outlay. Project costs will either be capitalised in the period of completion, or accounted for as incurred, depending on the accounting policies in place at CityGo. A net present value calculation would usually be used to appraise larger projects.

Quality - this is in reference to the outputs of the project and whether or not they perform to a desired standard. Quality with regard to computer-based systems would cover issues such as systems documentation and data integrity.

Risk - each project will have its own specific risk in relation to each element's degree of uncertainty. A project to completely change the whole computer system is likely to be more risky than simply upgrading an existing one.

The five elements can be seen to create conflicts against one another, such as time and cost. All possible conflicts can be avoided by correctly defining the project specification in the scope element.

Project management tools and techniques are available to assist in managing each element as follows.

Scope - at the initial planning phase, the project specification is drawn up. This will define the objectives and place limits on other elements, such as a timescale.

Time - there are various time-focused tools available, with the main one probably being critical path analysis. This tool will split the project into sections. Each section is given a specific time of completion, which will be in line with the overall project completion. Each element will then be measured against actual time as incurred. This is especially important when one element requires completion before another can begin. Current software available allows this to be computerised for additional ease of use.

Cost - the total cost will need to be divided into elements, which can then be used as a budget for the whole project. Actual costs incurred will then be monitored against budgeted amounts to ensure that targets are met.

Quality - the level of quality is set by the customer, because the customer determines whether or not it is 'fit for purpose'. There is little or no point in designing a higher level of quality than what is required. It is important however that the quality level is determined and defined in the project specification so that it can be monitored in light of the time constraint.

Risk - the risk of each characteristic within the project can be reduced by:

♦ improved working practices
♦ back-up systems
♦ high quality specifications.

The risk exposure that remains can be reduced or eliminated by the agreement of tight contractual conditions, and by the use of insurance.

Conclusion

Both the project management process and the project management tools and techniques can be examined under the headings of scope, time, cost, quality and risk.

Part (b)

Memorandum

To: Jim Ryan - CityGo Bus Company

From: Management consultant

Date: X October 200X

The responsibilities of a project manager include the following:

♦ *Agree the terms of reference of the project* - every project should start with Terms of Reference describing the objectives, scope, constraints, resources and project sponsor or client. It is the responsibility of the project manager to compile and agree these Terms of Reference. In particular he or she must be confident that the project can meet its objectives within the time agreed (a constraint) with the resources available. The Terms of Reference may be expanded into a Project Quality Plan, which will describe such issues as quality procedures, standards and a risk assessment. Producing the Project Quality Plan will also be the project manager's responsibility.

♦ *Plan the project* - the agreed project will have to be broken down into lower level tasks and activities, each of which will be given a time estimate. Precedents (which tasks must be completed before others can start) will also be agreed. The project task breakdown, the precedents of tasks, and task estimates will form the basis of the project plan. This will allow the project manager to determine the critical path and hence the elapsed time of the project. The project manager will also be able to see more clearly the resource requirements of the project. The project manager usually has the responsibility to produce and interpret the project plan, often using a computerised tool.

♦ *Monitor the project* - during the project the project manager must ensure that the overall project remains on target. Hence he or she will monitor the progress of tasks and record their completion on the project plan. Some of these tasks will over-run their original estimates and the consequences of this have to be carefully monitored and managed. The project will also be affected by new user requirements, staff illness and holidays and other external factors that cannot be predicted at the start of the project. The project manager has to reflect all these in the project plan and produce revised versions showing the effect of these changes.

♦ *Report on project progress* - it is usually the responsibility of the project manager to report project progress both upwards (to the project sponsor or client) and downwards (to the rest of the project team). Progress reports usually specify what tasks have been completed in the last period, what tasks have been started but not completed (with perhaps an estimate to completion) and what tasks are scheduled to start in the next period. Reports should also highlight problems and changes, showing the effect of these on the project plan and suggesting a course of action. The project sponsor can then decide whether such changes are implemented in the project or left until a later phase of the development. Project reports may also contain important cost and time information showing the overall cost of the project to date.

♦ *Undertake post-project reviews* - a post-project review usually takes place at the end of the project and it will be the responsibility of the project manager to organise and chair this review and report on its conclusions and recommendations. The post-project reviews will consider both the products of the project (such as the robustness of the software, the satisfaction of users, etc) and the organisation of the project itself. It may review the estimates of project cost and duration and compare these with actual costs and duration. Large variances will be discussed and analysed and any lessons learnt recorded and fed back into the project management method.

♦ *Motivate the project team* - usually a multi-disciplinary team has been brought together for the purpose of undertaking the project. Once the project is complete the team will probably be disbanded. During the project it is the responsibility of the project manager to motivate team members so that the tasks they are assigned are completed on time and to the required quality. Project managers have direct influence over the work that is assigned to the team members, the amount of responsibility individual team members are given and the recognition they are accorded on completion of their work. How the project manager goes about these management tasks will critically affect the morale and motivation of the team members.

Chapter 9

1   Systems development lifecycle

The systems development lifecycle, also known as the systems lifecycle, has several stages:

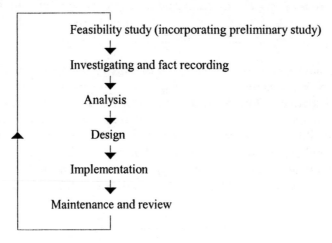

Feasibility study (incorporating preliminary study)

Investigating and fact recording

Analysis

Design

Implementation

Maintenance and review

(a)   *Feasibility study*

(i)   Introduction - an important step before committing resources to developing and implementing a management information system.

(ii)   Preliminary study - the scope of the MIS must be defined. Targets, ie objective measures of data processing performance should be defined. This is to enable reliable judgement of the success or failure of a system.

(iii)   The feasibility study of the MIS - the following questions should be asked:

♦   is it technologically feasible - easy to use, response time, high risk project, or tried and tested?

♦   is it economically feasible? (a cost benefit analysis must be performed).

♦   is it consistent with corporate objectives?

♦   is it consistent with existing and other proposed MIS?

(iv)   Analysing alternatives - alternative systems should be considered and accepted/rejected with reference to the above criteria.

(v)   The best alternative - this should be designed to the extent that forecasts can be made of the effect on the objective measures defined. Ensure there are no pitfalls.

(vi)   Planning - develop the structure for the main project; this helps with direction and control later.

(vii)   Reporting - the targets, design and plan should be documented so that they may be referred to in future by the project team, avoiding duplication of research and better analysis of the MIS when 'live'.

(b)   *Investigation*

During this stage of the cycle the analyst collects facts about the existing/proposed system, such as its objectives, input and output requirements, feedback and control mechanisms, and any other problems, either existing or perceived. The different methods of data collection that are used include interviews, questionnaires, observation and examination of existing documentation.

(c)   *Systems analysis*

The aim of this stage of the cycle is to build a logical model of the existing system. This involves:

♦   a review of the existing system;

♦   a definition of the system objectives;

♦   determination of the design constraints in terms of hardware and software availability and cost, development, operational and maintenance procedures and scheduling costs of the system;

♦   definition of requirements – definition of the logic of the system from the user's point of view in terms of inputs, outputs and information flow, ie a functional specification;

♦   user sign-off - authorised user states that the work has been examined in detail, that it is consistent with the user objectives, and that the user is committed to the specifications produced by the analyst.

(d)   *Systems design*

The aim of this stage is to design a new and better system for the users. This is done through a detailed outline of the new system and implementation. The actual design of the proposed system can be divided into four areas:

(i)   Description of the system at a logical level - definition of what the system will do.

(ii)   Refinement of the logical level with additional detail - assessment of all processing activities and definition of the relationships between the components of the system.

(iii)   Addition of physical detail - what the system should do and how it should do it, including design of the user interface.

(iv)   Completion of a structured walkthrough - to achieve input and feedback from users. Approaches to design include structured, top-down and hierarchical methods.

(e)   *Implementation*

This stage involves the co-ordination of the efforts of the user department and the computing department to put the new system into operation. The implementation procedure will have been stipulated in the system design phase and will involve the following components:

(i)   Staff training - the degree of training will depend on the complexity of the system and the ability of the present staff. Training will take the form of handbooks, 'hands-on' courses, or lectures.

(ii)   Programming - the programmer will design programs which conform to the requirements set out in the system specification. Alternatively, a standard 'off the shelf' package will often meet the requirements.

(iii)   System testing - to ensure that individual programs are effective, that the system as a whole will work, and that the clerical/manual procedures can be co-ordinated with the system.

(iv)   Master file conversion - there are three basic methods:

♦   parallel - the old and new systems are run concurrently using the same inputs, and the outputs are compared. Any problems can be rectified at this point;

♦   direct - the old system is discontinued altogether and the new system becomes operational;

♦   pilot - involves the changeover of a system, either directly or in parallel.

(f)   *Maintenance and review*

Once the system has been installed, it must be examined to see if it has reached its objectives, eg a comparison of costs and benefits. In future, the system will be changed and up-dated as problems arise and as the organisation's requirements change. Day-to-day operational tasks must be carried out to facilitate the efficient running of the system, eg file back-up, input of data, repair of physical breakdowns.

2   Structured approach

The main stages in the structured approach to systems analysis and design are as follows.

Stage 1: Problem definition

The aim of this stage is to produce a precise definition of the overall problem for resolution by the system to be developed. Overviews of the present systems and data structure are created and the current problems are defined.

Stage 2: Project identification

At this stage, the aim is to create a number of options to deal with the problems identified in Stage 1. These options are then evaluated and formalised for inclusion in the feasibility report.

Stage 3: Analysis of system operation and current problems

This stage involves the analysis of the existing system and documenting it in the form of dataflow diagrams (DFDs) and logical data structures (LDSs). Then a problems/requirements list should be produced by making a more refined identification of the problems found earlier.

Stage 4: Specification of requirements

Here the user requirements are defined in more detail. A data structure based on the LDSs created in Stage 3 is developed and the requirements of control, security and audit are considered and included as necessary into the systems specification.

Stage 5: Selection of technical options

There will always be several ways by which the required system specified at Stage 4 can be implemented. It is thus necessary for users and systems staff to select a suitable physical system. Generally it will be possible at this time to decide upon a hardware configuration and on the characteristics of the appropriate software. Also at this stage, the performance objectives based upon the hardware and software requirements are defined.

Stage 6: Data design

This is part of the logical design of the system. Data structures for the proposed system are designed by combining the top-down business view of the data derived from Stage 3 with the bottom-up view of data groupings, ie composite logical data design.

Stage 7: Process design

This is carried out in conjunction with the data design stage to utilise the composite logical data design. The processing identified in the requirements specification is detailed and the logical design is validated by means of a quality assurance review before proceeding with the physical design stage.

Stage 8: Physical design

In this stage, the logical design previously produced is converted into a physical design, ie programs and database contents. The data dictionary is updated and the design adjusted to meet performance objectives. Testing of systems and programs is carried out and operating instructions are produced. An implementation plan is prepared and the manual procedures are defined.

3   Prototyping

Report	Prototyping and its uses
To:	Management accountant
Prepared by:	Trainee
Date:	XX November 20X0

Introduction

This report aims to explain what is meant by the term 'prototyping' and give examples of situations where its use might be appropriate.

What is a prototype?

A software prototype is a limited model of the actual software required. By producing a prototype, the software designer can demonstrate the software to the user. The user is then able to experiment with the prototype in order to better assess his actual software requirements. The prototype is called a 'limited model' as many of the controls necessary for the actual software are left out. Nevertheless, it gives a much better demonstration of what the software will (or will not) do than abstract data models, for instance.

Prototyping tools

There are many tools used in the process of prototyping and these include:

(i)   an integrated data dictionary;

(ii)   screen generators;

(iii)   non-procedural report generators;

(iv)   fourth generation programming language;

(v)   non-procedural query languages;

(vi)   database facilities.

Uses of prototyping

There are two main forms of prototype:

(i)   throwaway prototypes; and
(ii)   developable prototypes.

The structured approach to systems design and development tends to use prototyping at a stage when only an outline analysis and design have been done. Use of 4GL allows the process of model development to be speeded up. Once the model has been developed the user is able to see what the working system will look like. Aspects of the system such as screen formats can be demonstrated and alternatives considered. Alternative transaction types can also be considered. This has obvious advantages over paper-based models such as dataflow diagrams.

Once the system has been agreed, the prototype is usually dispensed with and the actual system is developed using software engineering methods.

Software engineering allows provably correct programs to be developed. If the actual system were to be developed with the aid of a 4GL (as was the prototype) then, in a large system, the 4GL might impose unacceptable run-time overheads. Using a 4GL does take up large amounts of internal memory and needs to be translated into a code acceptable to the machine. It is the translation programs that would impose restrictions on the system being developed in this way.

However, some prototypes are used as a springboard for full system production. Changes needed to the system are developed iteratively. This must, however, be done within set budget limits.

This type of prototyping is considered as an alternative approach to the analysis phase of the requirements definition used by the structured systems approach.

This sort of prototype seeks to define the user requirements whilst allowing for expansion and modification. Also, it is intended that, as the user becomes more familiar with the system and his understanding develops, the system will evolve according to his definitions of his needs. This is seen as a heuristic approach to system modelling.

This type of prototyping is especially beneficial where:

(i)   the user is unable to specify his requirements;
(ii)   the user is unable to fully comprehend abstract paper-models.

Almost all prototypes are geared toward online database type systems rather than batch processing systems. In addition, where users are concerned with screen formats and layouts, prototypes are of particular use.

Conclusion

There are two main forms of prototype. One type (throwaway) is very much a tool of structured approach and is used to support other analysis tools. The alternative type is used to iteratively develop a requirements definition.

However, even when the developable prototype is used it would still be expected to dispense with the prototype model and completely replace it with the newly created production system. Although it is often tempting to use the prototype as the actual system, it will most often lack the capacity to handle large volumes of data.

Even when a prototype is used actual system development must be fully documented in order to provide a full and permanent record of the user requirements and specifications.

4   Database

A relational database can provide strategic management with summarised data from all functions within the organisation.

The database approach offers the following advantages.

Reduction in data duplication

Organisations by their very nature make use of and store vast amounts of information. In the past most of this information has been held on specific computer files. Very often the same information would be held by many different departments. For instance, the payroll department would hold data such as the employee number, name and address. In addition the personnel department would also hold this information, as would perhaps a number of different departments with whom the employee has dealings.

In effect this means that the same data has been duplicated many times throughout the files held by the organisation.

By using a relational database, the data duplication is minimised because all of the data, regardless of the applications served, is held in one central store. This central store of data is the database itself. All applicants wishing to access any part of that data would do so by going through the database management system (DBMS). The DBMS would be responsible for controlling the access to the data, thus playing an important role in the protection and security of the data held.

Data integrity

There is an increase in data integrity because there is only one store of data and all users of the system will access the same data. When specific files were in use, the situation would often arise where the various files would produce conflicting data. For instance, if the employee moved to a new address, he might inform the payroll department but might not necessarily think to inform the personnel department or any other department which held details of his name and address.

In addition, because there is only one store of data, keeping control of access and monitoring its use is much more easily done. Also, standards can be set and implemented.

Enhances system development

The organisation will hold vast amounts of data and by using a database system all of the data could be accessed by users (providing they have the authority). Therefore, if a new application is required, it is more than likely that the data needed is already held within the database. Users could use a structured query language to enable them to interrogate the database, and also the data dictionary would prove of particular use by enabling users to identify the items of data in existence within the database.

Data independence

Because the data is held separately from the applications accessing it, any alterations to the programs accessing the data would not affect the data itself. Likewise any changes to the way in which the data is being held would not affect the programs accessing the data.

Availability of information

All of the data is stored at one central point, which means that strategic managers are able to have summarised information concerning any aspect of the organisation. In previous times, when the data was held by the individual departments, a manager would have had to request a report from each department.

Obviously this would result in the manager having to wait for the information, and once received the information would soon be out of date.

Standards imposed

With a central database good standards are of vital importance. To some extent the standards which will need to be imposed may well be far higher than those previously in force in the different application areas.

5   DBMS

(a)   DBMS stands for database management system. A database is a shared, formally defined, centrally controlled collection of data used in an organisation. The database is organised and accessed through a generalised software package called a database management system. The DBMS provides access to the data for different application programs and users, together with security, back-up and recovery facilities.

(b)   Three advantages of a DBMS approach to data processing.

♦   Better exploration of the company's data allowing different parts of the enterprise to use consistent shared data.

♦   Easier enforcement of standards in systems development, data naming and program development. These issues are under the control of a centralised organisational unit (database administration) charged with the central control of data and responsible for deciding the information content of the database, the storage structure, defining security and integrity checks and producing a strategy for back-up and recovery.

♦   Controlled redundancy of data. Data used across several different application areas can lead to repetition of information, leading to inconsistency and duplicated data.

Chapter 10

1   Feasibility study

A feasibility study is an investigation of the current system and the way in which the system should be amended or developed so as to achieve some form of advantage, either in terms of cost reduction or competitive advantage, for the organisation.

The feasibility of the system development will be assessed from three different perspectives.

- Technical feasibility
- Economic feasibility
- Social feasibility

Technical feasibility is the matching of the system requirements to the performance that can be achieved from currently available hardware and software. For example the technical feasibility will be assessed in terms of how easily the resources can be upgraded and whether the organisation currently employs staff who are sufficiently technically qualified or experienced to deal with the new system.

Technically the project is feasible as the employees have the expertise and the system can be updated to meet the new requirements envisaged by the managing director.

Economic feasibility is the consideration of the various costs that will be incurred in the development and implementation of the new system, together with an assessment of the on-going running costs of the new system. It will also consider the various financial and non-financial benefits that the new system should provide once all of these costs and benefits have been established. They will be included within a full-scale cost/benefit analysis exercise – utilising the various project appraisal techniques of:

- cashflow analysis
- payback
- return on investment
- discounted cashflow
- net present value.

From the information contained in the question there is no urgent need for the new system, nor is there likely to be an immediate reduction in operating costs or greater efficiency. It is likely that some intangible long-term benefits may derive from the new system but at this stage these benefits cannot be established.

The project is not therefore economically feasible.

Finally *social feasibility* must be considered. This concerns assessing the impact of the new system on the organisation image, and on individuals both inside and outside the organisation. Based on the information contained within the question, it appears that user resentment will be high, because users have expressed their satisfaction at the way in which the current system functions.

It is therefore evident that whilst the proposed system development is technically feasible it lacks justification in terms of economic and social feasibility.

2   Cost benefit analysis

(a)   Factors to be taken into account under the various headings include the following.

Building the system

♦ The salaries of all the project staff.

♦ Built in time in the event of illness, holidays, etc.

♦ Time and cost to train the project staff in new methodologies and/or computing languages.

♦ The time used by the computer for system development work.

♦ New equipment which may be needed.

♦ Travelling expenses and accommodation costs which may be incurred by the project team when visiting remote user sites.

Installation costs

♦ Training of users and operating staff.

♦ Data entry costs at the conversion stage. If the data is already held on a computer then programming costs would be incurred when writing the conversion programs.

♦ General installation costs of computer vendors.

♦ Costs involved in planning and operating a parallel run.

♦ Costs involved in phasing the system in over a period of time.

Operational and maintenance costs

♦ Costs involved when renting or leasing equipment.
♦ Cost of maintaining the system in good working order.
♦ Costs involved in accommodating the system.
♦ Staff costs.

Cost of failures

♦ Cost of breakdown and repair.
♦ Costs involved in loss of computing power.
♦ People cost of time lost due to breakdown.
♦ Potential loss of custom due to system failure.
♦ Potential legal costs if system failure results in financial or other loss to customers.

(b)   Benefits fall into two main categories.

Tactical benefits

These are the benefits derived from being able to operate in the same way but at a lower cost, plus being able to process data more quickly thus providing better cashflow. Tactical benefits therefore allow for increased productivity at no extra cost or the same productivity at a lower cost. For instance, replacing an expensive mainframe which incurs many running costs with a mini computer which is virtually maintenance free would be a tactical benefit.

Strategic benefits

These are the benefits derived in being able to give a better service to customers, offer a wide range of products, attract new customers or prevent existing customers from being seduced by the competition.

Strategic benefits also include being able to obtain better information for decision making, being able to identify trends and patterns in the market place and being able to analyse the information produced.

3   Fact finding techniques

There are a number of techniques which a project team might use in order to gather detailed information about the existing system.

Information from documents

Analysts need to examine the 'hard data' contained in both quantitative and qualitative documents (reports, documents, financial statements, procedure manuals and memos). These provide information unavailable from any other fact-finding techniques.

Interviewing

This is a major source of information about both existing and proposed systems. The analyst listens for goals, feelings, opinions, and informal procedures, and attempts to sell the system and widen the knowledge of the interviewee.

Questions can be of two types: open, which leave all responses open to the interviewee; and closed, which limit the range of valid responses.

Interviews should be recorded, and reports written immediately afterwards to confirm what was said.

Questionnaires

These are useful if the people from whom the analyst needs to gather information are numerous and/or widely dispersed. They are most valuable when the information can be elicited by the use of simple, possibly multiple choice, questions.

The validity and reliability of the questionnaire is a problem of which analysts must be aware. Great care must be taken in their design, and they should be subjected to pilot test runs before being sent out.

Managers should have been consulted, agreed their use and made public their support for the technique in the particular context.

Observation

This technique provides analysts with an insight into what is actually done; they see at first hand the relationships between the various types of users; they perceive the day-to-day activities which together make up the system, and may differ markedly from what documents or interviewees may reveal. It is essential that the analyst understands the nature of what he or she is observing.

The analyst can make use of event or time sampling, observe decision-making activities, and body language. There are various methods of recording observations (eg category systems, checklists, etc).

Prototyping

This is a useful information gathering approach, which may replace several stages in the traditional systems development lifecycle. It enables user reactions, suggestions, innovations and revision suggestions to be obtained, to improve the prototype, and system plans to be modified with minimum disruption and expense. It will require the use of fourth generation languages with which to build the prototype.

A disadvantage of this approach is that managing the process is difficult because of the many iterations and the speed of the process. The user may pursue requests when the systems already fulfil the specified requirements. Sometimes an incomplete prototype may be pressed into service, and become regarded as the complete system.

Prototyping enables systems to be changed more easily during development, enables development to cease at an early stage if it becomes apparent that it is not progressing as required, and will result in a system that more closely addresses the requirements of the user.

4   Collecting information

(a)   In order to analyse a system the analyst will need to gather and evaluate information in relation to the organisation, and more specifically:

- the organisational culture

- the present economic climate

- results of previous investigations

- organisational structure

- management style

- requirements of the new system

- strategic plans

- short-term objectives

- details of departments and employees within the organisation (organisational chart).

The investigative techniques that can be utilised include the following.

Desk-based research

The study of previous system documentation, records, reports, information booklets etc. The company mission statement and policies could also be reviewed.

Interviewing

This is one of the major investigative methods and requires good communication skills from the analyst. Interviews should always be planned even when conducted in an informal manner. Whether to interview formally or informally by conducting a structured or unstructured interview will depend upon the type of person being interviewed and the atmosphere the interviewer wishes to create. This is where communication skills play a major part.

The interviewer needs to plan:

- whom to interview

- when to interview (avoid times which will be particularly disruptive to the day-to-day business of the company)

- what to ask (background information is needed concerning the interviewee prior to the interview)

- where to hold the interview (if the interviewee will need to demonstrate his tasks or refer to documentation then the interview is best conducted at the location of the interviewee)

- how to begin the interview (which questions will gain the best response, how to put the interviewee at ease, etc)

- how to terminate the interview

- how to analyse the notes, recordings, etc made during the interview.

Observation

Observe the system in operation within its usual environment. Human nature dictates that different behaviour will occur when an individual is aware that he is being observed - the results of the observation may therefore be distorted.

Questionnaires

These can be used to collect large amounts of information from large numbers of people. Questionnaires must be properly designed in order to extract meaningful information. The following factors should be considered.

♦ Tone of the questionnaire

♦ Objectives of the questionnaire

♦ Length of the questionnaire

♦ Whether to pilot run it

♦ The style of the questionnaire – easy to complete, free of jargon

♦ The way in which the responses should be analysed. Use of OMR might be appropriate

♦ Timescale for return and analysis.

Questionnaires are notorious for attracting low responses. The inclusion of a stamped addressed envelope might improve the response rate but cost should be an important factor.

Sampling

Where it is not possible to send questionnaires to or interview all the people concerned, samples are selected that are representative of the whole population under review. Use of sampling theory enables the required sample size to be calculated which, when the items are tested, will give statistically reliable results.

(b)   If the system under investigation is already computerised then the analyst would also fully investigate all the documentation relating to the analysis, design and development of that system. He would peruse the original system specifications and compare the requirements with the original test results. A review of the system documentation including dataflow diagrams, etc should also be undertaken.

The analyst would also run test data through the system, observe the operators of the system, observe the operation of the system itself and liaise with data processing staff and management. It is important to review all system documentation so as to ascertain where amendments have been made to the original specifications.

5   Mail order firm

(a)   The procedures outlined in the question are the procedures followed by the mail order firm's agents. These procedures can be depicted by way of a dataflow diagram.

The dataflow diagram is a tool used by the analyst, which takes a 'top down' view of the total system.

When the analyst has drawn the dataflow diagram he will use it as a means of communication with the users

The dataflow diagram for the procedures outlined would be as follows.

Note that

◆ The context diagram would be the agent system. This diagram is depicting the first level within that system.

◆ This dataflow diagram is examining the logical system and not the physical system. It is therefore irrelevant how the information is physically stored (which colour ringbinder is used); it is only necessary to state that the information is stored and this is shown by using a datastore symbol.

◆ Each process would be broken down into further levels of detail (exploded or decomposed). For example, the process of the agent verifying the items and resolving discrepancies would be shown at a further level within the process.

(b)   Tools that are used to describe the logic of the processes identified are as follows.

◆ Decision tables
◆ Decision trees
◆ Structured English

A *decision table* uses a set of rules. The rules define the decision to be made given a set situation.

The decision table is broken into conditions which might arise and actions which would be taken.

It is necessary for the decision table to be drawn in four parts.

Condition statement	Condition entry

Action statement	Action entry

A limited entry decision table means that condition entries are limited to Yes or No and action entries to X which indicates the course of action to be taken.

There are also extended entry and mixed entry tables but these do not ensure the same completeness and accuracy.

Some users might find decision tables difficult to understand; the same logic can be presented by using a *decision tree*.

The decision tree follows the same principles as a 'family tree' structure.

There is an 'act fork' and an 'event circle' as can be seen by the following diagram. It considers the consequences of each action.

It enables the user to see the potential outcomes of his decision. However, decision trees are not as good as decision tables for ensuring that all possible combinations of conditions have been catered for.

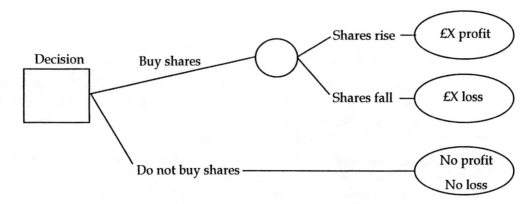

Structured English uses English words but in a precise and concise way. It removes the complexity and ambiguity from the English language. It omits all the frills so that the actual logic is apparent.

6 Car agency

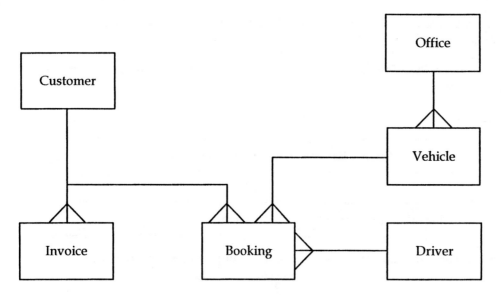

7 Explain in English

(a) The interpretation of the entity relationship model using a set of English statements is as follows.

- ♦ Each customer receives one or many invoices
- ♦ Each invoice is sent to only one customer
- ♦ Each invoice has one or many invoice lines
- ♦ Each invoice line is for only one invoice
- ♦ Each invoice is paid through one or many payments
- ♦ Each payment refers to only one invoice
- ♦ Each product is on one or many invoice lines
- ♦ Each invoice line is for only one product

(b) The relationship should probably be many to many so as to maximise the efficiency of the data.

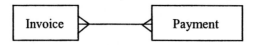

(c)   The many to many relationship can be decomposed into two one-to-many relationships with a new intermediate entity probably called allocation (or invoice or payment will do).

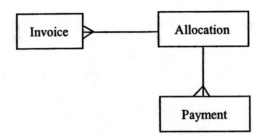

(d)   The likely contents of the entity 'Allocation' will be:

♦   payment number (the key of payment)
♦   invoice number (the key of invoice)
♦   amount.

Chapter 11

1   Training options

(a)   The four training options are as follows.

(1)   To send employees on the standard three-day training course offered by the software provider - the payroll manager has already attended one of the standard courses and so she is able to report on the effectiveness and quality of the course. Advantages and disadvantages of further employees attending such a course include the following.

Advantages

Training can be provided for one delegate at a time. Hence the majority of staff will still be in the billing office undertaking the daily routine business.

Each employee receives standard tuition of a known quality.

The delegate gets the opportunity to talk with other users of the software and so profit from their experience.

Disadvantages

Booking individual places will be more expensive than commissioning an on-site course. The cost of sending the remaining five billing office staff is £3,750 compared with £2,000 for an on-site course.

There are not enough presentations of the course to send one employee on each course before the deadline date. It appears that there will only be two further courses before the implementation date. Thus at least three employees will have to be sent on one course (perhaps causing some office disruption) unless the organisation decides to train some of the employees after the system has gone live.

The course is unlikely to be appropriate to the managers who only wish to interrogate the data. Hence a different method of training will have to be employed to fulfil this training need.

(2)   To arrange an in-house course - this is the standard training course run at the customer's premises.

Advantages

This option is cheaper than sending all the employees on individual bookings on public courses.

The content of the course can be tailored to the organisation's specific requirements, particularly concerning the training of the managers who will be discretionary users of the system. It may be possible to structure the course so that managers attend a self-contained session where all trainees learn about query and reporting facilities.

The users can all be trained before the proposed implementation date.

Disadvantages

It is likely that the payroll department will have to be closed down during the course.

There is no opportunity to learn from users from other companies.

Some delegates may find it difficult to learn with their colleagues and may feel inhibited by the presence of their peers and managers, particularly if they are having some difficulties with the concepts and functions of the software.

(3)   Use the payroll manager to cascade the course throughout the department - advantages and disadvantages include the following.

Advantages

It is probably the cheapest option, as it has no direct tangible cost.

Individual tuition can be provided so there is no need to shut the department down during the training period.

Tuition can be organised so that all employees are trained before the implementation date.

Disadvantages

The payroll manager is not a full-time trainer and may have no aptitude for training - she has only just learned the software herself and so may feel uncertain about her ability to effectively present the course. She risks exposing her own limited knowledge to her staff.

The payroll manager will have to prepare training material and courses. It is unlikely that she will have the time or the expertise to complete these before the deadline date.

(4)   To use CBT software produced by the independent training company - advantages and disadvantages include the following.

Advantages

Employees can fit their learning in with their operational job. There is no need for individuals to go off-site for courses.

Better assessment method - most CBT packages include tests, which are used to control progression onto the next subject. Delegates must pass these tests before they can continue. This limit on progression is not usually possible in taught courses.

The material remains in the company and so it can be used for staff who join in the future.

Disadvantages

A personal computer (PC) must be available for running the CBT software and time must be allowed for undertaking the learning programme.

There is nobody to answer specific questions about the operation of the software if employees are unsure or confused by certain features and facilities.

There is no opportunity to meet staff from other companies who use the software and hence profit from their experience.

(b)   This part of the question requires a coherent justification. Each of the four options could be justified. For example the organisation might elect to run an in-house course. This could be justified on the cheaper cost per delegate and it also ensures that all staff are trained before the system goes live. Training might be organised across two (or three) weekends to allow the continued operation of the department.

2   Data conversion

(a)   Current manual system to a computer one

Set up of master files. The task of file creation can be a daunting task. The resources of the department may not be sufficient or willing to undertake such activities on top of their daily work. The system is unusable until all such data is entered.

Entry of system derived fields. The operational use of the system may automatically create certain data values. For example, the date-of-last-order on the customer file might be posted into the field on receipt of order. However, at the start of the system this field will be blank in all the established customer records. Thus specially written file creation programs may have to be written to capture historical information into the system.

The lack of historical data may restrict use. For example, reports running off the date-of-last-order file introduced in the previous section may be of little use until the second or third year of the system's use.

(b)   Computer system to another computer system

♦ Technical feasibility of moving from one system to another. The developer has to investigate whether it is possible technically to take data from one system and put it on the target machine. It may not be possible to move information from a Unix machine to a Windows machine, for example.

♦ Data mapping and program testing. If it is possible to move from one machine to another then the developer has to carefully map the fields on the current system to the proposed one. For example, the field 'delegate' name may currently sit on a course file and this has to be transferred to a student record on the new system. The developer will have to formally map these relationships and write a program to move the data from the old to the new system. This program has to be tested and the test results carefully examined.

♦ Dirty data, different field lengths and empty fields. Problems can be caused by the transfer of incorrect data values, differences in field lengths between the new and old systems, and empty fields in the new system that have to be populated by specially designed data creation programs.

3   Payroll system

(a)   File conversion takes place during the last stages of systems development. Once the new system is in place then all data has to be transferred onto it. This process can take a considerable time when converting from a manual to a computerised system.

The way in which files are converted depends, to some extent, upon their size and complexity. In this case, there are 3,000 records for input onto a stand-alone microcomputer.

Assuming that there is only one input device, presumably a keyboard, the following sequence of events is likely to occur.

- The changeover will be thoroughly planned and a suitable time identified. In the scenario given, it would not be feasible to run any sort of parallel system and as the package being used is a bought-in package, then it will have been tried and tested and will be free from 'bugs'.

- Once a time has been chosen it is necessary to ensure that all the data held within the present system is accurate and up to date. Dead records should be removed from the system.

- The records will be in continuous use, therefore they will have to be entered in batches. Alternatively, all the cards could be photocopied and then entered onto the system.

- Initially, only the static data will be entered on the computer. This includes such data as name, address, personnel record number, etc. A record will be created for each employee containing all their personal static data.

- Once the static data has been entered then it will be a relatively easier task to enter the up-to-date variable information. This method avoids data becoming out of date before the system is in operation.

- Once all the data has been transferred to the computer, tests will be carried out using test data to ensure that the system is working correctly.

- Hard copies of all records would be printed out in order for employees to verify their record and also in order to comply with the terms of the Data Protection Act.

  Amendments will be necessary from time to time, as in the case of changes in tax tables and national insurance rates. However, there should be standard programs within the package to facilitate amendment.

(b)   Controls that would be incorporated into the process to ensure that the computerised master file is accurate, complete, up to date and suitable for running the live system would include the following.

- The controls exercised to check the completeness and accuracy of the existing manual system.

- The controls over the total number of records and the values imposed on certain key fields. Data entry should be controlled by use of a batch register to ensure that all records have been entered.

- Data should be validated by input programs to check correctness of input.

- Strict control should be exercised over any rejected records.

- Notes and records should be kept of any changes to the manual system prior to conversion.

- A check should be made by record once the data has been entered and this should be compared with the manual records.

- A full test run should be initiated in order to check the system's and operator's accuracy.

4 Testing

Testing goes through three basic stages.

Program testing

During the programming stage each programmer or programming team will perform their own program testing to the specification laid down by the systems analyst. This stage is concerned with validating the internal code of the program making sure that it conforms to the standards of the company as well as performing the functional business requirements defined by the analyst. The testing is performed through manual 'walkthroughs' of the program as well as the production of test plans and their result.

Systems testing

This is designed to ensure that the subsystems work properly together. This testing is performed against specification and uses test data and test results. Testing is performed over a single pass of data before progressing to cyclical tests (such as end-of-month and end-of-year routines) and volume testing. Testing may be performed by the systems analyst or by specialist quality and standards staff.

User acceptance testing

This is organised and performed by users. It is concerned with proving, to their satisfaction, that the delivered system meets the specification. The testing is again against test data with suitably prepared test results. The users check the outputs to prove the system against the day-to-day running of the system. User acceptance testing also allows for gradual user training and gives them experience of the system prior to implementation.

5 System changeover

(a) There are four basic approaches to systems changeover.

Direct changeover

At a given point in time the old system is abandoned and the new system commences. This would appear to be the cheapest approach but it is also the most risky approach and the balance must be considered between risk of breakdown or failure and economics of using alternative approaches. There are, however, some instances where there is little choice, if for instance the new system is radically different from the old, or if the organisation is moving from a centralised to a decentralised system or *vice versa*. With a department store which relies heavily upon continued sales and customer satisfaction it is unlikely that it could risk a direct changeover when it could use alternative methods.

Parallel changeover

This involves running both the new and the old system at the same time. The benefit of this is that the results can be compared. When the new system has proved that it is working well and can be relied upon, the old system can be abandoned. This is a relatively safe approach and has the added advantage that it allows the staff to become used to the system before abandoning the old system. However, to run two systems in parallel is costly: two lots of processing have to take place and there may be additional staff costs involved. For the department store this would probably be the best option.

Phased changeover

With this approach the new system is phased in department by department or subsystem by subsystem. This approach relies upon the fact that the old and the new system are compatible and can work together. Users get used to the new system on a gradual basis, but the benefits of the system cannot be fully felt until the whole system is in place. For the department store it might not be possible to phase the system in.

Pilot changeover

This approach involves running the new system on a sample of people or data, or at a particular branch. Potentially a pilot changeover can also include parallel runs. For the department store it would mean the introduction of the POS system at one branch, but keeping some old tills in place in case of breakdown or failure. Once the system had been tried and tested at the branch then a direct changeover could continue everywhere else. This would also appear to be a good option for the department store.

Whichever approach is adopted, managers will need to carefully control and monitor the changeover procedure to ensure successful completion.

(b) The activities which should be carried out during implementation are as follows.

♦ Creation of changeover timetable
♦ Creation of a changeover plan which involves all personnel
♦ Notify all employees of changeover plans
♦ Inform employees of progress by regular updates or bulletins
♦ Development of a training programme
♦ Employment of any additional personnel
♦ Take delivery of new POS equipment
♦ Test the equipment received
♦ Install software onto hardware
♦ Test software
♦ Complete documentation
♦ Train the systems operators
♦ Do trial runs
♦ Specify the changeover period
♦ Carry out acceptance tests
♦ Activate the new system

(c) The system will need to be evaluated after approximately three months. It is vital to ensure that the system is achieving the performance levels expected.

Criteria used to evaluate systems consist of the following.

Time

What is the time taken for a particular activity to be carried out? Response time is the time taken between the initial instruction and the performance of the activity. Response time is usually measured in seconds. Turnaround time is the time taken to provide the outcome to the instructions given. Response time and turnaround time will be important if customers are waiting at the tills.

Costs

This measurement determines whether the new system is meeting the financial expectations the company placed upon it. Overall costs of a system include costs of development, labour, maintenance, rentals, consumables, training, data entry, data storage etc. The new system should be more cost effective than the old system.

Hardware performance

This should be measured in terms of speed, reliability, maintenance, operating costs and power requirements. For the POS system, servicing of the system and its networking components should be evaluated.

Software performance

This should be measured in terms of processing, accuracy, speed, quality, volume of output, reliability, maintenance, and update requirements.

Accuracy

This is the measure of freedom from errors that the system achieves. It can be measured in several ways, but more importantly the system should be measured for the type of errors and volume of errors that occur. By highlighting these errors, early rectification of problems can be achieved. It is essential that the customers of the department stores are not inconvenienced by errors of the system.

Security

This is measuring the security of the data held upon the system. The system should be secure against illegal access or modification of data. Any personal data held on a system means that the company has to register under the Data Protection Act. It is essential that adequate protection is given against data corruption or virus infiltration.

Morale

This is measured by the levels of absenteeism and employee turnover. New systems, such as the POS, must be accepted by employees.

Customers

The reactions of the customers to the new POS are an important factor. If there were a large number of complaints from customers, the indication would be that the system is not working satisfactorily.

Data gathered during the evaluation should be studied to assess the success or failure of the system. In addition it should highlight any expectation failure for investigation.

6 Maintenance

(a) *Corrective maintenance* is the term often applied to the fixing of programming errors in the software. It can also be applied to hardware faults and to operational errors that cause the system to become unusable. Corrective maintenance is often required to return the system to a fully operational state. The system is 'down' until corrective maintenance has been completed.

Many companies log 'downtime' system failures. It must be determined whether these are due to operational problems (for example, the user switching the system off leaving files partially updated) or due to programming errors or mistakes in file use and updating. Each of these errors must be logged and investigated. The investigation must focus on the development and testing process so that it is understood how the error was introduced into the system in the first place. The results of the investigation may lead to changes in procedures and standards.

Adaptive maintenance is concerned with changing the software to reflect alterations in the business environment. These changes may be due to new user requirements or (more usually) refined user requirements in the light of experience in using the software. New user requirements are often triggered by changes in the business environment or perhaps by new users. In most instances the system can still be used whilst adaptive maintenance is performed.

Measuring the number of functional user changes after implementation is useful as long as the changes are correctly diagnosed and categorised. For example, some changes will actually be 'what we wanted in the first place'. In such instances there has been an error of specification and so specification methods must be reviewed to reduce these problems. In other instances the user's understanding of the requirements has only become clear after experimenting with and using the software. These changes can be expected although there may be a case for seeing whether these might have been uncovered earlier in the systems development lifecycle, perhaps through prototyping. Finally, there may be amendments due to unforeseen changes in the business environment. Hopefully a flexible design will reduce the effect of such changes but in general these amendments are difficult to predict.

(b)   Appropriate measures might include:

- Calls to the help desk.

    Calls to the help desk must be categorised and the statistics produced analysed. It may emerge that problems keep recurring and the reasons for this must be understood. There may be confusion or ambiguities in the dialogue, training may have been unsuccessful or inappropriate, or the system may not be able to cope with the variety of circumstances met in practical use. The reasons must be investigated and remedies suggested – changes in dialogue wording and structures, refresher training courses, new documentation, etc.

- Software monitoring of errors.

    Software monitoring of errors records information about what errors have been made. It will include errors that never get reported to the help desk because the user has solved the problem themselves – after some confusion and wasted time and effort. Consequently the help desk statistics and the software monitoring of errors are important complementary sources of information.

    The overall usability of the software can also be assessed through the following.

- Recording the time required for users to become proficient in the software. This may emerge from training courses, where users may still not be confident in the use of the software after the allocated course time. The trainers may also observe common problems and feed these back to the development team.

- Suitable questions in a user-satisfaction questionnaire.

- Software monitoring of the use of the system by discretionary users.

    The last of these examples illustrates how software monitoring can be used to assess the use of the system. For example, the number of times a particular report is requested can be logged together with the user and the time taken to produce the report or fulfil the enquiry. This can be used to provide statistics of actual use.

    This is very important with discretionary users such as managers who do not have to provide operational input into the system. Managers may elect not to use the system because of the following.

- It does not provide useful information. Hence requirements must be reviewed.

- It is too difficult to use. This may lead to changes in dialogue wording and structure.

- It is too slow to use. This may lead to changes in programs or data structures.

7 Performance criteria

This is a wide area for evaluation. There are many different 'systems' and as many different kinds of performance criteria utilised to assess 'success' of new systems. If we determine what the new system is supposed to do, however, we can then compare actual with expected performance.

A broad, overall review of performance would take into account the following aspects.

♦ In terms of system costs, the new system is expected to prove cost-effective, unless for example it is intended to promote the safety of aircraft passengers. Cost savings would be expected in, for example, staff, storage space for files of all kinds, and processing speed.

♦ As far as data processing is concerned, information for management decision-making should be carried out in an acceptable manner, for instance at a faster speed, which may well result in improved services to customers, clients and so on.

The handling of data volumes is also an important issue. Quantities handled during a given time period should be measured.

Benchmarks are frequently adopted to compare the performance of different systems which undertake the same tasks. A performance measure often adopted is 'millions of instructions per second' (mips), usually quoted by suppliers as an indication of the speed at which the CPU operates.

Other aspects of performance which are taken into account are response times (the time taken between the last input digit of a request to the first digit of the output; the response), levels of machine-usage and turnaround times.

8 Software selection

(a) Issues in software selection

Requirements fit

It is important to assess the 'fit' of the software to the requirements of the manufacturing company. It is unlikely that any of the packages will fulfil all the requirements defined in the invitation to tender and so the company has to decide to either make compromises and forgo certain requirements or to commission bespoke changes to produce a system that exactly meets its needs. The flexibility of the package may be an important issue in evaluating each proposal. Some packages allow menus, dialogues and reports to be tailored to each organisation's specific requirements. Some vendors will also build in changes at low cost in the understanding that such functionality can be passed on to other users, so that their product becomes more functional and hence attractive to other customers in the marketplace.

System performance

The functionality of the system must be supported by acceptable performance. The company must be sure that the system can cope with the volumes of data that will be processed and stored. Many suppliers have tables of performance statistics showing the response time of their software under different loadings and configuration. It may be possible to achieve acceptable performance by relatively cheap hardware upgrades and so it might be unwise to reject a package on system performance alone.

Compatibility with existing software

The company currently has inventory control software. This will be storing information about products, orders, despatch notes, etc which may still need to be accessed by the replacement system. Consequently the company needs to investigate issues of data conversion and compatibility, and the willingness of the supplier to provide such facilities and their cost.

Usability

Many software packages offer very similar facilities because they are supporting the same functional area. Consequently, differences may be confined to the user-friendliness of the software - general screen layout, meaningful error messages, context-sensitive help, report layouts, etc. In certain environments the package may be judged against de facto industry standards (such as Microsoft Windows). Evidence suggests that users are increasingly expecting packages to be consistent across applications, so that they can take their skills from one area to another.

Security and audit

Many competing packages offer different emphasis on the security aspects of the software. Some may offer only rudimentary password facilities (perhaps on initial entry into the package) whilst others provide layers of passwords, supported by encryption and other measures designed to protect the data. The audit trail should also be inspected and its content discussed with internal auditors or external advisers.

Supplier factors

Package selection should include a general evaluation of the supplier. This might include an assessment of the financial strength of the supplier, their experience in manufacturing industry and the number of solutions they have supplied to this sector. The supplier might also offer flexible supply options (for example, allowing the customer to rent the package for three months before deciding to purchase). Training, support and documentation can also be examined and assessed.

(b)   Weighted tables

The most common approach to assessing the strengths and weaknesses of each proposal is to compile a number of important factors and to weight their importance in the selection process. Here is an example.

Factor	Weighting
Functionality	10
Cost	8
Compatibility with existing software	8
Performance	7
User-friendliness	7
Flexibility	5
Security	5
Supplier issues	4

Each supplier is either given a rank or a score for each of these factors and a weighted total produced. The package with the highest figure is selected.

Benchmarks

Benchmark tests are undertaken by running competing software over the same data. The speed of response or function can be recorded and compared. There appears to be no plan to upgrade the current hardware in the manufacturing company. Consequently vendors can be invited to benchmark their software over the current configuration, providing statistics to supplement general tables of performance.

Chapter 12

1   Feedback control loops

(a)   Feedback loops are used to exercise control in both physical and organisational systems. In a business context the output of a system (eg a department) is monitored or measured and compared with the expected or planned performance. Based on the result of the monitoring and comparison, adjustments are made to the input side of the system if necessary. The process described is termed a feedback control loop and in an organisational system such a loop is based on information flows. The various parts of a control loop are shown in the following diagram:

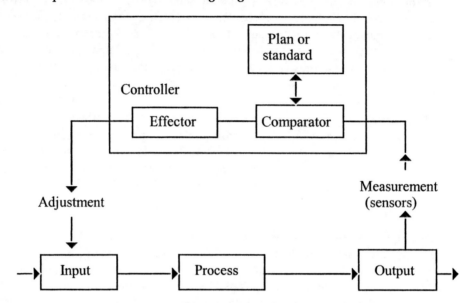

Sensors: the measuring devices of the system.

Comparators: the means by which the comparison of actual results and the plan is achieved.

Effectors: the means by which the results of the comparison initiate corrective action.

(b)   Importance of feedback

Some form of feedback is essential if there is to be any form of control in a system. Feedback which tends to dampen and reduce fluctuations around a norm or standard is called negative feedback and is the more commonly used because it tends to smooth out fluctuations and create more stable systems.   Using negative feedback, the corrective action would be in the opposite direction to the deviation.

On the other hand, positive feedback causes the system to repeat or amplify an adjustment or action. This can cause instability, but if used correctly positive feedback is useful particularly in the growth stages of a system.   All of the commonly encountered control systems, eg budgetary control, inventory control, production control, are based on information feedback loops.

(c)   Double loop feedback

Single loop feedback as described above is feedback regarding relatively small deviations from plan so that control may be exercised in order that the original plan is achieved. Double loop or higher-level feedback is concerned with feedback about larger variations and environmental changes so that the plan itself can be amended.

Double loop feedback does not always form part of the formal reporting system although from a system's viewpoint it is clearly very important to have some means of adjusting the plan or standard to meet changing conditions.

2   Open systems

(a)   Systems may be classified as 'closed' or 'open'.

A *closed system* is one which is completely self-supporting.

Open systems are those which interact with their environment and rely on this environment for obtaining inputs and for the discharge of their system-outputs. An example of an open system is a business organisation.

(b)   Katz and Kahn attempted to summarise the complexities of organisations as open systems. They identified the common characteristics as:

(i)   importation of energy and stimulation (eg organisational resources);

(ii)   conversion (eg the process of converting inputs into goods and services);

(iii)   negative entropy (entropy is the process by which all things tend to die) – developing negative entropy means developing mechanisms that enable survival (eg an organisation building up reserves);

(iv)   positive and negative feedback enables systems to correct deviations (eg organisations tend to develop control systems incorporating feedback);

(v)   equifinality – open systems do not have to achieve their goals in one particular way (eg organisations will set plans to achieve goals but will have contingency plans in the event of disturbances).

The above clearly indicates the concept of open systems to organisation theory.

3   Control

The statement 'control is the essence of management' implies that control is the main function of management.

Control ensures that management knows how the organisation is progressing towards objectives and what corrections need to be made to 'stay on course'.

Controlling activities are concerned essentially with measuring progress and correcting deviations. The basic functions of control are:

(i)   *To establish standards of performance*

Once plans have been made, standards of performance need to be clearly stated. Budgets are a useful means of setting quantifiable standards. Where standards are qualitative, they should be expressed in terms of end results rather than methods.

(ii)   *To measure actual performance against standards*

This involves analysing actual information in a manner which is consistent with the standards set. The most important source of information is the management accounting department. The measurement of actual performance depends on the accuracy, relevance and timeliness of information. The management accounting department will also be responsible for identifying and analysing variances, and for finding out whether they can be avoided if adverse or encouraged if favourable.

(iii)   *To take corrective actions where appropriate*

When comparing actual performance against standard, management will require action to be taken when the variances against standard are significant. This is known as the 'management by exception' principle.

The control function must be responsive to the environment in which it operates. Changes in the environment may result in the standards set being inappropriate. For this reason, the managerial control process must be flexible.

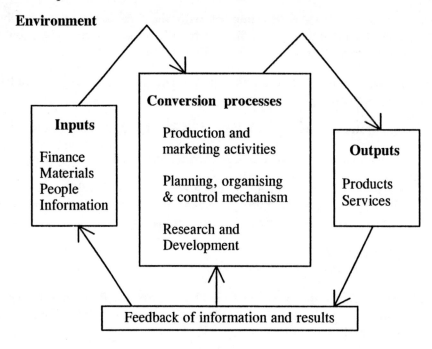

Chapter 13

1   The Highland Manufacturing Co

Report on suitable control procedures for the Highland Manufacturing Company

To: Management team

From: Management consultant

Date: 15th November 20X0

Terms of reference

In view of the change in the range of products now requiring expensive components, this report seeks to explain the types of procedures available and advise management on the most suitable.

Controls required

The controls required for the stock may be divided into seven main sections.

(i)   *Physical security* - safeguarding the physical security of the stock means controls over access to the storage area should be tightened up and strictly enforced.

          Supervision over stores staff should be intensified, especially at the end of the day to ensure that goods are not pilfered.

          External security on access by outside thieves should be improved.

(ii)   *Stock records* - adequate records should be maintained so that reordering, identification of slow-moving stock and stocktaking are facilitated. All forms used to support the recording system should be prenumbered. The records should include an indication when preset reorder levels are reached. It would be an advantage if such a system was computerised.

(iii)   Authorisation - all movements of stock should be properly authorised.

          These will include:

          ♦   requisitions for purchases (from stores for reordering of existing lines and from production control for new items)

          ♦   authorisation of orders, all of which will be placed by the buying department after checking of requisition form

          ♦   requisitions for issues, signed by factory supervisor.

          Authorisation is also required for the passing of invoices for payment after confirming that the goods concerned have been duly received in accordance with the order.

(iv)   Segregation of duties of those handling the stock - the work of maintaining the stock records and of dealing with the stock itself should be separated.

(v)   Supervision - all stages of the stock handling and recording operation should be supervised.

(vi)   Competence of staff - they may need training in the handling of the new stock lines to minimise damage or breakage.

(vii)   Internal audit - the whole process of stock handling and recording should be subject to internal audit. This should apply particularly in the weeks shortly after the introduction of the new system to ensure that any deviations from the system are detected and corrected.

Specific tasks for the internal auditors

These could include the following

◆   Checking of physical stock against records and investigation of discrepancies.

◆   Testing requisitions to ensure that all were properly authorised.

◆   Testing invoices to ensure that they have been properly checked against orders and against goods inwards records.

◆   Ensuring that returns from factory to store are duly accounted for. (This is frequently a point of weakness in stock control systems.)

◆   Observation of stock handling procedures to ensure that the controls built into the system are being observed and that supervision is adequate.

If internal audit staff are not available because the company is too small to have such a department, it is still necessary to have the checking tasks listed above carried out by staff independent of the stock handling and recording staff, especially in the early weeks of the system.

Further work

Further work, which provides additional evidence of the accuracy of the stock records, includes:

(i)   Comparison of stock usage over a period with expected usage as calculated by the production control department. (This work should be confined to the new high-value items, of course.)

(ii)   Reconciliation of opening and closing stocks with records of purchases, production and sales.

Conclusion

If the procedures recommended in the report are established and maintained, the management can feel confident that control is exercised from receipt to use of the items.

2   Internal audit tasks

(a)   Activities within the province of the internal auditor

　　(i)   Review of accounting systems and related internal controls.

　　(ii)   Examination of financial and operating data and detailed testing of transactions and balances.

　　(iii) Review of the operation of non-financial controls and the efficiency and effectiveness of business systems.

　　(iv)   Review of how corporate policies, plans and procedures have been implemented.

　　(v)   Special investigations.

(b)   Features of an internal control system upon which an auditor is likely to rely

    (i)   *Physical controls* - to ensure that assets and records are kept securely and that access is authorised.

    (ii)   *Authorisation* - a responsible person has been approved to give authorisation for all transactions. Limits on authorisation should be set down in writing.

    (iii)   *Personnel* - only properly motivated, competent personnel are employed, who have the necessary integrity for their tasks.

    (iv)   *Arithmetical accuracy* - the necessary arithmetical and accounting controls are in force to ensure the accuracy of records (eg control accounts).

    (v)   *Management* - the internal control system operates within a properly instituted framework of overall management controls, eg budgeting centres.

    (vi)   *Organisation* - there is a well-defined organisation structure within which the system works and which identifies responsibilities and authority.

    (vii)   *Segregation of duties* - when fixing responsibilities, no one person can fully record and process a transaction.

    (viii)   *Supervision* - the internal control system works with proper supervisory procedures.

(c)   Investigation of receiving, recording and banking of cheques

Management must provide a clear system for controlling cheque receipts and processing and ensure that only properly trained personnel of integrity are employed. There should be carefully defined areas of responsibility and authority.

When the mail is opened each day, this should be in a secure room under close supervision of an authorised manager. All cheques should be kept securely by one clerk and then transferred to another ledger clerk for processing (ie segregation of duties). As updating of records takes place, a pre-list total for arithmetical control should be prepared and the appropriate control account updated.

Cheques should then be passed to the cashier for preparation of paying-in documents. A security firm or guard would then take the cheques and documents to the bank. The cashier would then ensure that the debit to the bank account is recorded and that it agrees with the credit to the debtors control account prepared by the ledger clerk.

3   Internal audits

(a)   One definition of 'internal audit' is as follows: 'Internal audit is an independent appraisal function within an organisation for the review of systems of control and the quality of performance, as a service to the organisation. It objectively examines, evaluates and reports on the adequacy of internal control as a contribution to the proper, economic, efficient and effective use of resources'.

Internal checks are subsets of the whole system of internal control specifically designed to ensure that all errors or inequalities are identified and corrected and to confirm that all assets and liabilities recorded in the accounts do exist.

Both internal audit and internal check are elements of the overall internal control system which is defined as the whole system of controls, financial and otherwise, established by management in order to carry on the business of an organisation in an orderly and efficient manner, ensure adherence to management policies, safeguard assets and secure as far as possible the completeness and accuracy of records.

It should be noted that apart from a few special cases where internal audit is statutory, internal audit is a voluntary approach and service which is introduced by management to evaluate the internal control systems in force.

(b)   The types of internal control which may exist in an organisation are as follows:

   (i)   *segregation of duties* - a basic type of control ensuring that no one person should be capable of fully recording and processing a transaction through to completion;

   (ii)   *physical controls* - concerned with the physical custody of assets and ensuring that no unauthorised person can have access to them;

   (iii)   *authorisation and approval* - before any transaction is allowed, proper authorisation and approval should be given by a responsible official; clearly defined limits as to the extent of authority of any officer should be set out in writing;

   (iv)   *management* - the day-to-day routine of the system should be monitored from outside by budgetary control procedures and/or internal audit;

   (v)   *supervision* - responsible officials should be in charge of the day-to-day routine operation of the accounting procedures;

   (vi)   *organisation* - to ensure the identity of responsibilities and duties there should be a well-defined organisational structure;

   (vii)   *arithmetical and accuracy* - whenever possible and appropriate, checks on the arithmetical accuracy and correct procedures should be carried out by methods such as control totals, cross checks and reconciliations;

   (viii) *personnel* - only well-motivated, responsible and competent personnel should be entrusted with accounting work.

(c)   A wages system is an obvious set of procedures for illustrating the implementation of internal controls. Of necessity it must be the most efficient and reliable system in the organisation with no difficulties in any wages run - otherwise there would soon be problems with the workforce.

Following the order outlined in (b), the controls might be applied to a wages system as follows.

Segregation of duties - This should apply at all stages from calculation of gross wages through deduction to the assessment of net pay. No one person should have responsibility for all these tasks so that a control may be introduced to check the work at different stages.

Physical controls - These should be applied to the records particularly for the wages system to avoid tampering with items such as timesheets, tax-deduction cards and, of course, the final cash in pay packets or the BACS procedures.

Authorisation - This will apply to the authorisation of hours worked and any extra payments by the appropriate departmental manager. Also wage rates will be approved by the personnel department.

Management - Managers will keep a watching brief over the wages paid out and compare actual against budget. They will also ensure that all internal checks and controls are performed.

Supervision - The day-to-day operation of the wages system must be carried out under the control of a trusted supervisor.

Organisation - To ensure the segregation of duties, there should be a clearly-defined organisation structure in the wages department. This structure will also identify the responsibilities of supervisors and the fixing of levels of authority.

Arithmetical checks - These should be incorporated at all stages of the wages procedure.

Personnel - Only personnel of the highest integrity should be employed in a department which is responsible for the paying out of what may be the highest expenditure each week for the organisation.

4   Internal control

(a)   Substantive testing covers many techniques which are used to verify the figures appearing in the accounts and subsidiary records. There are four main methods of substantive testing:

♦   Inspection of documents - also known as vouching. The details on the document, eg names, dates and amounts, would be checked and any alterations or errors recorded. Normally more reliability would be placed on a document originating outside the organisation's business.

♦   Inspection of assets - the existence of physical assets such as machinery and stocks can be ascertained in this way.

♦   Direct confirmation - written evidence from third parties will vary according to their relationship/status.

♦   Checking calculations and reconciliations - this is checking the accuracy of both simple and complex calculations. It should be applied to both machine processed and manually processed items. Any discrepancies in a reconciliation require adequate explanation and follow up.

(b)   Analytical review - the purpose of this technique is to provide evidence as to the completeness, accuracy and validity of the accounting records and statements. It comprises a systematic study of the relationships among items and investigation of variations from the expected relationships.

The main stages in carrying out this type of review are:

♦   Assessment of the likely effectiveness of analytical review on particular items

♦   Definition of the items and relationships to be reviewed

♦   Estimation of the expected relationships or amounts, eg the gross profit percentage or the fixed overheads, and comparison of these with the actual figures

♦   Obtain and verify explanations of significant differences in the comparison above

♦   Decide whether the explanations are adequate or whether further substantive testing is required.

(c)   Compliance testing - this concerns the internal control systems. Note that compliance tests are **tests of controls.** They provide evidence as to whether or not the controls on which the auditor wishes to rely were functioning adequately during the period under review. Compliance tests check the functioning of a control, not the transaction itself. For that reason all exceptions revealed by the compliance testing should be thoroughly investigated irrespective of the amount involved in the particular transaction which is being used as the medium for carrying out the test.

If the compliance test reveals that no exceptions or deviations have occurred, then the auditor is entitled to rely on the working of that control. Any deviation or exception could be an isolated event or it could indicate the existence of errors in the systems and records, which may result in material error. The hypothesis that the deviation or exception was an isolated one can, and should, be proved by further tests. If one control cannot be relied upon, there may be alternative controls that are in force. These cannot be relied upon until they too have been tested for compliance.

Chapter 14

1   Internal audit interest

The internal audit function is an independent department set up within an organisation for the review and evaluation of operational, financial and accounting systems. The principal concern of internal audit would be the existence and effectiveness of each system with particular reference to the controls in the following areas.

Acquisition of computer facilities

♦   Project justification (statement of requirements)
♦   Purchasing procedures
♦   Appraisal and decision-making
♦   Installation of hardware and software
♦   Post implementation review

System procedural controls

♦   Input controls
♦   Processing controls
♦   Output controls
♦   Existence for an audit trail

System development controls

♦   Standards and documentation
♦   Project justification
♦   Project management
♦   Testing and proving
♦   Control of change and amendment
♦   Training

Administrative and operational controls

♦   Separation of duties
♦   File and software controls
♦   Operational controls (access to system)
♦   Terminal controls
♦   Environmental controls (temperature/humidity/fire/flood)
♦   Standby and recovery procedures

Use of resources

♦   Costing of projects
♦   Costing of human/computer resources
♦   Staff development planning
♦   Measures of performance (people/equipment/projects)
♦   Data (accuracy/relevance/timeliness)

2   Security

Briefing report

To: Head of Department

From   Trainee management accountant

Date: 2nd November 20X0

Security of an organisation's computer system

The factors which most affect the security of an organisation's computer system can be divided into three groups - physical, systems and human.

Physical aspects - these relate to the security risks to which the computer hardware is exposed. These risks mainly come from outside the system and include theft, fire, dust, humidity, flooding and earth movement damage to the building housing the computer.

Systems aspects - these relate to risks which are inherent in the system itself and include loss of data, loss of software and possibly damage to equipment; all caused by system malfunctioning brought about by either hardware or software failure or errors.

Human aspects - these include risks from inside and outside the organisation and risks arising from both intentional and unintentional actions. For example a large multi-user networked computer system is at risk from outside 'hacking' as well as from employees within the organisation. Unintentional damage to equipment, data and software, etc may be caused by accidents, eg spilling drinks into equipment, accidental changes to data, eg correcting the wrong file or deleting a file, running the wrong software, forgetting to run a particular process, etc. Intentional aspects include setting up fake accounts, causing unauthorised payments either as credit or cheques to be made, allowing favourable discount terms to particular clients and damage such as the deletion or corruption of data files and software.

Managing the risks associated with computer security

Managing the risks associated with computer security involves reducing the risks and the effects to the lowest possible levels. Three stages are necessary.

Risk assessment - a full examination of all the risks in the three groups above is made. Particular types of computer systems and particular locations and environments each have their own problems. The risks are, of course, different for a centralised system as against a distributed computing system.

Another factor is the importance of the work being done on the computer. For example if a personnel department computer went down, it would not be as serious as if the computer monitoring a production line failed, and there would not be such a need to get the personnel computer up and running again quickly.

Risk minimisation - this comprises the actions which may be taken when the risks to a computer system have been assessed. These actions include both taking physical and system precautions and providing fall-back and remedial measures. The list of actions includes:

♦   securing the building(s) housing equipment with bars, strong doors, locks, monitoring systems, access control, etc;

♦   provision of an environment suitable for reliable computer operation, having clean air at the correct temperature and humidity, and an electrical power supply that is both continuous and smooth;

- strict control of the quality of new software and on any modifications required to existing software;

- vetting of all computer staff appointments and the taking out of 'fidelity guarantees' with suitable insurance companies;

- access control for the system from terminals, etc. This will normally involve a system of passwords changed on a regular basis;

- a high level of training and education of computer staff;

- automated operating procedures with built in checks (probably utilising job control language 'programs') so that operators do not have to trust to memory and are given minimum scope for error;

- fully documented systems and procedure manuals including precise statements of actions to be taken for system recovery after breakdowns;

- provision of standby facilities and a reciprocal processing agreement with another organisation. (If the computer failed and it was expected that it would not be repairable for quite some time, then back-up disks would be transferred and processing carried out on the other organisation's computer, overnight or at the weekend - and vice versa.)

Risk transference - it is impossible to eliminate all risks, but it is possible to transfer the element of uncovered risk to another party through the medium of insurance, ie in the event of a computer catastrophe, the losses caused would be covered by insurance.

3 Control guidelines

(a) Systems controls should be designed according to the following guidelines.

- All transactions should be processed.

- All errors in transactions should be reported.

- Errors should be corrected and re-input.

- Fraud should be prevented.

- The likelihood of error should be estimated. This will depend partly on the location in which the source document is prepared and the type of person originating it.

- The importance of errors should be assessed. In accounting systems, 100 per cent accuracy may be required. In other systems (eg market surveys), a degree of error may be acceptable.

- The cost of control should be considered in relation to the cost of an error. The cost of 100 per cent accuracy is, in practice, usually too high.

- The controls should not interfere unduly with the progress of work.

- The controls should be as simple as possible, and acceptable to users.

- Auditors should be consulted and the system designed to meet their requirements.

(b)   (i)   *Incorrect customer account code*

This should be detected by a check digit. The account code would include an extra digit derived by calculation from the other digits. On input to the computer, the program would perform the calculations and, if the digit derived was not the check digit, an error would be reported. The system selected should minimise the possibility of undetected error.

(ii)   *Raw material quantity*

This should be detected by a reasonableness check. Upper and lower limits would be set, outside which a quantity should not lie. Since the entry of tons instead of pounds would result in a value 2,240 times as big as the correct one, it would be detected.

(iii)   *Product not stocked*

This would be detected by an on-file check. On input, the despatch note details would be referred to the stock master files, which would indicate that the product was not held in the warehouse shown.

(iv)   *Five-digit product code*

This would be detected by a format check. The validation program would have parameters for the size of fields, and would report the product code as being a digit short.

(v)   *Invalid expenditure code*

This would be detected by a range check. The validation program would have parameters showing the upper and lower values of expenditure codes. Comparison of the code with the parameters would reveal that it was not in the permissible range.

4   Food wholesaler (I)

Administrative controls

The objectives of administrative controls are to ensure that there is an acceptable level of efficiency and discipline in the day-to-day running of the department. The word 'acceptable' would be defined to fit a measurable set of objectives for a specific computer department.

♦   Standby procedures should be available in case of breakdown, with the ability to reconstruct data files.

♦   Security procedures should be set up. User numbers and passwords would be used to prevent or restrict access. Terminal 'handshake' procedures would identify special terminals that could access certain applications. Physical security could prevent unauthorised access to those terminals.

♦   Passwords should be regularly changed. They should be memorable to a user, but difficult for someone to guess. A secure procedure should allow a particular user to find out his or her password when it has been forgotten. If a password is written down, it should be kept in a secure location.

♦   Terminal and system usage should be logged. This can be used to allocate costs or to identify suspicious changes in usage patterns. There are computer algorithms that can identify automatically when usage patterns change suspiciously – they are currently used to identify credit card fraud.

Systems development controls

These are designed to ensure that there is a satisfactory standard at each level of the sys tems development process, including the analysis of needs, design of the system, project management, program specification, program writing, program testing, system testing, system implementation and documentation. Methods of ensuring good quality are as follows.

- A steering committee could be used to help allocate priorities for system developments. This would also be responsible for defining and enforcing systems development controls.

- A structured methodology such as SSADM could be followed in analysing, designing and developing a system.

- Specific projects would be carried out for individual project teams, which would be managed by a project management committee.

- A project time schedule would be set up, with control deadlines being overseen by the project management committee.

- Members of the department would be encouraged to build relationships with the users of systems, and should encourage users to become aware of the facilities that the computer makes available.

- Each program would be thoroughly tested, with a test log showing what conditions have been tested and what the result of the test was.

- The completed system would be comprehensively tested, with a test log being kept as above.

- Documentation would be created according to one of the published sets of standards (eg the relevant British Standard, the National Computer Council standard). Documentation should show what action should be taken in any eventuality (all types of errors should be foreseen and recovery procedures designed).

- Performance indicators should be built into the system, and a procedure designed for correcting any situation where the system is not meeting its objectives.

- All modifications to the system should be designed and documented to the same standard as the original. All original documentation should be updated to take account of the modifications.

Processing controls

The purpose of processing controls is to ensure that all data used by a system is accurately and completely processed from point of origin and that all data files are accurately maintained and updated.

Each application would have its own appropriate set of control procedures. A batch system would use different control procedures from an on-line system. Control procedures include the following.

Checks that the initial documents are correctly completed.

- Verification, which will check that data has been correctly entered. An on-line system will display the data on a screen and ask the user to verify that it is correct before it is stored. A batch system may require data to be entered twice.

- Batch totals will ensure that all data has been entered, and that it has been entered correctly. If the total being computed is meaningless (such as the sum of different account numbers) it is called a hash total.

- Batch listings are produced. These can be manually checked against source documents.

- Data can be validated (checked by the computer). Different techniques are used – check digits, reasonableness, existence, format, etc.

- Redundant data can be entered into the system. If the price per unit and number of units sold are entered, then it should be unnecessary to also enter the total cost, but this is sometimes used as a cross-check that the first two items have been entered correctly.

♦ Audit trails may be used to ensure that files are updated correctly, and that they can be reconstructed in the event of system failure.

♦ A log of runs on a particular system can be used to identify problems when they have occurred.

♦ Procedural controls are set up to ensure that output reports are complete, accurate and distributed appropriately.

5   Multi-user system control

The control techniques and safeguards used to protect a system where multiple users have access to centralised data through terminal devices at remote locations linked to a central computer system via telephone lines or other communication links are as follows.

♦ **Terminal physical security** - this covers two aspects. Firstly, terminal room access - the use of strict controls over the locking of the rooms in which the terminals are located and the distribution of keys to authorised personnel only. This is vital where the terminals are used either to access sensitive data files or to alter or develop programs. Secondly, terminal machine access - the restriction of access to and use of terminals by keys, cards and badges.

♦ **User identification** - this includes the positive confirmation of the identity of the user and the proof of his identification (authentication). The former includes the input of his name, employee number and account number. The latter includes the input of something that is known (eg passwords, question-and-answer sequences), something that is possessed (badges, cards), or something personal to the user (eg finger print, hand or voice features, signature).

♦ **Data and program access authorisation** - after identification of the user (as above), the privileges he has as to what he can access (files and programs) and what he can do during access have to be checked to ensure that he has the necessary authority. The user must be denied access if not specifically authorised.

♦ **Surveillance** - the detection of security violations by direct observation, by review of computer logs or by use of the operator's console to display current program and data usage.

♦ **Communication lines safeguards** - while impossible to fully protect communication lines, controls such as encryption, phone tap and bug checks should go a long way to prevent penetration of the system via the communication lines.

♦ **Encryption** - the transformation of a message or of data for the purpose of rendering it unintelligible to everyone but the correct users who are able to translate the message back to its original form.

♦ **Program integrity controls** - controls which ensure that unauthorised access and alterations cannot be made to programs.

♦ **Database integrity controls** - controls and audit techniques which protect database management systems software and data against unauthorised access, modification, disclosure and destruction.

♦ **Administrative considerations** - procedures which ensure that controls and safeguards are effective in preventing, deterring and detecting unauthorised or fraudulent systems data and program access and modification.

6   Food wholesaler (II)

The auditor should be able to objectively show whether the system is doing what is required of it, whether data has been accurately and completely processed, and when computer fraud has occurred.

Software that is useful for auditors includes the following.

Data retrieval software

This is used to extract data from files, and to prepare reports. These reports can be compared with the original data and processes that have been carried out since the last audit.

Parallel simulation

The auditor's own code is used to duplicate the results from the system being audited.

Embedded audit routine

Auditing procedures are included within the original program routines. They may produce an audit trail of transactions for later analysis, or may be used to display the procedures that are in operation within the program.

Test data

This is often used by the auditor to ensure that the program is producing the results that are expected.

Program review

Programs exist that will build structure diagrams from the original code. This will allow the auditor to make sure that the program performs according to its specifications, and that no undocumented modification has occurred. Programs also exist which can 'decompile' compiled programs into source code.

Program comparison

This involves the automatic comparison of two versions of the same program to show where unauthorised or undocumented changes have been made.

Debug programs

These can show a dump of what is happening in the memory of the computer as the program is being run.

Chapter 15

1   Quality costs

The four different types of quality cost are prevention costs, appraisal costs, internal failure costs and external failure costs.

Prevention costs - are the cost of any action taken to investigate, prevent or reduce defects and failures in the design and development phase of a product or service. These costs may include the following:

- engineering, drawing and design checks
- specification review
- supplier evaluation
- quality audits
- training and orientation

Appraisal costs - are the costs of conducting quality tests and inspections to determine whether the products and/or services conform to quality requirements. These costs may include the following:

- supplier monitoring
- inspection and test materials costs
- product acceptance testing
- quality department costs
- data processing of inspection and test reports costs

Internal failure costs - are costs arising within the organisation associated with the detection and rectification of items that have not been passed to the customer but do not conform to quality requirements. These costs may include the following:

- reviewing product designs and specifications costs
- re-inspection and testing costs
- scrap and lost materials costs
- losses incurred due to the failure of purchased items to meet specification
- losses due to non-conformance leading to reduced selling prices.

External failure costs - are those associated with the detection and rectification of the products/services that failed to achieve specified quality after they have been passed to the customer. These costs may include the following:

- complaints administration
- recall and refit costs
- the costs of analysing and repairing materials returned by customers
- service and warranty claims
- product liability and damages

2   Total quality

(a)   For an organisation, quality means satisfying the customers' needs and expectations. According to Crosby, it means 'getting everyone to do what they have agreed to do and do it right the first time is the skeletal structure of an organisation, finance is the nourishment, and relationships are the soul'.

In all of definitions of quality, the customers' expectations and specific requests are the main factors. Therefore it is important for an organisation to identify such needs early in the product/service development cycle. The ability to define accurately the needs related to design, performance, price, safety, delivery and other business activities and processes will place an organisation ahead of its competitors in the market.

(b)   There are four pre-conditions for quality to be fully accepted and absorbed into an organisation. They are commitment, competence, communication and continuous improvement (Kaizen).

Commitment - senior management must be committed to the quality philosophy so that their enthusiasm reflects on the workforce and makes it more likely that the customer requirements of quality will be met.

Competence - is gained with continual training and development of skills and experience. Without competence it would be very difficult to create quality in a product or service.

Communication - the quality message must be communicated throughout the organisation - operational to strategic levels. Communication improves the understanding of the purpose and benefits associated with the quality programme, and ensures that all members of the organisation understand the concept of quality and its importance to the organisation as well as the individual.

Continuous improvement (Kaizen) - Kaizen is a Japanese word meaning gradual and orderly, continuous improvement. As originally described in the book *Kaizen, the Key to Japan's Competitive Success*, Masaaki Imai stresses that Kaizen means continuing improvement in personal life, home life, social life, and working life. When applied to the workplace, it means continuing improvement involving everyone - managers and workers alike. It involves the continual analysis of organisational processes to obtain continued improvement in performance and quality.

3   Quality circle

(a)   A quality circle is a small group of employees who meet regularly to discuss problems they are encountering regarding the quality of their product and to suggest improvements. Quality circles generally extend the scope of their efforts to cover productivity, frustration, grievances, etc.

The idea of quality circles was developed in America but is now most frequently and effectively used in Japan.

Quality circles require the full backing of top management if resources, such as staff time, are to be made available for the process. Team members are volunteers who have been trained to identify problems and understand the techniques for solving them, and who are encouraged to contribute.

The result of meetings is a written report submitted to management suggesting alternatives for the correction of quality problems.

(b)   Quality circles have the effect of involving the workforce more in the running and operation of the business. Increased involvement leads to a better understanding of management and customers' concerns, frequently resulting in greater productivity, customer satisfaction, motivation and desire to see or suggest improvements.

The benefits arising from quality circles are usually expressed as:

(i)   improvements in quality;
(ii)   improvements in productivity and cost awareness;
(iii)   staff motivation and higher morale;
(iv)   improved communications.

(c)   Quality circles have not been as readily adopted in the UK as in Japan. It is believed that the reason for this is more to do with the culture and traditions of the work forces and their relationship with management.

Within the UK workers tend to react against new management ideas, being suspicious of their motives and aims. In addition they do not necessarily perceive that they will gain any personal benefit from the process, rather that this will all accrue to the business.

For quality circles to be effective demands a degree of commitment by management to its staff and products over some period of time to match the commitment asked of from staff. This attitude is uncommon in the UK.

4   Quality control

Quality control is now being viewed as an integral part of company strategy. As a result, quality control is being practised at each stage of the production process. Its role is to ensure that standards of quality are set and monitored.

There are a number of quality control techniques, which combine or include the following.

(a)   **Acceptance-sampling procedures** - These determine whether completed products conform to design specifications.

Standards vary enormously and the quality of the finished product will depend upon the standards set by management. An acceptance-level policy would need to be defined, this allows for a degree of variance in the standard achieved. There are two alternative policies.

(i)   A fixed-standard policy, whereby the item is either acceptable or not acceptable and there are no degrees of variation either way.

(ii)   A variable-standard policy, whereby the degree of standardisation is indicated. Degrees of 'goodness' are permitted before the items become sub-standard and therefore rejected.

(b)   **Process control procedures** - These monitor quality while the product is being produced or the service is being rendered. This technique is appropriate for products or services which are mass produced. The greater the degree of mass production, the more important it becomes to have 'built-in' quality to reduce the cost of large-scale sampling.

The aim is to ensure that products do not pass to the next stage in the production process if an unacceptably high proportion of them are sub-standard.

(c)   **Quality assurance (QA)** - This entails a total system necessary to assure customers that certain minimum quality standards will be met. Formal QA standards have been set by various bodies (including the British Standards Institution's BS5750), which specify that procedures for ensuring quality are implemented and monitored. The onus for achieving quality lies with all staff, and not just the quality department.

(d)   **Quality circles (QCs)** - These comprise small groups of operatives who meet on a regular basis to consider, analyse, investigate and resolve quality problems. The group is trained in problem-solving techniques and members may be required to implement decisions. Advantages of QCs include possible improvements in the motivation of employees and the application of workers' experience to problem solving. Kaizen systems are an extension of QCs, which seek to achieve continual improvements in quality through direct involvement of workers in a cycle of 'planning, doing, checking and actioning'. These systems are therefore an integral part of overall company operations and are also concerned with suggesting improvements to all aspects of working life.

5 Quality assurance

MEMORANDUM

To: Senior staff members
From: Product management accountant
Date: 20 November 20X0

Suggestions made by MD

In general terms, the suggestions made by the MD reflect a rather traditional view of quality and how it is assured. His emphasis is 'reactive' rather than 'pro-active', is 'feedback' based rather than 'feedforward', and is concerned with quality control rather than quality assurance.

Specifically:

(i)   His initial statement that 'something drastic has to be done about quality' does not seem to be based on any kind of systematic analysis or measurement. Nor does it suggest that the MD agrees with the normal meaning of quality, which according to Crosby is 'conformity to requirements'.

(ii)   His statement that 'quality is the responsibility of your department' ignores the fact that quality is the responsibility of all staff at all stages, in all departments and at all levels.

(iii)   The 'tougher line' suggests a punishment-oriented approach which contradicts the advice of Deming 'to drive out fear', and to seek co-operation.

(iv)   'Raising quality standards' without targeting particular areas, and without understanding why such quality improvement is necessary, is likely to be a costly and unproductive exercise.

(v)   'Increasing inspection rates' and 'giving greater authority to quality control inspectors' reinforces the 'control' approach, and the 'specialist' emphasis discussed earlier.

An alternative approach involves viewing quality control as part of a more strategic approach to quality, ie quality assurance. This requires:

(i)   An analysis of existing quality performance and problems. Such an analysis should involve all levels and all departments, and should concern itself with the customers, with the competition, and with suppliers as well as the activities of the firm itself. Crosby advocates the creation of 'quality committees' composed of members drawn from different departments.

(ii)   Calculating the 'cost of quality', which involves measuring the costs of not 'getting it right first time', and includes 'prevention costs', 'appraisal costs', and 'failure costs'. Such an analysis should identify a sizeable potential cost saving (or to quote Crosby 'quality is free').

(iii)   The careful selection and monitoring of suppliers, perhaps involving an 'active' rather than a passive relationship.

(iv)   The design of the product, to ensure an appropriate level of quality.

(v)   The installation of quality information systems which measure and feedback quality performance to those involved, and which can serve as the basis for targets.

(vi)   Quality improvement, perhaps involving the creation of quality circles.

(vii)   Quality staff, which involves investment in recruitment, selection, training, development, appraisal and reward.

In conclusion, such an approach is essentially long term, and requires a shift in thinking about quality at all levels. The essential ingredient in this cultural shift is a 'right first time' mentality, which encompasses all activities that impinge on quality. In short, the MD and other staff need to be encouraged to adopt the philosophy of 'total quality management'.

Index

Exam Text Review Form

CIMA PAPER 10 TEXT – SYSTEMS AND PROJECT MANAGEMENT

We hope that you have found this Text stimulating and useful and that you now feel confident and well-prepared for your examinations.

We would be grateful if you could take a few moments to complete the questionnaire below, so we can assess how well our material meets your needs. There's a prize for four lucky students who fill in one of these forms from across the Syllabus range and are lucky enough to be selected!

	Excellent	*Adequate*	*Poor*
Depth and breadth of technical coverage			
Appropriateness of coverage to examination			
Presentation			
Level of accuracy			

Did you spot any errors or ambiguities? Please let us have the details below.

Page	**Error**

Thank you for your feedback.

Please return this form to:

The Financial Training Company Limited
Unit 2, Block 2, Wincombe Conference Centre
Wincombe Business Park
Shaftesbury
Dorset SP7 9QJ

Student's name: ....

Address: ....

....

....

CIMA Publications Student Order Form

THE
FINANCIAL TRAINING
COMPANY
PUBLICATIONS DIVISION

To order your books, please indicate quantity required in the relevant order box, calculate the amount(s) in the column provided, and add postage to determine the amount due. Please then clearly fill in your details plus method of payment in the boxes provided and return your completed form with payment attached to:

THE FINANCIAL TRAINING COMPANY, 22J WINCOMBE BUSINESS PARK, SHAFTESBURY, DORSET SP7 9QJ

OR FAX YOUR ORDER TO 01747 858821 OR TELEPHONE 01747 854302

For examinations in Nov 03 ❑ May 04 ❑ Nov 04 ❑ (please tick)

FOUNDATION

PAPER	TITLE	TEXT ORDER	PRICE £	EXAM KIT ORDER	PRICE £	FOCUS NOTES ORDER	PRICE £	AMOUNT £
1	Financial Accounting Fundamentals		21.00		11.00		6.00	
2	Management Accounting Fundamentals		21.00		11.00		6.00	
3a	Economics for Business		21.00		11.00		6.00	
3b	Business Law		21.00		11.00		6.00	
3c	Business Mathematics		21.00		11.00		6.00	

INTERMEDIATE

PAPER	TITLE	TEXT ORDER	PRICE £	EXAM KIT ORDER	PRICE £	FOCUS NOTES ORDER	PRICE £	AMOUNT £
4	Finance		21.00		11.00		6.00	
5	Business Taxation [FA 2002] (May & Nov 2003)		21.00		11.00		6.00	
	Business Taxation [FA 2003] (May & Nov 2004)		21.00	Available Feb 04	11.00	Available Feb 04	6.00	
6a	Financial Accounting (UK Standards)		21.00		11.00		6.00	
7a	Financial Reporting (UK Standards)		21.00		11.00		6.00	
8	Management Accounting - Performance Management		21.00		11.00		6.00	
9	Management Accounting - Decision Making		21.00		11.00		6.00	
10	Systems & Project Management		21.00		11.00		6.00	
11	Organisational Management		21.00		11.00		6.00	

FINAL

PAPER	TITLE	TEXT ORDER	PRICE £	EXAM KIT ORDER	PRICE £	FOCUS NOTES ORDER	PRICE £	AMOUNT £
12	Management Accounting - Business Strategy		21.00		11.00		6.00	
13	Management Accounting - Financial Strategy		21.00		11.00		6.00	
14	Management Accounting - Information Strategy		21.00		11.00		6.00	
15	Management Accounting - Case Study		21.00					

Sub Total	£

Postage and packing – please note a signature is required on delivery

UK & NI   £5 for up to 10 books

If only Focus Notes are ordered, £1 each (max £5)

	First book	Each additional book
Europe	£25	£3
Rest of World	£40	£4

£

TOTAL PAYMENT	£

The following section **must be filled in clearly** so that your order can be despatched without delay.

TO PAY FOR YOUR ORDER TICK AN OPTION BELOW

A. I WISH TO PAY BY   MASTERCARD ❑   VISA ❑   DELTA ❑   SWITCH ❑

CARD NO. ⎕⎕⎕⎕ ⎕⎕⎕⎕ ⎕⎕⎕⎕ ⎕⎕⎕⎕ ⎕⎕⎕ (Some cards don't need all boxes)

EXPIRY DATE ⎕⎕⎕⎕   ISSUE No. ⎕⎕ (Switch only)   All cards - last 3 digits on signature strip ⎕⎕⎕

Cardholder's Signature _____

Cardholder's Name & Address: _____

Cardholder's Tel. No. (Day): _____

B. I WISH TO PAY BY CHEQUE ❑ Cheques should be made payable to *The Financial Training Company Ltd* and must be attached to your order form. Personal cheques cannot be accepted without a valid Banker's Card number written on the back of the cheque.

STUDENT NAME:
DELIVERY ADDRESS: (Must be the same as cardholder's address. Please contact us if you wish to discuss an alternative delivery address).

POST CODE:		TEL. NO. (Day):	

April 2003 (This order form replaces any previous order forms.)